S. Remington
To D. Henry Miller
1879

STEPHEN GANO.

Edw.d H. Fletcher, Publisher,
F. Michelin, Lith.

THE

BAPTIST PULPIT

OF THE

UNITED STATES:

ELOQUENT AND INSTRUCTIVE PASSAGES FROM THE SERMONS OF TWO HUNDRED BAPTIST MINISTERS.

BY JOSEPH BELCHER, D.D.,

Author of "Scripture Narratives," "Baptisms of the New Testament," &c., and the Editor of "The Complete Works of Rev. Andrew Fuller," "The Works of Rev. Robert Hall," &c., &c.

NEW YORK:

EDWARD H. FLETCHER,

141 NASSAU STREET.

1850.

Stereotyped by C. Davison,
33 Gold st., N. Y.

PREFACE.

In submitting this volume to the candid examination of the public, its editor would respectfully offer two or three remarks.

To three classes of persons he thinks this work may prove acceptable and useful.

Our families need more and better reading for the Sabbath than they generally have. It is more than time that tale-books, even though they may be embellished with religion, were dismissed. Nor is it of less importance that a class of works, not unfriendly indeed to piety, but entirely without it, should give place to volumes filled with holy truth. Here men eminent for talent, for learning, and, above all, for Christian devotedness, may be introduced to give their short but interesting addresses on topics of the highest moment.

Equally true is it that in many parts of our country, we have congregations meeting from Sabbath to Sabbath without a living teacher. Will not at least an occasional passage from this volume, well and seriously read, often tend to guard against error, to lead to the knowledge of truth, and to cherish a spirit of devotion and of holy love? Few of these passages can ever be inappropriate, while some one or other will be suitable for almost all the various states in which a church of Christ can be placed.

Nor can the volume prove unacceptable to the rising ministry. Here two hundred of the servants of Jesus, of every part of our country, and of more than one generation, in their varied phraseology, lead us around the cross of Jesus, and derive from it motives to the discharge of every Christian duty.

Many an important hint will be gleaned from the volume in reference alike to the subjects and the manner of the ministry, while all will be increasingly impressed with the importance of the office.

In the preparation of the work, its editor has been delighted with the unity of views and feelings manifested by those who have furnished its various parts. It is but justice, however, to say, that though the volume presents no mean specimens of fervid eloquence, the principal object has not been to select the most eloquent passages, but to prepare a useful book on as great a variety of topics as could be well included in it. Of course its editor will not be held responsible for every shade of sentiment it includes, much less for every interpretation of which its statements may be capable. All, however, must rejoice in a ministry which presents the characteristics here shown.

One source of regret, however, it has been the lot of the editor to discover. Not a few of the most eminent of our ministers have published no sermons, or a diligent inquiry has not been able to find them. It may be the case that some have thus appeared before the public whose names and labors are not in this volume. No small kindness will be shown by the transmission of such sermons to the editor, addressed to the care of his publisher; and should the public call for a second volume of the work, these will furnish materials in connection with new sermons constantly issuing from the press, for it.

With these statements the volume is now humbly commended to the blessing of God, and the kind consideration of its readers.

CONTENTS.

I.

THE CHARACTER AND WORKS OF GOD.

II.

THE NECESSITY, CERTAINTY, AND FACTS OF THE SCRIPTURES.

III.

THE RESPONSIBILITY, DUTIES, AND DESTINIES OF MAN.

IV.

THE CHARACTER, HAPPINESS, AND PROSPECTS OF THE CHRISTIAN.

V.

THE CHURCH AND THE MINISTRY.

VI.

THE DUTIES, DANGERS, AND PROSPECTS OF SOCIETY.

INDEX OF AUTHORS' NAMES.

THE BAPTIST PULPIT.

I.

THE CHARACTER AND WORKS OF GOD.

1.—THE IMMUTABILITY OF JEHOVAH.

W. SOUTHWOOD.

EVERY created object which passes before us, and challenges our contemplation as it passes, has the marks of mutability upon it. Do we press the yielding sand, or strike the rock of adamant, and inquire for immutability? The answer is, it is not in me. In every direction, in things animate and things inanimate; in the physical and intellectual world, we meet with evidences of mutability. The earth and the heavens shall perish, all of them shall wax old as a garment, and as a vesture they shall be folded up and changed. He who made all things, and who governs all things, is alone immutable, and this we know from his word, which he hath magnified above all His name. His wisdom and his power are discovered in creation, but revelation was necessary to make known to us the immutability of God. And it is no small consolation to the people of God to know, that revelation is made with a special reference to them. Indeed, all things are for their sake; and whether it be creation or revelation, they have an interest in all, because they have an interest in Christ through precious faith. "All things," says the Apostle Paul, "are yours; whether

Paul, or Apollos, or Cephas, or the world, or life, or death; or things present, or things to come; all are yours, and ye are Christ's, and Christ is God's."

That there is one Almighty Being, the light of nature will teach us; and that he made and governs the world, the heathen, in all ages, have acknowledged; but unassisted reason has drawn sentiments of the Deity from his power and vengeance; and men, in their blind attempts to propitiate him, have shown that their wisdom is folly, and that their tender mercies are cruel. Revelation has been given to exalt our reason; to place man upon an eminence, where, in the province of faith, the Almighty might be surrounded by a brightness and a grandeur which the light of nature could not bestow.

The immutability of Jehovah is an attribute of the most exalted nature, and of the purest excellence. In a peculiar manner it distinguishes him from all the creatures he hath made. Man, his fairest work, fell, because he was mutable; the angels, who kept not their first estate, were mutable; and those who remained faithful stood not by their own power, but because they were elect, and because they were sustained by him who had chosen them; whose prerogative it is, to be the same yesterday, to-day, and forever.

That the works of God, without his word, cannot sufficiently inform our minds of the unchangeableness of God, is clear from this circumstance—all his works are ordained to mutability. The heavens declare the glory of God, and the firmament showeth his handywork; but soon, the heavens shall be rolled together as a scroll, the elements shall melt with fervent heat, the world, and all that is therein, shall be burnt up. Then shall the sun start from his place, and the stars shall fall like falling leaves from off a fig-tree; then shall the hills melt like wax before the presence of the Lord, and the mountains flee from their station like chaff before the wind, and like a rolling thing before the whirlwind; then it shall appear, that all flesh is grass, and all the glory of man as the flower of the field; the grass withereth, and the flower thereof fadeth away, but the word of the Lord endureth forever; and this is the word, which by the Gospel is preached unto you.

Jehovah's immutability is the ground of security to the church of God. He who is unchangeable in his nature, is unchangeable in his purposes, and unchangeable in his covenant promises in Christ, to a thousand generations. Though worldly policy may sneer at such expressions, it is to be feared that the same philosophy, falsely so-called, will lead to the denial that one being or essence subsists in three distinct persons, Father, Son, and Holy Ghost, who are co-eternal, and co-equal, in all the properties and perfections of the Godhead; or, at least, to the keeping back of such truths of the Bible, as too antiquated for the popular taste; till on their revival, for revival there must be, they will be so far forgotten that, like the philosophers at Athens, Christian congregations will say—"May we know what this new doctrine, whereof thou speakest, is? For thou bringest strange things to our ears: we would know, therefore, what these things mean."

2.—JEHOVAH SEEN IN HIS WORKS.

J. MAXCY.

Well indeed is it said that the heavens declare the glory of God. This Great Being is everywhere present. He exists all around us. He is not, as we are apt to imagine, at a great distance. Wherever we turn, his image meets our view. We see him in the earth, in the air, in the sun, moon, and stars. We feel him in ourselves. He is always working around us; he performs the greatest operations, produces the noblest effects, discovers himself in a thousand different ways, and yet the real God remains unseen. All parts of creation are equally under his inspection. Though he warms the breast of the highest angel in heaven, yet he breathes life into the meanest insect on earth. He lives through all his works, supporting all by the word of his power. He shines in the verdure that clothes the plains, in the lily that delights the vale, and in the forest that waves on the mountain. He supports the slender reed that trembles in the breeze, and the sturdy oak that defies the tempest. His presence cheers the inanimate creation.

Far in the wilderness, where human eye never saw, where the savage foot never trod, there he bids the blooming forest smile, and the blushing rose open its leaves to the morning sun. There he causes the feathered inhabitants to whistle their wild notes to the listening trees and echoing mountains. There nature lives in all her wanton wildness. There the ravished eye, hurrying from scene to scene, is lost in a blush of beauty. From the dark stream that rolls through the forest, the silver-scaled fish leap up, and humbly mean the praise of God. Though man remains silent, yet God will have praise. He regards, observes, upholds, connects, and equals all.

3.—DIVINE BENEVOLENCE TO MAN.

M. R. SUARES.

The formation of man was the result of benevolence. The sources of his enjoyment are infinite; and the obligation consequent upon this gift is equivalent to his supreme affection for God. Men, however, looking at the evils of life, and regarding them as the absolute condition of our existence, have questioned the benevolence of man's creation. In their estimation, they can trace but few features in the whole relation of man, which they regard as benevolent. The sufferings perceptible in every department of human life, preponderate so much in comparison with the few blessings common to it, that they would do violence to their judgment to suppose life any other than a curse. This assertion is in opposition to truth, and derogatory to God. How poor soever a man may be; a subject of the severest affliction; destitute of friends; not having where to lay his head; yet his existence is a treasure which he values too highly to barter for the cessation of his sufferings. The pleasures of a conscious existence; the satisfaction of having lived; of knowing there is such a world as earth; peopled with such an order of beings, is a blessing with which all the sufferings of life, when contrasted, seem like an atom, compared with the immensity of infinity. Man is always partial to himself; and hence his conclusions are frequently erroneous. He looks at objects, not in their natural position. The rays of selfishness are too numerous and rapid in their convergency to admit those of truth; for this reason, and no other, he regards human existence a curse; and therefore feels himself under no obligation to love God with all his strength, and his neighbor as himself. A little reflection will convince us, that the unavoidable sufferings of life are essential ingredients to the right enjoyment of it. A poet, unknown to me, has no less beautifully than philosophically said:

"And if life's joy had no alloy,
We'd but half enjoy it;
We prize it now, because we know
Time may soon destroy it."

Those who have reflected upon the laws of physical nature, cannot fail to perceive the utility of those changes peculiar to it. They seem like so many blood-vessels, carrying the principle of life to every part of the system. The mountain torrent, rushing to the ocean, is again supplied by the principle of evaporation. The ocean is agitated by the silent, yet powerful influence of the moon. The clouds are constantly moving, and purifying the atmosphere by the explosion of their electric properties. The embowelled materials of the earth are silently gathering strength, and displaying their power in the eruption of volcanoes. All nature is active; and its activity is essential to its healthy existence. By a careful investigation into the philosophy of that moral system under which we live, we cannot fail to perceive that the necessary ills of life are essential to the production of reaction, on which depends the right enjoyment of life; for the action of one moral quality on another, is as requisite to the vital condition of the moral universe, as the action of one particle of matter on another. The ills which arise from the violation of moral laws, are injurious in themselves, as well as to others. The horrors of war; the inconveniences of idleness; the sufferings of drunkenness; and the pain consequent upon many offences too numerous to be mentioned, are the effects of our folly. To ascribe them to God, and say He made us miserable, when we have made ourselves so, is an act of injustice. A faithful observance of those laws under which we are placed, will conduct us to happiness; and we are to form our estimate of things, not by what they are, but by their obvious intention and design; by what they are capable of becoming. Hence we attach so much importance to man, because of the elements of greatness that are in him. God having made man susceptible of the highest degree of improvement—should man, through negligence or carelessness, plunge himself into misery, no fault can be ascribed to God; and man is under just as much obligation to love God supremely, as though he had arrived at that point of happiness of which his nature is susceptible.

The powers of man can never fully comprehend the nature and character of God. His works are the best representatives of him. They speak with a tongue too eloquent to be misunderstood, that He who made them is divine. God's power can never be withstood, either by men or angels. He said, "Let there be light, and there was light." The dark and confused mass of chaos became order and beauty; and the whole universe, with all its countless variety of grandeur, was created by the breath of his lips. The moral qualities of God are commensurate with the greatness of his power. He is not a creature of a sudden impulse, but firm and inflexible, governing the universe which he has made with a strict impartiality; aiming at general, not particular good. Benevolence is the most prominent feature in his character. It is legibly inscribed on all his works. But more especially is it illustrated in the noblest and best of all gifts, his Son. This is the consummation of all benevolence. It is the crowning gem in the diadem of his glory. Coming generations will gaze upon it as if lost in silent abstraction, wondering that God should so love the world as to give his Son to die for it. Men may boast of their benevolence. Their acts of self-devotion may be heralded, till vale and mountain shall echo with the sound; yet no form of benevolence bears any proportion to that which is embodied in the person of Christ. He is the sun of our moral existence, and we are the planets that reflect his glory.

4.—JEHOVAH'S REGARD FOR MAN.

H. J. RIPLEY.

THE souls of men are precious in the sight of God. Though they are sinful, he still cares for them. He remembers them as the work of his hands. He remembers them as endowed with noble faculties, and as formed for unwasting existence. His eye, that looks through infinity, sees the heights of glory and of bliss which they may attain. Their very guilt and danger excite an interest in their behalf. What man, if a distressed fellow-creature has somehow fallen into his care, and occupied his thoughts, does not feel an interest in his welfare, and a desire to afford requisite assistance? And if the supposed unhappy man be in danger of greater distress, will not his wants, and the solicitude which has hitherto been exercised, continue to call forth a tender concern for his welfare? To borrow an illustration from the Bible, (Luke, xv.) the woman who had lost the piece of money, felt more the value of it from its having been lost, and its having so much occupied her attention. The man, one of whose sheep had wandered from the fold, felt a more lively interest in that one sheep, thus exposed to danger, than in the ninety and nine that went not astray. And what father does not delight in the paternal kindness so abundantly excited towards the prodigal son, who had been reduced to the sad condition of envying even the swine their food, and who had returned in the woful garb of a wretched, outcast beggar? What though he had ungratefully forsaken his home! What though he had spent his substance in riotous living! His father had had many an anxious thought respecting him. His father's heart had felt many a pang while reflecting on his conduct, and imagining the distress to which he might be reduced. His father's concern in his behalf could not but increase. And now the sight of the returning son recalled the father's solicitude. The anxiety of which he had been the object, and the urgent need of kind attentions, which appealed to every feeling of a parent's heart, excited a painful interest, indeed; yet a more intense interest, than if his circumstances had not been so deplorable. Judge, then, of the deep interest which God feels for the souls of men. He pities them as estranged from duty, and consequently exposed to misery. For their restoration to holiness and happiness, he spared not his own Son, but delivered him up. Having thus provided for the welfare of men, you may well believe he watches with most tender regard and most observing scrutiny, those who engage in the work of their salvation.

5.—THE FOREKNOWLEDGE OF GOD.

J. R. GRAVES.

God does foreknow or foresee, but this foreseeing does not *force* our will to choose or refuse salvation. 1. God foresaw the ruin entailed by the fall; and he foresaw the means by which man could be redeemed from its curse. Here is God's *foreknowledge*. 2. He determines or purposes to adopt it:—here is his eternal and immutable purpose, *predestination*. 3. He declares this purpose:—here is his eternal *decree*. 4. He makes choice of the means—"the seed of the woman shall bruise the head of the serpent;" the person—his own Son, the time and circumstances—who shall announce his coming, and who shall be his apostles:—here we see God's sovereign, unconditional, personal, and particular election. To descend to particulars, Christ is to be made of a woman—made under the law. Now some particular nation must be chosen, from which he is to spring, and through which the knowledge and blessings of this sacrifice can be brought nigh and enjoyed. Of all the patriarchs of the east, Abraham is chosen. Why he was selected in preference to Melchizedec, none can tell. Abraham has two sons, Isaac and Ishmael; Isaac is chosen. Isaac has two sons, Esau and Jacob; Jacob is chosen in preference to Esau, which is the meaning of that Scripture, "Jacob have I loved, and Esau have I hated;" though Esau seems to have been the better character of the two. Here is particular, personal election. Jacob has twelve sons; these are chosen to be the progenitors of a large and peculiar nation. Twelve, and not thirteen, was God's favorite number.

Let us notice another eternal purpose of God. He foresaw that it was necessary or fit that this chosen people should suffer a cruel bondage, and then to be brought out of it with an outstretched hand, in order to impress most forcibly his glorious attributes upon their minds and memories to the latest generation. *Foreseeing* this, he determines or purposes it.

He declares this purpose,—this is his *decree*. We read it in Gen. xv. 13: "Know of a surety that thy seed shall be a stranger in a strange land, and shall serve them, and they shall afflict them four hundred years; and also that nation whom they serve will I judge; and afterwards they shall come out with great substance." Now this was God's decree, made known hundreds of years before its accomplishment, and it must needs come to pass just as he determined it. He accordingly elects or chooses the means,—that is, time, persons, nations and circumstances. In due time Joseph is sold into Egypt,—God preserves and raises him to the second place in the kingdom. Famine is brought upon the land. This ultimately brings Jacob and his family into Egypt, where he is finally enslaved. At the expiration of the four hundred years, Moses is born, preserved, raised and educated a prince. God reveals his purpose to him—and finally redeems Israel, overthrowing Pharaoh in the sea. The descendants of the twelve sons become a great nation, divided into twelve tribes,—from one of these tribes is the Messiah to be born. Judah is chosen. From all the families of Judah, Jesse's family is selected; of all his sons, David; of all David's sons, Solomon;—and when the time had fully come when Christ should appear, of all the villages of Judea, Bethlehem is chosen; and of all the virgins of the line of Jesse, Mary alone found grace in the sight of the Lord to be the mother of Immanuel.

Thus have we seen, by simply citing one event, eternal, absolute, particular, unconditional, personal election, which no one can deny. God determining to bring it about, none could "stay his hand"—He governed and controlled the circumstances which brought it all forward, just as he willed it. It all pertained to his *sovereignty*, and he accomplished it Christ died by the determinate will and purpose of God—to bring in a new and better covenant, which God decreed from the beginning; and is it not rational to suppose that he, from the beginning, also fixed, determined, or decreed the conditions of that covenant, in and through which lost man might be saved? We have thus seen that God can act the part of a sovereign, rule and direct his own affairs, without infringing upon the *moral* will of the creature,—that is, compel the creature to love or hate him.

6.—DOCTRINE OF SPECIAL PROVIDENCE.

A. M. POINDEXTER.

THE providence of God, it is sometimes said, is general, respecting only great events and distinguished persons. It is thought beneath the Great God to notice trivial matters. To this, in the language of a heathen philosopher, we might reply, "great things cannot be taken care of without taking care of small; and in all cases, the greater any artist is, the more his skill and care appear in little as well as in great things." Let us not, then, conceive of God as less than even mortal artists.

This objection to a particular providence, originates in low and contracted views of the divine character. It implies, that providential government requires an *effort* of attention. It supposes a defect of knowledge in the Omniscient. It presumes, that to God, some beings and events are more important than others—a supposition entirely inapplicable to him to whom all things are infinitely important. It is as great condescension in God to notice an archangel as the mite that floats upon the breeze of summer. He "humbleth himself to behold the things that are in heaven and in the earth." And after all, what events are unimportant? Who does not know that the greatest revolutions have arisen from causes, seemingly, the most trivial? How often, in ancient times, did the appearance of the entrails of a beast decide the march of armies and the fate of empires? The life of Mahommed was preserved by a spider's web. By preventing Oliver Cromwell, then an obscure individual, from embarking, an exile from his native land, for America, Charles I. lost his crown and his head. And to the same act may be traced the mighty Revolution which placed the Protector on the throne of England, and affected the condition of the whole civilized world. There is, perhaps, nothing unimportant; nothing, but is concerned, remotely or immediately, in the production of everything important. And were the smallest link in the great chain of cause and effect taken away, or in the slightest degree altered, it may be, that consequences would follow, at which all intelligent creatures would be struck with horror. Each being in this vast world, is the centre of an influence ramifying throughout the whole range of connected being. *He* is what he is through the influence of other, and to those yet to come, he shall be the medium of union with all that is past. Any man who will reflect, must be convinced, that whatever he may now be, his character and condition have been materially shaped by those of his progenitors, and others with whom he has been connected. A difference in these would have made a difference in him. Nor is this obvious connection the only one of which we have plain indications. To what Christian has not the history of Abraham, of Jacob, of Joseph, been an incentive to faith, to prayer, to steadfast integrity? To the end of time, and for ever, many a heart will glow with pious emotion over the simple annals of the poor. Angels are interested in the concerns of earth. The conversion of a sinner imparts new melody to the harps of heaven. To use the language of a distinguished writer, " the same law of interminable connection, a law of moral gravitation, stretches far beyond the limits of the human family, and actually holds in unison the great community of intelligent beings." Now this universality of influence makes it indispensable that there be a particular providence, shaping the course of each individual with a view to the whole. Let us illustrate by a single case. The greatest event which ever transpired in this world, the manifestations of the Messiah, depended upon the marriage of Boaz to Ruth! Upon the determination, so beautifully expressed by the affectionate Moabitess, " whither thou goest, I will go; where thou lodgest, I will lodge; thy people, shall be my people, and thy God, my God;" depended the salvation of the world! and this again, upon the education of Ruth.

Every argument which can be adduced, sustains the doctrine of a particular providence. The character of God establishes it. We can conceive of no reason why he should exercise a providence, which does not equally involve its extension to all things. An imperfect government is inconsistent with the perfection of his nature; but a partial government, one that overlooked some things and excluded others, would be imperfect. The constant representations of Scripture, prophecy, prayer, each of these requires a particular providence.

An observation of the course of events may strengthen our convictions of the truth of this doctrine. " A man's heart deviseth his ways, but the Lord directeth his steps." Who is in just the condition he would choose? How many are constantly struggling in vain against what they deem adverse fortune? How often, too, have we known instances of preservation from danger, and deliverance from peril, where all hope of escape had fled. There is not, perhaps, a reflecting person but has exclaimed:

> "There is a Providence that shapes our ends,
> Rough-hew them how we will."

Instances, too, are not wanting, in which somewhat of retributive justice is manifest in the course of human affairs. We speak not now of such punishment of crime, nor rewarding of virtue, as is common. These are under the divine supervision, but they occur as matters of course. This, we know, is not the state of retribution. But there are instances in which the greatly-wicked have been stricken down in the height of their daring impiety, like the oak scathed and blighted by heaven's bolt, and we have felt "the Lord hath done it." There are cases in which distinguished piety has been specially rewarded in such a manner as to show the hand of God. As an example of the former, may be mentioned the horrible death of Herod; of the latter, the preservation of Paul amidst all the dangers of his perilous voyage.

7.—RESTRAINING PROVIDENCES.

C. F. STURGIS.

UNDER this head of restraining providences we arrange all those instances wherein the Almighty, for wise and gracious purposes, pleases to interfere in the conduct of human affairs, so that the disastrous consequences which would have resulted as the legitimate fruits of the errors, or sins of men, are overruled in such a way as not to produce those results which would naturally belong to them. In the examination of this large class, we see that some of the richest blessings we enjoy have been conferred upon us through the good providence of God, making "the wrath of man" praise him, and bless the world, and *restraining* the remainder of wrath. See the avarice of Balaam and the treachery of Judas for illustrations under this head. Observe how the former made repeated efforts, for the sake of filthy lucre, to curse Israel, whilst God as frequently changed the curses into blessings. And in the case of the treachery of Judas, how delightful to contemplate, by far the most glorious event in the history of man, if not of the universe! And all was brought about by God *overruling* and *controlling* his malignity! It would seem to be a reflection on the understanding to do more than merely to suggest, that in all such instances the intention of the *actor* is turned aside, and results are produced foreign, yea contrary, to any purpose desired or even contemplated by him. Here, we may observe, an indirect but very considerable proof of the truth of the doctrine we contend for, inasmuch as these plans are often so deeply laid, and the spirit with which they are prosecuted so hostile to the interests of society. The termination of those plans in anything short of wide-spread misery among men, is perfectly astonishing; and we can account for it only on the hypothesis that the Almighty exercises *a restraining providence.*

While upon this train of reflections, it might be appropriate to direct the pious mind to a contemplation of the almost innumerable instances in which the providence of God has warded off those evils which were justly to be anticipated. Let any candid man look over the history of his own life, and he will find, in instances not a few, that he has, by his own folly or sin, been brought into circumstances where, but for the intervention of divine power, he must have suffered the most serious evils. And thus, like Israel of old, with mountains on either hand, the sea before, and an infuriate enemy in the rear, refuge having failed, and destruction appearing inevitable, the Almighty has opened a pathway, as it were, through the mighty waters, so that even the irreligious have been led to feel, if not to exclaim: "This is the finger of God!"

Observe another class of events in which the kind providence of God interposes. How many and how violent the convulsions which seize upon the elements! and how few, comparatively, the calamities that ensue! Storms appear to be indispensable to the purification of the atmosphere, and to the maintenance of animal and vegetable life, and they are common, both at sea and on land; yet how rarely do they involve man unavoidably in their dreadful consequences! We see the knotted oak prostrated—a mass of ruins; but how often is it that man is involved? We see, too, the lightning's fiery bolt fly flaming athwart the darkened sky, and the tall monarch of the forest receives the blow. The shivered trunk flies in atoms, and falls in dreadful confusion to the ground; but rarely does the flaming bolt fall upon the traveller's path. "These speak the dreadful God," and warn the sinner how dangerous it is to provoke his wrath. They say, in no unintelligible accents;

> "Hast thou an arm like God?
> Or canst thou thunder with a voice like him?"

8.—IMPORTANCE OF THE DEITY OF CHRIST.

S. GANO.

The doctrine of the Divinity of our Lord is Scriptural, and is placed before you for your reception or rejection. Compare it with those passages from which we derive our knowledge of the true God, and upon which we build our hope of everlasting blessedness. If Jesus Christ be our all, God blessed for ever; if he possesses all the fulness of the Godhead, a rejection of him must be attended with the most awful consequences. If we reject the arm of Omnipotence, what can save us? My fellow-mortals, we stand on the brink of eternity."

"A point of time, a moment's space,
Removes us to yon heavenly place,
Or shuts us up in hell."

The sentiment I have been presenting to you, and which I have feebly supported in this place, and from this pulpit, for more than twenty-five years, is now the only ground of my own hope, and that which I wish to commend when the messenger of death shall summon my soul to an account before the only wise God my Saviour. I mention this, not as an argument for the veracity of the doctrine, for I am fully sensible that the most abominable and vile sentiments may be sanctioned by the most hoary antiquity, and adhered to with a pertinacity of enthusiasm that outbraves death; but if I may possess any claim to honesty, I express it as my settled confidence in what the Scriptures reveal, and what is intimately connected with our eternal condition. The Scriptures we must understand for ourselves. To our Master we stand or fall. An attempt to explain what is inexplicable, is absurd; but to believe what is inexplicable, is rational, and what we all do daily. You are entreated to believe in Jesus Christ, as revealed in his word. Believe in him as God manifest in the flesh, as one with and in the Father; as the eternal life which was with the Father. In such a being as this, who would not trust? Turn your eyes from all worldly objects to behold Him who is glorious in holiness, fearful in praises, doing wonders. Fear not, ye humble and trembling souls! your salvation is sure. So wondrous is his power, that no part of the planetary system varies in its course; so wondrous his love, that nothing can either wander in disorder, or be wanting to complete his system of grace. Join, then, with the prophets: How great are God's signs! How mighty are his works! His kingdom is an everlasting kingdom, and his dominion is from generation to generation.

9.—THE TEACHING OF CHRIST.

J. DOWLING.

WITH what inimitable beauty and skill does "The Great Teacher," who spake as never man spake, employ the parabolic mode of enlightening the ignorance, rebuking the ingratitude, or condemning the obduracy of his hearers. True, the result was not always to produce the contrition and the penitence of a David; for, sometimes, when the reason was convinced, and the conscience was compelled to make the application, the pride and obduracy of the heart were still unsubdued. Thus did it happen, that after our blessed Lord had exposed the madness and the cruelty of the Jews, and foretold their approaching fate, in the parable of the vineyard and the husbandmen, who destroyed, first the servants, and then the beloved son of their Lord;—that his auditors were compelled to self-application, and perceived the justice and felt the severity of the reproof, while they still hated the reprover. For "the chief-priests and the scribes, the same hour," says the evangelist, "sought to lay hands on him; and they feared the people; for they perceived he had spoken this parable against them." —Luke xx. 19; Mark xii 1–12.

The richness and beauty, the instructiveness and variety of our Saviour's parables, is a theme too copious even to touch upon in the present discourse. It is sufficient to say, that they constitute a complete and invaluable model for the study and imitation of all whose duty it is to teach and to preach the truths of that gospel which Christ himself proclaimed, in such a way that the multitudes hung upon his lips, and

JOHN DOWLING.

Pastor of the Berean Baptist Church, New-York.

Edw H Fletcher, Publisher.

F. Michelin, Lith.

"the common people heard him gladly." And it is, certainly, a sufficient reply to those who affect to undervalue or to despise the illustrative mode of preaching or of teaching, that of the public instructions of our Lord Jesus Christ, the only perfect preacher that ever lived, a very large proportion, probably more than one-half of all that are recorded, were delivered in the form of comparison or parable.

Why is it, I have often thought, that some men of education and study, seem almost entirely to neglect, if not to despise, a mode of teaching, so constantly adopted in the instructions, and so eminently sanctioned by the example of Christ himself, that Divine Master, from whom they profess to hold their commissions to preach, and who has said, "As my Father hath sent me, so send I you?" Why is it, that some of our young men, fresh from the University, or the Theological Institution, with the ink of their diplomas scarcely dry, imagining that because they have completed a course of study, they must now be, of necessity, profoundly intellectual, and wondrous wise—look down, with ill-disguised contempt, upon men vastly their superiors in all that constitutes ministerial efficiency, and affect to exclude them from *their circle* of intellectual preachers, simply because—avoiding the abstract and the dry—they aim, like their Master, Jesus, to adapt their discourses to the comprehension of all, by familiar and appropriate illustrations, drawn from the common affairs of every-day life? Let me be understood. I do not mean to assert that it is, by any means, a frequent failing among *really intellectual* men, thus to despise the faculty of illustrating truth by familiar and well-chosen analogies. It is generally the sciolist, the *would-be-intellectual*, the man who has not yet shaken off, by contact with men as they are in this every-day world, the starch and the stiffness of college-halls; who, from his imaginary height among the stars, thus looks down upon those homespun preachers, who dwell among men, and deal in the things of real life, and who dare to eschew scholastic distinctions, and metaphysical subtleties, at the fearful risk of being punished for their temerity, by the charge, hurled at their heads by these self-same intellectuals, of "catering for the popular taste."

10.—THE EXAMPLE AND TEACHING OF CHRIST.

A. CAMPBELL.

EXAMPLE is a more powerful teacher than precept. Now Jesus Christ has afforded us an example of human perfection never witnessed before. He gave a living form to every moral and religious precept, which they never before possessed. In this respect he was the distinguished prophet, to whom Moses and all inferior prophets referred. In entering on his prophetic office, he taught with a peculiarity unexampled by all his predecessors. He spake as never man spake. The highest commendation he gave of Moses, was that he wrote of him, and that he was a faithful servant in Christ's house. From the beginning of his ministry to the end of his life, he claimed the honor of being the only person that could instruct men in the knowledge of God, or of his will. He claimed the honor of being the author and finisher of the only perfect form of religion; the Eternal Father attested all his claims, and honored all his pretensions. Respecting the ancient rules of life, the law and the prophets, he taught his disciples they had lived their day—he taught them that they were given only for a limited time. "The law and the prophets prophesied until John"—then they gave place to a greater prophet and a more glorious law. Malachi, the last of the ancient prophets, informed Israel that they should strictly observe Moses' law, until a person should come in the spirit and power of Elias. Jesus taught us that John the Baptist was he, and that the law and prophets terminated at his entrance upon his ministry; for since that time the kingdom of God is preached, and all men press into it. To attest his character, and to convince the church of his being the great prophet, to whom all Christians should exclusively hearken as their teacher; to weaken the attachments of his disciples to Moses and the prophets, it pleased God to send down Moses and Elias from heaven; the one the law-giver, the other the law-restorer, to resign their prophetic honors at the feet of the Messiah, in presence of select witnesses. "Jesus took with him Peter, James and John, into a high mountain, and was transfigured before them; and his face did shine as the sun, and his raiment was white as snow, and behold there appeared Moses and Elias talking with him." Peter, enraptured with these heavenly visitants, proposes erecting three tabernacles: one for Christ, one for Moses, and one for Elias. But while he was thus proposing to associate Christ, the great prophet, with Moses and Elias, inferior prophets, a bright cloud overshadowed them, and a voice out of the cloud, an indirect reply to Peter's motion—"This is my beloved Son, in whom I am well pleased, *hear ye him.*" Thus, when these ancient and venerable prophets were recalled to heaven, Christ alone is left as the great teacher, to whom by a commandment from the excellent glory, the throne of the Eternal, we are obliged to hearken. That this transaction was significant of the doctrine we have stated, must be manifest, when we take into view all the circumstances. Might it not be asked, why did not Abel, Abraham, or Enoch, appear on this occasion? The reason is plain—the disciples of Christ had no hurtful respect for *them.* Moses and Elias, the reputed oracles of the Jewish nation, were the only two in respect of whom this solemn and significant revocation was needful. The plain language of the whole occurrence was this: Moses and Elias were excellent men—they were now glorified in heaven—they had lived their day—the limited time they were to flourish as the teachers of the will of Heaven was now come to an end. The morning star had arisen—nay, was almost set, and the Sun of Righteousness was arising with salutiferous rays: let us then walk in the noon-day light—let us hearken to Jesus as our prophet and legislator, priest and king. He shall reign over the ransomed race. We find all things whatsoever the law could not do are accomplished in him, and by him—that in him all Christians might be perfect and complete. "For the law was given by Moses, but grace and truth came by Jesus Christ."

II.—OBEDIENCE OF THE LORD JESUS.

T. MEREDITH.

We propose to consider the example of Christ, in reference to his obedience to his Father's will. "He took upon him the form of a servant, and was made in the likeness of men;" that he might be "obedient unto death, even the death of the cross." This expresses, not only the extent, but the completeness of his obedience. As death is the last and highest sacrifice that can be made; so the making of this, as an act of obedience, implies the performance of all the rest. Christ rendered exact and complete obedience to the will of his Father, expressed in his holy law. He obeyed this law under its diversified appellations, of moral, ceremonial, and remedial.

The moral law he kept without sacrifice; it being agreeable to his holy nature, and adapted to his humbled condition. It was holy, just, and good. He was holy, harmless, undefiled, and separate from sinners. Having obeyed it in its greatest strictness, both in letter and spirit, he could say, even to his bitterest enemies, "which of you convicteth me of sin?"

Its ceremonial features he also observed, with their various rites and exactions. According to their requisitions, he was circumcised, attended the Jewish festivals, visited on the Sabbath the temple and synagogues; and even observed its judicial features, performing a miracle to meet its exactions. Thus far the obedience of Christ was comparatively easy. It is true, it required infinite condescension to leave the heights of glory, and descend to the depths of humanity to be—"made of a woman, made under the law;" it also required labor and toil, perseverance and abstinence; but all this was the lesser part of his obedience, and may be considered as easy, when compared with the obedience he rendered as the "propitiation for sin"—the satisfaction which he made in behalf of the sinner, to the claims of divine justice—obedience unto death, even the death of the cross! This part of the divine law which he undertook, as our Redeemer, to satisfy, required not only holiness, but suffering; not only obedience, but obedience unto death! Offended justice could not be propitiated without blood. "Without shedding of blood there is no remission." When the period arrived for him to render obedience to this part of the divine law, then was the time of his agony. He prayed fervently, "and sweat as it were great drops of blood, falling to the ground;" saying: "O my Father, if it be possible, let this cup pass from me;—nevertheless, not my will, but thine be done;" and also the second and third time, "O my Father, if this cup may not pass away except I drink it, thy will be done." In our Saviour's prayer and agony in Gethsemane, we see the shrinkings of humanity, from the dreadful sufferings of Calvary; but we behold, also, his complete and unreserved submission to the will of his Father. He was ready to meet the most awful summons—to meet death in its most terrible form—the death of the cross—death with the severest torments, and the greatest ignominy.

Christ, in his death upon the cross, has set an example to the universe of the true spirit of obedience; obedience which was perfect and complete in every respect; which originated in his infinite love and holy submission; and, after encountering every variety of temptation and trial, met death in its most appalling and terrific form. Now, my brethren, what is there in heaven or on earth, that can move our wills to entire obedience, if this marvellous example do not affect us? "Let the same mind be in you, which was also in Christ Jesus."

12.—SUFFERINGS OF MESSIAH.

G. F. DAVIS.

The most impressive figurative use of the word baptism, is made by the blessed Saviour in reference to his expected sufferings. Luke xii. 50. "I have a baptism to be baptized with; and how am I straitened till it be accomplished!" Now let me solemnly ask, what did he mean by calling his sufferings a baptism? Did he mean to say—"I expect a little pain—to breathe a few sighs—to utter a few groans—to shed a few tears—to endure a partial withdrawing of my Father's face?" O ye that depend on his sufferings for eternal salvation, ye do not believe this. Whatever may have been your practice in reference to baptism, ye do not believe that the baptism of your Saviour's sufferings was a mere sprinkling or effusion of scanty drops. Ye believe that something more than pouring even, was intended, when he said, "I have a baptism to be baptized with, and how am I straitened till it be accomplished!" He expected not only to drink the cup of bitterness, but to sink in deep waters of affliction, and to have all the waves and billows of sorrow roll over his head. His calling the sufferings which he was to endure a baptism, gives you his definition of the word.

Any one who wishes to know how his Lord and Master understood the meaning of the word *baptism*, has only to consult this passage, and he has the definition given in the most affecting terms—terms which, I confess, would carry the fullest conviction to my mind in favor of immersion, if there were no other passage in the Bible. I love to have my Jesus define words; and his definition is far better to me than that of lexicons or historians. And when I read this passage, I know just what he thought of baptism—I know that he considered it nothing less than a total immersion.

13.—NECESSITY OF CHRIST'S DEATH.

A. FISHER.

It was necessary that Christ should die, because the maladies of men could not be cured by less effective means. The object of God in the plan of Redemption was doubtless the salvation of sinners. In devising the means by which the object could be attained, he would no doubt adopt such as would meet the case. The difficulties, as well as the nature of the means, would be considered. When disorders are deeply-seated and violent in their nature, they require powerful remedies, but when they are slight and easily cured, less solicitude is felt. If man had been only partially disordered, some slight remedies might have answered the purpose; but such is his disorder, that no such remedies would reach the seat of the evil. The disorder of sin is seated in the heart. By the apostacy of our first parents, all their posterity was tainted with sin, for they communicated to them a love for the evil. In consequence of this, all the generations of men before Christ were disposed to pursue sin, and did pursue it. The world was full of violence. Guilt, as is always the case, was the concomitant, so that every individual became hardened with the guilt of his own sins. The law of sin, which was natural to man, discovered itself in innumerable ways; it produced all the crimes which were committed against God and man. The world in general, and all the individuals composing it, were deeply involved. The evil inflicted by the fiery serpents on the Israelites was but a faint emblem of the evil of sin. In order to the restoration of man to holiness and the favor of God, powerful means were necessary; those of a different description could never accomplish the end. This is evident from experience. Innumerable laws have been framed to stop the current of human depravity, but it bursts over all barriers, and carries every thing before it. Human inducements have been held up to men to keep them from committing crimes, but they also prove ineffectual. Innumerable ways have been devised to remove human guilt, but alas! how unavailing have they been! All the superstitious rites which men have observed, in different ages and countries, are designed to propitiate the favor of the Deity. But these are all without effect. The all-important question still returns, "How can man be just with God?" Now the exhibition of Christ is the only remedy which has been found of sufficient efficacy to remove the love and guilt of sin. In order, therefore, to make men holy, and deliver them from death, Christ must be crucified. As this was an important object with God, his death became necessary. The death of Christ removes the love of sin, by procuring the Holy Spirit, by whose influences men are made new creatures. Without such influence, men would forever remain at variance with God and holiness, and of course under the dominion of sin. But by these influences an immense multitude of the human family have been effectually cured of the evil of sin, made completely holy, and so prepared in this respect for the enjoyment and business of heaven. By the agency of the Holy Spirit, men are made to believe in Christ, and so to become heirs of eternal life. Nor is the death of Christ less effectual in removing the guilt of sin than its dominion. Indeed, in this respect it has a more direct influence. In the Scriptures, all other means are represented as being unable to wash away sin; but this is represented as effectual. The blood of Christ cleanseth from it, is the repeated doctrine of revelation. This effect is produced by believing on Christ; the moment faith is exercised in his atonement, sin is taken away. There may not be at the time an exact view or feeling of it, but the effect is nevertheless produced. No sinner is ever savingly benefited by the sacrifice of Christ without faith in him, but every one who does believe will be saved. This is the only way in which the sinner can be delivered from death, and received to heaven. This last reason why it was necessary that Christ should be crucified, will be rendered more clear, by adverting again to the brazen serpent. When an Israelite had received a wound from one of the fiery serpents, he could not expect healing without a view of the brazen serpent, and his looking at that implied an acquiescence in the appointed method of cure, and faith in it; so the sinner's looking to Christ implies the same. When the wounded Israelite looked at the serpent on the pole, he immediately lived, that is, he felt his disorder abate, and assurance of a cure. So when a sinner looks to Christ, however deep his stains of sin may be, he will find relief. If the serpent had not been erected for the people to look at, all bitten must have died; so had not Christ been slain for the sins of men, all the human race must have perished. We see, therefore, the propriety of the text: "As Moses lifted up the serpent in the wilderness, so must the Son of man be lifted up, that whosoever believeth on him should not perish, but have eternal life."

14.—DEATH CONQUERED BY MESSIAH.

J. LELAND.

It was necessary for Christ to conquer death. Persecutions, captivity, and anarchy, are called death, as well as the dissolution of the body, the apostacy of the soul, and the punishment of both soul and body in hell. These deaths all entered among men at the door of sin. But that all these deaths were contained in the first threatening of God to man:—"In the day thou eatest thereof thou shalt surely die," is more doubtful. It is pretty evident that the depravity of the soul took place before the test of Adam's obedience was broken; for, if his mind had not first been corrupted, he would not have rebelled. Lust did first conceive, before it brought forth the action of sin. If, therefore, the internal depravity precede the transgression of eating of the prohibited tree, death could not be the penal consequence thereof.

And further, it is difficult to distinguish between moral depravity (often called spiritual death) and sin itself. Now with what propriety could God have said unto Adam, "In the day thou sinnest, thou shalt surely die." Nor is this all. "To be carnally-minded is death." "The carnal mind is enmity against God." Here the inspired description of spiritual death is, to be under the government of a carnal, envious, irreconcilable mind. If spiritual death, therefore, was included in the threatened penalty, God must have said, "In the day thou eatest thereof, I will make thee a carnal, irreconcilable enemy to myself." Supposing a father should lay his injunction on his child, not to leave the place where he was and go to a certain tree; to make this injunction effectual, he should, moreover, threaten him with stripes if he disobeyed. The child, however, violates the prohibition of the father, and runs to the interdicted tree; on his way a poisonous adder leaps at him, and injects a deadly poison into his flesh and blood. In this supposed instance, it could not be said that the deadly poison was any part of the father's threatening, nor could the calamity of the child exempt him from the threatened stripes. From these remarks, it is safest to conclude, that, although the world is in a deplorable state of depravity, yet moral depravity, which is called spiritual death, was no part of the threatening of God to Adam.

There is a doleful state of existence, frequently spoken of in the Scriptures, as hell, hell-fire, everlasting fire, eternal fire, everlasting punishment, everlasting destruction, and the second death; as also other names descriptive of this awful state. In common conversation it is most frequently called eternal death, and this death is supposed by many to be included in the threatening of God to man, which we are treating of. But if *moral* death is excluded, *eternal* death cannot be included; for moral death is such an essential part of eternal death, that the last cannot exist where the first is absent. Furthermore, the death which was threatened, was to take place on the day of transgression; whereas Adam and Eve did not experience eternal death on the day in which they fell; if they had experienced it, their bodies must have been immortalized, and their souls been in a state and condition that they could not have propagated their species.

But natural or corporeal death was included in the threatening. Whether there was a poisonous quality in the fruit which grew on the forbidden tree, which made Adam and Eve mortal, from which death immediately began to prey on them by disease; or whether disease was the penalty inflicted on them for transgression, are questions attended with some doubt. If the fruit was poisonous in its nature, and tended to mortality and death, then the prohibition of God was only cautionary, to preserve the new made pair from poisoning themselves to death; and if this was the case, then, if there had been no prohibition, and they had eaten of it by mere accident, it would have had the same effect. But if all this was true, which to me is highly probable, still the prohibition was made the test of Adam's obedience. So the rainbow, though depending on a natural cause, was made the token of a covenant made with Noah. If, on the other hand, there was no poisonous quality in the fruit, but it was prohibited, simply as a test to Adam; then, by eating, he did not make himself mortal, but only rebelled against his God, and for his rebellion, mortal disease was that day implanted in him, which neither food nor physic could remove. In either of the cases, death began his career on the day of transgression; a career which, if I may be allowed to personate death, he has unweariedly been pursuing ever since, and which he will pursue until Adam and all his offspring shall fall before him.

The first great threatening of God to man has its full accomplishment without abatement. In this instance the Almighty does not recede from his word. The coming of a Mediator into the world has no ways mitigated it, for the blessed Saviour did not come to save men from dying, but leaves them all to die as universally as though he had not come; but he came to destroy death and raise the dead—to swallow up death in victory—to take captivity captive, and to deliver those who are appointed to die. As death came by *man*, so by *man* shall death be destroyed;

for as in Adam all died, so in Christ shall all be made alive. Christ came to destroy death.

He first destroyed death in himself; he had power to lay down his life and take it again—he died through weakness, but rose again by the power of God. The resurrection of Christ is abundantly proved in the Scriptures; and let the man who can comprehend eternity, and mete out immensity—who can conceive of the mode of eternal existence, and account for the creation of the world—who can tell where the winds began to blow, together with their destination, and measure the depths of the sea—who can fill the high heavens with loud thunder, and dart the shafts of lightning through the ethereal vault—who can shake the earth to its centre, and swell the seas into raging fury;—let such, and none but such, contend with their Maker—exalt reason above revelation, and deny the resurrection from the dead.

But aside from revelation, the resurrection of Christ can be supported by as good evidence as any other great events which have taken place on the earth. Great events are preserved, in succession, by history, periodical days, and emblematical institutions. All these concur in the resurrection of Christ. The history of the New Testament has handed the event down to us. The first day of the week has been regarded, in commemoration of it, from that time until now. Baptism is our emblem of it. Buried with Christ by baptism, we rise to figure the resurrection of Christ, by which we are saved. This also has continued from the beginning of the gospel until the present time; but, if the dead rise not, why are we baptized for the dead?

As Christ was the first-fruits from the dead, he has also given assurance unto all men, that they shall be raised by his power. The hour is coming when all that are in their graves shall hear the voice of the Son of God, and come forth; they that have done good to the resurrection of life, and they that have done evil unto the resurrection of damnation. All will be raised to life, and death shall be no more.

15.—POWER OF THE CROSS.

R. FULLER.

THINK of the enterprise on which Jesus came, and the cost at which that enterprise was achieved. The enterprise! think of that; it was the salvation of man. The devils saw him, and exclaimed, "What have we to do with thee?" as if they had said, "thou hast not come to save us." No, they had nothing to do with him; but we have every thing to do with him; since he came for us once as our salvation.

The enterprise—and then the cost—those sufferings which destroyed his life, though they could not destroy his love—think of these, and how are you affected? "Christ," says Peter, "hath once suffered for sin, the just for the unjust;" but in that *once*, what sufferings were not concentrated! Ah! miserable sinner! from eternity had the only-begotten reposed in the bosom of the Father, and now see him leaving that bosom and taking the form of a servant for you. From eternity had the fairest among ten thousand and altogether lovely, been rich in the glories and hosannas of the skies, and now see him becoming poor for you;—so poor, that living he had not where to lay his head, and dying he would, but for charity, have been buried like a common malefactor, by the highway-side. Follow the adorable Jesus from scene to scene of ever-deepening insult and sorrow. Trace his footsteps, marked by his own blood. Behold his sacred face swollen with tears and stripes. And, last of all, ascend Mount Calvary, and view there the amazing spectacle; earth and hell gloating on the gashed form of the Lord of glory; men and

RICHARD FULLER.

Pastor of the Seventh Baptist Church, Baltimore, Md.

Edw.d H. Fletcher, Publisher.
F. Mic.elin, Lith.

devils glutting their malice in the agony of the Prince of life; and all the scattered rays of vengeance, which would have consumed our guilty race, converging and beating in focal intensity upon him, of whom the Eternal twice proclaimed, in a voice from heaven: "This is my beloved Son, in whom I am well pleased." After this, what are our emotions? Can we ever be cold or faithless? No, my brethren, it is impossible, unless we forget this Saviour, and lose sight of that cross on which he poured out his soul for us.

16.—A MESSAGE FROM THE CROSS.

W. F. NELSON.

To the once glorious, but now condemned race of men, comes the herald of the cross, the minister of reconciliation, to proclaim deliverance to the captive grinding in Satan's prison-house—to break from his neck the iron bondage, and reinstate him in the favor of God, pointing him, through the blood of atonement, to a seat at the right hand of the Majesty on high. He beholds man, steeped in crime, led a willing captive by the devil at his will, and rushing madly on from present calamities to a fate still more dreadful—to endless misery—to eternal death. Moved with compassion, like his Master, he comes to a race that has defied the mercy and wisdom of its Creator; that has abused his goodness; has cast off, cast down, and trampled under foot the authority and solemn sanctions of his law, and in its madness impugned the justice, imprecated the vengeance, and defied the fierceness of the indignation and wrath of Almighty God. The glorious gospel of the blessed God takes its stand in the dreadful breach, and, stooping to the lowest depths of the abyss of human guilt and wo, it lays hold of the poor infatuated wretch, madly rushing on to irretrievable ruin, and rending the veil in which sin has enshrouded his understanding, reveals to him the full extent of his wretchedness; then, when his fainting heart is just ready to sink under the crushing burden of its guilt and misery, it turns his despairing eye to Calvary—shows him there his incarnate Creator, *bleeding*, GROANING, **DYING**, *for his rescue!* And while, thus all-wrapped in amazement at the stupendous scene, the still, small voice of God whispers in his ear that peace-speaking, life-giving sentiment, "God so loved the world, that he gave his only begotten Son, that whosoever believeth on him might not perish, but have everlasting life;" and as his soul drinks in the joyful sound, which, like angel music, thrills through his inmost soul, love, joy, and peace spring up like a fountain of life in his heart. The spell of sin is broken—the sting of death is taken away—and from that glad moment begins the life of God in the soul of man. Christ is formed in him the hope of glory. Life and bliss eternal are his; and from strength to strength he goes on in his heavenly career. He learns, even while a pilgrim on earth, to cheer his heart by the prelude to that song—"Unto him that loved us, and washed us from our sins in his own blood, and hath made us kings and priests unto God, to him be glory and dominion forever and ever."

17.—EVIDENCE OF MESSIAH'S RESURRECTION.

R. B. MANLY.

THE expression of Luke, that "with great power gave the apostles witness of the resurrection of the Lord Jesus," may refer to their *earnestness.* This was produced by a sense of the importance and certainty of the fact to which they testified. If the views comprehended in the new testament scheme of truths connected with the resurrection of Jesus be correct, where, among all possible stimulants, can any thing be found so suited to rouse and engage the slumbering energies of the mind? Nothing more elevated, more sublime, and important can ever be conceived of; and if energy depend on truth and certainty, that which animated and sustained their testimony is of the highest degree. To be convinced of this, let us for a moment take a view of the circumstances in which they were placed, with regard to this fact. They had known the Saviour intimately for three years, and had had their attention particularly turned to the identity of his person, by a thousand touching circumstances and wonderful events, so that it seems impossible they could mistake another for him. They saw him apprehended from among them, and never lost sight of him until his body was deposited in the sepulchre. They saw him expire, and observed the soldiers omit to break his legs under the conviction he was already dead—and if this had not been sufficient to convince them, yet when they saw the blood and water issue from his wounded side (an evidence that the pericardium had been pierced), no doubt could then have been harbored that he really was dead. The sepulchre in which the body was laid, they knew had been closed and sealed, and guarded by a strong detachment of Roman soldiers, selected for the express purpose of preventing the disappearance of the body. After the third day it could not be produced. They certainly knew that *they* had not taken it away, and with equal certainty almost, must they have known that neither the guard, nor the priests, nor any of his enemies *would* take it away; since this would have manifestly tended to prove that doctrine to be true, which they were laboring to prove an imposture. They saw that the only account of the event, besides their own, carried in it its own refutation; and that within eight years it could be openly published and recorded as perjury, and the authors pointed out in the very place of their residence, no man contradicting.

Their own account, they must have felt, was not made up of romantic anticipations, and the welcome illusions of excited imaginations, but was *forced* upon them after the event by evidence which they could not resist. That they did not expect him to rise, is evident from preparations made at great expense to embalm the body, and the unaffected astonishment and unbelief excited by the first reports of his resurrection. Every motive of temporal interest combined to make them wish those reports untrue. They were, therefore, prepared to question all testimony, and none but such as should be absolutely unquestionable would establish their faith. Accordingly it is wonderful to observe from how many sources testimony came to their relief. The *sense of sight* furnished its aid; they saw he was not in the tomb—and he was afterwards seen by different individuals of their number on as many as *ten* several occasions, sometimes in Jerusalem or its neighborhood, and sometimes in Galilee; some of them saw him eat in their presence, wearing all the distinct marks of his identical body. They *heard* him speak, knew his voice, and followed him from Jerusalem to Bethany, listening to his instructions just before his ascension. They *touched* him—putting their fingers into the nail-prints, holding his feet, and worshipping him. Their faith was also assisted by *testimony;* they saw a vision of angels who said that he was alive; and by *memory*, for they afterwards called to mind that he had often told them he would die, and on the third day rise again. To these we may add their frequent *intercourse* and *conversations* with him, during forty days, on various subjects which had mutually interested them before his death. Under these circumstances how could *they*, how could *we*, avoid saying, that it was "by many *infallible* signs he showed himself alive after his passion?" How could they have spoken otherwise than *earnestly*, and "with great power?"

18.—CHRIST THE RIGHTEOUSNESS OF BELIEVERS.

J. S. BACKUS.

PURE as the world may have been when it came from the hand of its Maker, or man when formed in the image of God, all now lie in wickedness. "There is none righteous, no not one; for all have sinned and come short of the glory of God;" so that "by the deeds of the law no flesh can be justified" in his sight. All who have opened their eyes upon the world at large, or been brought to know the deceitfulness of their own hearts, must have seen and felt the necessity of a righteousness, such as is not to be found in this wicked world. And when taught that all must meet a righteous God, who has appointed a day in which to judge them, when he who has offended in one point shall be regarded as guilty of all, and those who have not continued in all things written in the book of the law to do them, be punished with everlasting destruction, must have felt to ask, who then can be saved? Or when that great day of his wrath has come, who then will be able to stand? But dark as the picture may be, or hopeless and helpless as men may appear, there is a righteousness in which the soul may stand justified before God, on earth and in heaven; a righteousness not the least part of which is from works that we have done, either before or after conversion. "Not of works, lest any man should boast." Nor is it angelic, or a righteousness that angels have prepared. It is "the Lord our righteousness." "Christ, who of God is made unto us wisdom, righteousness, sanctification, and redemption"—"Who has become the end of the law for righteousness to every one that believeth." And to all who are found in him, not having their own righteousness, which is of the law, but the righteousness which is of God by faith, he says, "No weapon that is formed against thee shall prosper, and every tongue that shall rise against thee in judgment shalt thou condemn. This is the heritage of the servants of the Lord, and their righteousness is of me, saith the Lord." While to all without Christ, he says, "Hearken unto me, ye stout-hearted and far from righteousness, I bring near my righteousness." This righteousness offered unto those who will hearken unto the Lord, is "an everlasting righteousness," and therefore cannot be of men, for even Adam's before the fall was not everlasting. But according to the prophet, it is "the Lord our righteousness;" and according to the apostle, it is a righteousness that God imputes to those who with the heart believe unto righteousness, without the works of the law.

19.—CHRIST THE CENTRE OF THE CHRISTIAN SYSTEM.

J. S. MAGINNIS.

Whoever will prosecute an attentive study of the sacred volume, cannot be long in perceiving that all its stupendous developments are made with respect to one great Personage—the Mediator between God and ruined man—the Lamb that was slain from the foundation of the world, who liveth, and was dead, and is alive for evermore. It may justly be said, therefore, that the specific object of biblical theology is, to acquaint us with the pre-eminence which the Bible assigns to the character and offices of Christ as the Redeemer of lost sinners, and with the relations which all its other instructions sustain to him. Little respect is due to any system of theology which has not Christ for its sun and centre. Little regard can be paid to any doctrines which do not, directly or indirectly, relate to Him. Little importance can be attached to any moral principle which does not draw from Him its life and power. Let no one suppose that this view of the subject is adapted to contract the field of theological investigation; it only directs us to an eminence from which our horizon continually recedes, while every object upon the expanding surface presents itself with new distinctness and beauty. Paul did not restrict himself to a narrow circle of thought, when he announced to the Corinthians his resolve to know nothing among them but Christ and him crucified. The universe, surely, is not less broad to him who finds its true centre, than to one who would make all the heavenly revolve around some inferior planet; the difference would be, the former only could see its regularity and its order. It is to Christ that all the doctrines of the Bible relate—from him they all proceed—to him they all return. However important these doctrines may be in themselves as distinct and separate topics of consideration, and whatever interest of a historical, moral, or philosophical character may attach itself to each, they all derive their chief and special importance from the relation they sustain to Christ and his cross—a truth which must be generally felt and acknowledged before the science of theology can ever be brought to its highest perfection.

20.—PERSONALITY AND WORK OF THE HOLY SPIRIT.

WILLIAM R. WILLIAMS.

We fear that Christians, even the most orthodox, allow themselves to think or to speak of the Holy Ghost, as if but an attribute or influence of the Deity, or as an abstraction in theology. But the Bible, to our view, teaches emphatically his existence as a Divine person. He is as really a person as Abraham or David, or any of the patriarchs, or as Paul, John, or either of the apostles. Is the Son distinguishable from the Father, so is the Spirit also. When you were baptized, it was into his dread and distinct name, invoked upon you, as you sunk beneath the entombing waters, and rose again to the upper air. You were not, as Unitarianism would make that form to mean, immersed beneath the baptismal flood in the name of God, a man and an attribute, just as the arch-sceptic Voltaire blessed the young son of our own Franklin in the name of God and liberty, or, in other words, in the name of a reality and a metaphor, and with the blessed titles of a Being and an abstraction, a divine personage and a human personification. But you were baptized into the doctrine of the Spirit, just as much as into the doctrine of Christ or Christianity; and you were received into the fellowship of the church, just as much upon your faith in the Deity of the Spirit, as upon your faith in the Deity of the Father; and our churches can therefore no more tolerate your denial of the one, than they would your denial of the other. You cannot be a Christian and reject Christ. You cannot be a Christian and reject the Spirit. The Lamb was needed to die for you in redemption. The Being, whose emblem is the dove, was alike needed to live for you in regeneration. Just as it was the peculiar office of the Second Person in the adorable Trinity to make the atonement that cancels sin; so it is the peculiar office of the Third Person of the Trinity to work the regeneration that changes your hearts. Blasphemy against the Father may be forgiven; blasphemy against the Holy Ghost has no pardon. The latter is, therefore, something more than a mere emanation from the former. The graces of the Christian, and the endowments of the Christian ministry are peculiarly *His* gifts. When the Saviour withdrew his presence from the church, the Holy Ghost came in to supply his place as the teacher of the church. And such were the advantages this successor of the Saviour brought with him in his train, that our Lord assured his disciples, it was better for them that He himself, endeared as he was to them, and many as were the blessings they had received from him, should go away, that room might be made for the coming of the Comforter. And to commend and enhance in the eyes of men the worth of this new Teacher and Guide, the Saviour spoke of him by the most expressive titles. The intellect of man craves the truth. Even the most besotted and wilful disciples of error cannot content themselves without having some show of truth. And therefore the new Guide of the church was described to them as the Spirit of Truth. The heart of man craves peace. Amid the cares and strifes, and tumults and conflicts of life, the soul yearns after consolation and repose. And therefore the new Guide of the church was described as the Comforter. As the author and dispenser of truth, he met the wants of man's intellect; as the giver of consolation, he satisfied the longings of man's heart; and the understanding and the affections alike found their cravings met in the influences of the One Spirit. In some sense, then, it may be said that the church is now living in the third dispensation. Before Christ's advent and incarnation, the church was under the dispensation of the Father, when the Son was seen but remotely and indistinctly, through emblems and shadowy ordinances, and promises of distant fulfilment. On Christ's coming in the flesh began the dispensation of the Son, when it was distinctly announced, that all men should honor the Son even as they honor the Father, and the Mediator, intimated and predicted under the preceding economy, was now made visible to the eye of sense, and his claims and nature were more fully taught than of old. And on the day of Pentecost, the last and existing dispensation, that of the Holy Ghost began. Not that Christ loses his Headship over the church; he was in patriarchal times, and will remain in the millennial days "Head over all things to the church." But his bodily presence was withdrawn on his ascension; and, as he himself told the Apostles, it was so withdrawn "that the Comforter might come." And as we pass we would say, one of our manifold objections to the Romish doctrine of Transubstantiation is this, that it contravenes the dispensation of the Holy Ghost, by contradicting that bodily absence of the Saviour, upon which the Saviour himself predicated the coming of the Paraclete. Romanism asserts that the church has still the bodily presence of Christ in the sacrament. If so they do not need, and, according to the intimations of Christ himself, could not rightly expect the coming of the Comforter.

The personality and personal presence and agency of the Holy Ghost, are then important truths to the welfare and peace of the Christian church. In the allegories of our own Bunyan, how vividly and beautifully is this distinct personal existence of the Holy Ghost presented. The pilgrim, on passing through the narrow wicket gate that stands at the head of the way, enters into the Interpreter's House, where he is shown the mysteries of Scripture. The Divine Agent here appears not as an abstraction, but as having personal existence; and as the Interpreter, presenting in emblems and pictures the great truths of the Bible, he takes of the things of the Father and the Son and shows them to the eager and inquiring mind of the convert. So in the other of his narratives, my Lord Secretary appears as the channel of intercourse between Mansoul and its sovereign my Lord Shaddai. And here we have the work of the Spirit as the Intercessor inditing our prayers, as before we had him presented in his offices as Interpreter of Scripture.

21.—WORK OF THE HOLY SPIRIT.

Z. BRADFORD.

THE Holy Spirit is the great agent in the conversion and salvation of men. He was the sole, ultimate agent in erecting the temple by Zerubbabel. This I consider the doctrine of the text—"Not by might, nor by power; but by my Spirit, saith the Lord of hosts," Zech. iv. 6; and as a scriptural doctrine, I shall not therefore attempt to counterpoise human instrumentalities against the Spirit's agency, or compound them, deciding their ratio, or harmony, in the work of salvation. I understand the text to say, that the Holy Spirit is the one and only agent, by whom God's intentions of grace are brought about. This will not militate against the doctrine of free agency, or obedience, or the use of means, more than the fact that God governs the seasons, the light and winds of heaven, precludes the importance of our improving them, to gain his blessing. So far from this, it inspires and nourishes hope; is a lure to action; reveals the source of our strength, the author of our blessings, and can but lead us to acknowledge and honor the Divine Spirit. The object of informing Zerubbabel of this truth, was to quicken, not slacken and unman him for labor. The design of God in revealing the doctrine of the Trinity, appears to be, that we may discriminate the office of each of the *Three-One* in the work of salvation. It eminently facilitates our understanding of the subject. God the Father originates, the Son comes forth to execute, and the Spirit applies.

22.—THE HOLY SPIRIT IN CONVERSION.

I. W. HAYHURST.

Let Christians attempt to effect a revival of religion without the heartfelt acknowledgment of their dependence upon God for success, and like the disciples, who, in the absence of their Master, toiled the weary night in vain, they will accomplish nothing. Neither zeal nor skill will compensate for the want of the Holy Spirit. Whosoever plants, the increase is of God. That increase can be expected only when the need of the Spirit is felt, and his aid sincerely sought. If in his absence they should appear to succeed, and multitudes should be added to the church, it will not be "of such as shall be saved." The converts will be like the bodies in the prophet's vision before the Spirit resuscitated them. There will be "no breath in them." Or, like the fabled creations of Prometheus, before animated with the divine fire, they will be mere lifeless statues. Having a name to live, they will still be dead—and dead weights to the church's prosperity, instead of adding to her strength.

God has given us no means by which the conversion of sinners, or the general revival of religion can be effected, irrespective of the direct agency of the Spirit. The gospel itself will not do it. It is indeed a system of truth, divinely planned and promulgated—truth concerning matters of infinite moment, the soul and the awful realities of eternity. As such it is calculated to have an influence upon the minds of men. Too much can scarcely be said in reference to its adaptation to fill the place which God has assigned it—making it the means in his hand of the salvation of souls. So far as the means of a revival are concerned, too much reliance cannot be placed upon the faithful preaching of the pure Gospel. Still it is not the native energy of even

A. D. GILLETTE.

PASTOR OF THE ELEVENTH BAPTIST CHURCH, PHILADELPHIA

gospel truth that is to secure its triumph over sin. When Paul accounts for the wonderful effect of his preaching at Thessalonica, he ascribes it not to the inherent force of the truth that he taught, but to the fact that the gospel came unto them, "not in word only, but in power, and in the Holy Ghost"—in the power of the Holy Ghost. The gospel is the power of God to every one that *believeth.* The hearts of sinners must be prepared for its reception--else by whomsoever preached, it will fall like seed by the way-side. Experience teaches us that there may be evangelical teaching without revivals of religion. The oft-quoted instance of the Moravians in Greenland, who changed the subject matter of their preaching, began to proclaim the doctrines of the cross, tell of Christ's matchless love to guilty sinners, and witnessed as the result of the change, a great revival of religion, proves only that God is ready to bless his own appointed means of salvation. It does not prove any inherent efficacy even in evangelical doctrine to save man, irrespective of the direct agency of the Spirit. In some instances, the gospel has been preached by men of learning and eloquence—even by the apostles themselves—in vain. Again it has been preached by plain, comparatively unlettered men—its truths imperfectly taught, but being accompanied by the power of the Holy Ghost, has exhibited an influence over the characters of men never effected by any human means whatever.

While then, dear brethren, our earnest prayer is, "Lord revive thy work," let us be careful not to grieve the Holy Spirit. Let us employ such means as he can sanction. Let us rejoice that as the gift of Christ's love, he is to abide with his church forever. Let us earnestly implore his aid, pleading the gracious promise of the Saviour, "Ask, and it shall be given you; seek, and ye shall find; knock, and it shall be opened unto you."

THE BAPTIST PULPIT.

II.

THE NECESSITY, CERTAINTY, AND FACTS OF THE SCRIPTURES.

1.—NECESSITY OF A REVELATION FROM GOD.

J. L. WALLER.

THE question of the existence and character of God has been one of anxious solicitude, and was much debated by the ancient heathen philosophers. They found that a tradition had long been in the world, that there was a God, who in the beginning had made the heavens and the earth, and all the hosts of them. And this tradition, too, professed to trace its origin to a divine source. In far remote antiquity, ere man had much degenerated from primeval rectitude, celestial messengers, it was said, had borne intelligence to earth that there existed a holy and righteous One, dwelling in empyreal light and splendor, the builder and father of nature. Philosophy seized hold of this tradition, and sought by its suggestions to correct and modify the absurd superstition of the million. But who, by searching, can find out the Almighty. Who, without the light which revelation alone imparts to the mental vision, can look through nature up to nature's God? "The world by wisdom knew not God." Professing themselves wise, the philosophers became fools. They reasoned of God and the origin of things, until they found themselves involved in the mazes of a labyrinth from which they could not escape. To the anxious inquiry respecting the truth of God, propounded by suffering and degraded humanity, philosophy gave every variety of answer, and the mind stood bewildered at the myriad different lights every where kindled in the gloom, to each of which it was pointed as the beacon-fire of truth—uncertain which to follow, and dissatisfied with them all. Indeed, when our Saviour came, the prevailing opinion of the learned was that *truth* was all a chimera—the abortive phantom of a diseased brain! The dark cloud of scepticism overshadowed the world. But men were not satisfied with this decision. Reason sickened at the speculations of a philosophy which spoke

> "Huge folios of nonsense every hour,
> And left, surrounding every page, its marks
> Of prodigal stupidity."

Besides, it was denying to men what they most needed, and what they felt to be essential, if not to their being, at least to their happiness. It was commending a cup of gall to their parched lips.

Men, therefore, desired a revolution to satisfy their minds on this all-absorbing question. They felt that it was as unsafe as it was uncertain to follow the guidance of mere human reason. They needed divine illuminations. It is evident that those philosophers of antiquity who wrote most wisely upon the Deity, borrowed their knowledge from traditional revelation. Those of Greece were accustomed to travel among the nations of Asia, and Plato admits that they learned many things pertaining to God from the oriental sages, and also from "ancient and venerable tradition." From the regions of the patriarchs and prophets—among their acquaintances, their kindred, or their descendants—in those places or their neighborhoods where God has only condescended to hold converse with man, and to pour celestial splendors into the night of the mind—were gathered all those exalted truths in relation to God which gild with diamond beauty, certain portions of the speculations of Socrates, Plato, Cicero, and kindred sages of Greece and Rome. But philosophy was still at fault. The full idea of God was too mighty for its grasp. Proud as it was, it had to acknowledge its impotency in grappling with a theme so superhuman and divine. Hence that great philosopher Plutarch, remarks, that "it becomes all persons that have any understanding, to ask all good things of the gods; but that especially we should pray to obtain from them a knowledge of the gods, as far as men are capable of attaining to it, since neither man can receive, nor God bestow, any thing greater or more venerable than truth." The great mind of Plutarch felt the necessity of divine revelation to enable it to understand the truth in relation to God. And during the last century, when a pseudo-philosophy spurned the light of revelation as a guide to its researches, it forced many of its victims to assume the monstrous proposition, that "there is no God, and death is an eternal sleep!" It is difficult to conceive at what point short of this horrible abyss infidelity can consistently pause. All the later Platonists and Pythagoreans, though enemies of Christianity, owned the necessity of a revelation from God to lead men into a knowledge of divine truth.

And the conviction has prevailed in all ages and countries, that Heaven did, or would, in some way, impart revelations to man. The religious rites and ceremonies of the heathen were supposed by their observers to have come from above. Hence, also, the most celebrated law-givers of antiquity thought it necessary to profess some intercourse with heaven, in order to obtain from the people greater reverence for their institutions. Among all nations methods have been devised by which to ascertain the will of Deity —to brush away the cloud intervening between man and the celestial abodes. The extensive prevalence of omens, auguries, oracles, soothsaying, and astrology, proves that the human mind feels its need of a light over and above that ordinarily emitted by nature. The very fact that our species have been made the dupes and the victims of such gross imposition and fraud, establishes, beyond all evasion, their intense desire for divine illumination. The famished will relish even tainted food. And however we may smile at the simplicity of an augur, pretending to learn the secrets of futurity by the feeding of chickens, or attempting to reveal some decree of fate by prying into the reeking entrails of some recently slain calf or lamb—however we may be amazed that the croaking of a raven, the hooting of an owl, or the chirping of sparrows should startle with alarm, or inspire with enthusiasm mighty and chivalrous armies—and however gross and absurd to us may appear the superstition which supposes the fates and the fortunes of men and of empires were indicated by the motions of the heavenly bodies—yet, in this very folly we recognize the existence of a strong and universal conviction of the human mind, not only of the necessity of divine illuminations, but that a power somewhere resided that was inclined and competent to unfold the will of Heaven to man.

The desire of men for the truth in relation to God —for the light of revelation—may be learned from the very moral degradation of earth's teeming millions. "*We want the truth!*" comes in piercing and plaintive tones from all the dark places of heathendom. The myriads of altars, and images, and temples—the monuments of man's folly and the means of his misery, are so many mute orators imploring the light of God's word. In the sufferings of the pilgrim traveling in torture to some distant shrine—in the self-immolation of the enthusiast—in the groans of the poor wretch being crushed to death beneath the car of Juggernaut—in the shriek of the widow burning upon the funeral pile of her husband—in the heart-piercing cries of innocent infants offered in sacrifice by their ignorant and superstitious mothers—in that general wail of wo and wretchedness, ascending from suffering and agonizing humanity, the supplicating voice of mankind is heard, crying from the depths and darkness of superstition, "Give us the truth in relation to God! We are robbed of our property, defrauded of our happiness, deprived of our most sacred privileges; our children, our lives, our *souls* are constantly exposed to destruction! We are without God and without hope in the world!" Such is the voice of man's misery where the Bible is not.

2.—HISTORY OF THE SCRIPTURES.

S. JONES.

THE ancient Greeks had one sentence which they believed, though without foundation, to have descended from heaven; and to evince their gratitude and veneration for this gift, they caused it to be engraved in letters of gold, on the front of their most sacred temple. We, more favored than they, have not a sentence only, but a volume, that really descended from heaven, whose author is God; and in accents soft and sweet as the melody of angels, this blessed volume proclaims that "God is love." Then let us, my beloved brethren, search its sacred pages, and learn his most gracious will concerning us.

"O for a strong, a lasting faith,
To credit what the Almighty saith;
To embrace the message of his Son,
And call the joys of heaven our own!"

Whether we consider the Scriptures in reference to their subject-matter, eloquence, antiquity, or influence on society, they stand alone in their glory, having no equal, nor any to be compared with them. They tell us whence we came, what is now our duty, and whither we are going. They tell us of the creation of the world, the formation of man, and the providence of our all-wise Creator. They stretch forward to the destruction of the world, the closing scene of time, and they open to our astonished views eternity with all its tremendous realities. Their voice is as "the voice of many waters," and yet so exquisitely melodious, that thousands have listened until they have both wept and fainted in the excess of feeling. Like the fabled pillars of Seth, which are said to have bidden defiance to the deluge, they have stood for ages, unmoved in the midst of that flood which sweeps men with their labors into oblivion. In their light it is that the philosopher is enabled to tread his way through the intricate maze of nature. To them the politician is indebted for all that is valuable concerning human rights. And *we*, my brethren, especially owe to their kindly influence the free institutions under which we have the happiness to live, and which have now become the last hope of the friends of human liberty. To the church in the wilderness, through the influence of the Scriptures, must be ascribed that light which conducted our revolutionary fathers into the temple of liberty; and while truth has a votary, or liberty a friend, the memory of our pilgrim fathers will be revered for the share they had in reflecting on the government of this, our dear native land, the light which they themselves had received from the lively oracles of God. And here it is that the moralist drinks of healing waters, and in their strength he cries to the famishing multitudes as they pass along, "Ho, every one that thirsteth, come ye to the waters; and he that hath no money, come ye, buy and eat; yea, come, buy wine and milk without money and without price."

Though written by various authors, in different languages, during the space of about fifteen hundred years, and forming a collection of sixty-six different books—though their subjects are by far the most sublime and important that ever engaged the pen of man—and though their authors were not in kings' houses, nor heeded by the great men of this world, yet they have left us the only perfect system of morals the world has ever seen. Like Aaron's rod, it swallows up all opposers—and, like the sun, its influence is one, and most benign. Much has been written, and many labored efforts have been made with a view to exhibit discrepancies in the sacred text. The boldness and frequency of these attempts have been equalled only by the ignorance and imbecility of those who made them. That the Scriptures should contain "some things hard to be understood" by men of dark and prejudiced minds, is by no means surprising, nor does it argue any thing against their consistency. Hence, many have found fault with what they did not understand, and they have made *that* the reason of their implacable hatred to the gospel. To be consistent, such persons should neither converse, nor walk, nor eat, nor drink, nor sleep; for if we would comprehend these admitted laws of our nature, we must trace them up to nature's God. Had the sacred volume contained nothing beyond the stretch of man's puny intellect, then God must have refrained from revealing any thing of himself, or of those eternal realities that so deeply concern us. Then would the scoffer have boasted over that poverty, the want of which now so much offends him. And then the world would have been shrouded in moral darkness, far more dark than "the valley of the shadow of death." For the most part, the most reckless opposers have been the most ignorant of the Scriptures. Some have confessed that they had never *read* them—others that they *despised* them, and therefore were too prejudiced to be impartial judges—while many have commenced their perusal with the avowed intention to write against them, and in the end were convinced of their truth, and won over to their support.

3.—PRESERVATION OF THE SCRIPTURES.

A. D. GILLETTE.

THE marvellous preservation of the Scriptures from entire destruction, previous to their being collected into one book and translated into the common language, a period of about nine hundred years after the advent of our Lord Jesus Christ, shows the constant care of God over them. From the time that the Scriptures of the Old and New Testament were written, to the tenth century, each book was separate from the rest, written upon scrolls of parchment, and generally found only in the libraries of churches and monasteries, or belonging to persons of great wealth or distinction, and sometimes not even kings were able to possess the whole work, its value exceeding their ability to purchase.

No other work, in so many departments, could have so long survived the waste of time, and the decay that hath almost all things else destroyed; but God inclined the hearts of many to love this holy treasure; and although immense numbers of human writings of eminent authors, have floated down the current of time into oblivion, or suffered great changes from the mutilations of men, this polished mirror of truth and holiness, is now as bright as it came from the hands of its Author; yet pure as it was, and all-essential to the well-being of society, Christians were either so straitened that they could not, or so ignorant of their duties that they would not, invent or employ means to render them accessible and effective to the minds of the people. The slow and tedious process of transcribing, by hand, every line and every letter, was the cause for the general scarcity of the word of God, and consequently few copies were in circulation; and as the multitude had not learning, the number was very small who could read in their own language the wonderful word and works of the Lord. Truly did Jehovah almost by miracle display his regard for the inspired word, by preserving it from alterations and oblivion, when so much ignorance prevailed among the people, and many in power were in their hearts and lives so opposed to its exalted principles and sanctifying effects. Had not the Lord—may we all now say—had not the Lord been favorable to the Scriptures, and on our side, we should have been as dark in mind, and deluded in religion, as the nations are who have not the Holy Bible "as a lamp to their feet, and a light unto their path."

4.—THE CERTAINTY OF GOSPEL TRUTHS.

J. COOKSON.

THE religion of the gospel is calculated to promote the happiness of man, because it removes from the mind all doubt and painful suspicions, as to the way of our acceptance with God and the enjoyment of his power forever. A state of doubt and uncertainty of mind relative to subjects of such acknowledged importance, is peculiarly distressing. In such a state of mind we can enjoy no rest, nor be conscious of any security. But the gospel brings these blessings. Of the divine origin of its doctrines the Christian is certain. The fulfilment of prophecy, the most stupendous miracles, and the purest morality, are proofs of the divinity of our religion. And on this glorious body of evidence we fix our faith, and here it rests unshaken. To this we may add the internal witness of its truth, existing in the heart of every true believer, which to the disciples of Christianity is equal to a thousand arguments.

All doubts and hesitations are forever dissipated, and what to the most sagacious and enlightened amongst the heathen only glimmered, here shines with the most glorious lustre, what with them was but a feeble effort of hope, is with us the stability of faith.

We have already said, that the principles of the religion of Jesus are distinguished by the most infallible certainty. Those truths, which, previous to the revelation of the glad tidings made known to the shepherds, were involved in mystery and darkness, are now distinctly declared by the authority of Jehovah, and cordially received by every humble believer. In fact they never could have been made plain to our minds, but by a communication from Heaven. Nature could not enlighten us here, because it was not in her power. But respecting our immortality, and the certainty of justification through faith in the Son of God, these are truths which are now indisputably established.

Revelation does not ground these doctrines upon metaphysical speculations, or upon a long train of refined reasoning ; if it did, what better should we be for its assistance ? But it grounds them on the only possible conclusive principle, and that is the will of God. Hence, the Christian believer is not agitated by the most corroding anxiety about his future character and prospects. He feels not for one moment the agitations of fear lest his soul should become extinct at the dissolution of his body ; but with reference to all the doctrines of Christianity, he can exult and say—"Though uncertainty hangs on all mortal things, and obscurity too often involves all human speculations, yet here there is no uncertainty, there is no obscurity:" we have heard it from heaven, that "God so loved the world, that he gave his only begotten Son, that whosoever believeth in him should not perish, but have everlasting life." And the "angel of the Lord said, Behold, I bring you good tidings of great joy, which shall be to all people." The best and most enlightened heathen could never attain to any satisfactory conclusions on these supremely interesting subjects. Not so the believer; with an unfaltering tongue he can affirm, "Though our outward man perish, our inward man is renewed day by day. For we know that if our earthly house of this tabernacle were dissolved, we have a building of God, a house not made with hands, eternal in the heavens. Blessed be the God and Father of our Lord Jesus Christ, who, according to his abundant mercy, hath begotten us again unto a lively hope by the resurrection of Jesus Christ from the dead, to an inheritance incorruptible, and undefiled, and that fadeth not away, reserved in heaven for you who are kept by the power of God through faith unto salvation." Then let the Christian triumph, though in a world of evil, in the immutable treasure laid up in heaven for him. And let him rejoice with exceeding great joy, in those immutable principles of the gospel, on which his hopes of immortal blessedness are founded.

5.—THE MORAL EVIDENCE OF CHRISTIANITY.

E. BAPTIST.

We mention, as a strong evidence of the divine origin and character of the gospel, its divine efficacy manifested in the sanctification of believers. Wherever the truth is cordially embraced, it always produces an ameliorating effect on the believer. It is a mortifying fact, that many a hypocrite has imposed on mankind by a form of godliness while destitute of the power. But for this true religion is not to blame. The Bible curses all hypocrisy and deceit. Indeed, it is an evidence in its favor, for every counterfeit presupposes a reality, and a reality of excellence. For it would be impossible to counterfeit that which has no existence, and there could be no inducement to counterfeit that which is of no value. Hypocrisy is the homage which vice pays to virtue. Conscious that it does not possess the reality, it assumes the semblance of virtue. But in your intercourse with the world, have you ever known any person whom you have believed to be a genuine Christian, or have you not seen under the influence of the gospel a wonderful transformation of character? The drunkard becomes sober, the thief honest, the liar a man of veracity, the impure adulterer chaste and virtuous, and the profane swearer one that reverences an oath; in short, he who was a pest to the community, becomes an ornament to society, and an example of Christian virtue. Such being the general effects of the gospel, how important that it be published to all men, that it be cordially received by all, and that in obedience to its precepts, we "place our affections on things above, and not on things on the earth." Remember the transitory and perishable nature of all terrestrial objects. Change is the prominent feature of nature. The infinite and eternal God alone remains unchanged, and unchangeable; while "the fashion of this world passeth away." While we are discussing events, they cease to be. While we are criticising customs, they become obsolete. While we are adopting fashions, they vanish. While we are condemning or defending parties, they change sides. While we are contemplating feuds, opposing factions, and deploring revolutions, they are extinct. Of all created things mutability is their character at best; brevity their duration at the longest. "But the word of the Lord endureth for ever." All that the heart craves, that word supplies. Then let us take the Bible for the subject of our meditation, for the ground of our prayers, the rule of our conduct, the anchor of our hope, the standard of our faith. Fixed on this rock, we may smile at the ruins of nature, we may see this world with all its pride and pomps and pageantry vanishing into fumes and vapors, while we rise upon the wings of hope and love to a better and an enduring substance.

6.—REASONABLENESS OF FAITH.

S. G. HILLYER.

THE divine arrangement of walking by faith and not by sight, is exactly adapted to our condition as sinners. We shall find that our being shut out from absolute knowledge of those truths which respect God and our relation to him, is an arrangement of mercy. Remember, mere knowledge enriches the intellectual powers only. It is not its *property* to purify the heart. If, then, God had bestowed upon our race the highest degree of intelligence, so that we could comprehend all mysteries, it does not follow that we should have been any the less sinners. Yet, continuing transgressors under such circumstances, must have aggravated, beyond measure, our iniquities. A sinner's knowledge unsanctified, has no other moral power, but to magnify indefinitely the enormity of his guilt; and thus to make him ten-fold more the child of wrath.

In proof of what is here stated, let us look at the condition of the fallen angels. We cannot suppose that they were deficient in knowledge. They walked not by faith, but by sight; yet their exalted privileges neither shielded them from transgression, nor inclined them afterwards to repentance. To this hour, with certain knowledge of those great truths, which are to us objects of faith only, they continue the same lost spirits. Nor have we the slightest evidence that a token of mercy was ever tendered to them from on high. They seem to have sunk unpitied to their eternal doom. Now, who can say that our condition would not have been equally hopeless, if we had enjoyed equal knowledge? There are in scripture, impressive intimations that such *would* have been our unhappy destiny. What mean the woes denounced upon the unhappy cities of Capernaum, Bethsaida, and Chorazin? The judgment shall be more tolerable for Sodom and Gomorrah than for them. Why? We do not pretend that their knowledge was perfect; yet they did enjoy, in the person and conduct of Christ, a far greater light than that which the little household of Lot was able to shed upon the benighted regions of the plain. Therefore they were more guilty. We cannot fail to notice, that while the greater privileges of the Galilean cities do not seem to have inclined them to the service of God, or to have exerted any wholesome moral effect upon them, yet in proportion to the superiority of these advantages, the judgment of heaven becomes more fearful and unforgiving.

We infer, that when knowledge of divine truth becomes so far complete as to remove all occasion for the exercise of faith, God finds no place for the exercise of forbearance towards the sinner. This is corroborated by the fact, that there is no hope for the wicked beyond the grave. When such a one enters on the scenes of the invisible world, he is no longer required to walk by faith—perfect revelation of the whole truth bursts upon his mind. But *then*, God will show no mercy. He that is guilty must be guilty still. Our Saviour gives us another intimation to the same effect, which is yet stronger. In his dying prayer he said, "Father, forgive them, *for they know not what they do.*" Satan, who instigated this deed, did know. The misguided people who were his instruments did not. The latter were, therefore, the objects of his compassion, while Satan was the serpent under his heel, fit only to be trampled. Thus it appears, that a want of knowledge, when not voluntary, is made a ground of clemency. Hence, says Paul, I found mercy, because I did it ignorantly, in unbelief. From all which we conclude, that that very state of things which shuts out from the perception of our senses the propositions of religion, and makes them the objects of enlightened faith, is the only state of things in which the Almighty would ever have devised in our behalf any scheme of redemption. If so, that we are in such a state, becomes an indication of divine goodness. That we are required to walk by faith and not by sight, is the glory of religion—showing that our God is not "an austere man," but a compassionate Father. Surely, then, it is our highest duty, and our best interest, humbly to embrace the plan which God has so wisely adapted to our condition as sinners, and in which he so kindly offers to us eternal life.

7.—THE AUTHORITY OF RELIGION.

J. P. TUSTIN.

THERE can be no religion without authority to enjoin it; and the doctrines of religion, to have any influence, must rest on authority of the highest order, and the religion that is from God, has such authority. Jesus Christ proclaimed himself as the only Mediator between God and man, and the only Lord of the human conscience. When his disciples professed his name, they declared their allegiance to him, and their internal faith, by public baptism. This was the order in which Christ himself connected the conditions of obedience:—"He that believeth, and is baptized, shall be saved." And his inspired apostles observed the same principles, in the same order. They always regarded baptism as the outward act of internal faith; as the test-oath, and naturalization act, by which a stranger and alien declared his allegiance to Christ his King, and became a naturalized citizen of the visible church. Thus the apostle Paul declares it, as the act of the soldier who has put on the regimentals of the army, into which he has been sworn; or as the act of the servant assuming the livery of the master, whom he has bound himself to serve. "For as many of you as have been baptized into Christ, have put on Christ." Nay, the very method by which baptism was administered, declared its significance and its binding obligation. It was a solemn act of burial in water, by which a man declared his belief of the burial and resurrection of Christ; his own deadness to the world, and his rising again to newness of life. "Know ye not, that so many of us as were baptized into Jesus Christ, were baptized into his death? Therefore we are buried with him by baptism into death; that like as Christ was raised from the dead by the glory of the Father, even so we also should walk in newness of life. For if we have been planted together in the likeness of his death, we shall be also in the likeness of his resurrection."

8.—CLAIMS OF THE GOSPEL.

H. KEELING.

It is not wonderful that mistakes have existed concerning religion, even among those possessing the Bible, and perusing it with care. Under similar circumstances, the appearances of nature have been misunderstood, and the volume of inspiration can scarcely be expected to be plainer. Religion, in its fundamental principles, is plain; but as a science, whose laws may be investigated, or as an art, whose principles are to be practised, it involves much intricacy. It is precisely so of other subjects, which claim our daily attention. Law is an abstruse subject—but no one is in danger of a criminal offence, through mere mistake. Morality is more so: yet men rarely err through their ignorance. Few things are more complicated than machinery: and yet the mechanical powers are resolvable into three, or at most six.

Among the most common mistakes of modern times, is this: that religious discourses are intended to be mere orations, delivered either for amusement or instruction, or at most to convince of some one great truth or duty, and to persuade to its belief or performance; and that such discussion may be safely left for future action, when the interview has passed.

It is clear that the gospel has to do with but two classes of men—the church and the world; and the objects it proposes are likewise two—the edification of the church, and the conversion of the world. It claims the immediate conversion of every sinner to whom it addresses itself.

My business here to-day is with the latter class. I am come on a distinct errand. Although I am not an apostle, or a prophet, I have a message; and to each one present, I affirm, that although I am come on a very different errand from that of Ehud to Eglon, yet "I have a message from God unto thee." My object is perfectly intelligible, and it deeply concerns *you.* My business with each is particular and exclusive, as if he and I were alone. I am not come to prescribe a remedy for a disease, otherwise mortal; nor to vindicate rights of person or property; nor by my testimony to wipe off reproach from injured reputation. I am here to tell you how you may be saved; upon what conditions; and why you ought, without delay, to comply. The documents are ready; your signature is requisite. Our Master makes a just, reasonable, benevolent proposition. It is for you to agree or disagree, and abide the consequence.

Accordingly, I am to show you *the precise thing the gospel requires you to do*, that you may be saved. On this subject the Bible is explicit, but the public mind confused. Repentance, faith, love, trust in God, external obedience—each of these, and of many other things, is supposed by many to be the *hinge* upon which salvation turns. But if you carefully compare all that the Scriptures teach, you will find that they reduce all mankind to *one* class, and suspend the salvation of every rational creature, to whom the gospel comes, on *one* condition. All, whether Jews or Gentiles, are reduced to one class. Scepticism, idolatry, worldliness, profligacy, morality, thoughtlessness, ambition, love of pleasure—it matters not what predominates, if obedience to Christ is withheld—they are all so many different aspects of the same thing—*a heart opposed to Christ and to God.* All stand on the same level before the Omniscient Judge—all guilty and exposed to hell. As the *disease* is one, so the *remedy* is one—that is, *a cordial reception of Jesus Christ as the only Saviour.* This is the paschal lamb—the brazen serpent—the floating ark—the altar—the sacrifice—the priest; every allusion, every service, every truth, every duty, every thing looks to Christ. And whatever we are required to do, it all amounts to nothing, except as connected with our cordial reception of him as our only Saviour. The figure is changed, but the idea is always the same.

I would show you, also, *when* this thing is required to be done. Our text is to the point. "*To-day—now*," is the time. In every view you take of the gospel, it claims *instant* regard. *Invitation.* Does it invite? The guests are expected to accept. Not to accept is insult. What else is meant by the parable of the supper? "Ho, every one that thirsteth." *Command.* "God commandeth all men every where to repent."

Is the command *present* expecting future obedience? Is God to be served on credit? It might as well be by proxy. "To-day if ye will hear his voice, harden not your heart." *Warning.* "O generation of vipers, who hath warned you?" "The axe is laid at the root of the tree; every tree that bringeth not forth fruit, is hewn down and cast into the fire." *Remonstrance.* "Turn ye, turn ye, why will ye die?" "What more could I have done to my vineyard, than I have done in it?"

9.—THE EFFICACY OF THE GOSPEL.

FRANCIS WAYLAND.

We see that all which is really terrific in the misery of man, results from the disease of his moral nature. If this can be healed, man may be restored to happiness. Now the gospel of Jesus Christ is the remedy devised by Omniscience specially for this purpose, and therefore we do certainly know that it will inevitably succeed.

It is easy to be seen that universal obedience to the command—Thou shalt love the Lord thy God with all thy heart, and thy neighbor as thyself—would make this world a heaven. But nothing other than the gospel of Christ can persuade men to this obedience. Reason cannot do it; philosophy cannot do it; civilization cannot do it. The cross of Christ alone has power to bend the stubborn will, and melt the frozen heart to love. For, said one who had experienced its efficacy, the love of Christ constraineth us, because we thus judge, that if one died for all, then were all dead; and that he died for all, that they who live should not live to themselves, but unto him who died for them and rose again.

The preaching of the cross of Christ is a remedy

for the miseries of the fall, which has been tested by the experience of eighteen hundred years, and has never in a single instance failed. Its efficacy has been proved by human beings of all ages, from the lisping infant, to the sinner a hundred years old. All climates have witnessed its power. From the ice-bound cliffs of Greenland to the banks of the voluptuous Ganges. the simple story of Christ crucified has turned men from darkness to light, and from the power of Satan unto God. Its effect has been the same with men of the most dissimilar conditions ; from the most abandoned inhabitant of Newgate, to the dweller in the palaces of kings. It has been equally sovereign amidst the scattered inhabitants of the forest, and the crowded population of the densest metropolis. Every where, and at all times, it has been the power of God unto salvation to every one that believeth.

And lastly, we learn from the word of the living God, that it will be successful until this whole world has been redeemed from the effects of man's first disobedience. As truly as I live, saith Jehovah, all the earth shall be filled with the glory of the Lord. Ask of me, saith he to his Son, and I will give thee the heathen for thine inheritance, and the uttermost parts of the earth for thy possession. In the revelation which he gave to his servant John of things which should shortly come to pass ; I heard, said the apostle, great voices in heaven, saying—The kingdoms of this world are become the kingdoms of our Lord, and of his Christ, and he shall reign forever and ever. Here then is the ground of our unwavering confidence. Heaven and earth shall pass away, but one jot or one tittle shall in no wise pass from the word of God, until all be fulfilled. Such, then, are the means on which we rely for the accomplishment of our object.

10.—POWER OF TRUTH ON THE CONSCIENCE.

B. MINER.

CONSCIENCE is the most authoritative of all the faculties of the mind. Even amid the wild commotion of perverted faculties and depraved passions, each striving for the ascendency, the voice of conscience is heard, and its authority felt, if not obeyed. The most guilty and depraved men, in whose minds judgment was dethroned and passion swayed the sceptre, have exhibited the power of conscience.

When Ahab was walking in the vineyard of the murdered Naboth, the sight of the prophet roused his conscience to condemn him. And Ahab said unto Elijah, "Hast thou found me, O mine enemy?" When Belshazzar, the King of Babylon, was feasting with a thousand of his lords, there came forth fingers of a man's hand, and wrote an unknown sentence on the wall. "Then the king's countenance was changed, and his thoughts troubled him, so that the joints of his loins were loosed and his knees smote one against another." Why this sudden and great effect upon the king? There was nothing in the writing to alarm him so suddenly, for he could not read it; nor in the writer, for that was only "the fingers of a man's hand." But all his terror was caused by conscience. The frenzy of Nero, and Caligula, and other tyrants, is believed to have been the effect of a guilty conscience. And all this confirms the truth of the poet's declaration—

"Conscience, tremendous conscience, in his fits
Of inspiration—wheresoe'er it came—
Rose like a ghost, inflicting fear of death
On those who feared not death in fiercest battle,
And mocked him in their martyrdom of torments:
That secret, swift, and silent messenger
Broke on them in their lonely hours;—in sleep,

In sickness; haunting them with dire suspicions
Of something in themselves that would not die;
Of an existence elsewhere, and hereafter,
Of which tradition was not wholly silent,
Yet spake not out: its dreary oracles
Confounded superstition to conceive,
And baffled scepticism to reject.
What fear of death is like the fear beyond it?"

The murderer sees the ghost of the murdered man every time he closes his eyes. He shudders at the imaginary sight of the ghastly features, and bleeding wounds, and imploring attitude of his victim. He hears dying groans in the roaring of the waters, in the howling of the winds, and in the voices of men. No lapse of time, no distance of place, can satiate the gnawing vulture, *remorse*, or prove to be the *Lethean* waters, to obliterate the memory of the past. All this was for a single sin; and a sin, too, which, in the sight of God, is not more heinous than the sins which every man commits. The reason why the murderer feels it more deeply is, that his conscience is more enlightened on that particular sin. But who will say that the sin of rejecting Christ, discarding the gospel, and resisting the Holy Ghost, is not worse? And if the power of conscience is so great when aroused by a single sin, what will it not do when the preacher aids it in confronting the sinner with all his sins? Though the conscience has become seared as with a hot iron, there are seasons when even that conscience can be reached. God has chained this part of our moral nature to a throne of justice, and truth, and holiness. The sinner may strive to lose sight of that throne, by urging his way on in sin; but the distance only increases his guilt and the weight of his chain. A poet has well said—

"The farther off we go,
The swing of justice deals the mightier blow."

The man who preaches to the conscience has the greatest power over his hearers. Bishop Butler says of the conscience—"Had it *strength* as it has *right*, had it *power* as it has manifest *authority*, it would absolutely govern the world." One great design of preaching is, to restore conscience to its rightful supremacy; to seat it again on the throne of the mind, and to bring all the other faculties under its control—and to seat it there, an enlightened and holy sovereign, educated by divine truth, and sanctified by the Holy Ghost. What would be the effect, if a church were composed wholly of members so governed? fully recognizing every obligation to God, and to their fellow-men, and laboring to discharge these obligations? All this every church should be, and will be, when, by manifestation of the truth, we commend ourselves to their consciences, in the sight of God.

11.—THE ATTAINMENT OF TRUTH.

C. D. MALLARY.

Many powerful causes combine their influence to betray men into error upon almost every subject that engages their inquiry. One cause is to be found in the limited powers of the human mind. How difficult, with the feeble and beclouded faculties which we possess, so to investigate important and intricate subjects in all their various relations and tendencies as to defend ourselves against mistake. With the imbecility of the human mind, how many other things co-operate. Indolence checks investigation; early education warps the judgment; the opinions of revered associates, public sentiment, and the authority of great names, often rear their formidable ramparts against the truth.

And how strong are the manacles which the depraved heart of man rivets upon his understanding.

Pride dictates opinion with amazing power; prejudice darkens the mental eye; passion clamors for a verdict in accordance with its blind impulse; and self-interest seizes the scales of judgment and casts in her unequal weights. All these influences have deeply affected the religious opinions of men, and given origin and perpetuity to innumerable errors. Where truth has not been wholly extinguished, how often is it sadly beclouded; and even when it seems to shine forth with full-orbed brightness, prayerful and patient scrutiny may reveal upon the disk many an unseemly spot. In relation to the same point, men have entrenched themselves at a distance from each other almost infinite. Nor is it certain when we correct ourselves in one extreme, that we shall not fall into another equally absurd. How often does the human mind, when routed from one mistake, swing off, like the pendulum, to an opposite position, just as distant from the truth, and as dangerous to the cause of Christ. The strongest intellects have put forth their might in the defence of error, and wit and learning have gathered many costly materials to embalm and consecrate the most futile delusions. And as error is often united to great intellectual attainments, so is it sometimes associated with eminent piety. It is not strange that considerations like these should suggest discouragement and fear, and induce the honest inquirer after truth to exclaim, "Who can understand his errors?" How shall I arrive at the right knowledge of divine things? Can I hope to go right, where the wisest and best have wandered? Can I hope to stand firm, where the mightiest have stumbled? We would say, "Let no man's heart fail him for fear." The views which we have presented should inspire watchfulness and self-distrust; but they should not induce despair. We have in our possession (thanks to the Great Father of lights) an infallible standard of truth, and there is a way in which its most important instructions may be learned. "The law of the Lord is perfect, converting the soul; the testimony of the Lord is sure, making wise the simple." And that word which stands before us as the rich store-house of eternal truth, reveals to us in its very portal the sacred key by which we may unlock its golden gates, and enter in and be wise. "Wherefore, laying aside all malice and all guile, and hypocrisies, and envies, and all evil speaking, as new-born babes desire the sincere milk of the word, that ye may grow thereby. If any man will do his will, he shall know of the doctrine, whether it be of God, or whether I speak of myself. The meek will he guide in judgment, and the meek will he teach his way. Take my yoke upon you, and learn of me." We cannot mistake the purport of those instructions; it is plainly this, that a sincere desire to know the truth, connected with a meek, gentle, obedient, and teachable temper, will render us successful and profitable students in the oracles of God. Such a spirit as this is always needful, but never more so than when we come to the investigation of those doctrines which particularly involve the sovereignty of Jehovah. They are revealed, and are therefore to be contemplated and believed; yet they are mysterious and awful, and should never therefore be approached in the spirit of cavilling, of levity, and pride. With what sacred awe, with what holy reverence, with what deep humility, should we gaze at those grand revelations which exhibit God in the sovereignty of his grace and the glory of his dominion, having mercy on whom he will have mercy, doing according to his will in the army of heaven, and among the inhabitants of the earth. Without this disposition of soul, we shall be likely to object, and contend, and err as thousands have done; or if we should render a formal assent to the truth, we shall come short of those inestimable benefits which a devout, humble, and reverential consideration of it will never fail to impart. In our investigations upon these subjects we must be carefully guarded against those two great errors which in all ages have so much dishonored God, and impeded his righteous cause; on the one hand, such views of his character and instructions as would annihilate the obligations of his creatures and tend to soothe the sinner in his rebellion, and the professed Christian in his antinomian indolence; and on the other, such views of the creature's power and worthiness as tend to encourage his pride and self-righteous presumption; and by exalting man, to invade the sovereign prerogatives of Heaven.

12.—THE OPERATIONS OF PRINCIPLE.

W. J. HARD.

PRINCIPLE is the mind's devotion to truth or to falsehood, and is called pure or the contrary, in accordance with the character of that which it has embraced. I would describe one possessing pure principles thus; one whose mind is under the constant influence of moral law. They are active and equable. The regularity of their developments affords the tests by which judgment shall be passed upon them. The *measure* of devotion affords other distinctions; such as these, firm or weak principles. The highest degree of the soul's consecration to the truths of the decalogue, is possessed by the perfect man. It is expressed by the Psalmist thus, "The law of God is in his heart." Such is his undying attachment to its precepts, that they are ever present to the mind's eye, and may be said, in the figurative but appropriate language of the Bible, to be written on his heart, as perpetual remembrances, as infallible guides, and as constant excitants.

Pure principles conduce to distinguished excellence,

in the first place, by giving *proper direction to the mind.* Where religious truths exert their influence, this will be had. For the realization of our agency, and the conversion of our hearts, will direct the soul to other and nobler objects—to higher aims and more arduous efforts, than selfish nature would desire or make. They lead one beyond the circumscribed sphere of personal desire, to the extensive field of obligation and duty. Such direction will secure more than *partial virtue*, which, alas, is the only wages of many minds of great ability and untiring industry. "Whatsoever things are honest, whatsoever things are just, whatsoever things are pure, whatsoever things are lovely, whatsoever things are of good report," are the objects of the perfect man's thoughts and aims; and they throw back the mind upon the lustre of their purity. Attention to all these things is enjoined by Paul. The disputing Greeks would make this and that the basis of virtue; but this distinguished Christian philosopher made it consist in the union of every thing excellent, and taught that devotion to every particular is necessary for purity of character.

Pure principles conduce to zeal in the performance of duty. Let it be remembered, that zeal is not so much the result of mental temperament, as it is of a proper state of mind. That which is scriptural and worthy of commendation, results not from constitutional order, but from the love of purity, and from hatred to its opposite. These strongest passions of the heart afford it perpetual aliment, and keep it ever vigorous and active. In the being of pure principles, it is not a flickering light, but an imperishable flame. Success does not enervate it, nor does disappointment destroy it. It cannot be conquered; for it is always warmly "affected towards a good thing," is always on the field warring in its favor, or advancing its conquests. If it does not extend its triumphs *abroad*, it is always exulting in victories at *home*. To call it deathless would be but half commendation; like the path of the just, it shineth brighter and brighter unto the perfect day. If success be possible, this will ensure it; for it enlists all the faculties of the mind, employs all proper instrumentalities, and improves all opportunities. This is the martyr-spirit which animated prophets, apostles, reformers, and patriots. Its triumphs are recorded in the history of the world and of the church. Individuals actuated by it, cannot but be distinguished for virtue and for usefulness. Without it, splendid abilities can achieve but little; with it, inferior talents will accomplish wonders. Relative perfection is its certain reward, engaged as it is in the promotion of every thing which is excellent. True, one of this stamp may not command the popular favor. He may not win golden opinions from the fickle multitude; but he secures character, which, though aspersed, is not defiled. He leaves behind him monuments of his worth, which shall outlive the malignities of men. His name, identified with whatever is excellent, and pure, and honorable, shall not perish. The virtuous will embalm his memory, and it shall be said of him, though "dead, he yet speaketh."

They will conduce to perseverance. For continuance in well-doing, no substitute for purity of principle can be relied on. Selfishness, when satisfied, may be won to sloth, or lured to open profligacy. Too frequently are its subjects seen ruining the characters they have won, with more awful celerity than they acquired them. The reason is, the impetus given being only sufficient to reach a desired elevation—the force expended, they fall like lead in the abyss beneath. Interest is a feeble barrier against strong temptations. Ambition may be hurled from high distinction by favor or disappointment, to perish miserably in the dust. Not a few victims in private and public life, confirm and illustrate the insufficiency of such considerations for the maintenance of unswerving rectitude. Every graveyard has given them a resting-place, and every heart has been called on to mourn their untimely and dishonored end. He who would secure moral excellence, must be prepared for universal resistance. Virtue must be loved for itself, and not for the advantages it confers. The soul must be devoted to this, come weal or come wo, or some opportune temptation will lead it to irrecoverable dishonor—will fix upon it shame indelible in the memory of man. In every thing dreaded, or desired, there is danger to frail humanity. Prosperity and adversity, popularity and persecution, have laid many low. Reputation itself, precious as it is, may beget self-confidence and pride, dangerous to virtue—let the bloody and ignominious death of that talented English clergyman, Dr. Dodd, suffice for confirmation. Self, as well as all allurements prejudicial to integrity, must be watched and guarded. Conscience must be a faithful sentinel, which will repeat not only the daily admonition of Philip's servant, "remember thou art mortal," but the needful caution of our religion, "let him that thinketh he standeth, take heed lest he fall." The praise of virtue is vigilance—vigilance over the heart—vigilance over the smiles of friends and the frowns of foes—vigilance over that which seemeth good—over that which appeareth evil. Let the priest, whose duty it is to guard the sacred fire, slumber, and the temple will be darkened, and its glory obscured. The minister must love the temple more than himself—the holiness of the altar more than his repose. He must feed the celestial flame, from the moment of the soul's consecration, until the decree of God brings it to exist in the light of his immediate and personal glory. Who is that faithful minister, who guards the virtue of his heart? He in whose bosom purity dwells, not as a cold abstraction, but as a living principle? He who not only admires it, but loves it. He who makes this the object of his existence, and his pleasures and pursuits subordinate to it. Such a one will maintain his integrity—" none of his steps shall slide." His soul firmly fixed on the Source of purity, shall receive such accessions of strength, that it shall make perpetual progression—it shall run and not be weary, it shall walk and not faint.

An exalted state of excellence is the legitimate sequence of pure principles : for the objects to which they direct the mind, will impart their coloring to it, and increasing excellence will ensue. This is the instruction which mental philosophy affords. Again ; the perpetual exercise of the moral faculties will be succeeded by additional strength and lustre. This is likewise a result of mental law, as determinate as the effects of physical causes. The Scriptures teach, that this submission of the soul to God, will receive his special blessing—that he will not only produce in it virtuous aspirations, but invigorate its virtue, and excite it to continuance in well-doing. This is clearly matter of experiment, susceptible of sensible confirmation. "If any man will do my will, he shall know of the doctrine." It is to be wished that men would not leave these things solely to the moralist and the theologician. They are perfectly consistent with every honorable pursuit. They constitute the safeguards of honor—the ægis of integrity—the infallible mentor of the judgment and conscience. They will aid mind in all its efforts, by subduing its disorders, by defending it against all assaults, and by prompting it to noble acts. Could it be proved by reference to the comparative merits of men, engaged in the same pursuits, that the neglecters of moral law had won more laurels, and had contributed most to the well-being of mankind by their attainments and example, we would not improve this mournful occasion * with the subject which we have selected. But the testi-

* Funeral of a Christian physician.

mony of every age and of all history, harmonizes with the injunction of the text, and bids you mark the perfect man and the upright. On the pages of our country's history, the names of the greatest and best were men whose minds were subjected to the gospel of Christ. To these the patriot directs the minds of the rising generation, knowing that the existence of the republic depends on their conformity to the principles and actions of such men as "the father of his country." There are others, great in debate and in council as they have been, apostles of freedom though they were, for whom, on many accounts, the cheeks of their countrymen must be tinged with shame. The mantle of political and literary distinction is not large enough to cover moral turpitude. Their reproach co-exists with their greatness, and detracts largely from their fame.

13.—MYSTERIES OF THE BIBLE.

J. N. SEAMAN.

God is incomprehensible in his word! How interesting to trace the hand of the same all-wise and powerful Being in nature, providence, and his word! In reference to each it may alike be said—"He holdeth back the face of his throne and spreadeth his cloud upon it."

We cannot comprehend the union which exists between the three Divine persons in the Trinity. How there can be a Trinity, three persons equal in power and glory, and but one God, and one God existing in three persons, is a mystery too profound for finite reason to develope. It is mysterious why sin was ever permitted to enter the world. Who can comprehend "the mystery of godliness, God manifest in the flesh," the union between the human and the divine natures in the person of Christ? Why did not God, who is infinite in goodness and power, provide efficiently for the salvation of all mankind, and not a part? In reference to these and other truths, we must say—"He holdeth back the face of his throne and spreadeth his cloud upon it."

But, my brethren, are these all the mysteries contained in the Bible? "We speak," says the Apostle, "the wisdom of God in a *mystery*, even the *hidden* wisdom which God hath before ordained unto our glory." Who of us can comprehend the length, and breadth, and height, and depth of "the love of Christ, which passeth knowledge?" We may look a little way over the surface of the *immeasurable ocean*, but we cannot take into view its utmost extent, nor understand the countless treasures which lie concealed in its bosom. We can behold a few of those resplendent orbs which glitter on the outskirts of this universe of glory, but it can be *fully* comprehended by none but by him who formed it.

We freely admit that the Bible contains mysteries. But the objection, we think, comes with an ill grace from the mouth of the infidel, that the Scriptures ought not to be believed, because they are full of mysteries. Is not nature full of mysteries, and are not the providences of Heaven inscrutable? Why not, then, disbelieve in the existence of a God who has created and who governs the universe? We deny not, that in the Bible, as in nature, there are mysteries which we cannot unfold. But this fact is no argument against the inspiration of the Bible, but one which tends rather to confirm it. In every revelation of an infinite Being to finite creatures, there must necessarily be a mixture of light and darkness, of clearness and obscurity. It is so in nature and providence, and why should it not be so in the kingdom of grace? God has stamped this mystery upon the face of his word, to teach us our own littleness, while he has rendered many things most important for us to understand, sufficiently plain, that we may be encouraged to draw nigh unto him in confidence and prayer.

We read in the word, "God so loved the world that he gave his only begotten Son, that whosoever believeth in him should not perish, but have everlasting life. He that believeth on the Son hath everlasting life, and he that believeth not the Son shall not see life, but the wrath of God abideth on him." The truth conveyed in these passages is plain. There can be no difficulty in understanding it, if our hearts are sincerely disposed to receive instruction; and it is infinitely more important, my hearers, that you should understand and believe this truth, than that you should be able to comprehend the Trinity. Attend, then, to these truths of the Bible which are simple and essential to salvation, and which nothing would prevent you from embracing, but "an evil heart of unbelief" —a heart which is at enmity with God, and is not subject to his law, neither indeed can be.

14.—SOURCES OF ERROR AMONG CHRISTIANS.

J. J. WOOLSEY.

THE more common sources of error, or the main causes why some Christians, enjoying the same advantages as others, from acquaintance with the teachings of Christ and his apostles, are betrayed into mistaken views respecting the doctrines and institutions of the gospel, may be briefly comprehended as follows.

The pride and selfishness of man; an improper reliance upon the reputed correctness of others' opinions, without strictly examining for themselves; the influence of early religious instruction, and the force of custom, which, when combined, powerfully control even the sincere, binding the understanding, and chaining it down to a degree of ignorance and prejudice the most incredible, were it not for the unquestionable testimony of the facts themselves; a prevailing desire to make the Scriptures speak that *sense* which is held by some favorite party, or friends, rather than embrace the obvious meaning which the inspired writer intended to reveal; daring to trifle with conscience, suppressing her convictions of duty and truth, on the ground that the thing required is not indispensable to salvation, and therefore of little consequence, quite a matter of indifference, whether it be received and obeyed or not; a disinclination, if not a settled determination, to hear and read only such instructions as shall favor their own pre-conceived opinions, and build up the party to which they chance to belong; a confounding of the literal and figurative sense of Scripture; an attempt to support some favorite sentiment by probabilities, suppositions, inferences, and analogy, where there is no plain command, nor yet example for any such sentiment.

These are the more usual sources of error in doctrine and practice among those who acknowledge the authority of the Bible, and profess to take it as their guide. So long as these things exist, we can never come to the unity of the Spirit in the bond of peace. It becomes every one, therefore, who desires the peace and prosperity of Zion, not only to adopt the Bible as his own authority in matters of religion, but also to see to it, that he does not make the Bible speak what it does not contain; that he gives to every part of the word of God that obvious sense which the Holy Ghost indited in the minds of the sacred penmen: "For whatsoever is more than these, cometh of evil." Let it not be forgotten by the Biblical student, that substantial interpretations of the word of God must rest upon their own intrinsic evidence; in the use of words employed; in philological or grammatical construction; in agreement with the immediate context; and in perfect harmony with other parts of Scripture. Whoever shall carry out his interpretations upon principles like these, shall see and know their practical utility in acquiring that positive sense which the inspired writers intended to communicate.

15.—THE SOURCE OF HERESY.

J. PARKHURST.

It is sometimes insinuated by men of extensive influence, that though we embrace different and contradictory systems of faith, we are equally under the guidance of the Holy Spirit—equally the objects of the Divine complacency. But this is a mistake which must be rectified—a delusion which cannot be too strongly resisted. It is dishonorable to God, and dangerous to souls. When once a man persuades himself that religious error is harmless, he ceases to feel the importance of the truth, loses the studious zeal of the noble Bereans, is likely to adopt any sentiments but such as are correct, and is fit to be led by any one except the Spirit of the Most High. But the insinuation is dishonorable to God. What! does the selfsame Spirit originate the various and jarring tribes of Christendom? Incredible. This would make him the author of confusion—the abettor of strife and discord. Truth is not thus ductile in its nature, and accommodating in its genius. It presents itself in the excellence of perfection as the mirror of the Divine glory, and varies not to suit the convenience of rebellious men. The world must yet bow to its majesty. And when that happy era shall arrive, foretold by ancient seers—when the earth shall be filled with the *knowledge* of the Lord which shall dissipate the shades of ignorance and error—the partition-walls of sectaries shall be broken down, and the happiness of union shall be universally enjoyed.

If men embrace erroneous sentiments, let them not look to Heaven for justification. Heresy was born in a different world; and let them know, while they patronize her delusions, that they, not the firm adherents of truth, stand charged with the guilt of scattering the seeds of discord among the people. When any number of Christians move under the guidance of the Holy Ghost, they move in concert; and when any portion of them break away from his sacred guidance, they submit, though unaware of it, to the father of lies, and may expect that their end will be according to their ways—a scene of bitterness and strife. In this way we may account for the varying sentiments of men, without dishonoring God, without reproaching religion, or checking the holy zeal of saints in their investigations of the Bible.

16.—PERNICIOUS INFLUENCE OF ERROR.

J. D. KNOWLES.

O HOW dreadful has been the sway of error over the human mind, from the beginning of time to this hour; and how awful is the evidence thus furnished of the moral depravity of mankind! What else could impel them to repress the instinctive craving of the mind for truth, and yield themselves to the dominion of debasing and ruinous delusions? The first act of sin was the immediate result of the belief of a falsehood, uttered by that powerful and malignant spirit, whose pre-eminent odiousness and hostility to God and man are summed up in the title given him by our Saviour himself—*the Father of lies.* The very essence of all the forms of idolatry, which have covered the earth with crimes and mourning, is falsehood—*falsehood* to God, for it has changed his glory into the likeness of corruptible man, and beasts, and creeping things—*falsehood* to man himself, for it has deceived him in regard to his condition, his duties, and his destiny—*falsehood* to the very nature of man, his interests and his best affections, for it has urged him to inflict tortures and death on himself, and on his fellow-men: it has impelled the mother to throw her living babe into the flames, or into the jaws of the crocodile—falsehood to the eternal principles of morals, for it has sanctioned and fostered every species of vice, which can debase human nature. The Jewish religion, in its present form, is founded on falsehood, for it denies that Jesus is the Christ. Mahommedanism is a rank imposture, with just enough of truth to make the darkness of the whole system more hideously visible.

And how large a mixture of error has infused itself into the principles and practices of men who call themselves Christians! How much is there, even in Protestant Christianity, which has no warrant in the word of truth! Is it wonderful that there have been bigotry, and persecution, and alienation among the disciples of our Lord? What other fruit could be expected from the errors which they have incorporated with the pure truth of God? The natural effect of error is to contract the understanding, and close the heart, and thus engender bigotry, and impel to persecution. What wonder is it that the standard of Christian morality has been so depressed, and that the disciples of Christ have exhibited so little of his spirit! It is the *truth* alone which can purify the heart, and mould the moral nature of man into a lovely image of Him who was "full of grace and truth." Why should we marvel, that darkness still covers so large a part of our globe? The truth has not yet been sent forth into all lands, to expel the darkness, and pour light on the dwellers in the shadow of death.

17.—IMPORTANCE OF THE SCRIPTURES TO THE MINISTRY.

J. LUMPKIN.

THE word of God is that sword of the Spirit which God has directed to be used by all his servants, and on which, under his direction, they are to depend for success in all their labors—"For the word of God is quick and powerful, and sharper than any two-edged sword, piercing even to the dividing asunder of soul and spirit, and is a discerner of the thoughts and intents of the heart." But they cannot use this powerful, this efficient weapon, unless they have a knowledge of that word. And although the great end for which the Almighty has called men to labor in his vineyard, is to destroy the works of the devil, and to build up and establish Immanuel's kingdom, yet we are not from this to infer, that a superficial or a general acquaintance with the Bible is enough. No, my beloved brethren, against such an inference as this, some of us in this assembly, from experience, would feel it our bounden duty to enter our solemn protest. We cannot subscribe to such a sentiment—for we go forth with our heads bowed down like a bulrush, with language like this in our hearts: "Alas for me, that my knowledge of the word of the Lord is no greater!" Neither does it require any extraordinary exertion of mind to discover, that the preacher of the gospel should have a particular knowledge of all the Scriptures.

In sustaining this position, we shall adduce only two or three texts. The Saviour, when tempted in the wilderness, in repelling effectually the assaults of Satan, makes this declaration—"It is written, man shall not live by bread alone, but by *every word* that proceedeth out of the mouth of God." From this passage, this conclusion is unquestionable—that *every word* of God is of use to man, especially to the minister of the gospel. In Paul's address to the elders of Ephesus, at Miletus, he calls upon them to bear witness that he was pure from the blood of all men, for this reason—"I have not shunned to declare unto you *all* the counsel of God." This text teaches us that the apostle's confident appeal to those who were well acquainted with his ministry, did not relate exclusively to his faithfulness, in that he had not preached any thing "save Jesus Christ and him crucified," but that he had preached "*all the counsel of God;*" which we conceive no man can do, unless the word of Christ dwell in him richly. Once more: "All Scripture is given by inspiration of God, and is profitable for doctrine, for reproof, for correction, for instruction in righteousness; that the man of God may be perfect, thoroughly furnished unto every good work." The sentiment which we adduce from this text, is this—that although there is an ample fullness in the Scriptures to afford the gospel minister all necessary information, there is no redundancy; hence he ought, like Apollos, to be "mighty in the Scriptures," and thus be qualified to convince those who oppose themselves.

18.—THE FACTS OF THE GOSPEL.

G. W. EATON.

A GREAT portion of this wonderful book is occupied by a simple narration of facts—the principal of which relate to the birth, the life, the doctrine, the death, the resurrection, and the ascension to heaven of Jesus of Nazareth, and the subsequent spread of his doctrines through the instrumentality of his chosen apostles and disciples. Let us look at some of the more prominent of these facts. And that we may have a nearer and more vivid view, let us in imagination

G. W. EATON.

PROFESSOR IN MADISON UNIVERSITY.

transport ourselves back in the history of our world somewhat more than eighteen centuries, and to the land of Palestine, then nearly the geographical centre of the civilized portion of the globe. In the vicinity of Bethlehem a group of pious shepherds are watching their flocks in the solemn stillness of the night. Suddenly a dazzling radiance bursts from the dark skies above them. And as every eye is turned upward to the brilliant phenomenon, a glorious being from the upper world is revealed to their astonished gaze. Every heart sinks, congealed with terror; but hear that voice in tones of seraphic melody—"Fear not; for behold I bring you good tidings of great joy, which shall be to all people. For unto you is born this day, in the city of David, a Saviour, who is Christ the Lord." And as the sign is given by which the reality of the vision might be tested, around the celestial messenger, and stretching away on either side, thronged a vast concourse of shining ones robed in the splendors which heaven alone can furnish. Hark! they are singing! What words are these which come floated down on waves of heaven's music? "Glory to God in the highest, and on earth peace, good-will towards men." The wondering and ravished shepherds hasten to Bethlehem to see with their own eyes the thing which the Lord had thus made known to them. There, precisely as the angel said, they find the *babe*, but in all external circumstances, how great the contrast to the scene they had just witnessed! Here the human eye sees nought but poverty, obscurity, desertion, and humiliation. Let us pass on some twelve years. The babe of Bethlehem has grown into a manly and ingenuous lad. We see him sitting modestly, but independently, among the renowned doctors of the nation, in the then hall of instruction in the temple, filling them with unutterable astonishment at the profoundness and reach of his understanding, and his familiar acquaintance with the mysteries of divine science. We pass over a score of years. A man of peculiar and unearthly aspect appears in the desert country of Judea, east of the city of Jerusalem, proclaiming an entirely new message to the people—"*Repent*, for the kingdom of Heaven is at hand." He arrests universal attention, and produces a profound sensation in all classes, from the lowest to the highest. He is acknowledged as a messenger from God, and immense multitudes resort to him, and beg to receive the new rite which he declared he was commissioned to perform upon all who obeyed the great injunction of his message. While the eyes of all are intently fixed upon him, and their ears eagerly catching every word that fell from his lips, he solemnly declares he comes but as a herald to proclaim the approach of another infinitely his superior—for whom he is not worthy to perform the most menial of offices. Directly that person is seen advancing from the crowd. In his mild and serene aspect we at once recognize the features expanded and matured of the remarkable child we saw among the learned doctors. He asks to receive himself, at the hands of the holy man, the rite he was administering to the multitude; but, divinely perceiving his true character, the baptizer shrinks in profound humility from the service. Being assured it was the Divine will, he reverently acquiesces, and lays the sacred body of the mysterious individual beneath the yielding waves of the Jordan, and as he rises from the crystal waters, behold an impressive wonder—the heavens are opened, and a glory descends and settles as a lighting dove upon his head, and a voice is uttered from the viewless air—"This is my beloved Son, in whom I am well pleased." Henceforth this *man*, thus accredited by the Divine testimony, appears as a public, independent teacher of the people, and is known to them by the name of *Jesus of Nazareth*. For three years he unremittingly discharges this office, setting forth and inculcating a code of moral doctrines which reflect the purity, the spirituality, and eternity of Heaven itself; perfectly, beautifully, and most impressively exemplifying them all in his own person; performing, the mean while, a series of the most stupendous and beneficent miracles, and uttering predictions concerning himself and future events entirely beyond the reach of human sagacity, and human probability. He gathers round him a small number of disciples, chiefly from the humbler walks of life, takes them into the most intimate friendship with himself, carefully instructs them in respect to his seal character and mission, and the nature of the kingdom he had come to establish on earth, and unequivocally declares himself to be the Son of God, and claims the highest prerogatives of divinity. But strange and inexplicable contradiction! Just as the clear conviction of his true character had taken possession of the minds of his disciples, and they were exulting in view of the honor and glory which awaited them as his peculiar favorites, he declares he is about to be delivered into the hands of his implacable enemies, and to suffer the most horrible and shameful death. His own soul is seized with an insupportable anguish, and expressions escape him of mysterious and unaccountable import. As he predicted, the proud and carnal rulers of the people, who had long been offended and exasperated with his independent teachings and utter disregard of their authority, and his severe rebukes of their carnality and hypocrisy, after various fruitless efforts succeed at length in apprehending him. To the utter amazement of his disciples, whose still carnal views prevented them from understanding his predictions, he unresistingly yields to the violence of his enemies, meekly bears their cruel indignities and mockings during a protracted trial, in which every principle of justice is shamefully violated, is pronounced worthy of death by the great national council, and sentence extorted from an unprincipled Pagan ruler that he should be *crucified.* In this trial and death there was concentrated upon the meek and unresisting victim every ingredient of humiliation, of ignominy, and pain. Successful and frantic malice left nothing out that could add intenseness and bitterness to the cup of shame and agony which it pressed to his lips. Terrific phenomena of nature attend his expiring agonies. The sun is supernaturally darkened—the earth trembles and heaves—rocks burst—the great vail of the temple, which curtained from human view the holiest place, by unseen hands is rent in two from top to bottom. His bleeding and mangled body is taken from the cross and securely entombed. But on the morn of the third day—wonder of wonders—he appears to his disciples *alive,* with the marks of his cruel wounds still upon him. He manifests himself to them, in various ways, times, and places, during a period of forty days. He leaves no possible room for a supposed delusion. Every proof of which the case is susceptible is applied. The most doubtful are convinced, and rest in satisfied confidence and joy. Having completed and given his final commission in respect to his kingdom and its extension, he gathers round him his reassured and rejoicing disciples, ascends with them the Mount of Olives, and before their eyes, while intently gazing on him, he is taken up, and a bright cloud receives him, and he is lost to their view.

19.—THE BRAZEN SERPENT.

W. COLLIER.

ONE of the first exercises of a mind blessed with saving faith, is that of uneasiness and anxiety respecting his state and condition as a sinner, and his accountability to his Maker, whom he knows to be the rightful Sovereign and moral Governor of the universe. He sees the law of God to be holy, just, and good; and becomes deeply sensible, that, if he were suffered to sink into the regions of wo and despair, he would have no cause of complaint against the government of God towards him. He is affected with his situation; mourns for his sin and transgression; and asks with intense anxiety, "What shall I do to be saved?" He feels the sting of sin; and knows that it is death. Like the Israelite bitten with the fiery serpent in the wilderness, he feels the mortal wound—the poison of sin rages till death stares him in the face. He reads the sacred word—"The Lord said unto Moses, Make thee a fiery serpent, and set it upon a pole: and it shall come to pass, that every one that is bitten, when he looketh upon it shall live." "When he looketh upon it," directly showing that whosoever believeth in Jesus Christ might not perish, but have everlasting life. He feels as sensibly that he must perish as did the bitten Israelite, unless he looks to the cross of Christ, as the only appropriate and efficient remedy which God hath provided for the salvation of the guilty. He looks and lives. No one can doubt for a moment, but the Israelite, when he received the sting of the fiery serpent in the wilderness, felt assured that the wound was mortal—that he must die, unless he looked to the brazen serpent erected upon the pole, so that it might be seen from every part of the camp of Israel, as the only remedy for such a disease. All earthly physicians were of no value. A sight of the brazen serpent upon the pole—the eye of the bitten Israelite directed to this extraordinary remedy—allayed at once the inflammation, extracted the venom from the blood, saved the subject of the disease from death, and restored him to soundness of health. There is something very similar to all this in the experience of every one sensible of the moral disease of sin, who receives the healing balm of the gospel, by faith in the death of Christ. The language of the Saviour to Nicodemus, in his application of the figure to the gospel remedy for the wounded sinner in his distress, is peculiarly striking. "And as Moses lifted up the serpent in the wilderness, even so must the Son of man be lifted up; that whosoever believeth in him should not perish, but have eternal life." He *feels* himself to be in a perishing condition, and it is the sight of Jesus upon the cross alone that can save him from perishing. He must sink—he must die—he must *perish*, unless he receives help from Christ. *His* death is the believer's life. He looks and lives.

20.—PETER AND THE KEYS.

J. YOUNG.

The Lord Jesus Christ appointed Peter to a peculiar duty—that of first opening his kingdom, and laying down the principles which were to regulate its communion. This transaction is recorded, Matt. xvi. 16. Peter, on that occasion, was the first to make that all-important Christian confession, "Thou art the Christ, the Son of the living God." His Lord informs him that upon the basis of that confession he will build his church, and make it indestructible; and further adds, "and I will give unto thee the keys of the kingdom of heaven; and whatsoever thou shalt bind on earth, shall be bound in heaven; and whatsoever thou shalt loose on earth, shall be loosed in heaven." The power of the keys has been claimed by many of Peter's supposed successors. The pope informs us, that the keys were left as a legacy to him, to descend without wear or tear along the line of popes forever. Most Protestant denominations have asserted their right to them, with, perhaps, about equal degrees of probability, but Christ gave the keys to Peter, and to Peter only. He only could use the keys aright, being under the guidance of inspiration. Let us then ascertain how he used the keys, that we keep the door as he left it.

The gospel kingdom, or Christian church, was set up and regulated on the day of Pentecost. Some imagine that it commenced earlier; this could not be, as the works were not finished, the vail of the temple was not rent, the earthly things were not shaken, until the moment of Christ's dying upon the cross. Then the types and shadows of the former dispensation were fulfilled. Consequently before this the language of both John and the disciples of Jesus was—"The kingdom of heaven is at hand." After his death, he informs them, when they inquire of him concerning the restoration of his kingdom, that they will receive power from on high in a short time; and commands them to tarry at Jerusalem, and not to attempt to lay a single stone of the spiritual building in their own wisdom, but wait for the promise of the Father.

When the Spirit descends with the shaking force of a tempest, it gathers together a great multitude of the Jews, not only in Jerusalem, but those come up from Judea, and all the surrounding region; that unto that nation might be first opened the gospel kingdom. Beautiful is it to trace the wise, though sometimes minute arrangements of Providence. Who stands forth on this occasion to open up the great truths of the Gospel? Lo! even Peter, who had been designated to the work by the giving of the key. Again, God intends to receive, not only Jews but Gentiles, under the new dispensation. Cornelius, a Gentile, is praying; God desires to open to him the glorious truths of gospel salvation, and introduce him, together with all believing Gentiles, into his church; who is the apostle selected to do this? None else but Peter; again must Peter open the door, but now to Gentiles, a people whom he hated and regarded as unclean. A sheet and unclean beasts is let down from heaven, and by that his bigotry is removed, and he is taught how to use the key. All, then, is plain and simple to us; we have only to ascertain the fundamental truths which the apostle laid down on those occasions, as the basis of their faith, and the ordinance by which he introduced them, and our work is done.

---

21 —PRESERVATION OF THE INFANT JESUS.

J. H. T. KILPATRICK

It is night, and all nature sleeps. But what or who is that I see passing with hasty step, thus hid from public gaze, and the searching eye of persecution? It is a delicate female, and with a tender infant pressed to her maternal bosom, and accompanied by one lone person else, but who is she? Oh! it is Mary, the mother of Jesus! She carries in her arms the *only hope* of a ruined world! Here is a strong case. Herod is out, or about to be, on the work of infant murder, and this very infant is the sole object of pursuit. In the history of man's redemption a wondrous page is here turned up to view. It would appear that this matter has now to be settled, as it were, between the Great Jehovah, and Herod, whether God's eternal purposes of salvation shall all fail, and the whole scheme of mercy be thwarted by Herod! No! brethren, we tell you, no! And though things appear, humanly speaking, to be thus hair-hung, as it were, yet Herod can no more murder *that* infant, than he can pluck the strong pillars from the throne of Jehovah. This same infant Jesus is the incarnate God—is God as well as man—is called Wonderful, Counsellor, the mighty God, the everlasting Father, the Prince of Peace.

Now we hold it as a truth, that Herod could no more destroy God the Son, than he could destroy God the Father, contrary to the counsels of the Godhead; and that God the Son would as surely finish the great work of the atonement upon the cross, burst the bands of death and return to the Father—we say we hold these things just as certain, as that the Lord God omnipotent reigneth. And we all agree that if God had seen proper, he could have destroyed ten thousand such as Herod in a moment of time. But notwithstanding all this, it was absolutely necessary that the infant Jesus should be carried to Egypt, beyond Herod's jurisdiction? Why? Because God commanded it to be. Because it was His will who worketh all things after the counsel of his own pleasure. Because this was one link in the great chain of God's economy of grace, and if one link be gone, the chain is broken. Because the Scriptures must be fulfilled, "Out of Egypt have I called my Son." And we might add, because God intended to teach that his purposes and sovereignty do not supersede the necessity of man's agency.

22.—DETERMINATION OF MESSIAH'S ENEMIES.

E. KINGSFORD.

It appears evident from the brief history which the sacred writers have furnished of the Saviour's life, that at an early period of his public ministry, his death was seriously resolved on in the secret councils of his bitter and implacable enemies, the Scribes and Pharisees. He incurred the hatred of this sect, by unmasking their hypocritical and base pretensions to exalted piety and expansive benevolence. To accomplish their cruel purpose, no act which envy and malice could suggest, or vindictive feelings mature, was left untried. The rapid succession of splendid miracles which the blessed Jesus performed on the blind, the deaf and dumb, the halt and the maimed, and in a word, on all who were diseased, and who sought relief at his hands, as well as the instructive lessons of wisdom which he graciously taught, gave the Pharisees frequent opportunities of watching narrowly his movements. On some of those occasions, they cherished the hope that a favorable season would present itself to entangle him in the net which they had industriously prepared.

There were two points which these ferocious pretenders to philanthropy kept constantly in view, and to the attainment of which they addressed themselves with untiring zeal. The one was to destroy his popularity and credit with the people, by holding him up as an enemy of Moses and a subverter of his laws; and the other was to awaken the jealousy of the Roman government, by representing him as a sower of sedition amongst the people, and above all, as being himself a pretender to the Jewish crown. Thus we find them at one time suddenly demanding his opinion as to the right of the Romans to exact tribute from the Jewish nation; at another, requiring him to decide whether the law of Moses, which condemned to death an adulteress, should be carried into execution or not. Baffled in every attempt by the wisdom of his answers, to surprise him into an unguarded expression upon which they might construct a charge against him, they nearly despaired of success, when the treachery of a follower and professed friend effected that which their concentrated efforts were unequal to accomplish. Judas sold his master for thirty pieces of silver; and the chief-priests and rulers placed their long-expected Messiah, and the desire of nations, before the bar of Pilate, as a blasphemer and a traitor!

By the following examination, according to Dr. Campbell's translation of a portion of the eighteenth chapter of the gospel by John, we are made acquainted with the grounds upon which the Jews founded their hopes of a capital conviction: "Then Pilate entered into the judgment hall again, and called Jesus, and said unto him—Art thou the king of the Jews? Jesus answered—Sayest thou this of thyself, or did others tell thee so concerning me? Pilate replied—Am I a Jew? Thine own nation, yea, the chief-priests delivered thee unto me; what hast thou done? Jesus answered—My kingdom is not of this world, or my adherents would have fought to prevent my falling into the hands of the Jews; but my kingdom is not hence. Pilate therefore said—Thou art a king, then? Jesus answered—Thou sayest that I am a king. For this I was born, and for this came I into the world to give testimony to the truth: whosoever is of the truth, hearkeneth unto me."

Pilate was evidently convinced by this answer, that whatever might be the regal pretensions of the prisoner, or the nature of his kingdom, the Roman government had nothing to fear from either; for it is said that he went out again to the Jews, and declared his full conviction of his innocence. In the foregoing examination, two very important facts were elicited. The first relates to the kingly office of Christ; the second to the nature of his kingdom. "My kingdom," says he, "is not of this world."

23.—THE SEPARATION OF JESUS FROM HIS DISCIPLES.

B. T. WELCH.

ALTHOUGH the sufferings of Jesus were immediately before him, distinctly foreseen in all their intensity, yet his bosom glows with a generous sympathy for his disciples. In the assurance he gives them of his continued protection and love, he addresses them in language and manner the most delicate and affecting. "Let not your hearts be troubled; ye believe in God, believe also in me." He assures them that the great design of his death, and the dreadful scenes they were about to witness, contemplated their salvation and everlasting happiness. "I go away" through a fearful conflict; the sorrows of death will encompass me, the pains of hell take hold upon me, but it is "to prepare a place for you, that where I am there ye may be also." He encourages their hearts with the assurance, that in every danger and under every trial the provisions of his grace were ample for their safety and peace. If they were exposed to danger from the errors of the world, the sophisms with which their faith would be assailed, when they no longer enjoyed the advantages of his presence and instructions, he would neither leave them comfortless, nor defenceless; he would "pray the Father" as their great Intercessor on high, and He would send them another Comforter, even the Spirit of truth, who would dwell with and in them. If they were exposed to suffering from the hatred and persecution of the world, his grace would be found sufficient for them, his presence and love would be their support. "Peace I leave with you, my peace I give unto you —let not your heart be troubled, neither let it be afraid"—or, "Let it not shrink back," as the expression imports—let not your hearts be appalled at the fiery trial through which you are to pass. In a few hours you will see your Lord sustaining the attack of the powers of hell, and an ungodly world in furious combination, but fear not; let your faith in that dark hour be firm and unyielding. The conflict, the humiliation, the suffering *is mine;* the salvation, the peace, the glorious results are *yours.* "I go away" through a death of shame and agony, but "I will come again" in the power and glory of my resurrection! This to you should be a cause not of dismay and grief, but of holy exultation and joy. "If ye loved me, ye would rejoice, because I said I go unto the Father."

What love was here, how forcibly and yet how delicately expressed! In their imperfection and weakness, ever mistaking their Master's designs, their views were confined to earth; but He would elevate them to heaven! In that hour of gloom and peril, they would be prone to concentrate their thoughts upon their own forlorn condition; upon their deprivation of one they loved, the apparent prostration of their hopes. He would direct them to his own exaltation, elevate their views above every earthly, every selfish consideration, and teach them to derive consolation and joy from his glory. "If ye loved me, ye would rejoice to see my sorrows and labors terminate, and to follow me in your faith to the presence of my Father. I go to ascend my throne, to secure your complete redemption, to receive for you a kingdom that cannot be moved. I go to be exalted a Prince and a Saviour; to sit down on the right hand of the Majesty on high; to receive the dominion, power, and glory forever; to be revealed amid the splendors of heaven, and to the principalities and powers that be in heavenly places, as the head of the divine administration; the object of all adoration and praise; the brightness of the glory of the invisible God!" Such, in the light of the Scriptures, is the comprehensive import of this expression of the Saviour! He had come down from heaven upon a mission of infinite love; his return to those bright abodes in the nature he had assumed, and in all the glory and grace connected with his triumph over sin, death, and hell, constituted a part of the joy that was set before him, for which he endured the cross and despised the shame. Now, as love must ever delight in the elevation and happiness of its object, the inference is just and forcible—"If ye loved me, ye would rejoice, because I said, I go unto the Father." Thus does he manifest his love and encourage their hearts; nor is he less gracious, less mindful of the welfare of his people, or less generous and tender in his sympathies with their afflictions, now that his work of redeeming mercy is completed, and he has entered into the holy place, than when on earth he comforted his disciples. Let, then, this truth, expressed with characteristic sweetness, from the lips of the Saviour, furnish to us a motive to submission, and a source of consolation.

24.—THE LOVE OF THE FIRST CHRISTIANS.

BARON STOW.

ON no part of the Christian character does the New Testament so frequently and strenuously insist as on love—on none does it pass so many and deserved encomiums. Whatever else a man might have, if deficient in love he was regarded as defective in the primary and essential element of evangelical godliness.

They understood that "love is the fulfilling of the law."

The early Christians had great love to *the Saviour*. They remembered the thrice-repeated and searching interrogation, proposed under the most impressive circumstances, on the shore of Tiberias—"Simon, son of Jonas, *lovest thou me?*" It burned deep in their souls the conviction that love to him must be the fundamental element of their character, the mainspring of all their action. Hence we find them uniformly and studiously cultivating this affection, that so they may never be lacking in the impulsive power appropriate to their calling—that so they may ever with sincerity appeal to the Searcher of hearts, "Lord, thou knowest all things, thou knowest that we love thee." When Dr. Doddridge entered the dungeon of a prisoner, with a reprieve which he had obtained for him, the poor man fell down at his feet and exclaimed—"I will be yours! Wherever you go, I am yours! Sir, every drop of my blood thanks you, for you have had mercy upon every drop of it!" Similar were the feelings of the first Christians towards their redeeming Lord—similar their protestations of gratitude, attachment, and allegiance. "My beloved is mine, and I am his." The love of Christ—both his love to them, and their love to him—the latter being only a reduplication of the former—constrained them to live not unto themselves, but unto Him who died for them and rose again. To please him was their primary object. To please him they cultivated personal holiness. To please him they labored for the conversion of souls. To please him they urged their missionary inroads into remote regions, encountered the most appalling dangers, endured the severest hardships, and faced death in its fiercest forms.

This love unquestionably exists in modern Christians in a degree, but alas! in a too diminished degree. It is not in us, as it was in them, a burning passion, a fire-giving impulse to the whole machinery of our being. If it were, it would impel us onward to similar sacrifices, labors, conflicts, victories.

They had great love to *one another*. Brotherly love is seldom seen in our day just as it existed among the early Christians. With them it was a test of discipleship, an elementary principle, devoid of which, a man could not obtain, from saint or sinner, from angel or devil, even the name of Christian. Without this, they did not pretend to consider themselves as the children of God. "We know," said they, "that we have passed from death unto life, because we love the brethren." The absence of brotherly love was one of the criterions by which Antichrist was to be known. Its presence was to furnish indisputable proof both of the Divine mission of their Master, and of their attachment to his cause. Jesus prayed that his disciples might *all* be one, to the end that the world might believe that the Father had sent him. And to them he declared, "By this shall all men know that ye are my disciples, if ye have love one to another." And the world, as they beheld the chain of fraternal affection running through all hearts, uniting them firmly to each other, and connecting the whole inseparably with the throne of love, felt and confessed the force of the demonstration. Their brotherly love—which was really a divine instinct, an essential property of their new nature, and therefore spontaneous and unmodified by external circumstances—stood forth in strong contrast with the selfishness of the world around them, like the verdure of paradise set in the desert, and drew forth from their bitterest enemies involuntary expressions of wonder. An unbelieving historian, attempting to account for their astonishing success in propagating their religion, alleges as one of the most powerful causes, their affectionate union. Then there was but one denomination of Christians. "One Lord, one faith, one baptism."

Consequently there were no clashing creeds, no sectarian bickerings, no rival interests, no party plottings and counter-plottings, no wasteful expenditure of time, and feeling, and moral energy, in attempts to maintain and fortify party positions. "By one Spirit" they were "all baptized into *one* body," and they regarded themselves, and were regarded by all around them, as members of *one* harmonious and devoted brotherhood. Christ was the centre of attraction, around which they rallied and united, and, like the radii of a circle, the nearer they drew to the centre, the nearer they were to each other. Assimilated by the grace of God, and fused and welded by the fires of persecution, their affinity and cohesion rendered them the admiration of the world that hated them, and gave them a moral power which the modern church does not possess, and never will possess, until brotherly love shall resume its ancient influence, and become, as it then was, a "bond of perfectness"—until "the multitude of them that believe" shall be "of one heart and one way," keeping "the unity of the Spirit in the bond of peace." O when will "the whole family" of Christ become one, and with "hearts knit together in love," discontinue their petty controversies among themselves, and following their one Leader, converge and direct their whole energies towards the one point—the salvation of the human soul? We may speculate as we please about the incidental advantages of our division into sects or denominations, comparing them poetically to the prismatic hues of the rainbow, and from the pulpit and the platform shouting in ecstacy, "*E Pluribus Unum!*" But the practical man will tell us that if we would dissolve the intractable substances of earth, we must have the colorless ray of virgin light.

25.—DEATH OF STEPHEN.

ENOCH HUTCHINSON.

The Sanhedrim, or council of the nation, had not, in the days of Stephen, the right of judging in capital cases, such power having ceased when Judea was annexed to the Roman empire; and though they might have thought that Stephen should be put to death, they could not have condemned him. This the procurators or governors could only do. These officers were Romans of the equestrian order, or freedmen of the emperor, not appointed by the senate, but only by the Cæsars, and had great power. While the proto-martyr stood before the council, the artful witnesses, to vary their false accusations, declared that he spake "blasphemous words against this holy place (meaning the temple), and the law," and that they heard him say that Jesus would destroy the temple, and change the customs which their fathers had received from Moses. The members of this august body looked steadfastly on Stephen, and his face appeared like that of an angel. He was so full of faith and love to God, that all these officers of state beheld the brightness of his countenance, and doubtless had misgivings while proceeding with the trial. The high priest, then, according to the judicial custom on such occasions, asked the prisoner, if these things which had been testified against him, were so? Stephen then proclaimed the gospel faithfully to this council, and to great numbers of the common people, who were probably allowed to witness the revolting scene. He charged them in severest terms, with constantly resisting the holy messenger from heaven, and told them that they had cruelly betrayed and murdered Jesus Christ. Such language cut them to the heart, and made them gnash upon him with their teeth. But as their violence increased, his views of Christ and heavenly things were still more glorious, until, at last, as Luke informs us, "he looked up into heaven, and saw Jesus standing at the right hand of God," and declared this fact to all the people. A strange, tumultuous scene ensued. The council seem to have been changed into a mob. The multitude cried out with one accord, stopped their ears, ran upon him, cast him from the city, and stoned him. In accordance with the law of Moses, the stoning was commenced by the false witnesses (Deut. xvii. 7), who laid their clothes at the feet of that chief opposer, Saul of Tarsus. While the foes of Stephen were thus taking his life, he kneeled and prayed, as did our Saviour, for his persecutors—"Lord, lay not this sin to their charge." These seem to have been his last, his dying words. He had long been toiling as an instrument to save his fellow-men, and now about to leave the world, he still endeavored to do good to those who sought to take his life. What disinterested kindness! It was religion—ardent piety—an overwhelming sense of man's accountability and the value of the soul, which made him disregard the sorrows that were heaped upon him. He was *happy* in the midst of all his sufferings. His biographer describes his death in three short words—"He fell asleep." How beautiful! and what volumes in praise of his untiring zeal, Christian firmness, and triumphant faith, which alone could raise him far above the waves of sorrow that were dashing over him, and impart that peace which passeth understanding. "Devout men" consigned him to the tomb, and made great lamentation. Though the disciples mourned his loss, they did not cease to toil for their ascended Lord amid those awful persecutions which followed his untimely death.

26.—CONVERSION OF SAUL OF TARSUS.

NATHANIEL COLVER.

A FEW brief years have passed, and the number of the apostles is broken. Treachery and desertion have left the place of one of them vacant; the officious attempt at the Pentecost to fill it, has been unsatisfactory to Christ; he will make his own selection. In his view, an instrument varying, in many respects, from those already chosen, is *now* demanded. One must be set for the defence of the gospel, possessed of such a mind as is developed in the epistle to the Hebrews or to the Romans, in the inimitable defence before Agrippa, or in the debates of Tyrannus; or such a mind as was exhibited in that steady light which could not be smothered by the walls of a Roman prison, or extinguished by the crimson fountains which gushed from the altar of Nero.

But where shall such a man be found? Hitherto, the Lord had chosen the weak things of this world to confound the mighty. Not many mighty, not many noble, had been called. The eye of the Lord is over all the churches; but he looks in vain to find the man. He is not among them. But ah! that eye has found him—yonder he sits at the feet of Gamaliel. But, for such a work, can that young man be obtained? Consider his circumstances. His education is just completed. He has mastered the philosophy of the Greeks. With a mightiness of thirst, he has drunk at the fountains of Judaism. He has threaded the mazes of Jewish law and Jewish tradition.

With the wisdom of the schools and the pride of the Pharisee, none were better prepared to stumble at the cross, or to spurn him who was there bruised. Nay, the humbling doctrines of the cross have already aroused him. The fires of resentment are already kindled in his bosom. He has heard of the successful preaching of Stephen, and he makes haste to confront him before the council. His eloquent appeals against the dying martyr have won for him the marked distinction of keeping at his feet the clothes of the young men, while they stone him to death. The struggles of the dying saint are hardly over, ere he speeds him onward in his mad career of blood. In the fury of his zeal, he has forgotten the dignity of the lawyer, has espoused the office of the sheriff, and is hot in the pursuit of men and women for the slaughter. This young but furious wolf is eager for the blood of the lambs of the flock. Oh! can that young man be had, for the high purposes of the Son of God? Can that wolf be tamed? Can that pride be made to kiss the cross? Can those fearful energies be withdrawn from that mad career, and made subservient to the ministry of peace and love? To these thrilling interrogations our text is an answer—"For necessity is laid upon me"—the necessity of the Son of God. Oh! what a necessity! What majesty in grace! What might in all-conquering love! The Lord, even Jesus, has met him *by* the way. That plaintive appeal, "Saul, Saul, why persecutest thou me?" has reached the heart, flinty as it is; it has reached it, and done the work. "Behold, he prayeth!" The proud Pharisee is the weeping penitent, and the devouring wolf is henceforth the tender shepherd of the flock. To that heavenly vision he is not disobedient. He cannot be. "Necessity" is laid upon him; a necessity, not of wealth, that he could better obtain in some other way, but a necessity demanding the loss of all things—a necessity, not of honor, but to lay his honor in the dust. No, his "Lord had need of him," and he would have him. He lays *his* necessity upon him, and he cannot resist; the call is honored, and the Saul of Tarsus is henceforth the "Paul" of the Gentile world—"a preacher and a teacher of the Gentiles in faith and verity."

27.—INFLUENCE OF THE GOSPEL ON PAUL.

R. H. CHRISTIAN.

We have only to look at Saul of Tarsus, and compare him with Paul, the Christian, to see a most beautiful and striking illustration of the excellency of the gospel. Contemplate for a moment the character of the persecuting Saul. He is a young man of no ordinary intellect, highly cultivated in the best schools, learned in the Jewish law, and accustomed to the most refined society; yet such is the ferocity of his unrenewed nature, such the malignity of his heart, that he can sit quietly and encourage an infuriated mob, whilst engaged in stoning to death a poor, meek, unresisting disciple, whose only fault is, that he worships the God of his fathers, according to the dictates of his own conscience, and who, whilst the work of death is going on, is actually engaged in prayer for his murderers. Nor is this all. We presently find him, under the influence of the same vile passion, engaged in binding, and delivering into bonds and prisons, all whom he found worshipping in this way; and such is the ferocity of his disposition, that even helpless woman does not escape his wrath. Both men and women are bound and delivered unto prison. Neither is he content with pursuing his victims in his own country, but persecutes them even unto strange cities. Now when we have pictured in our minds this mad persecutor, let us turn and contemplate the same individual, in the person of the meek but manly Paul, as he winds his way through the earth, testifying to small and great, repentance towards God, and faith in our Lord Jesus Christ. Himself now the object of the cruellest persecution, we behold him flying for life, from city to city, the Holy Ghost testifying to him, that every where bonds and afflictions await him. Yet amidst all this, how patient, how meek, how unresisting, and yet how determined in his object! How little of self in all he does! How regardless of suffering, how faithful! It matters not what may befall him, so that Christ is preached. In this he will rejoice, although it may add to his afflictions! Look! he is at Thessalonica—he preaches Christ to that people—the Jews are stirred up against him—he flies for life to Berea—his life is in danger—he flies to Athens, and even in that learned city, before the great of the earth, he still lifts up his voice in behalf of the despised Nazarene! Now who can contemplate this great change, without being convinced of the excellency of the knowledge of Jesus, the means by which it had been accomplished?

28.—THE CRUCIFIED REDEEMER PREACHED AT CORINTH.

E. T. WINKLER.

Corinth was the wealthiest and most beautiful city of Greece. It is not to our purpose to expatiate upon the extent of that commerce, which constituted this city a great treasure-house of nations, and made her merchants kings; or upon that culture which gave generals to head the armies of the republics of Greece, or on that refinement which filled her streets and palaces with the choicest and most beautiful productions of art; but we would speak of her religion. It was the religion of their fathers, and therefore venerable; it was the religion of art, and therefore beautiful. The imagination regarding it, became entranced and lost in its exceeding loveliness. The reason, nicely scrutinizing it, on a sudden shrinks back, appalled from the presence and by the fear of those awful beings, the objects of a people's admiration. For century after century, it had been interweaving the threads of its mythology among the fibres of the national heart. It was the theme of those popular ballads, that, more efficiently than laws, mould and determine public character. It had inspired those loftier poetic strains, which, requiring centuries for their production, never die, and never lose their influence. To a people passionately fond of beauty, it had given streets adorned with colossal monuments, and religious emblems; and had thrown open temples, in which the architect, and the painter, and the sculptor had combined to exhibit the beauty of classic taste, and upon which the merchant had lavished the treasures of commercial opulence.

And when we remember that the Corinthians sang the poems which Homer sung, and admired the works which Phidias and Protogenes wrought; that the sculptured majesty of Jupiter hurling his thunderbolt, and the Apollo touching his marble harp, towered from their temple pavements, and the pencilled loveliness of the sea-born Venus smiled on them from the temple walls; that every grove, and spring, and mountain had its genius; that the stars were ruled by awful spirits, and the caves of the ocean inhabited by lovely shapes; and when we remember, too, that all these forms of beauty and of awe were the offspring of their religion, we can readily imagine how it must have interwoven itself into the hopes and fears, the admiration and love, of this classic people. We can readily imagine with what a mixture of horror and disgust they saw the apostle attacking, beneath the very shadow of their gods, the religion of their fathers. A foreigner (*a barbarian*, as the Greeks termed him), standing in the midst of the splendors of Paganism, assaulted the religion of poetry, of beauty, and of art!

The inimitable productions of the Grecian masters were all around him, but he passed them coldly by. The pompous processions, and the Isthmean games,

Lith. of T. Bonar 121 Nassau St.

N. COLVER

and the imposing ceremonies of Paganism, would naturally have attracted the curiosity of a stranger, but they had no charms for him. The sophist reasoned in the groves and porticoes, upon the principles of nature and philosophy, but the apostle neither to dispute with the sophist, nor to gain instruction from the lips of the philosopher. Paul was a man of refinement, and versed in Hebrew, and to a considerable extent in Grecian literature; but he looked upon the refinements of Corinth as vanities; and all that was imposing to the Grecian idolater, was to him but as the sounding brass and the tinkling cymbal. Pervaded by one great idea, animated by one astonishing fact, he said nothing, heard nothing, cared for nothing, but what pertained to the great object of his mission and apostolic labors. For "I, brethren, when I came unto you," he says, "came not with excellency of speech or of wisdom; declaring unto you the testimony of God. For I determined not to know any thing among you save Jesus Christ and him crucified."

It is utterly impossible for language to express the claims of Christianity more forcibly and fully than they were expressed, under these circumstances, by these words. It is as if the apostle had said: "The religion of Jesus comprehends facts, and involves duties, compared with which, human enterprise and human thought, the accumulated wealth of centuries, and the grand intellectual and moral progress and works of a nation, sink into insignificance. I see the wings of your commerce whitening the Mediterranean—I behold the labors of the husbandman, adorning your fields with nodding harvests—I see the immortal works of art, that beautify the streets and temples of your city—but they are to me as if they were not. Another subject, better and nobler, occupies my thoughts and inspires my actions; it is the religion, that, turning away from the marble and the canvass, from the altar and the temple, takes up its abode in the heart, even of the humblest of men, and makes it the temple of the living God. It is the worship of a Spiritual Deity. It is the doctrine, that taking its place at the feet, looks upward ever to the countenance of Jesus, that surrounds with glory the cross on which they have crucified my Lord. And this religion is the one thing needful; this is the all in all."

29.—PROGRESSIVE NATURE OF RELIGION.

E. G. SHIP.

EVERY thing in religion is progressive. Hence the apostle Peter exhorts us to "grow in grace, and in the knowledge of our Lord and Saviour Jesus Christ." I shall define the word "grace," to be favor, free love, and affection. The grace of God denotes his free favor and love to us. The word grace in the text more particularly means our reconciliation with God and favor with him—the influence of his Spirit on our hearts, the holy principles, qualities or habits, of faith, hope and charity, and the fear of God which we possess, inasmuch as all these blessings proceed from the undeserved favor of God. I shall define the word "knowledge" to be a spiritual and experimental apprehension of divine things, whereby through the teaching of God's Spirit and word, we are enabled not only to perceive, but also powerfully and kindly disposed to believe in, and love God in Christ, as our God.

Having thus briefly defined the words grace and knowledge, I remark that they are inseparable companions. It is impossible to possess that grace spoken of, without possessing at the same time some knowledge of ourselves, of the evil of our own hearts, and the goodness of God; and we cannot possess a spiritual and experimental knowledge of God unless we have the grace of God. But while these facts are admitted, let it be remarked that these graces are progressive. "The path of the just is as the shining light which shineth more and more unto the perfect day." A desire after perpetual progress in religion is an effectual antidote to a spirit of declension; and St. Paul exhorts the Hebrew converts to diligence in seeking after a full acquaintance with the whole Christian scheme: "therefore," says he, "leaving the principles of the doctrine of Christ, let us go on to perfection."

Again, we oppose the maxim of the text to the sloth and apathy of those who regard past experience and former attainments as though they constituted the whole of religion. There are many, I fear, of this character. They tell with much accuracy and precision, the date of their spiritual birth. They point out and dwell with much emphasis on the various circumstances connected with their conversion. Such persons very frequently recur to their former experience, sometimes with self-complacency, and sometimes, it is to be feared, with a spirit of indolence and satisfaction entirely inconsistent with all religious improvement. Now, my brethren, the attainments which we have already made, should be considered valuable no farther than they are stepping stones preparatory to future attainments. In order to give a scriptural representation of the progressive state of the Christian, listen to the prayer of the apostle for the Ephesian brethren: "For this cause I bow my knees unto the Father of our Lord Jesus Christ, of whom the whole family in heaven and earth is named, that he would grant you according to the riches of his glory to be strengthened with might by his Spirit in the inner man; that Christ may dwell in your hearts by faith; that ye being rooted and grounded in love, may be able to comprehend with all saints, what is the breadth, and length, and depth, and height, and to know the love of Christ which passeth knowledge, that ye might be filled with all the fullness of God." We know what we mean when we apply the word "grow" to vegetable productions. We attach precise ideas to the word "grow" when applied to the human or animal species. We know the difference between the stature of a child and a full-grown man, and between the strength of the intellect of a child and the intellect when brought to maturity. So it is in regard to the Christian. We are to grow in grace and in the knowledge of the Lord and Saviour Jesus Christ. We should grow in the grace of faith, until all the dark clouds which so often hover over our minds are scattered and driven away; and until the eye of our faith is purified from every obscuring film. In knowledge, too, we should seek to be men, "strong in the Lord, and in the power of his might," until "we reach the stature of a perfect man in Christ." To know God as he is revealed in the gospel record of his love to a lost and ruined world, is above all things most desirable. "This," says the Saviour, "is life eternal, to know thee, the only true God, and Jesus Christ whom thou hast sent." We should grow in the grace of love; love should absorb all the powers of the soul, fixing them upon God. I shall conclude my remarks on this topic by a quotation from the second epistle of Peter: "And besides this, giving all diligence, add to your faith, virtue; and to virtue, knowledge; and to knowledge, temperance; and to temperance, patience; and to patience, godliness; and to godliness, brotherly kindness; and to brotherly kindness, charity. For if these things be in you and abound, they make you that you shall neither be barren nor unfruitful in the knowledge of our Lord Jesus Christ. But he that lacketh these things is blind and cannot see afar off, and hath forgotten that he was purged from his old sins."

30.—LABORS OF THE APOSTLES.

D. D. PRATT.

HUMAN nature, in the days of our Lord and his apostles, was substantially what it is in ours. When they commenced laboring in behalf of men, evils already prevailed, sins as enormous as were ever committed, and yet no direction is given by our Saviour to his apostles to form a society for the removal of any one of them. Had they lived in this day, they might have been represented as being in favor of all these practices! And indeed, they did not escape such a charge even then! The censorious and self-righteous Jews accused our blessed Lord of violating the Sabbath—of intemperance in the use of wine—of licentious intercourse with the world—and of an alliance with the devil! But our Saviour still prosecuted the great work of human salvation; and though the commandments, from the first to the tenth, were daily violated—the dreadful scourge of war devastated the earth—and slavery, in its most cruel and intolerable forms, was supported by the Roman government—the very government under which he and all his apostles lived, and which even gave the master the terrible power of the life of the slave—things at which our inmost soul shudders even to mention—and though, no doubt, our Lord and his disciples mourned that such wicked practices prevailed in the Roman empire, and throughout the world—and that they did prevail, is matter of historical fact—yet, they took no step, as I can learn, to form a society for the suppression or removal of any one sin in particular. But they taught a religion that laid the axe at the root of the trees—a religion whose legitimate influence would prove the wisdom of God, and the power of God unto salvation, to every one that believeth, whether Greek or Jew, bond or free, and hasten on that glorious, promised, predicted, foreordained time, when the wolf and the lamb shall dwell together, and the lion eat straw like the ox. But what is the tendency of many of the present schemes, in their bearing on this sublime subject? What is their influence on the morals and religion of the community? Unfavorable, as it appears to me. Itinerant lecturers, and floods of party and passionate papers, leave but little time for domestic duties, and for prayer meetings; nearly the whole of solid reading, even the Holy Scriptures themselves, must give way to all these engrossing themes, and in my humble view, the effects on morals and piety are most disastrous. The cross, the cross of Christ, that great, that spiritual, that mighty weapon of our warfare, is the chief scriptural instrument to be employed in subjugating the kingdom of darkness—in bringing down lofty imaginations—and in laying low every high thing that exalteth itself, and in ushering in the glorious reign of Messiah, till his kingdom shall fill the universal world.

31.—THE PREVALENCE OF CHRISTIANITY.

W. T. BRANTLY.

VERY shortly after the return of our Lord to heaven, the preaching of the gospel by his apostles was attended with such extraordinary success, as to excite the apprehension of the Jewish rulers lest the new religion should supplant the faith of their ancestors. They had already given orders to the heralds of the cross to quit Jerusalem, and to desist from the publication of their offensive doctrines. But acting from the highest convictions of duty, the apostles persisted in preaching Christ crucified. Perceiving that their injunctions were disregarded, a council was convened to devise a plan for the suppression of the troublesome heresy. After some deliberation, it appeared to the assembly that the most effectual method of extinguishing this religion, was to put to death its preachers—the obstinate advocates of its claims. They were about to carry this measure into effect, when, as we are informed by the narrative, Gamaliel, a doctor of the law, held in high reputation among the people, urged the adoption of a different course. He reminded the council of several impostors, who had previously risen up and caused them much trouble by seducing the people; but who, having been put to death, their followers were in a short time dispersed. He brought to their notice the case of Theudas who had enlisted in his cause about four hundred disciples, who continued faithful during the life of their leader, but who were disbanded shortly after his death; he adverted also to Judas of Galilee, who, in the days of the taxing, drew away much people after him, but who were scattered when he died. From these cases he inferred, that if Jesus Christ was really an impostor, inasmuch as he had been crucified, the believers in what he published would soon be dispersed, and there was no necessity for shedding their blood. If they were not thus disbanded, they might take it for granted that he was no deceiver. In view of these facts, I say unto you, "refrain from these men, and let them alone; for if this counsel or this work be of men, it will come to nought; but if it be of God, ye cannot overthrow it; lest haply ye be found even to fight against God."

The advice of Gamaliel, though agreed to in this instance, was soon forgotten. These men were not let alone. Every conceivable obstacle was thrown in their way. Ridicule, wit, learning, wealth, secret treachery, open malice, industrious violence, were all excited against them. Persecution in its multiplied forms, torture of every species, the most malignant passions of the human heart, have been arrayed against this work; but has it been overthrown? What has been the result of this contest? At the lapse of nearly two thousand years since Gamaliel gave this advice, have the developments of this long period, permit me to ask, evinced this to be the work of man, or have they demonstrated it to be the power of God? I put the question this morning: has the combined hate of its uncounted foes been sufficient to accomplish its annihilation? No, my hearers. The trophies of redeeming love in every age cry, No. The unnumbered multitudes who through faith in the cross of Christ, this day exult in the hope of a blessed immortality, cry, No! The tens of thousands now in glory, from their exalted abode echo back the cry, No! No!! In vain have the kings of the earth set themselves, and the rulers taken counsel together. Victorious over every foe, trampling down every obstacle, this despised gospel has lived, and still lives, and will continue to exert its saving power when time shall be no more.

Christianity, then, is a fact whose existence demands explanation. When I find it flourishing in the world notwithstanding the opposition which it has encountered; when from century to century I see it subjected to the most rigid scrutiny—tried by the severest tests which man or devil could devise; when I look at its advocates hunted down with the most unsparing fury; when, notwithstanding every effort which has been made for its suppression, I find that the religion of Christ still triumphs, I can account for that triumph but from one consideration; and that is—that it has been preserved in the world by the power of Almighty God. He who resists the force of evidence like this, I must pronounce hopelessly sceptical. He would not believe Christianity to be a divine revelation, though one should rise from the dead and assert the truth. His unbelief is as wilful and as obstinate as that of the man, who, at mid-day, should plunge into the dark mines of the earth, and contend, in the face of truth and of reason, that the sun did not shine.

32.—THE APOSTLES JAMES AND JOHN.

ROBERT TURNBULL.

It is not surprising that the apostle James, and especially his brother John, notwithstanding their great simplicity and tenderness of character, should be described as "sons of thunder." Were they not, after all, men of iron mould, of lofty intellect and sovereign will, who for Christ and his cause perilled their lives in the high places of the field, and who, when they contended for the truth, or preached the gospel to the hearts of men, spoke with a fervor and a power which was best likened to the light flashing from a darkened hemisphere, or the thunder leaping and reverberating among the mountains? Indeed the strongest natures are always the calmest, like the electric spark, which is rather seen than heard, when it rends the rock or prostrates the forest; or like the comet, which rushes amid the constellations with less of noise than the fall of a leaf in the silent woods. Gentle as he was, the apostle John possessed a strength of intellect and an energy of passion, which, sustained by the grace of God, braved the anger of kings, held him up in the solitudes of Patmos, amid the visions of death and hell, and winged his words with apocalyptic fire. "To him it was given," says Robert Hall, "not only to record the life of our Saviour, in common with the other evangelists, but to transmit to future ages the principal events and vicissitudes which shall befall the church to the end of time, in a series of visions which revived the spirit and manner, and more than equalled the sublimity of the ancient prophets. Endowed with a genius equally simple and sublime, he mingles, with ease, among the worshippers before the throne, communes with beings of the highest order, and surveys the splendors of the celestial temple with an eye that never blenched." That lofty repose, that serene gentleness of spirit which distinguished him as "the beloved disciple," and which made him so dear to the church at Ephesus, in which he spent his latter years, was but the finished result of that native energy which formed the principal element of his character. This it was which fitted him at once to lean upon the bosom of Jesus, and mingle in the visions of eternity—to become the guardian of the Virgin mother, and reveal the destinies of the church to the end of time.

33.—PAUL AND JAMES ON FAITH.

J. E. THOMAS.

A DIFFICULTY arises from the epistle of James, who seems to teach a different doctrine from that of Paul, when he says, "Ye see how that by works a man is justified, and not by faith only." The difference between the two apostles is only apparent; their writings perfectly harmonize, as you may perceive by giving attention to the following remarks:

1. Paul and James had not the same design in view. Paul insisted on justification by faith in Christ, because it was a fundamental article of the Christian religion, and a doctrine strenuously opposed by certain teachers, who affirmed that men are saved by works. James addressed professed Christians, who had imbibed dangerous views concerning faith. They imagined that we are justified by a mere assent to the Gospel; or that faith consisted in an orthodox belief. To the carnal mind this was a welcome notion; for the indulgence of sin might continue through life, and be followed by the rewards of glory. The apostle throws his might against this error, and declares that it is in vain to suppose a person justified, while his faith was of such a nature as to leave him in a state of alienation from God.

2. Paul and James do not speak of the same faith. The faith which, according to Paul, is the instrument of our justification, is a fruit of God's Spirit, the faith elsewhere called "the faith of God's elect," "precious faith;" a living, active principle, which purifies the heart, and excites to universal obedience. But to the faith of which James speaks, these exercises and this character cannot be ascribed. And the reason that this faith cannot save is, because these properties do not belong to it. This faith is exhausted in empty professions; it is dead—a body without a soul. To deny justification to this faith, and ascribe it to the faith spoken of by Paul, are not inconsistent. There is no contradiction between two men, when one affirms that man thinks and speaks, and the other denies it, if the former means a real man, and the latter means only that which is painted.

3. The two apostles do not speak of the same justification. Paul discusses the question, how we receive the pardon of our sins, and our justification *before God?* which question he answers, "by faith in Christ." James does not treat of justification before God, but of justification *before men.* His inquiry is into the *faith* by which we are justified, and the way in which it is evinced to be genuine, which is by our works: How other men may know that we are justified. Or, how can our professions be justified before men? James answers, "by our works." This is evidently the meaning of the apostle, which may be clearly seen from the instances to which he appeals. "Was not Abraham, our father, justified by works, when he had offered Isaac, his son, upon the altar? Seest thou how faith wrought with his works, and by works was faith made perfect? And the scripture was fulfilled, which saith, Abraham believed God, and it was imputed unto him for righteousness; and he was called the friend of God."—James ii. 21, 22. This justification is declared to have taken place when Abraham obeyed the

command of God to offer up Isaac in sacrifice. But Paul and Moses declare that he was justified by faith about thirty years before this transaction, even before Isaac was born.—Gen. xv., Rom. iv. Observe here, that James quotes the same passage from Moses which Paul does, and adds, "and the scripture was fulfilled, which saith, Abraham believed God, and it was imputed to him for righteousness." The scripture affirming that he was justified by faith, was "fulfilled" when Isaac was offered. This can mean nothing else than that the scripture was *illustrated and confirmed*, which declared him justified many years prior to this act of obedience. The justification of which James speaks, must relate to a different transaction, namely, his justification before men, the manifestation of his sincerity, and the living character of his faith, and consequently, of his acceptance with God; for faith can be shown only by works. His justification was known to God and to himself only, prior to offering his son; but this act made the fact known to others. This was the way his faith was made perfect. Works did not supply any defect in faith, and concur with it to recommend him to the favor of God; but they proved it to be not a mere assent, but a full, practical persuasion of the truth of God's promise. The other instance referred to by James, is the case of Rahab, who was justified by works, when she received the spies, and sent them another way. In Heb. xi. 41, Paul informs us that she received them by faith. Hence her justification by works must mean, as in the case of Abraham, the manifestation of her faith. By works she was justified before men, or proved to be a believer; but she was justified before God by faith, prior to the performance of works. James uses the term justification, not in the sense of acceptance with God, as Paul does, but in the sense of *declarative justification* before men.

Paul treats professedly the question, how a man is justified before God? And he stabs the pride, and scatters the foundation of those who put undue value upon works. The whole truth must be sought there from him who professedly enters into the subject. James seeing justification by faith abused by those who professed to be justified by a mere assent to the truth, unaccompanied by the purifying effects of true faith—these were a kind of Antinomians, who undervalue works—he scatters their foundation, and withers their hopes. He speaks of faith "alone," and "dead;" but the faith of which Paul speaks, is never alone or dead, but is always accompanied by good works, to which its vitality prompts. Justification before God is attributed solely to its own actions instrumentally. But while it converses with supernatural writers, and receives blessings from God directly, it moves on in acts of obedience, and thus justifies its professions before men.

THE BAPTIST PULPIT.

III.

THE RESPONSIBILITY, DUTIES, AND DESTINY OF MAN.

—THE STUDY OF MAN.

J. C. CLOPTON.

It has long ago been said, that "the proper study of mankind is man." As a being possessing only a physical organization, how wondrous is he! how well calculated to impress us with feelings of admiration and love for our Great Creator! Well might David exclaim, in viewing his physical construction, "I am fearfully and wonderfully made."

But it is not so much as a creature possessed of body as of mind, that man becomes an object of study to the minister of the gospel. The mind is the great inlet to the heart. This enables man to rise above all other animals, and to feel that he is allied to creatures who are entirely spiritual. Men have minds which are ready to *perceive* whatever is stated from the pulpit, and not only so, but this power enables them to detect the least impropriety in gesture or in feeling. They can perceive when a man is proud, or when he is humble; when his manner is affected, and when it is simple; when his feelings are sincere, and when they are hypocritical. They have memory also, which enables them to retain what is said, and to recall trains of thought and reflection which may have been long forgotten. Father Abraham, in addressing the rich man, takes advantage of this capacity, and wakes up the rich man's thoughts to reflect on his career on earth. "Son," says he, "*remember* that thou, in thy life-time, receivedst thy good things, and likewise Lazarus evil things; but now he is comforted and thou art tormented." Peter refers to this power of the mind several times in his second epistle, as it enabled him to stir up the Christian by way of remembrance. The power to compare one object with another, or thought with thought, and to deduce proper conclusions, is also an attribute of mind, called *judgment.* Luke refers to this when he says of the Bereans that they were more noble than the Thessalonians, because they searched the word with all readiness of mind to see if those things were so. Unlike many professors in our day, they read and thought, and judged for themselves. He who acquaints himself with man as he ought, must take these things into consideration, and make them the subject of patient investigation. There is an advantage in the study of mind which is formed in the study of no other science; it can be done without books. The mind is its own library, and its own laboratory. Investigation and experiment can be conducted when alone. It is because of attention to these things, that many ministers are useful, who are precluded from securing knowledge directly from books. In the shop, or at the plough, or as they journey by the way, the mind is absorbed in contemplating its own powers and operations, and thus, as it enlarges itself, it raises its possessor to distinction and usefulness. But man must be studied, not only as a mental, but also as a moral agent. Men have feelings deep and very excitable. The heart is the seat of these feelings. It loves and it hates, it rejoices and it mourns. Out of it are the issues of life and death. All thoughts are rendered virtuous or vicious, according to the purpose or design of the heart. A knowledge of the powers and operations of the mind, and the corresponding affections which certain thoughts are calculated to excite, together with a proper judgment of corresponding action, is a knowledge of *human nature.* The Bible excepted, this is the most important study to the gospel minister. Paul was so well versed in this knowledge that he could say, "I am become all things to all men, that I might by all means save some. To the weak became I as weak, that I might gain the weak. To the Jew, became I as a Jew, that I might gain the Jew." If he was with the Jew, such was his knowledge of their thoughts, feelings, and prejudices, that he could accommodate himself to them. And if ministers accommodate themselves to their hearers, it must be from a knowledge of human nature. Whoever is ignorant here, cannot shape his course properly, but will often become an object of ridicule to the world. A knowledge of what was in man, enabled the Saviour to rebuke his adversaries successfully, and to triumph over them in every effort to entangle him. There are three ways in which we may study human nature. First, as it is presented in the Bible; second, as seen in the acts of men, when witnessed by us, or recorded in history; and lastly, by studying our own hearts. In the study of character in profane history, we labor under some disadvantage, resulting from the unfaithfulness of historians, and our inability to judge of motive, even when the act comes under our own observation; but in studying the character of man, as it is recorded in the Bible, and on the tablets of our hearts, we have more infallible guides. In our own mental operations we can observe the first traces of thought, and as it darts in among our moral powers, we can discover the first ebullition of feeling, and as that feeling is embodied in action we learn the motive, which motive gives character to our action, and it is pronounced to be right or wrong accordingly. Viewing this process in various instances, we soon learn to apply our knowledge to others in similar circumstances, and thus judge of their acts. Hence, a man with the most enlarged experience, who has been placed in the greatest variety of circumstances, is better prepared to form a proper judgment of man, than he who has mingled little with the world.

2.—FREE AGENCY OF MAN.

W. B. JOHNSON.

As a free agent, man has life and death set before him, with the liberty of choosing the one, and rejecting the other. As a fallen creature, he is an enemy to God, and without the provision of mercy in his Son, would for ever remain such. Descending to the abode of the devil and his angels, as a company of kindred spirits, he would for ever unite with them in their unhallowed opposition to their common Creator. Mutual crimination and joint blasphemy against their Maker, would render them as miserable as their capacity would admit. But now, the announcement of pardon and restoration invites him to return. "Come now, let us reason together, saith the Lord; though your sins be as scarlet, they shall be white as snow: though they be red like crimson, they shall be as wool." "Ho, every one that thirsteth, come ye to the waters; and he that hath no money, come ye, buy and eat; yea, come, buy wine and milk, without money and without price."

As moral agents, for whom there is hope, I call upon you, then, fellow-sinners, to turn to the Lord; for thus saith the Lord, "Say unto them, as I live, saith the Lord, I have no pleasure in the death of the wicked; but that the wicked turn from his way and live; turn ye, turn ye from your evil ways; for why will ye die?" Your God commands, invites, entreats.

Open your ears, and hear the word of this salvation which is sent unto you—"Kiss the Son, lest he be angry, and ye perish from the way, when his wrath is kindled but a little." As disobedient subjects, as prodigal sons, come back. Your Sovereign is ready to receive you—your father's arms and house are open to embrace and entertain you. Come, then, the fatted calf shall be killed for you, the best robe shall be put upon you, joy and gladness shall thrill through your ransomed, heaven-born souls. The church on earth shall rejoice. Attending angels shall bear the tidings to the throne of the Eternal, and the holy company of cherubim and seraphim in his presence, shall make all heaven resound with hallelujahs of praise to God and the Lamb.

But if ye refuse the invitations of love and mercy, and will not have the man Christ Jesus to reign over you, if ye will continue in sin, ye must receive its wages—*death—eternal death.* You must see that man Christ Jesus on the judgment-seat, and hear from his sacred lips the sentence—"Depart, ye cursed, into everlasting fire, prepared for the devil and his angels." But you will be your own destroyer; the Judge will only, as the organ of insulted justice and violated law, pronounce the sentence which you will have drawn down on your own head.

Now, now, O fellow-sinners, you have it in your power to place yourselves under influences that are spiritual and saving; or under influences that are carnal and damning. You can read the Bible, or the book of infidelity; the sermon of truth, or the novel of fiction; you can attend the party of sinful pleasure, or the meeting for holy prayer; you can go to the midnight revel, or to the house of God. You can lift up the prayer of the publican, or the howl of the bacchanal. You can utter the praise of the Most High, or belch out the blasphemy of the arch-fiend. How solemn the responsibilities that are upon you! Under what awful accountability does your free agency place you! The freedom to choose is the freedom to reject. O, exercise this freedom aright! Pause, consider your latter end. "Choose you this day whom you will serve. If the Lord be God, serve him; if Baal, follow him." Difficulties attend the decision. For their removal, search the Scriptures, implore the teaching of that Holy Spirit, whom God will give to all who ask for him in sincerity. And O, may He enlighten the eyes of your understanding, and give you to see Christ in the Scriptures as your "wisdom, righteousness, sanctification, and redemption."

3.—THE VALUE OF THE SOUL.

C. B. SMITH.

We may profitably consider some of the properties of the soul which render it of great value.

Its faculties and powers may be increased in vigor and in strength beyond our present conception. At present we are shut up within a very narrow limit. The clearest mental vision is greatly beclouded, when compared with the angels of heaven. But we cannot suppose the intellectual height of the angels will be the highest point to which the mind may attain. There have been intellects developed in this world, by such men as Newton, that have astonished the world. They were like the bright stars that break out from amid the cloud, and whose brightness is increased by the surrounding darkness. Some of the purest, strongest, and finest sentences in any language, are to be found in the writings of the prophets. The sweet singer of Israel brought out strains that have never been equalled. Paul's eloquence was never surpassed. But contemplate these same individuals now in heaven! Freed from every thing which impeded their course while on earth, instructed by a God of infinite wisdom, they have been mounting upward and upward for ages. Can any man conceive even the height to which they have already attained? Can we conceive the sweet, thrilling, and heavenly strains that David is now capable of producing from the harp of praise? Paul, the master-spirit of his age, now capable of fathoming some of the deep mysteries of God, may almost vie with Gabriel in his efforts to glorify God. The objects for contemplation which are presented to the mind, both in heaven and in hell, are calculated to call forth every energy and faculty, and thereby increase its strength. Objects which are grand, glorious, and sublime—objects which will keep the mind on the stretch, on the wing continually—and then with the fact that eternity is before us, what height may we not attain? In this view of the subject, is not the soul valuable?

The soul has the power of choice, or election, which renders it of not a little value. God has enstamped upon it *freedom*, and placed life and endless happiness within its reach. Joy and sorrow, life and death, happiness and misery are before us; we have the power and privilege of choosing either. Without a soul, we should follow the mere impulse of nature. We should, like the brute, eat, drink, and enjoy life, and die, and exist no more. In such a case, our happiness is not under the control of ourselves. We are then creatures of circumstances. But now we can obtain that which is beyond the reach of any enemy. Though we have not yet learned in this respect what our soul is worth, yet its intrinsic value is not lessened by this ignorance.

The soul is capable of the greatest possible enjoyment; we know of no bounds to its happiness. Brutes are happy when their passions are gratified—so are men; but the enjoyment derived from the possession of a soul is almost infinitely superior to this mere animal enjoyment. We may join in the songs of angels and of heaven. Without a soul we could not unite with that which is entirely spiritual. Those who are unacquainted with any happiness except that which is derived from the senses, have an instrument in their possession, the value of which they have not yet learned. Hence Satan succeeds so easily in destroying the immortal soul. The landholder will part with his farm for a very small price compared with what he would ask did he know that a little under the surface existed a mine of gold. So of persons in parting with their souls. We could be of no possible benefit in the world without souls. Like brutes we should live, and like them die.

Especially does the soul bear the image of God, and hence its inestimable value. Every work of God bears the impress of intelligence and wisdom. Not only do the heavens declare his glory, but even the single blade of grass shows the perfection of his workmanship. Solomon, in all his glory, could not compare with a single flower. But when we have passed through the departments of Jehovah's works, and come to gaze upon this last picture—the soul of man, we see that it bears the very image of its Creator. It infinitely surpasses any and every other of his works. It is that alone which will outlive time. What must be the guilt of him who will suffer the very image of God to be destroyed?

Contemplate for a moment a corpse—a lifeless lump of clay. Remember its former greatness. It was the soul within him that made him what he was. Deprived of this soul, the body returned to dust. The brute never makes any improvement upon former generations. The first race were as perfect as they are now. Not so with man. He is constantly making advances, constantly increasing in intelligence and strength. He has tamed the winds, subdued the ocean, hewn down the forest, soared amid the stars, chained the lightnings, and subdued kingdoms. Was all this accomplished by brute force? We must attribute all this to the soul. What more sublime and grand than a thinking, reasoning soul?

---

4. DEPRAVITY OF MAN.

JOSEPH A. WARNE.

THE doctrine of human depravity is proved by observation. It is only necessary to reflect on man's intellectual and moral nature, and its depravity is obvious. If the whole nature of man is comprised in the terms, understanding, will, and affections, what does observation teach us respecting them? It teaches the exact truth of the declarations of Holy Writ: That his "understanding is darkened," being alienated from the life of God through the ignorance that is in him; that the will is hostile and rebellious; and that the affections are "earthly, sensual, devilish." Imagination cannot picture a perfectly depraved being, if one, all of whose powers are thus alienated, be not so depraved. But it may be said, that this classification of man's powers is suited to periods which are past; that new light has been shed on this subject; and that it is now ascertained that the fundamental powers in man, are very much more numerous than was formerly supposed; and that, therefore, it does not suffice that we find, in general terms, that the will, the understanding, and the affections, are depraved. We answer that these are terms which are general and comprehensive: they include the moral, and intellectual, and animal nature of man. If, by induction, we find all these depraved, man's whole nature is depraved; unless it can be shown that his nature embraces more elements than the moral, the intellectual, and the animal. It is true that modern philosophy has greatly enlarged our acquaintance with the fundamental powers of man; but it still recognizes in him a moral, intellectual, and animal being; and classes all the fundamental powers it has traced under one or other of these heads. But lest it should be supposed that we fear to examine our doctrine in the light of truth, whencesoever derived, we will briefly advert to some of these fundamental powers; and we are greatly in error, if we shall not find the proof of human depravity accumulate upon us.

Man is a *reflecting* being: he is endowed with a fundamental faculty of tracing back effects to their causes, and of following out causes to their consequences. He loves to *think;* he *must* think; but he does not love to think on God: "God is not in all his thoughts." He reflects on the works of God, and discovers the traces of power, and wisdom, and goodness: but ascribes them to an imaginary being whom he designates Nature! Or if God be recognized, it is as a mighty *Genius*, and not as a *moral Governor;* as one to whom gratitude is due as *our* Benefactor, but not admiration and love for *his own* boundless excellence. Man is an *active* being; activity is his element; but *never*, in a state of nature, does he act *for God.* He is a *social* being; "the countenance of a man sharpens that of his friend." Poets have sung of "the feast of reason and the flow of soul;" but alas! among the unregenerate, this "feast" seems to be turned into the apples of Sodom, and this "flow" to be suddenly and magically arrested, on the introduction of conversation respecting God, his perfections, and claims, and benefits: man "desires not the knowledge of His ways." Man is a being endued with a faculty of *appreciating the beautiful* and the vast; yet has he no inclination to scan the moral beauty and incomprehensible vastness of his Maker. He is a *conscientious* being, endowed with perceptions of *right* and *wrong*, yet are these perceptions, in the unregenerate, never called into exercise with regard to God. The rights of men may be regarded with a scrupulousness which merits our highest praise; but the claims of God on the homage of the man are never recognized, till genuine conviction for sin takes possession of the soul; and then, its anguish may all be resolved into the consequence of a perception that the rights of God have been disregarded. Man is even by the constitution of his nature a *religious* being; he is endowed with a faculty which teaches him, instinctively, the necessity of *a God:* that is, of some object of religious worship. Hence the fact that all nations, even the most barbarous, have always had their theology. But no nation, in any age, has evinced a supreme regard to the *true* God. On the contrary, the nation of Israel, when made the sole depository of the oracles of God and the institutions of religion, were continually evincing a tendency to fall into the idolatrous practices of the surrounding nations; and when those nations were instructed as to the nature of Jehovah, and the service he required, they rejected the instruction or poisoned the knowledge they obtained from it, by mingling with the worship of the true God the abominations of idolatry. Of this a striking instance is afforded, 2 Kings xvii. 24—29.

How could these things be thus, if man loved God supremely! Could a reflecting being reason, ascending, to causes, or descending, to consequences, and never advert to the object of his supreme affection, while yet, that object was the great First Cause? Could he admire his natural perfections, and overlook his moral ones; while, yet, these latter were the object of his highest love? Could he act instinctively and voluntarily, and yet *never act for God*, the object of his warmest affection? Could converse be his delight, and yet, could he loathe conversation respecting the object of his highest admiration? Impossible. And yet these are facts which observation daily confirms: observation, then, proves that God is not supremely loved by men; and if not, as we have already seen, human nature is depraved; and the multiplication of the fundamental powers discovered by the investigation of modern research, does but confirm the doctrine of the text: "Every one of them is gone back; they are altogether become filthy; there is none that doeth good; no, not one."

5.—DOCTRINE OF HUMAN DEPRAVITY.

A. HALL.

The doctrine of human depravity is fundamental, and lies at the very foundation of the Christian Religion; insomuch as a practical conviction of its truth, may be considered as the first step towards the reception of the offered mercy of the gospel. By it we understand that man by nature is wholly corrupt and depraved; not only destitute of love to his Creator, but actually opposed to his laws, and at war with his perfections: that man's whole nature and attributes, animal, intellectual, and moral, are perverted. His understanding is darkened, his imagination beclouded, his memory impaired, his reason dethroned, his will perverse, his conscience defiled, his affections estranged, his heart polluted. In his thoughts he is impure, in his words filthy, in his actions vile. In short, that he is "earthly, sensual, devilish." Let Paul, with the pencil of inspiration, draw his portrait: "There is none righteous, no, not one: there is none that understandeth, there is none that seeketh after God. They are all gone out of the way, they are together become unprofitable; there is none that doeth good, no, not one. Their throat is an open sepulchre; with their tongues have they used deceit: the poison of asps is under their lips: whose mouth is full of cursing and bitterness: their feet are swift to shed blood: destruction and misery are in their ways: and the way of peace have they not known: there is no fear of God before their eyes."—Rom. iii. 10—18.

But let another sacred writer fill up the back-ground, and deepen its shades still darker, if possible. "Hear O heaven, and give ear O earth, for the Lord hath spoken: I have nourished and brought up children and they have rebelled against me: the ox knoweth his owner, and the ass his master's crib; but Israel doth not know, my people do not consider. Ah sinful nation, a people laden with iniquity, a seed of evil-doers, children that are corrupters! They have forsaken the Lord, they have provoked the Holy One of Israel unto anger, they are gone backward. Why shall ye be stricken any more? Ye will revolt yet more and more. The whole head is sick and the whole heart faint. From the sole of the foot, even unto the head, there is no soundness in it; but wounds and bruises, and putrifying sores: they have not been closed, neither bound up, neither mollified with ointment.—Isa.i. 2—6. 'Tis done—the canvass is full—the picture complete—drawn from life—*daguerreotyped.* Behold the portrait! Whose is it? It is yours—it is ours—it was Paul's and Isaiah's too, in a state of nature.

Pelagius, in the fifth century, denied the doctrine of original sin, and asserted that the consequences of Adam's transgression were confined to himself, and did not affect his posterity, and that the favor of God was bestowed upon men according to their merits. A doctrine so much in unison with the feelings and bias of the carnal heart, found many advocates, and finally obtained such an ascendency in the world, that the church itself was corrupted, and on the verge of ruin, and would have perished in the vortex of error, and superstition, and vice, had not God been her defender and deliverer. As he had raised up Moses, and Aaron, and Joshua, to be the guides and deliverers of ancient Israel in the wilderness, so he raised up Luther, and

Melancthon, and others, to oppose and root out this heresy from the church, and to establish again the doctrines of grace and truth. This humiliating doctrine is confirmed by the history of all nations and religions, whether Pagan, Mahommedan, Jewish, or Christian; else why those scenes of war, of rapine, and bloodshed, that fill the pages of history, sacred and profane? Surely, if any record could be found free from such recitals, it might be found, at least, in the history of that favored nation, God's peculiar people, the Jews. Read those records, my hearers, and deny, if you can, that man by nature is totally depraved. Yes, ancient Israel was not more distinguished for her high and exalted principles, than for her ingratitude, rebellion, and idolatry. If further proof be necessary, look for a moment at the history of individuals, from the highest to the lowest station in society; and, without specifying as to names among so many, you will find, from the king to the peasant, predominant in the heart of man by nature, pride, malice, envy, deceit, treachery, and revenge. Nor is this depravity the effect of education and example. These may tend greatly to augment the evils of sin, but they are not the cause. The disease is hereditary. We are "born in sin, and shapen in iniquity;" and before we can discern to know good from evil, this hereditary bias is plainly developed. "The wicked are estranged from the womb; they go astray as soon as they be born, speaking lies."—Ps. lviii. 3. We do not mean that man is naturally so depraved in degree that he cannot grow worse; on the contrary, man does, in time, and probably in eternity, "wax worse, and worse, deceiving and being deceived; but by total depravity we mean that every faculty of man is corrupt. The whole head is sick, and the whole heart faint. A stedfast conviction of this doctrine is necessary, to tear away from self-righteous man the leaf-covering of his own righteousness, and to make him see himself in all his native deformity and pollution, that so he may duly value the atoning righteousness of the Lord Jesus Christ.

6.—INFIDELITY.

W. L. DENNIS.

THE masses of society regard it as a dreadful thing to be an infidel. They have, however, extremely vague conceptions of the process by which infidels are made—and equally vague conceptions of the thing itself. If they do not always expect to meet, in an infidel, an aged and dissolute man, openly profane and blasphemous; they do expect—the masses—to find an infidel ready to declare his unqualified unbelief in the Bible, and his hearty opposition to its circulation and credit. This is the point, of all others, to be guarded; because, the infidelity most to be dreaded, is the infidelity that steals the livery of the heaven it derides, to people the hell it smiles at—the infidelity that pretends to a more enlightened piety, and a deeper philanthropy than can elsewhere be met. Such men as Kneeland and Owen; and such women as Wright and Restell, will do but comparatively little harm. They throw off all disguise, and appear just what they are: while hundreds and thousands, who are not a tittle better than they, who believe, essentially, what they believe, and practise as they practise—except so far as prudential considerations restrain them, are nevertheless unsuspected of infidelity, merely upon a declaration, that they habitually make; viz., that they are the friends of religion, and believers in the Bible. Friends of religion! What kind of religion? A religion, that, if it obtained universally, would drive the religion of the cross from the earth. A religion that denies the atonement; the necessity of repentance, and faith in Christ; the depravity of man, the future judgment, the doctrine of eternal rewards and punishments; a religion that smiles at tears of penitence, and unblushingly ridicules every consistent effort to enlighten the world, from the giving of a tract, to the preaching of the gospel to the heathen on the plains of India; a religion with but one article for its creed; which is, to gratify, so far as possible, every present desire, and let another world take care of itself. And its faith is in keeping with its work. It believes the Bible. Yes, it believes the Bible is a book; but it does not believe that it is God's book—the product of plenary inspiration. They believe in the Koran and the Shasters as they believe in the Bible.

An infidel is a person who disbelieves a revealed truth, that is essential to the harmony of God's perfections and attributes, and the uncorrupted maintenance of his moral government. He may yield the assent of his judgment to every fundamental truth in the Bible except one; if he disbelieve that one, he is an infidel. Because the cardinal points of revelation are constructed with especial reference to each other, and you cannot annihilate one, without rendering the remaining ones nugatory. For example: every fundamental doctrine in the Bible is intimately connected with God's omniscience. Suppose a person to admit every thing that is said in the Bible concerning both the Creator and the creature, except God's omniscience—His infinite knowledge—who does not see that the unbelief in this perfection of the Deity, has vitiated every essential doctrine of the Bible that remains; for these doctrines are just as intimately connected with the infinite knowledge of God, as is respiration with animal life. For instance, what is the doctrine of repentance worth, if it be disconnected with God's omniscience? Why, the transgressor says, at once, if God's knowledge is not infinite, I may sin, and He not know it; or the penitent may say, I may be sorry, and God not discover it. Hence all is gone, the sanction and the hope. I am anxious to impress this point, and to do so, I give another example. Supposing an individual to believe, or to say that he believes all the Bible, except the declaration that, without holiness no man shall see the Lord. Where shall we put such a man? Unquestionably among infidels; for He disbelieves *the truth* upon which the whole Gospel structure rests. Deny that holiness of heart is essential to God's favor here and hereafter, and you have drawn the last drop of blood from the Gospel, and have left it a dead letter; unmeaning in its import, and unsatisfying in its reception. Viewed through such a medium, the death of Jesus Christ was more than worthless. It was a work of supererogation; for the Bible—such portions as such a person would admit—declares that Christ suffered that God might be just in regarding those as righteous who believed in His name. And yet they refuse to believe that purity is essential to salvation. Prove that without holiness men can see God in peace, or believe it, if you cannot prove it, and the Bible and the sanctuary are without spiritual value; and faith, repentance, prayer, and a good hope through grace, obsolete or unmeaning terms.

A person who should say that he believed all the Bible except the truth to which I have referred, would come no nearer being a believer, than he would being an American in heart, who should strike out from our bill of rights its first sentence; viz., "that all men are born equal, that they possess certain inalienable rights, among which are life, liberty, and the pursuit of happiness;" and should coolly tell us that he believed all of that document that remained. Would you call him a republican, who should deny the first principle upon which our free institutions are based? Certainly not. You would say that the place for such a one would be among the crowned heads of Europe. And so we say of the rejecter of a single essential truth of the Bible. His place is among infidels. Such a rejection amounts to positive infidelity.

It is not necessary to stop a single moment, to vindicate the definition given. If it be new to many, it must yet commend itself to the sober judgment of all. If we take any other ground, we are afloat without chart, compass, sun, moon or star to guide us. If we affirm that a person may disbelieve a revealed truth, that is essential to the harmony of God's perfections and attributes, or to the uncorrupted maintenance of His moral government, and not be an infidel, we affirm that infidelity is not unbelief; that the rejection of a portion of God's word, deemed by Him essential to its completeness, and revealed that it might be believed, is no bar to Christianity. What would be the consequence? Why, a score of persons, each rejecting some important truth, might, as a company, disbelieve the whole of the Bible, and yet none of them be pronounced infidels. God's perfections, attributes, and moral administration, might be upturned and thrown into chaos, and yet the members of the confederacy vindicate themselves from the charge of infidelity, by declaring that they each reject but a single essential truth — one asserting that there is no hell; another, no heaven; a third, that God is not in every place beholding the evil and the good; a fourth, that he is not strict to mark iniquity; a fifth, that he is not out of Christ a consuming fire; another, that Jesus Christ was not God manifest in the flesh, and that He offered no atonement for sin; and so on, until the last truth of revelation is sacrificed. Who does not recoil from such a conclusion, that must follow unless our definition be adopted,

7.—ABSURDITY OF INFIDELITY.

W. C. CRANE.

We are gravely told by infidels, that a miracle is contrary to experience. Hume, especially, remarks, that he could not believe any testimony which is contrary to universal experience, because, says he, it is infinitely more probable that the witnesses are mistaken, than that the laws of nature have been violated. It is also asserted that the course of nature is fixed and inviolable, and that it is inconsistent with the immutability of God to perform miracles. Thus, the evidence of the senses is made the standard by which, from a residence of half a century on one speck of the illimitable universe, a *very mote* in creation, we are to deduce the inviolability of God's laws, through infinite space and eternal duration. To employ the indignant language of one of the most distinguished men of the age, "a mole, or gnat, or insect may then, from the image of this great world painted on the retina of its eye, philosophically depose that the universe is self-existent and eternal." If the being of a God is admitted, the possibility of a miracle must also be admitted. If the omnipotence of God be conceded, the possibility, nay, even the probability of a change in his laws must be conceded. Can it be possible to conceive that God would ordain such general laws for his own operation, as will effectually exclude a change of those laws, where a great and important end could be answered thereby? The very creation of the world was a change in the course of existence, yet what sane man denies that the world was created? Hence, according to infidel logic, the laws of nature were violated, which is contrary to universal experience. If the definition of a miracle which has already been given, be correct, then the creation of this terrestrial planet was a miracle. To prove to common sense that blind chance brought out of the womb of eternity this footstool of God, will puzzle all the pagans and infidels, philosophers and wise men, from this time until the judgment day.

But let us for a moment examine the reasoning, that miracles are opposed to experience and the common course of nature. Is experience the only teacher from whom we obtain knowledge? If so, our lot is indeed most lamentable. The past is all a fable; historians are ingenious novelists; travellers are arrant liars; to those of us who have not crossed the great deep (indeed the very existence of the deep is problematical), Europe, Asia, and Africa, are regions, the fairy creations of a poetical fancy. Alexander and Cæsar, Washington and Napoleon were not. The future cannot be, because not experienced. The future! it is a horrid, hideous vacuity. Has memory no share in obtaining knowledge? Why then send your children to schools and colleges? Is faith of no avail in amassing intellectual treasures? Then the world is hardly less than the burning reality of hell, exhibiting all the awful proofs of enormous guilt and distressing crimes; and man is but a single remove from the monkey tribe. "But," says the sceptic, "when we speak of experience, we mean universal experience." Who will deny that universal experience is the experience of *all* men, in *all* places, and at *all* times? And what man of threescore years and ten, and of no greater dimensions than ourselves, has stood over this narrow world like a mighty Colossus, one foot on the plains of Hindostan, and another on the wine-fields of France, and in all ages, and all times has observed all changes and all events, and from this far-reaching point of observation has gathered and concentrated upon his own brain the accumulated treasures of universal knowledge? The wisdom of that conceit which makes experience the only teacher, is well illustrated in the story told of the emperor of Siam. An Englishman, in whose society he delighted, informed him that in England water congealed into ice, and was so hard and thick, that men and cattle walked upon it. This was so glaring a falsehood in the eyes of the emperor, and so distinctly opposed to his experience, that he pronounced it a *lie*, and refused to believe any thing the Englishman thereafter would say. Surely that emperor must have become a wise man!

Hume, who attempted in all his writings covertly to inculcate his sceptical sentiments, disproves his own theory by his own practice. In his works upon "Human Nature," his inquiry concerning "The Human Understanding," and the "History of England," he very plainly contradicts his own favorite argument from experience, in the credit he attaches to a multitude of facts, of which it was impossible for him to have had any experience. Did he ever see William the Conqueror? Did he ever attend the court of Richard III., and witness the machinations of that wicked man? Did he ever shake hands with Queen Elizabeth, or drink wine with Queen Anne? If he had not seen them all—been an eye-witness of their administrations—how dare he, in the face of his great principle, attempt to describe what he had never personally observed, nor experienced?

8.—THE POWER OF CONSCIENCE.

J. SHANNON.

It is hard to pursue a course of sin in opposition to the dictates of conscience. There may, no doubt, be some transgressors, who, by a long-continued course of sinning, have acquired a character for sinning so desperate, and attained to a pre-eminence in guilt so fearful, as to be seldom annoyed with the visits of remorse. Their situation is truly terrible; terrible beyond all description, and hopeless, I had almost said, as if they were already damned! The heart sickens at the contemplation of their wretched case, and we hasten to consider the transgressor in a condition less fearful, where he has not yet been utterly deserted by the Holy Spirit, nor had his conscience seared as with a hot iron. This is a more favorable view, which charity would fondly take of the greater part of the family of transgressors. How fares it, then, with the sinner even in this state? Although he may be surrounded with all those circumstances, which make him an object of envy to the unthinking multitude, the eye of faith can easily discover that his way is hard. Created by God, sustained by him, and redeemed by the blood of his dear Son, reason tells him that he should pay supreme regard to the will of his Creator, Preserver, and Benefactor. Memory recounts the innumerable blessings his heavenly Father has lavished upon him from time to time, reminds him of his entire want of suitable affections to that Father, and the many crimes he has shamefully committed against him; points him to the blackness of darkness, that might have been his portion; bids him look to bleeding love on Calvary; and conscience asks, Is it reason, is it gratitude, that such a friend should be so requited?

Oh! there are seasons when the ungodly, even in his most prosperous state, must feel under the lash of a guilty conscience, that the curse of Cain is on his path; and that fugitive and vagabond in the sight of heaven, is the character of all who walk in it.

But the sinner stops not here: every day's experience teaches him, that earth is by no means a state of permanency; that here he has no abiding city; and that could he possess all things under the sun, and enjoy them to the greatest possible extent, it would avail him but little; for soon he must bid them an eternal farewell, and take his departure for an unseen world. In the Bible he reads, or hears read, the story of a character that much resembles his own. He reads of a rich man, clothed in purple and fine linen, and faring sumptuously every day, whose history is closed in the words, piercing like a dagger to his soul—"He also died, and was buried; and in hell he lifted up his eyes, being in torments."

How knowest thou, O foolish man, says conscience, that ere long thy case may not be like his? Why shouldst thou run so fearful a hazard? Dost thou, indeed, as a rational being, prefer the body to the soul, earth to heaven, and the short and fleeting moments of this life to the never-ending duration of eternity? And the poor man, although conscience tells him, and the scriptures tell him, that this night his soul may be required at his hands, yet he still continues to drudge and toil more laboriously than a galley-slave in the way of transgression, that in the end he may reap the wages of eternal death! Surely if there be a hard way on earth, it is that of the transgressor against God? Did he enjoy peace of mind, it would, at least for the time, be some alleviation. But there is no peace, saith my God, to the wicked. At war with himself and with his best interests, at war with his better judgment, his conscience, and his God, he is doomed, under the influence of a wretched infatuation, to walk self-condemned in a path, where he enjoys not one particle of true happiness in time; and at the end of which he can look for nothing but blackness of darkness, the bitter pangs of remorse, and the stings of an accusing conscience throughout eternity. From the hard, miserable fate of transgressors may the good Lord deliver us.

9.—IMPORTANCE OF EDUCATION.

D. CHESSMAN.

Solomon was a careful observer of human nature, and he dwells much upon the subject of the education of youth and children. And it is certainly of as much importance as any other subject—involving the most serious consequences.

In the *first* place, the happiness of youth in the present life, is involved; if they are not brought up in the way they should go, it is almost certain that they will pursue a course of vice and misery.

In the *second* place, the happiness of the parents is involved. It is evident that some of the severest afflictions arise from the misconduct of wicked children; those which wring the heart with agony, destroy all earthly comfort, and bring down the gray hairs with sorrow to the grave. While, on the other hand, the happiness of having children walking in the path of virtue, is indescribably great; because they are the support of age, alleviate its infirmities, and repay, as far as possible, all former attentions. If, therefore, parents neglect their children, they not only see them ruined, but know that they have been the authors of their destruction.

In the *third* place, the happiness of their circle of relatives and friends is involved; all of whom are affected by the disgrace and misery which disobedient children bring upon themselves.

In the *fourth* place, the happiness of the community and the country is involved. One vicious child has a pernicious effect on many. In consequence of the depravity of the heart, vice is like a contagious disease; or like a fire passing through stubble, or a spark on gunpowder. And if, in any country, a majority should become vicious, there would be an end of law an government. Especially would this be the case in a republic, where the power is in the people; and where no small degree of virtue, as well as knowledge, is necessary to the very existence of the form of government. Statesmen, therefore, as well as Christians, ought to feel deeply interested in this subject.

And in the *last* place, the everlasting happiness of youth is in a great degree involved. We do not mean to say, that no vicious child will be reclaimed; or that God cannot, or will not pluck the most hardened criminal as a brand from the burning. But while we know that the supreme authority has power to pardon the murderer, we also know that it is seldom exercised. And where one is pardoned, thousands suffer the just sentence of the law; so that murderers have reason to consider their doom to be certain. And for the same reason, those children who tread the paths of vice, and those parents who suffer them to do it, have reason to fear in the future world the most awful consequences. Even if the parents are saved, it will be indescribably dreadful to know, that their children are lost, and that they, by the neglect of their duty, have, in any measure, contributed to the awful catastrophe.

10.—THE ABUSE OF THE TONGUE.

D. F. RICHARDSON.

An abuse of the tongue is destructive of an individual's own happiness. That heart alone can be happy, that looks with kindness upon the world, and delights in promoting its enjoyment. God has so constituted us, that when we breathe good will toward our fellow-men, ardently desire their happiness, and never injure them in word or deed, we promote our own happiness in a most successful manner. But that individual who indulges unkind feelings toward any of his fellow-creatures, and employs harsh, bitter remarks against them, whilst he makes others unhappy, makes himself the most wretched.

All the moral sensibilities suffer when 'the throat becomes an open sepulchre,' sending forth its pestilential effluvia through a community. Whilst poisoning others, the individual himself is sadly contaminated. All that is lovely in the heart will droop and die, when bitterness and wrath is continually vented against others. Some seem to delight only in dwelling upon the faults of others, and in seeking to cast their virtues into the shade. Nothing pains them more than the praise of others. We need no better evidence that happiness is a stranger in their bosoms, and that base passions are destroying all moral excellence, than the exhibition of such a spirit. Such fountains, we may rest assured, are impure, where deadly exhalations are ever issuing forth. A contemplation of goodness communicates goodness to the heart; whilst a consideration of what is base, leaves a pernicious influence upon the mind, unless it is viewed solely with a benevolent desire to remove it. The abuse of the tongue is awfully offensive in the sight of Heaven, and cannot fail to accumulate a fearful amount of guilt. Some, from malignity of heart, indulge in abuse toward their fellow-men. Such individuals are exceedingly sinful in the sight of Heaven, and exert a baleful influence around. Others, for the sake of amusement, are prone to abuse their fellow-men. They delight to take up a character, and show their dexterity in dissecting it, and exposing its faults and defects to the ridicule and laughter of all others. Although such persons may show no unkindness of feeling toward those they thus treat, yet they often do them serious injury. It is difficult for us to respect those we often hear ridiculed. The use of such a weapon, where no good is to be accomplished, and much injury may result, is exceedingly wicked, and cannot fail to exert a depraving influence upon the heart. The odium of a community will, sooner or later, settle heavily upon one who thus trifles with the character of others. God will show how guilty such conduct is in his sight, by suffering him to feel severely the dislike of others. Jehovah has said, speak evil of no one, and a disobedience to this command cannot fail to meet his disapprobation.

11.—A COMMON MISTAKE.

J. PEAK.

THERE is a class of professors of religion, who, nevertheless, manifest great indifference to it, both in sentiment and practice. They tell us, that it is of no consequence what a man's faith is if his practice is but good, or if he leads a good, moral life. This they say, not that they are in any way remarkable for good works, except in theory, but to manifest their indifference to the peculiar doctrines of the gospel. With them it seems to be a matter of no importance whether we worship and adore the Son of God as a divine person, or consider him as a human or angelic being; whether we acknowledge ourselves partially, or totally depraved; whether salvation be by grace alone, or partly by grace and partly by works; whether the promise is sure to all them that believe, that they shall be saved, or whether real saints may fail of the grace of God, and be finally lost; so of the state of the righteous and wicked in the future world. These are considered by some as merely speculative opinions of no great consequence in religion. We see not why a scheme of sentiments, entirely opposed to the gospel in all respects, might not fully answer all the purposes of these indifferent people, providing it were honored with the Christian name. Nor are they more conscientious in their practice in some respects. Not to enlarge upon their sinful and shameful conformity to this vain world, in their idle customs and fashionable amusements; but even in matters of religion, we should suppose, from their manner of treating this subject, that it is of no great consequence whether we adopt, for our rule of conduct, the customs and traditions of men, or the word of God, providing that we have stupidity and ignorance enough to persuade ourselves that we are sincere, and mean well. All this is called a Catholic spirit, a noble mind, generosity, liberality of sentiment, condescension, Christian forbearance, moderation, and I know not what; and it is sometimes more profanely called charity. But it argues the want of sanctification. It is thought, that if such people should ever realize this gracious work upon their hearts, they would see and feel more sensibly the importance of divine truth and a holy life.

12.—DANGER OF NOMINAL CHRISTIANITY.

T. ROBERTS.

No external privilege can entitle you to membership in the church of God. Are you, my friend, placed by a kind providence in a neighborhood where the pure word of God is faithfully dispensed? And are you a constant attendant on the word so preached? Truly your advantage is great; but if you remain impenitent and in unbelief, your condition is truly awful. Your responsibility has been swelling as your advantages have been multiplying; and if you die in your sin, you will surely meet a fearful reckoning. Where much is given, much will be required.

Has God blessed you with pious parents, who are consistent members of the Church of Christ, and who have prayed with you and for you, and have taken pains to lead you in the way that you should go? Great as your privilege is in this particular, it does not give you the least title to any of the blessings of the covenant of grace. If you are without personal faith in Christ, and holiness of heart, you are a stranger from the covenants of promise, and an alien from the commonwealth of Israel; without God and without hope in the world, a child of wrath, and not a child of God.

John the Baptist faithfully warned his hearers against trusting in the faith and piety of parents. "Say not in your hearts, we have Abraham to our father: for I say unto you, that God is able of these stones to raise up children unto Abraham. And now also, the axe is laid unto the root of the trees; therefore every tree that bringeth not forth good fruit is hewn down and cast into the fire." The rich man, who cried from the abyss of hell for a drop of water to cool his tongue, was a descendant of Abraham, and the glorified patriarch recognized him as such, but this availed him nothing. The gulf was fixed, O, for ever, for ever fixed! They, and they only, that are of faith, are blessed with faithful Abraham.

Dangerous in the extreme is that doctrine which asserts that unconscious babes have a right to membership in the church of God, and that attaches holiness to what is born of the flesh. Have they not yet heard, that "that which is born of the flesh, is flesh?" And then, to complete the climax, they put into the mouths of the poor deceived children, in answer to the question, "Who gave you that name?" the reply, "My godfathers and godmothers, when I was baptized, and made a child of God, and a member of Christ, and an inheritor of the kingdom of heaven." A more deadly dose of opiate never was administered to lull the conscience in careless security, and to usher immortal souls into the presence of their final Judge with a lie in their right hand. I speak, my brethren, in part from my own experience. I have swallowed the dose, and for years have felt its deadening influence on my soul. But

> O, to grace how great a debtor,
> Daily I'm constrained to be!

My heart bleeds for youth that are similarly situated. O Spirit of our God! rend the veil from their hearts, and undeceive them; show them that except they are born again, they cannot see the kingdom of God.

13.—DOGMATISM OF SUPERFICIAL RELIGION.

J. RICKER.

FIDELITY to truth prompts the further remark, that superficial religion is extremely prone to be *dogmatic.* It is apt to be self-sufficient and positive. It is impatient of any attempt to instruct its ignorance. Indeed, ignorance is something to which it does not commonly confess. In its very cradle, it is wiser than all its teachers. Destitute of true self-knowledge, humility is, of course, out of the question. As in the case of a certain king of Israel, thrown by a violent revolutionary convulsion from the lowest regions of society, upon the giddiest heights of power, the cry which rises above, and drowns every other, is, "Come and see *my* zeal for the Lord!"

Deep rivers move silently, while the brooklet that owes its very being to the passing shower, brawls along its noisy bed, as if to proclaim, first its existence, and afterwards its importance, to the whole surrounding region. Just so is it in religion. The man who has the deep waters of piety in his soul, is commonly slow to speak. He thinks little of himself, and much of his profession and his Master's service. There is abundance in his heart, though he is more prone to withhold it when it is needed, than to make an ostentatious display of it to the world. But in the man whose religion is chiefly external, all this is reversed. His Christianity is mainly objective—something to be looked at and talked about, rather than felt as an inner and spiritual being, a well of water springing up into everlasting life. Hence his dogmatism, his over-confidence in himself, and the censorious bearing with which he often treats others. He has somehow become possessed with the idea that he is the man, and that wisdom will die with him; when, truth to tell, spiritual ignorance is the most marked feature in his character. Remove it, and you deprive him in fact of his very religion—or what he has cherished as such—and reduce him to the wholesome extremity in which Job found himself, when forced to exclaim, "I have heard of thee by the hearing of the ear, but now mine eye seeth thee; wherefore, I abhor myself, and repent in dust and ashes!"

14.—OBLIGATIONS OF THE YOUNG.

THOMAS BALDWIN.

[*Delivered at an Ordination.*]

MANY there are in this dear assembly, who are now in the bloom of life. Who can forbear reminding you of the importance of remembering your Creator in the days of your youth, and of devoting your early years to his service? You this day behold one of your fellow-youth publicly engaging in the cause of Christ, and devoting his service to your best interests. Despise not his youth; but as you have opportunity, listen to his instructions and counsel.

As you, my young friends, have been favored with a religious education, and enjoy the blessings of a preached gospel, your obligations must be great. O, let not all these advantages be lost, and your souls lost for ever! To-day, if ye will hear his voice, harden not your hearts. It is yet an accepted time, and a day of salvation. Your hearts are now susceptible of the impressions of truth; but a habit in sin may render them callous.

You may fancy to yourselves that the bright scene of life is now but just opening; but remember, it may close ere you are aware, and all your future prospects close with it. The awful hour is fast approaching, when conditions of pardon will no more be offered. The mild tone of mercy which has so long sounded in your ears, will give place to the stern voice of justice. Then he that is unrighteous, must be unrighteous still; and he that is holy, must be holy still.

15.—RESPONSIBILITY OF YOUNG MEN.

ROBERT W. CUSHMAN.

You are not merely to be pitied in yielding to temptation, but you are to be blamed. You are not simply unfortunate, but you are guilty. The instances of ruin by temptation in a Christian community, without a conviction of wrong, if such exist at all, are very rare. We would present to you, therefore, the consideration, that you are responsible for your actions; and, consequently, if you yield to temptation, you will be called to answer for it to God.

A temptation cannot deprive you of your freedom. Its assault is not on your liberty, but your choice. It deals not blows, but pleas. However strong the influences it brings to bear upon you, it directs them upon your will. You cannot be overcome without your consent. The key of your citadel is in your own hands. The enemy cannot enter but by the gate, and that opened from within.

Temptations, moreover, like poisonous plants, have their localities; and tempters, their haunts like beasts of prey. And, if you know your temperament or weakness to be such that you cannot pass through them with safety, you have the means of security by keeping out of their way. If, then, you expose yourself, when you know your danger, you are a transgressor, and God will bring you into judgment for it.

The temptation of intoxicating drinks, for example, may be too strong for you. Then keep out of the way of them. Have nothing to do with strong drink. Touch not; taste not; handle not. Look not upon the wine when it giveth its color in the cup. Keep away from the places where intoxicating drinks are sold, and shun the companionship of those who frequent them. If you will do this, you will be safe. But if you will not do it, but will expose yourself when you know your danger, you are guilty; and, if you fall, you are a victim *self*-immolated; and you go into eternity as a breaker of the law which says, "Thou shalt do no murder," with the folly as well as the guilt of one that dies by his own hand.

For known and voluntary transgression of the laws of God there is a retribution beyond the evils it brings in the present life. "We must all appear before the judgment-seat of Christ, that every one may receive the things done in his body, according to that he hath done, whether it be good or bad." "He hath appointed a day in which he will judge the world in righteousness by that man whom he hath ordained; whereof he hath given assurance unto all men, in that he hath raised him from the dead." And this seat of judgment, and this day appointed, are beyond the grave. "For it is appointed unto men once to die, but *after* this the judgment." The reception of the things done in the body, therefore, at that judgment-seat, must be something beyond what is suffered by the body, or by the soul while in the body. To that day, then, my young friends—to its righteous decisions, and its unavoidable retributions—let me entreat you to turn your eye whenever temptation is spreading its lures before you; and your ear to the impressive warning that has been given forth from that dread authority before which you must appear, which bids you beware that you be innocent, while it wishes you happy. "Rejoice, O young man, in thy youth, and let thy heart cheer thee in the days of thy youth; and walk in the ways of thy heart, and in the sight of thine eyes: but know thou, that for all these things GOD WILL BRING THEE INTO JUDGMENT."

16.—REALIZATION OF DIVINE TRUTH.

PHARCELLUS CHURCH.

OUR spiritual nature, like our animal, depends for its subsistence and growth on substances foreign to itself. The influx and incorporation of the divine doctrines into its affections, is what sustains it; and hence we are said to live by every word that proceedeth out of the mouth of God. But this process of spiritual digestion and incorporation cannot go on apart from the continued agency of the Holy Spirit. *That*, and that alone, can take of the things of Christ and show them to us, or so inweave them into our experience as to give them substance and reality in our minds. To make plain and real what is already revealed in the Bible, and not to add new revelations, is the sole work of the Spirit. Hence our Saviour says, "he shall not speak of himself," or shall not add to the facts or to the matter of the revelation, which is already complete in me; "but whatsoever he shall hear, that shall he speak."

Complete as is the revelation of God's word for all the purposes of faith and duty, no man can so enter into it as to feel its life-giving power, without the teaching of the Holy Spirit. His office-work, in the plan of our redemption, is like to local authorities of a distant province of a vast empire, carrying out in form and in fact the will of the crown. Without them, laws and statute book would be in vain. The Bible can do nothing effectually for the salvation of this lost world, apart from the accompanying Spirit. The church, without his agency, is a mere collection of dead corpses, impregnating the moral atmosphere with a malignant malaria. My God, how shall we make this a practical sentiment throughout the different branches of thine Israel? How shall we draw off thy professed children from running round in the perpetual circle of their own feelings, sympathies, and intellections, to launch out into the open sea of thine infinite fulness, thine almighty love? How shall we inspire them with a just appreciation of what they might become, in the use of the word, and by the power of the Holy Ghost?

What living Christian has not felt the difference between receiving the gospel in word only, and receiving it in power, and in the Holy Ghost, and in much assurance? Those promises which the Spirit has applied to sustain us in our sinking moments, seem to us the sweetest of all those doctrines which have been so wrought into our experience as to give us peace and assurance, we can never forget; and those precepts which have occurred at a moment of suspense as to the course of duty, to relieve our doubts, and to fill us with the joy of knowing and doing our Master's will, peer aloft in the horizon of our recollections, like some delectable mountain, from whose clear summit we caught glimpses of our everlasting rest. Now those parts of the Bible which have thus imparted to us spiritual strength, are the only ones which we are capable of using effectively, for our own good or the edification and salvation of others.

Says an old divine, "preach only what you have experienced." You are as incompetent to preach any thing else, as a blind man is to lecture on colors. A sickly taste for variety leads us to preach many things in which we have no vital experience, and consequently no power. We supply by a meteoric brilliancy, what we lack in the genial warmth of heaven's own sun. But no plants of grace vegetate under our ministry; no flowers bloom; no loaded sheaves reward our toil.

It has been said, "Look out for the man of one idea." One Bible idea—justification by faith—wrought into the soul of Luther by the Holy Spirit, broke up the slumber of ages, shook thrones, inflicted a thousand wounds on the old red dragon, of which he continues to bleed to this day, and brought about one of the greatest revolutions ever experienced by man. Better preach the same thing from sabbath to sabbath, than preach any thing beyond the energy of Christ working in us. Let us expatiate more and more on the office-work of the Holy Spirit. Let this be a subject of private thought and prayer, throughout our ministry and churches, as well as of public preaching and conversational discussion, that if possible we may enter fully into the spirituality and power of our faith; and we may expect as a consequence, that an influence will diffuse itself among us, which will cause the cold and dead masses of crude and shapeless matter, that now encumber our churches, to start up into new forms of life, beauty, and efficiency.

It is here, in the Spirit's work, that we must look for strength to convert the world. And there is no danger of turning too much thought, too much sympathy, or too much labor in this direction. To nourish a sickly thirst for various discussion upon plans, organization, fixtures, money, and outward agencies of the kind, instead of turning our concentrated forces upon making enlarged spiritual acquisitions, is like a nation laying up in its arsenals the material of war, when the martial order and discipline necessary to wield it efficiently does not exist. The least of its foes might laugh to scorn the puny accumulations of such a nation. Christians, we must become the organs of the Spirit, or nothing we can do will be effectual. The Bible in our hands, instead of being an instrument of evangelization, will point its thunders at our own head, producing the contortions of secret guilt, by making our duty plain, without revealing our power to do it. How, therefore, can we talk of the remedial influence of gospel provisions, so as to win men to their acceptance, when we ourselves are bleeding within from the wounds inflicted by an indignant law? Never did the taunting proverb, "physician, heal thyself," come with such force, as to those Christians who undertake to teach Christianity as a means of salvation from sin, while they themselves are the slaves of lust and unbelief. O, that this slavery may instantly terminate in our churches, through a larger development of the Spirit's power! O, that we understood what some of the holy men who penned our creeds meant, when they constructed those articles which have reference to sovereign, efficacious grace! And may the Spirit deign to make us, even *us*, his organs for extending the empire of righteousness and peace here below! May He wield the studies, preparations, and public preaching of our ministers, modelling their voices to tenderness and love, and filling them with "thoughts that breathe and words that burn." Yea, may he distil his genial influences over all the parched places of our Zion, to render them blooming and beautiful as the garden of the Lord.

17.—THE DIGNITY OF MAN AN ARGUMENT FOR ZEAL.

J. BUTLER.

In attending to our obligation to do all we can for the benefit of our fellow-men, we ought to consider the dignity of the human mind. Man, by Divine appointment, must, through all time, inherit the dominion of the world. His powers are intelligent and his origin divine. He is capable of the noblest employment, and of participating in celestial pleasure; yet the beasts over whom he rules might blush in view of his follies and crimes, and many of them are happier than he, while destitute of the knowledge of God. Inferior beings may be instructed, but it is in those acts which, like the paths they tread, lie in the dust. But the human mind is capable of turning the eye of intelligence to heaven, and of receiving rays of divine light from the Fountain of infinite wisdom. In natural science, it is capable of high degrees of improvement, and of everlasting progress in the knowledge of God—of being adorned with the beauties of holiness, and made happy in divine fruition; but it is a slave to sin and suffering. The darkness of a hundred generations lies upon it; and if some favored parts of the earth have been illuminated by the light of religion and of science, if holiness and happiness have there produced a scene of moral beauty which charms the eyes of angels, it becomes a sight by which we discover more distinctly the deep and awful gloom which lowers upon the rest. Christian benevolence is called upon to make an effort to deliver the suffering nations from moral slavery, from mental darkness and the shackles of superstition; to restore the human mind to its original moral dignity and happiness.

In contemplating the subject of our labors, we discover upon the features of the soul the impress of immortality. It is true, that when a few short years have passed, then does the dust return to the earth as it was; but the spirit ascends to God who gave it. At the beginning, beauty and worth appeared upon the whole creation of God; but man sinned, and all nature felt the shock. Then began the work of dissolution; then was vanity inscribed upon all beneath the sun. But the spirit of man then stood forth alone; and, though he no longer reflected the moral image of his God, but was clothed with the guilt and shame of disobedience, he was not deprived of the distinguishing attribute of immortality. Annihilation was not contained in the Divine threatening, and the most ignorant, superstitious, degraded nation in the Pagan world, is a generation of immortal beings. Yes; in the savage of the woods, and the voracious cannibal of Africa, there is a soul of divine origin, of exalted capacity, and of undying existence. And while they roam the solitary desert, spending their days in superstition, cruelty, and degrading vice, they fix their characters for eternity, and seal their endless doom. The value of the soul baffles the highest power of calculation, while eternity opens on our view. O, who can look over the immense field, and extend his thoughts along the everlasting tract of duration! At the end of a thousand ages, let a single particle of dust be separated from the great mass of creation, and at the end of a thousand more let another be separated, and should you continue, at this ratio, the work of numeration, the distant period will at length arrive, when you shall have counted every sand and every dust, and measured out the waters of the great deep by single drops. It might seem that when this work is done, your existence must cease; but it will then be in its commencement, and the end thereof as far distant as when your spirit left its house of clay.

18.—INGENUITY AND ENTERPRISE OF MAN.

A. T. HOLMES.

AN encouraging evidence of the final conquest of the world for Christ, may be found in the ingenuity and enterprise of man, as exercised with reference to commercial intercourse. The facilities of transportation, by the overruling providence of God, are made tributary to the advancement of his course; and there is no extravagance in the belief, exultingly entertained, that the progress of truth henceforth will be most decidedly accelerated. Nations, heretofore the very antipodes of each other, are brought into comparative proximity, and the intervention of mountains and deserts and oceans is disregarded, in view of the conquering power of steam. Important intelligence flies upon the wings of the wind, and events affecting the commercial relations of respective nations, are communicated with a dispatch only surpassed by the flight of thought, or by the lightning's flash. But, as the various ends of secular interests are thus promoted, so is the cause of the Redeemer's Kingdom promoted. Gospel news is conveyed as all other news is conveyed; the car, the steamboat, and the magnetic wire, are alike available to the votaries of pleasure, the worshippers of mammon, and the friends of Christ; and upon the deck of the same ship that spreads her canvass to the breeze, in search of some distant, foreign port, stand, side by side, the man of business and the man of God. In connection with, and in confirmation too, of this fact, it is worthy of remark, that in those countries where the spirit of enterprise and ingenuity has been most extensively cherished, and most obviously developed, there, also, has the spirit of Christian benevolence been most decidedly awakened and acknowledged. In the United States and in Great Britain, more than elsewhere, the spirit of internal improvement prevails. Railroads, canals, and telegraphic offices, are soon to effect one continuous chain of communication throughout these respective countries; and from them, as from common centres, the gospel of the kingdom will radiate its beams of heavenly light; and, as the claims of the Lord Jesus upon his followers are more fully recognized and more sensibly felt, and all these advantages are brought to bear upon the cause of truth, the language of the prophet will become more intelligible, as, contemplating the end from the beginning, it is announced, "And I will cut off the chariot from Ephraim, and the horse from Jerusalem, and the battle bow shall be cut off: and he shall speak peace unto the heathen: and his dominion shall be from sea even to sea, and from the river even to the ends of the earth."—Zech. ix. 10. "The Lord hath made bare his holy arm in the eyes of all the nations; and all the ends of the earth shall see the salvation of our God."—Isa. lii. 10.

19.—PARENTAL OBLIGATIONS.

W. STAUGHTON.

PARENTS, the obligations by which you are bound to seek the present and everlasting welfare of your children, are firm and solemn. God has said, "Train up a child in the way he should go;" but what is that way? Should he go to the tents of wickedness, or to the house of God? Is it the disgrace, or honor—the defilement, or purity—the ruin, or felicity of thy child that thou art commanded to make thy aim? An answer need not be given; but we must affirm, that that parent deplorably neglects his duty, who does not train up his children in the habit of attending the worship of Jehovah. Often, when the Saviour appears in his courts, the eyes of the young are opened, that they may behold his beauty, and their tongues are loosened, that they may sing hosannas to his praise. Often, at a period much earlier than expected, a course of piety and virtue commences, for which the world and the church, the subject himself, and the happy parent, have ten thousand reasons to be thankful. And even in those rare instances, in which a virtuous education is followed with a life devoted to profligacy, the remembrance of parental instruction, and of the instructions received in the house of God, will always check, will often reform, and will sometimes, through divine grace, effectually reclaim the prodigal. First impressions are always deepest, death will soon take us from our children: it becomes us, therefore, to endeavor that such sentiments may be rooted in their tender minds, as may be serviceable to them, and to our children's children, when we are sleeping with our fathers; that, when led by dutiful remembrance to visit the hillock that rises over our dust, the tears of affection and gratitude may flow together. Many parents, it is to be feared, by the indulgence of a sinful, because an unwise and injurious fondness, suffer their children to continue at home, to visit the house of God, or to pursue almost any other course which puerile caprice may fancy. Very differently did the Psalmist train up young Solomon. He has recorded the circumstance among his proverbs, to the immortal memory of his parent. "I was my father's son, tender and only beloved in the sight of my mother. He taught me also, and said unto me, let thine heart retain my words."—Prov. iv. 3, 4. O beware, lest your indulgence indirectly prove the damnation of your children. By how much they are dear, very dear to your hearts, by so much the more be concerned to instruct them. Say with the Psalmist, "Come, ye children, hearken unto me, I will show you the fear of the Lord." Complain not that you cannot compel your family to attend the temple of the Lord. God has clothed you with authority; he has commanded your children to honor you, and of this they are easily made conscious. Let but your righteous injunctions be early, affectionately and perseveringly imposed, and you may hope for continual obedience. If, however, after such deportment, a child should prove rebellious, you will be able to derive consolation from reflecting that your record is on high and your witness is in heaven.

Children are ever imitating and cleaving to those whom they love. If you are but door-keepers in the house of God, your little ones will take hold of the skirts of your garments; and if you enter the dwellings of sin, doubt not but they will follow you. Paul argues, in his epistle to the Romans, that "a teacher of babes" should be a consistent character. "Thou, therefore, that teachest another, teachest thou not thyself? thou that preachest a man should not steal, dost thou steal? thou that sayest a man should not commit adultery, dost thou commit adultery?" Admonition unenforced by example, will be unavailable. Conduct at night will unravel the texture that precept wove through the day.

Perhaps there are parents who never admonish their children—who forbid them from attending God's house, or if not, leave them to the operation of that native depravity, which will of itself prefer sabbath-breaking to devotion. Alas, what thousands of young children are there who are walking in the wicked ways of their fathers! How often are they heard practising articulation with oaths, and with all the impurities of the tongue! O parents! where is your natural affection? Instruments of the earthly existence of your babes, will you be the means of their destruction? O have pity, have pity upon them! Ahaz led his son to be burned to an idol in the valley of Hinnom, but you are leading your children to a more fearful flame. If you will not train them up virtuously for their sakes, do it for your own. Think how degraded is your condition, when, if a child would obey God, he must be disobedient to you; when, if he would enter into heaven, he must look with horror on the behavior, and fly from the resorts of him that begat, and of her that bare him.

Without staying to portray the wretchedness of your offspring in future life, or the remorse which you will probably feel in the hour of death, suffer me to lift up the curtains of the invisible world. I cannot but believe, that there are degrees in the happiness of heaven. I cannot but conclude that the joys of pious parents will be heightened, when they witness in glory the triumphant arrival of those children, whom on earth they had so often led to the sanctuary, and commended to God in fervent prayer. I must believe also, that there are degrees in the anguish of hell. The rich man feared lest his five brethren should come to his place of torment, because he knew their miseries would increase his own. The parents that are now "drinking down iniquity," are on their way to the pit; but, O, how will their pains be increased, when they behold their children descend after them into the same hopeless regions. Bunyan, in his "Progress," brings his pilgrims to a mountain, on the side of which was an opening into hell. Mercy is instructed to hearken; she hearkened, and heard one saying, "Cursed be my father, for holding back my feet from the way of life and peace." Much of the misery of futurity will, probably, consist in reproach. Some, says Daniel, will awake to shame and everlasting contempt. Tormented with the devil and his angels, how will your heart endure to hear the cries of your children for ever lost? "O cruel father, O unfeeling mother, you never taught us the way to heaven—we lisped no prayers in our childhood—a holy hymn we never learned—you never offered a petition for us in the closet, or in the family—the Bible you never read to us, nor caused us to read it—vou never led us to the house of God; but made a mock alike at sin and at religion. We saw you enter the tabernacles of transgression; unsuspectingly we followed: you handed to us the poisonous potion, and our corruptions relished it. We saw you draw iniquity with cords of vanity—we applied our hands also to the rope, and, as the fruit of those sins to which you have been accessary, we are, by a righteous God, tormented in this flame!" * * * I will not enlarge. Permit me to appeal to you all, to-day, whether king David be not justifiable in asserting, he had rather be a door-keeper in the house of his God, than to dwell in the tents of wickedness.

20.—SELFISHNESS OF MAN.

J. N. BROWN.

SIN is but selfishness in its ten thousand forms; and every selfish spirit acts upon a latent maxim the very reverse of that inculcated by the Lord Jesus, when he said, "It is more blessed to give than to receive." The maxim of selfishness, brought out from its disguises, and put into words, would be, It is more blessed to *receive*, than to *give;* or, as the modern phrase is, "Keep all you can get, and get all you can."

Now for the application of this principle in practice. "Keep all you get;" that is to say, let no one be the better for your strength, talents or learning—for your labor, skill or experience—for your prayers, property, or influence. Happiness is your being's end, and happiness consists in the free gratification of your favorite desires. If your taste be for good eating and drinking, for fine clothes, houses, furniture, or equipage, indulge yourselves, without regard to others, except to see that you lose nothing by them. Waste nothing upon the wants of the improvident poor, who are only idle, impudent, and ungrateful. If your taste be for books, gratify yourself alone. Shut yourself up n your library. Never lend a book, for it will be sure to be injured or lost; never communicate your knowledge, for people always hate to be told the truth. If you care for none of these things, and love nothing but money, secure your drawers and chests; see that your securities are good, and your stocks safe; comfort yourself with looking over your notes and bonds, your deeds and mortgages, your houses and lands, your silver and gold. Never think of any good your money might do to others—how many destitute sufferers it might relieve—how many schools it might establish—how many tracts and other useful books it might procure for the benefit of thousands—how many evangelists and colporteurs it might send out in our neglected settlements—how many missionaries it might support among the heathen—how many Bibles it might translate, print, and circulate in the languages of the perishing people, to make them wise unto salvation. No, these are all visionary schemes, with which no prudent man will trouble his head. Keep all you get for yourself; and when you must leave it in the course of nature, leave it all to your children or family connections—whether they need it or not—whether it will be likely to benefit or ruin them. In a word, you may be a glutton, you may be a book-worm, you may be a miser, only keep all you get.

But the one-half of this miserable story is not yet told. The latter part of the maxim of selfishness infinitely exceeds the former. "Get all you can;" that is to say, be the spunge of the community. Stick at nothing to get along in the world; drive your business night and day, early and late; allow yourself no pause for prayer, no parenthesis for reflection. Determine to be rich; no matter though thereby you plunge yourself into temptation and a snare, and into foolish and hurtful lusts, which, the Bible says, drown men in destruction and perdition; all this is nothing, if you can only become independent—if you can only acquire the character of an industrious, sharp, and stirring man, who knows how to do his own work, and drives his own bargains. But you say you cannot dig. Never mind, then beg. Be a drone in the hive of society, and suck the honey from every one who is generous enough to feed you. Ask favors and kind offices of all, but render as few as possible in return. "Get all you can." But you say, perhaps, to beg you are ashamed. Well then, continues the lying spirit of selfishness, since you must live in some way, and cannot afford to live honestly, get over all scruples of conscience, as you have those of honor—covet that which is your neighbor's, and get all you can. Steal, lie, cheat, swindle; be a forger, a counterfeiter, a highwayman. Or, if you despise being a vulgar villain, be a genteel one. Get into some lucrative office, no matter what, or how; never trouble yourself about discharging its duties beyond what is unavoidable; neither be scrupulous about accounting for all that you receive—that is the concern of your employers. If ejected at length for abuse of trust, be sure to get all you can. If that be not sufficient, resolve at least "to die game;" gamble, drink, quarrel, kill your man like a hero, or be killed yourself; as to consequences, you have nothing to fear after death—hell is all a bugbear—heaven a dream—death an eternal sleep—religion superstition, and of all superstitions, that of the Bible is the worst.

Do you say, hold! this is too horrible. I know it is, most horrible. But it is a most horrible reality. All this is but selfishness fully acted out. All this is the natural, and alas, too frequently the actual consequence of the diabolical principle—it is better to receive than to give. How many thousands has it landed in irreligion, libertinism, atheism? All these forms and more, selfishness assumes; to all these tremendous results it necessarily tends; and, however kept under check and restraint by the benignant providence of

God, still every desire, every thought, that springs from this odious principle, has essentially the same hateful and abominable character. O, how can we expect the church to prosper; how can the world be made happy; how can we hope for the approbation of conscience, the esteem of virtuous beings, or the blessing of a holy God, till we from the heart abjure all the specious and glozing maxims of selfishness, and mourn in brokenness of spirit that the time past of our life has been so much under their accursed and withering dominion?

21.—MORAL PRINCIPLE AND COURAGE.

L. C. STEVENS.

A GREAT want of moral principle characterizes the age.

What is moral principle? It is a determination to do right, because it is right to do right; it is a determination not to do wrong, because it is *wrong* to do wrong. Let it not be supposed that every action in itself is the result of correct moral principle. An action, considered apart from the motives which prompt it, may be a worthy action—an action fraught with good to many a soul. But that same action *considered in connection with the motives that prompt it,* may be wicked and exceedingly displeasing to God. For example: a man contracts a debt of fifty dollars, and gives his note for its payment in three months, and when the three months are expired, upon presentation, he pays the note. He may, or he may not, act from moral principle in the matter. Does he pay the note because he loves to do right, and would on no account do wrong? If so, he acts from moral principle. But he may pay the note because, if he refuses, he is liable to a suit at law; or, because, if he refuses, he is liab!·

to a loss of reputation ; or because he foresees, if he pays it, he may hereafter be successful in defrauding his creditor out of twice the sum now due to him. In such a case as either of these, he is as absolutely destitute of moral principle, as if he should refuse peremptorily to pay the note.

A man may tell the truth, not because it *is* the truth which he utters, and still less because he loves the truth and hates falsehood ; but because to tell the truth will promote his present interests. Were he placed in different circumstances, so as to deem a falsehood necessary to promote his present interest, he might give utterance to it, without hesitation, *provided* only that he has no fears of detection and exposure.

Now where this want of moral principle exists in a professedly good man, what is the result? He "becomes all things to all men," in a most wicked sense of these words of Paul. You will find him *one* thing to-day, and *another* thing to-morrow, and never *twice* alike, unless indeed it suits his interest and convenience to appear twice in the same garb. He will accommodate himself to any thing and every thing, to all sorts of people, good, bad, and indifferent. Ask him what you will, and he will always answer to please you, never saying *yes* when you wish him to say *no*, never saying *no*, when you wish him to say *yes*. If you apprise him of his contradictory statements, he will always have an explanation ready—an explanation which, he will assert, fully justifies him for doing what is an outrage upon the commonest principles of reason and right. In one word he is a *Jesuit*, understanding intrigue, and manœuvre and twistification, as well as did the Spanish Loyola himself.

A great want of moral courage is characteristic of the age.

By moral courage we mean a braving of the dangers of doing right—a firmness and resolution which bear a man forward in the path that God has marked out for him to walk in, without regard to consequences. This is an element of character which was conspicuously exhibited in Daniel, and the three worthies at Babylon, and by Paul when he declared "none of these things move me." It has been exhibited by every man, more or less, who has lived to any good purpose.

But what we now assert is, that this element of character is greatly wanting in multitudes, who appear to *mean well.* They see what ought to be—what the word of God requires—what their own consciences approve. Still they are timorous—fearful—cannot do it. If some persons would go before them and lead the way, perhaps they would follow after. Let them be placed somewhere in the rear, where the weapons of the enemy could not reach them till the front ranks of the whole army should be destroyed, and then they might possibly nerve themselves up to the work of standing in opposition to a threatening foe.

22.—APPEAL TO THE UNCONVERTED

HOWARD MALCOM.

It is not to be questioned that all men are bound to humble themselves, and accept the gospel. "Repent and believe," is a plain command. "He that believeth not shall be damned," is a plain warning of the penalty of neglect. No soul will be lost, but by its own impenitence and perversity. "Ye will not come unto me that ye might have life." While alarming denunciations of wrath are uttered for our warning, the most cheering and positive invitations and promises are offered for our encouragement. "Look unto me and be ye saved, all the ends of the earth." "Ho, every one that thirsteth, come ye to the waters." "He that believeth and is baptized shall be saved." The proclamation of mercy is without the least restriction to classes of men. It is "good tidings of great joy which shall be to all people." There is nothing either in the doctrine of election, or particular redemption, which makes it in vain for any son of Adam to seek eternal life. Your sole concern is to submit yourself at once to God, and apply earnestly for mercy. Why should we disbelieve God when he says, "Whosoever will, let him come and take the water of life freely?" "It is impossible for God to lie." His word is, Christ "is able to save unto the uttermost all who come unto God by him." "Come now, and let us reason together, saith the Lord: though your sins be as scarlet, they shall be white as snow; though they be red like crimson, they shall be as wool."

How amazing that such a Redeemer, and such declarations should meet a cold and stupid reception! How strange is the unbelief, and contempt, and opposition, and hatred, and ridicule, with which the gospel of God is received! What ingenuity is displayed in the invention of excuses, the discovery of flaws, the explaining away of precepts, and the perversion of truth! Fearful must be the guilt of thus treating a message of infinite mercy! The case of heathens is sad enough. But what shall we say of men, who thus spend their entire lives, while from the cradle to the tomb they are surrounded by the meridian splendor of revelation, and are fully, freely, daily, urged to lay hold on the hope set before them. O sinners! receive not the grace of God in vain. Spend not your hasty moments in questions and doubts suggested by Satan, and nourished by pride. The kingdom of God must be received by you "as a little child," or not at all. He who, instead of praying, is considering the compatibleness of prayer with Divine immutability, loses the blessing which God ordains to them that ask. Though no toil can make the seed to grow, yet he who neglects to plant shall have hunger instead of harvest. He who neglects to accept "so great salvation," while he pries into its extent, dies unredeemed. How can we understand what "angels desire to look into?" First obey intelligible calls, and then commend yourselves to the teachings of that Spirit who is to "guide you into all truth." Lazarus, though *dead*, was *commanded* to come forth. The *withered* arm was commanded to be stretched forth. You are required, O sinner, to forsake your way, and "turn unto the Lord, who will have mercy."

If you still say there may be no atonement for you, then see that this alone keeps you from the skies. So perform all that *is* in your power, that if turned into hell it shall not be your fault. Slight no warning, refuse no instruction, omit no endeavor. Repent and turn from all your sins. Believe on the Lord Jesus. Watch unto prayer. Live in love, and die casting yourself on the mercy and merit of a Divine Saviour. Then, if lost, the rigors even of hell would be mitigated. Yea, you might triumph in your overthrow, and all the rebels thenceforth have some joy. For your condemnation would prove the gospel a deception, its invitation mockery, and its promises untrue. It would shake the throne of the universe, and tarnish the character of the Almighty!

Why complain, dear fellow-sinners, of limited powers, when what you know you *can* do, is omitted—omitted from choice, not necessity, as yourselves even insist. Why cavil, when judgment and conscience approve? Believe on the Son of God. You are deciding your eternal doom by rejecting this Saviour. Your path is the road to hell. You are hasting away from the presence of God, and all felicity. There is but a step between you and death. Look aloft at the promises; look round at the brevity of your probation; look back at your sins, and "flee from the wrath to come." Sport not away these precious moments, while toppling on the verge of opportunity.

How can you behold hell and destruction at your feet, and feel no anxiety? Arise and call upon God. To-day you may die. O look to Jesus, and be saved! Frail, irresolute, exposed, dying mortal, come taste and know that the Lord is gracious. How often would he have gathered you "as a hen gathereth her chickens under her wings, and ye would not." Proceed not, until, smitten of God, you sink on a death-bed of damnation, and in the agonies of dissolving nature, realize the fearful sentence, "Because I have called and ye refused, I have stretched out my hand, and no man regarded, I also will laugh at your calamity: I will mock when your fear cometh."

Now, now "is the day of salvation." "To-day, if ye will hear his voice, harden not your hearts." Begin this moment, and never cease to make salvation and the service of God the business of your life. Wait for no better opportunity—seek no present carnal indulgence—contrive no sophistry—listen to no seduction—allow no discouragement—desire no relaxation of terms—make no reserve—wait no further impulse. Begin, not by laboring of yourself to grow better; but by pressing to your heart and conscience the consideration of your great guilt, and the blessed message of the text—that "Christ Jesus came into the world to save sinners." Begin at Christ, or you miss "the way." "Strive [*agonize*] to enter in at the strait gate." If even the reading of religious books, or an attendance at inquiry meetings, leads you to a dependence on these things, they lead you astray. If even your solemn resolutions of self-dedication, induce you to postpone the act, they are not of the Lord. Fall down at the foot of the cross. There the Christian race begins. There go for cleansing, and for spiritual life. "The blood of Jesus Christ cleanseth from all sin." "He that hath the Son hath life; and he that hath not the Son of God hath not life, but the wrath of God abideth on him."

23.—A WORD TO THE THOUGHTLESS.

D. SHAVER.

WILL those who have hitherto "thrown their inch of time away," suffer a warning, and a plea of Christian affection? My hearers, all who hope to rejoice with Paul, must first tremble with him. How numerous are the considerations which speak thunder in your ears! Record the magnitude and enormity of your transgressions. The righteous judgment of the day of wrath, when the heavens shall be bowed with the burden of Divine majesty, and the heart of the wicked with the more fearful burden of Divine vengeance, shall "render to every man according to his works." While, therefore, unbelief is the ground of condemnation to the impenitent, while it must bind them in chains under darkness for ever, the intensity of the fire which shall kindle upon them will be aggravated by *all* their unrighteousness. Every sin of thought, of word, and of action, shall find its own retribution; shall add bitterness to the cup of sorrow; shall introduce another arrow into the quiver of holy anger; shall open a lower depth before the fall of the shrinking spirit, which reaches forth after hope and grasps the stings of despair; shall increase the wretchedness which even without it is untold, immeasurable and fathomless. Your iniquities have increased over your head, and your trespass is grown up unto the heavens. Can you look upon the reckoning which awaits you and feel no dread? You feel no dread? Tremble, then, that you do not tremble! It is no task of difficulty to preserve this composure of mind, until it shall have destroyed you. Scarron, the poet, who spent his life in merriment, resolved to be gay upon his death-bed. Almost with his latest breath he said, "I never thought it was so EASY a matter to *laugh at the approach of death.*" So EASY a matter! In this or another state of being, the sinner shall employ similar language. I never thought it was so easy a matter to make my heart hard against all fear. I never thought it was so easy a matter to brave the terrors of the Lord, what time they come nigh to us. I never thought it was so easy a matter to step into hell with smiles. I never thought it was so easy a matter to be damned before we are alarmed. I never thought! If I had, I would not now be found in this condemnation. I NEVER THOUGHT! O ye dying souls—dying, yet laughing—THINK! THINK! Subdued, as Paul was, cry this day, "Lord, what wilt thou have me to do?" And may He who has saved the chief of sinners, save all ye!

24.—VANITY OF THE WORLD.

T. CURTIS.

WE are ever needing the lesson, both in the aggregate and the detail, that all about us is unreal, as a foundation for permanent plans—the whole circuit of earthly things a very vanity. At the tomb, what interest of man, out of the ten thousand jarring concerns of a worldling, does not terminate for ever! And that tomb, how nigh! In youth, intent on interests peculiarly personal, we plan naturally for a whole life: and Hope crowds into her canvass whole groups of future events in which we shall be prominent and successful, no one of which is transferred to the picture of our history. We plan for a whole life—but "a worm is in the bud of youth." The average of young people do not live half a life. At maturity, we become domestic, agricultural, commercial—political. We must be settled and require a home. Now we share awhile our personal interests with another and another, with a second and a multiplied self. But the original ingredient of vanity is so perpetuated as to blight the exercise of our most honorable affections. We are scarcely *united* with any thing human, before the tie is broken. Two become one, but to give agony to the grasp of death that soon tears them apart, as how many feel! and parents rear the most hopeful of all children for early graves! Thus of our other pursuits. How full, under favorable circumstances, of abortive labor—of charge with little hope and no improvement! And how soon will a fit of sickness, sometimes, wind up every passing interest we feel in them!

Reason and philosophy may teach us enough of the vanity of the world to distract or paralyze us. The ancients, therefore, when they were excited by argument, "felt after" a better system; but as they cooled, and became more serious, they were sceptical. "Reading arguments," says Cicero, or to this effect, "we become convinced of the immortality of the soul, but we lay aside the book and the conviction is gone." Our moral circumstances, how superior! The living God steps in at once to cheer our hopes and to prescribe our duty. Of all, even the vain things of life, he assumes the final direction, and teaches us both to use the world and be useful, however transitory our personal interests in it. Philosophy had no curb of divine authority to place upon any of our selfish feelings—and those which the world's vanity will exasperate are not few nor weak. But the noble lessons of a Christian self-denial educate us at once for two worlds.

25.—MAN A SOJOURNER.

EDWARD SAVAGE.

ONCE I saw an old man. A hundred and eleven winters had bent and withered his form and whitened his locks. Other aged men stood around him with grey heads and trembling limbs, but these were not the companions of his youth. He had seen a whole generation pass away before they were born. I asked myself where are the companions of his youth; those who began to live when he began, with as much apparent certainty of life, and as bright, joyous hopes, as he? They had gone, all of them. Death, in unnumbered forms anticipated or unforeseen, had taken them away, and none of them could redeem his brother, or define the period of his sojourn here. Many of them, doubtless, had calculated upon long life, but quickly had they been hurried away, while he stood a lonely monument to point back and tell us of the brief day of their pilgrimage.

But will any of us be mocked by this flattering illusion? Will we suppose that we can lay hold on life with a strong hand, and not let it go until we have outlived all of our generation, and consigned the last one to the grave? The instances of mortality now before us say, "that even in the midst of life we are in death;" that at any age, in any moment, we may be taken. A few days since, and those whose funeral we now attend were busy in the scenes of life. But they are now dead. Their life has sped like the flight of a weaver's shuttle. With railroad speed, their souls have fled into eternity to their God never to return. How short and uncertain, then, is human life. Surely, with Moses, the man of God, we should each one pray, "So teach us to number our days, that we may apply our hearts unto wisdom."

26.—EXPECTATION OF A FUTURE STATE.

S. HALL.

If a man loves God he will rejoice in the doctrine of the gospel, concerning a future state of existence, the resurrection of the dead, and eternal judgment. If I love God supremely, I shall desire to be with him, to know more and more of him, to approach nearer and nearer to him, and to sustain a greater likeness to him. If I love God with all my heart, I shall listen with joy to those tidings which assure me that I shall live after I am dead—that I shall behold the King in his beauty—that I shall gaze upon his excellence for ever—that I shall enjoy his friendship, world without end—that I shall enter deeper and deeper into the mysteries of his incomprehensible nature—that I shall lay my heart upon the heart of him whom my soul loveth—that I shall be surrounded and protected by his almighty energy and presence—and that my life of blessedness shall be extended to immortality. If I love God with all my heart, I shall certainly be happy to know that death is not an eternal sleep; that my grave shall, by and by, be opened, and my body come forth, fashioned into an incorruptible, spiritual, strong, and honorable body, capable of sustaining a far more exceeding and eternal weight of glory, and that, reunited to the soul, it shall be for ever employed in the praise and service of God.

If I love God, why should I object against a future judgment? It is a rational doctrine. We are accountable beings. It is right that we should be accountable. We could not be happy in God unless accountable to him. If we are accountable to God, it is right and proper that he should call us to give account to him. There is no more impropriety in calling us to account, than in making us accountable. If we are accountable to God, and if he is our governor, it is right and proper that he should *appoint a time* when he will call us to give an account to him. If a man loves God with all his heart, he will not be afraid to come to judgment. Holy angels never object against the judgment. It is the love of sin and a consciousness of guilt, which make men fear the judgment and object against it. In that great day, for which all other days were made, God will display his goodness and glory, and vindicate the reasonableness and benevolence of his government. He will show that the interests and privileges of holy beings are in his hands. He will show that he is worthy to receive everlasting honor, praise, and homage from all intelligent beings. He will then take away the reproach of his people, and bless virtue and piety with everlasting joy. He will show his love of holiness, and his infinite and unchangeable hatred of sin, and that he has no fellowship with sinners. He will then, more than ever, expose the evil, criminality, and guilt of sin, and doom it to its proper place. Is not this a day greatly to be desired by those who love God? Can a man love God, and not desire to see the goodness, holiness, and justice of his nature, character, and government vindicated, honored, praised, and glorified? Will not a holy man be willing that God should judge the world *in righteousness?* The gospel preaches such a day. If we love God, we shall certainly love such information. But if we hate the Father, it is easy to see that such information will be very unwelcome. We shall not cordially receive him who brings such tidings.

27.—IMMORTALITY OF THE SOUL.

J. J. JAMES.

Is the soul immortal? This was the great problem which agitated for ages the minds of heathen philosophers, and to establish which they exerted their utmost powers. To settle this question many of them spent the best portion of their lives in patient and laborious study. They probed into the secrets of nature with the most careful research, and drew from all her accessible resources whatever might tend to elucidate the subject. But after all their labors, the light which they received from nature and reason was still unsatisfactory. They were left somewhat in darkness and in doubt. Many pious heathen endeavored to believe in the soul's immortality, and sometimes professed to do so, as did also some of their philosophers; but some of the wisest of these often doubted their own reasonings. To be convinced of this, we have only to examine their writings; and not to do more, let us listen to the declarations of a few of their most enlightened reasoners.

Cicero, the orator of Rome, when treating on this subject, says, "I do not pretend to say that what I affirm is as infallible as the Pythian oracle, I speak only by conjecture." Cyrus, in his address to his children, says, "I know not how to persuade myself that the soul lives in this mortal body, and ceases to be when the body expires. I am more inclined to think, that it acquires after death more penetration and purity." We hear also the immortal Socrates, the prince of all heathen philosophers, when taking leave of his judges, who had wickedly condemned him to death, say, "And now we are going to part, I to suffer death, and you to enjoy life. God only knows which has the happier lot." Thus we see that on a subject the most intensely interesting and deeply important, which poor mortals can contemplate, nature has not satisfactorily taught her most intelligent disciples. With the strongest desires to believe in the immortality of the soul, they have been compelled, in their most honest moments, to confess the insufficiency of their reasonings. The light which nature gave them did not penetrate through the dark valley and shadow of death.

How completely does revelation dissipate all this obscurity! It clearly teaches that the soul is immortal, and that its immortality is based upon the will of its Creator; that He who made it, made it immortal; and that nothing but the same almighty power can annihilate or destroy it. Of the numerous passages which might be quoted from the sacred scriptures, setting forth the soul's immortality, we select the following, which we think amply sufficient. "Then shall the dust return to the earth as it was, and the spirit shall return to God who gave it."—Eccles. xii. 7. "Fear not them which shall kill the body, but are not able to kill the soul; but rather fear Him which is able to destroy both body and soul in hell."—Mat. x. 28. "For what is a man profited, if he shall gain the whole world, and lose his own soul; or what shall a man give in exchange for his soul? For the son of man shall come in the glory of his Father, with his angels; and then shall he reward every man according to his works."—Mat. xvi. 26, 27. "For we that are in this tabernacle do groan, being burdened; not for that we would be unclothed, but clothed upon, that mortality might be swallowed up of life.—We are confident, I say, and willing rather to be absent from the body, and to be present with the Lord."—2 Cor. v. 4, 8. "They stoned Stephen, calling upon God and saying, Lord Jesus receive my spirit."—Acts vii. 59. "Who hath saved us, and called us with an holy calling, not according to our works, but according to his own purpose and grace, which was given us in Christ Jesus before the world began; but is now manifest by the appearing of our Saviour, Jesus Christ, who hath abolished death, and hath brought life and immortality to light, through the gospel.—I know whom I have believed, and am persuaded that he is able to keep that which I have committed to him against that day."—2 Tim. i. 9, 10, 12.

28.—THE WAY OF HAPPINESS.

D. WILLIAMS.

THE way of obedience is the only way of true happiness. The world, in various ways, is in pursuit of this, but "following lying vanities," they forsake the way of mercy and real enjoyment; only the true Christian has pleasure, pure and refined in its nature, and eternal in duration. He has such a principle, that his happiness consists in making others so. Thus the father's ebbs and flows with the son's, and the husband's with the wife's; and so of the rest. Thus to be holy is to be happy, and there is no luxury like doing good. This disposition exists in God, and is seen in his address to his people. "Oh that my people had hearkened unto me and kept my ways and commandments, then had their peace been as a river, and their righteousness as the waves of the sea." The river deepens and widens as it rolls to the ocean. So would the peace of the Christian be, until it empties in the boundless ocean of Deity, whence it rose. And lastly, reverse the text, "If ye know these things, happy are ye if ye do them," and you draw aside the curtain which conceals the source of unhappiness. Let us try this. "If ye know these things and do them not, ye are unhappy." In heaven the will of God is perfectly known and universally observed: and so all these are completely happy. In hell it is known and universally violated: and all these are "weeping and wailing and gnashing of teeth" in torment endless. In this world the Divine will is partly known and observed; and so far happiness prevails. But as there is much ignorance and disobedience, there is much misery in our world. "There is no peace, saith my God, to the wicked;" but "peace shall be upon Israel."

29.—SORROWS OF AGE.

JOHN STANFORD.

It frequently happens that the best of men have their greatest afflictions reserved for them until heart and flesh begin to fail beneath the weight of years. Like Job, they lose their children, their worldly property is removed, friends are unkind, diseases attack them, and a desponding spirit presses them down to the very dust. It was so with David in his latter days, and this, possibly, in some degree, may be the case with you; and it is very natural for you to wish a little revival in your bondage, or, as Zophar expresses it, that your age may be clearer than the noon-day, and that you may shine forth as the morning, in health and prosperity. The Lord granted such a favor to good old Jacob, who, after more journeyings and afflictions than fell to the common lot of other patriarchs, was permitted to spend his last seventeen years in peace and comfort with his once lost beloved son Joseph, in the fertile land of Goshen, so that his age was indeed clearer than the noon-day. And certainly Zophar's wish for Job was eventually verified, for the Lord turned his captivity, and made his latter end twice better than its beginning. Let this encourage your hope, and be assured, that if such earthly comforts shall comport with your best interest, the Lord is able to do so to you, and more also.

30.—PROSPERITY OF THE WICKED.

S. CHAPIN.

A SEVERE trial of the mind of man is produced by the prosperity of the wicked, compared with the adversity of the righteous. Many persons often fail to cherish a practical belief, that this life is not a state of retribution. Hence they are prone to judge of men, according to their temporal circumstances. Those who are the most successful in their pursuits and experience the fewest reverses of fortune, they are ready to consider as the greatest favorites of Heaven. And on the other hand, those who are the most frequently defeated in their designs, and suffer the greatest calamities, they are equally ready to consider as the greatest offenders in the sight of God. This, it seems, was the opinion of Job's friends. For they undertook to measure the degree of his guilt by the severity of his sufferings. Said they, "The work of a man shall God render unto him, and cause every man to find according to his way." Some are apt to judge not only of men by what they experience, but also of the character of measures by the manner in which they succeed. If the adopted measure prosper, they at once conclude that it is good; but if it fail, they pronounce it bad. This was the way in which the wicked of ancient times judged of the character of measures. While they and their offspring were permitted to spend their days in wealth, and to chant at the sound of the harp and organ, they fancied that they were pursuing the best course to promote their highest interest. Therefore they said unto God, "Depart from us, for we desire not the knowledge of thy ways," and "what profit shall we have, if we pray unto him?" So, too, the Jews, in the days of Jeremiah, concluded that the worship of idols was better than the worship of Jehovah; because, while they adhered exclusively to the worship of the latter, they were in want of all things; but while they poured out drink-offerings to the moon, they had plenty of victuals and wanted nothing. They therefore renounced the service of the true God, and resolved to pay their homage to the queen of heaven. In this way, even good men have often been strongly tempted. Asaph was greatly stumbled, when he saw the prosperity of the wicked. He says, "My feet were almost gone, my steps had well nigh slipped. For I was envious at the foolish. They are not in trouble as other men; neither are they plagued like other men. Their eyes stand out with fatness, they have more than heart could wish." But while he said this, he and other godly men of the times, were plagued all the day long, and chastened every morning. When he sought to know this, it was too painful for him. He therefore concluded that those were in a better condition who lived as they pleased, than were those who attempted to practise the duties of religion. He was even ready to give up his God and all his hopes of heaven, and to join the standard of the wicked. Saith he, "Verily, I have cleansed my heart in vain, and washed my hands in innocency." And it was nothing but his visit to the sanctuary, where he learnt the end of the ungodly, that prevented his complete apostacy,

---

31.—THE NECESSITY OF DYING.

J. R. SCOTT,

HUMAN life, however lengthened out, *must* come to an end. Our lives, as compared with the lives of others, may be long, but impartial death will come to us at length. Mortality is our common lot. There is no discharge in this war. "His days," says Job, "are determined; the number of his months are with thee, thou hast appointed his bounds that he cannot pass." The days of our years may be threescore years and ten; they may reach even to fourscore; nay, they may be increased even very considerably beyond that; but the shaft of the insatiate archer cannot be escaped; sooner or later, it will pierce us, and we must fall.

But he is only the messenger of another. It is God who issues the decree. It is the author of life who is the arbiter of life's close. "*Thou* turnest man to destruction, and sayest, Return, ye children of men." It is the same Being in whose hand is the soul of every living thing, and the breath of all mankind, who taketh away their breath, so that they die, and return to the dust. And *why is it that death is thus inevitable?* The reason is suggested in the connection of our text. "We are consumed," says the psalmist, "by thine anger, and by thy wrath are we troubled. Thou hast set our iniquities before thee, our secret sins in the light of thy countenance." When we consider the goodness and the power of God, in connection with the fact of our mortality, we cannot but feel that in some way our race has been subject to his displeasure, and that this is the cause of our mortality. Such we find to be the case. It is because we are a corrupt and sinful race, that we are a dying race. We inherit depravity, and this has infused the poison into our veins which must issue in our dissolution. The sentence pronounced originally on our general father in Eden, was pronounced on him as the representative of our race—"Dust thou art, and unto dust shalt thou return." That sentence continues in full force against all his posterity. "By one man sin entered into the world, and death by sin; so that death hath passed upon all men, because that all have sinned." It was part of the direful penalty of Adam's transgression, and probably no little aggravation of his own personal punishment, that he should transmit to the remotest generation of his descendants, a sinful, diseased, and mortal constitution; that he should not merely die himself, but that all who should trace their origin to him should die.

My hearers, it is not for us to arraign our Maker, and question the equity of this arrangement. That the principle holds, not only in our relation to Adam, but in all the relations of life, is beyond dispute. It is one of the great principles of God's moral government. Our Sovereign has so ordered it, that no one of us can sin, without others being more or less affected by the consequences. The child must feel the effects of the father's vicious excesses. He feels them in the diseased and debilitated body he has derived from his parent. The spendthrift head of a family not only brings penury and sorrow upon himself, but also reduces all who are dependent upon him to want and wo by his prodigality. And so throughout society. We may presume to question the justice of this arrangement as much as we please, but we cannot deny that it exists. God has so constituted us, and has so constituted society, that it must be so—it cannot be otherwise. But is there nothing to counterbalance this gloomy and mysterious part of his plan? It is true that we suffer from sins and vices not our own. Is it not equally true that we derive benefits from good deeds and virtues not our own? Does the child profit nothing from the excellences of the parent? How many owe their fortune, and good name, and standing in society far more to others with whom they are, or have been connected, than to themselves. The jealous God, who visits the iniquities of the fathers upon the children unto the third and fourth generations of them that hate him, delights also to show mercy unto thousands of them that love him and keep his commandments. What claim have these latter to the blessings which fall to them? And what claim, we demand, has the child, on the score of equity, to be freed from the inconveniences entailed on him by his father's vices, which does not prove also that he has no right to derive advantages from his father's virtues? Men do not complain of this arrangement so far as it affects them favorably; but when it involves them in misery, they hesitate not to murmur, and accuse their righteous sovereign of injustice; and this, notwithstanding the plan is so admirably adapted, at once to restrain men from wickedness, and excite them to the highest moral excellence.

And has God revealed nothing in his plan, as an offset to the unhappiness of our condition, in consequence of our relation to Adam? Yes, dear hearers, there is not only a first Adam in whom we fell, but there is also a second Adam, in whom we may be restored. A glorious provision has been made for our redemption. As in Adam we have death, so in Jesus Christ we may have life, and life eternal. The original sentence must indeed be inflicted on our bodies; but if we believe in Jesus, the day is coming when both soul and body shall be gloriously wrested from the hand of the destroyer. Hear the voice of death's Conqueror. "I am the resurrection and the life: he that believeth in me, though he were dead, yet shall he live; and he that liveth and believeth in me shall never die." Hear an apostle. "If by one man's offence, death reigned by one; much more they that receive abundance of grace and of the gift of righteousness, shall reign in life by one, Jesus Christ. Therefore, as by the offence of one, judgment came upon all men to condemnation, even so by the righteousness of one, the free gift came upon all men unto justification of life. For as by one man's disobedience many were made sinners, so by the obedience of one shall many be made righteous." Here, my friends, you see the offset to the unhappy consequences of Adam's fall, which accrue to us.

32.—THE DEATH OF GREAT MEN.

JESSE MERCER.

If great and good men are to be regarded as the blessing of God to a people, their continuance must be signal of his favor, and their removal of his displeasure. Their fall can be considered in no other light than a public calamity. It has in it a warning voice, and should excite lamentation. This solemn fact is exemplified in the histories of Greece, Rome, and all other ancient nations, which approximated the nearest in civil government to that charter of equal rights, which Heaven donated to man. From their highest eminence of republican glory and plebeian freedom, these nations commenced their downward aim, in the loss of those great men, whose sterling knowledge and equanimity of soul enabled them to establish and direct their destinies to glory and renown; and terminated their mad career in ruin, under the dominations of men ruling in power rather than right; whose ambition and self-adulation acted the most destructive influence on the liberties of the people, and even on the national existence. But God, in his sovereign and good pleasure, has afforded to some nations a long and happy succession of great and good men to rule over them, by which they are distinguished in the scale of nations, as the preserved of the Lord. But evils seldom come alone; and so in the fall of nations there is often a fearful concatenation of evil events. When great men of renown are taken away by the stroke of the Almighty, it is frequently followed by the ingress of men whose pusillanimity and vile habits render them to the nation a double curse. Thus when God announces his displeasure against Israel, in taking the mighty man and the man of war, the judge and the prophet, the prudent and the ancient, and the honorable man, and the counsellor, and the eloquent orator, he threat-

Eng.[d] by H.S. Sadd, N.Y.

Printed by W. Neale, N.Y.

ens to give them children to be their princes, and babes to rule over them. And as a cousequence of such a calamitous state of things, he declares the people shall be oppressed one by another, and the child in politics shall behave himself proudly against the ancient; and the base ruler against the honorable. Thus Israel was given up to the scourge of her own sins, and chastised by national corruption. Her rulers were the rulers of Sodom, corrupters, oppressors, and even murderers. The whole body politic became diseased. The whole head was sick, and the whole heart faint. There was no soundness, and the wound was incurable. And the nation was devoted to ruin—such a ruin as whosoever heard the report of it, both his ears should tingle. Thus the death of great and good men has in it a warning voice. The flight of doves to their windows indicates approaching storms—when nations go to war, they call their envoys home. When God calls his ministers of state away, it suggests troubles at the door. Thus saith the prophets: "The righteous perish, and no man layeth it to heart; and the merciful men are taken away, none considering the righteous are taken away from the evil to come." The warning continues—"The good man perisheth out of the earth; there is none upright among men; they all lie in wait for blood; they hunt every man his brother with a net. That they may do evil with both hands in earnest, the prince asketh, and the judge asketh for a reward; and the great man (in wickedness) uttereth his mischievous desire; and so they wrap it up." "The best of them is as a briar, and the most upright sharper than a thorn hedge: the day of thy watchmen, and of thy visitation cometh; now shall their perplexity be."

33.—FAMILIES SEPARATED BY DEATH.

J. BRADLEY.

DEATH is an enemy, because it separates the best and dearest friends from each other—destroys their plans, and closes up their prospects of enjoyment. At its approach, brethren, sisters, parents and children, husbands and wives, must part for ever. No sigh of sentimental attachment, no groan of deep and pathetic affection, can avert these awful consequences of his apparently barbarous, and palpably tremendous award. Tears may flow, warm and copious from the fervor of mental anguish, but they flow in vain. The heart, seized with trepidation and alarm, at the solemn, the painful, the distressing, the distracting thought, may, like the mariner's compass in a tempest, heave, and totter, and tremble in its frame; still the doom is inevitable, the blow must fall, the fatal stroke be struck; and honors, and rational enjoyments, virtuous pleasures, and reciprocal love, like the expanded leaves of the forest when stricken by the frost of autumn, must lose the vivifying hold that sustained them, fall into the ground, sink into the earth, and mingle with the clods of the valley.

This enemy deprived Abraham, the father of the faithful and the friend of God, of his beloved Sarah. While sojourning in a far country, in a strange land, his bosom companion, the sweet response of a kind and gracious soul, his fond and dutiful wife, was cloven down by the ample scimiter of death. With the tenderest and most grateful sensations of the best of husbands, he gazed upon the beauteous ruin. Though the rich melody of her voice could no longer charm him; though the willing effusions of her plaintive goodness could no more administer to his consolation, and beguile the rugged incidents of an arduous and ruthless journey; yet would he fain have preserved the lifeless remnant of her earthly existence, and carried it along with him. But death, having performed his ungracious office, had consigned it to corruption. He, therefore, in the bitterness of affliction, was compelled to say unto the sons of Heth, "Give me a possession of a burying place with you, that I may bury my dead out of my sight."

This last enemy, in all his movements, spreads desolation and unspeakable distress. When he stalked round the habitation, and through the family of the pious Job, destruction and wo followed in his train. But Job knew that he was irresistible, and therefore submitted to his ravages with resignation and composure. He rent his mantle, shaved his head, and fell upon the ground. His friends, having heard of his calamities, came to mourn with him and comfort him. "And when they lifted up their eyes afar off and saw him, they lifted up their voices and wept, and rent every one his mantle, and sprinkled dust upon their heads. So they sat down with him upon the ground seven days and seven nights, and none spoke a word unto him; for they saw that his grief was great."

Death not only cuts asunder all those strong, endearing ties which unite mankind together and to the world, but goes still further, and reaches the whole mechanism of man. Even the latent and mysterious bond of connection, which holds in unity the spirit, soul, and body of man, must at last give way, and the whole of his material system experience a total demolition. From this once lively, admirable, and fearful structure, but now inanimate and deformed mass of clay, the renewed soul ascends—rises above the stars, and flies with ineffable velocity through all the splendor of the planetary system, till it enters the vast assembly of departed spirits, and stands in the immediate presence of the Lord of Hosts.

34.—THE SINNER'S DEATH BED.

C. P. GROSVENOR.

I AM not disposed to amuse you, my auditors, with that in which you have no personal concern. Those of you, who, till this hour, have been living without God, may, at some not distant day, experience the truth of what I have already stated, in relation to the awakened and dismayed sinner. And here permit me to add—but if I declare not what is attested by facts, I ask not your credence—that the most obdurate, the most daring opposer of God and his Christ, while in health and worldly prosperity, and among his associates in sin, usually becomes the most timid, weak, insipid coward in sickness, and on the approach of death. While in health, the preaching of the cross was to him foolishness, superstition, or priestcraft, and the worship of God but dull, unmeaning formality, or the obsequiousness of slavery. *His* lofty spirit moved in a higher and more extensive sphere. The Lord's day was to him a day of conviviality ; and if he visited the house of God, it was an act of great condescension, and done only to fill up the hour with recreation, which would otherwise have been filled up with *ennui*. When in the house of God, if the services be not very amusing, he contrives to occupy his mind with something else, for the worship of God and plain truth are not suited to his high-minded soul. He judges of the worship of God's house as of theatrical performances, and retires disgusted or amused, as he is pleased or displeased with the external character of the performances. How many have sat for this painting, it is unimportant to inquire ; but, that originals exist, I think, will not be disputed. These outlines are sketched to be filled up at leisure by each person concerned, before that mirror of the heart, *conscience* enlightened by truth.

We may now look at such men on the bed of sickness, premonitory of death. How is their countenance changed? They can now invite the plain, truth-telling minister, for they dare no longer be deceived. "O tell me, tell me *truth*! O give me the interpretation! What is this religion you preach? I cannot understand it. What must I do to be saved?" This man has at length come to see that ignorance of God not safety; that unblief is the fatal sin; that neglect of God is not the means of preparation to meet him at his tribunal. But he is unprepared. It is the last night, although he may be unapprised that death is so near. He hears the interpretation of repentance and faith; a new heart; the blood of atonement; the work of the Holy Spirit; the law and its penalty; eternal punishment; the Gospel and its gracious rewards; eternal life;—but the dew of death is on his brow; reason has left her throne. The next rising sun lights only the death-colored *clay* of the unbelieving man. But whither? O whither went the spirit?

Belshazzar, too proud to acknowledge the sovereignty of the true God, calls in the magicians, to obtain from them an explanation of the phenomenon of the writing; but, like Nebuchadnezzar, was utterly disappointed. Imagine the state of his mind at this juncture. His doom was written before his eyes, but he could not read it, neither could all of his wise men understand a syllable of it;—and yet an internal monitor spoke and urged a loud, and still louder, "Beware, beware the strength of the unseen arm, whose fingers wrote those unknown words." All is darkness and mystery; but the very fact and its attendant circumstances are enough to imply some hidden yet important truth. The words are written; "fingers of a man's hand" were seen to write on the palace wall. The fingers are gone, but the words are indelibly written.

So, my hearers, is the truth of God, relating to every individual character in this assembly, written in this *Bible ;* written, too, by fingers sent from God—indelibly written. "Heaven and earth shall pass away, but the word of God shall not pass away." To the sinner there is no hope from this quarter. The Bible is written, and the doom of the impenitent, as well as the hope of the believer, is here. Do you gaze at this mysterious book, and does your conscience sometimes tell you that you have a personal concern in what is written here? and do you say, It is mysterious writing, I cannot understand it? You must all be satisfied that the Bible is written by fingers sent from God, and that you have a personal interest in its contents; and that, since it is from God, its import must be momentous. So far, reason and conscience will conduct every reflecting mind. But that, to some, the Bible is a sealed book, will not, I think, be disputed. Do you all understand it, my friends? "If our gospel be hid, it is hid to them that are lost: in whom the god of this world hath blinded the minds of them who believe not." If you do not know its meaning, who shall be its interpreter? You will not call in the magicians and soothsayers, and other wise men of the world, who are not furnished with an interpretation from heaven. From the history of the kings of Babylon, you know how unavailing that would be. "The interpretation" must come from God. The wisdom of men cannot unlock the mysteries of heaven.

35.—DOCTRINE OF THE RESURRECTION.

R. T. DILLARD.

THE resurrection of the body is a doctrine clearly taught and positively asserted by the writers of both the Old and New Testaments; and its vast importance in the scheme of redemption is most evidently set forth by its prominence among the doctrines of the cross. Denied by the ancients, and ridiculed by the philosophers of the Apostles' time, it nevertheless triumphed over the theories of the Pretorium, the vagaries of the portico, and the dogmas of the synagogue. A band of men, gathered from the humblest walks of human life, made it a Corinthian pillar in the Christian temple, demonstrated its just proportions, and entwined around it the evergreens of an endless day.

While infidelity is making such inroads on the human mind, and marshalling its forces against the church of the living God, is it not important that the main argument in favor of a doctrine so essential to human happiness, be clearly stated and understood by the disciples of Jesus Christ? In all ages of the church, there have been those who wrested the scriptures and made them bend to their own crude and false opinions. Thus the Sadducees rejected the Old Testament, except the Pentateuch, because they conceived that these five books of Moses did not teach an existence after death. But Christ reproved their ignorance when, in their hearing, he quoted the words of the Almighty, "I am the God of Abraham, of Isaac, and of Jacob," thus showing that these ancient patriarchs were still alive; for he is not the God of the dead, but of the living.

A species of modern infidelity is gradually insinuating itself into the public mind, forcing holy scripture to bow to the supremacy of human reason. It vaunts of the grand discoveries of the age—the unparalleled march of the human intellect; and covering itself with the halo of its own glory, attempts to throw in the shade prophet and apostle, and to become dictator to the Eternal mind.

How soon the doctrine for which we this day plead may be assaulted openly, as it has been covertly, none can tell. But let the friends of the Bible, having on the whole armor of God, meet the enemy in the gate, and defeat him with arguments drawn not only from the word of God, but even from nature itself.

36.—THE GENERAL RESURRECTION.

A. WILLIAMS.

We are referred to the analogy of nature, as an argument for a future state. And the argument is indeed a strong one; but its strength may be used with the greater advantage in favor of the resurrection of the dead. The vegetable kingdom, which appears to remain dead through the freezing months of winter, revives again with returning spring, and nature is made lovely with the blooming flower, and the soft green of the forest and meadow. The animal which we beheld a few days ago, a helpless worm feeding on the dust, having lain for a season in the tomb which itself constructed, is now the gay butterfly sporting in the sun, and deriving its pleasure from the sweets of every flower. The farmer buries his grain of corn in the earth, and after a season beholds it shoot up in a more beautiful form, and gathers from it an abundant crop. The body which to-night lies helpless, and unconscious of every thing around, having upon it the very image of death, rises again in the morning to the duties of life, refreshed and strengthened by its long repose. All the laws and operations of nature are perfectly analogous to the doctrine for which we are now contending; and they evidently point to a time when that inanimate body which is now laid in the grave, shall awake from the long slumber of death, and bursting through the confines of its narrow home, and shaking from it the dust of the tomb, shall arise a glorious body, in obedience to the voice of the Son of God.

Do we then confine ourselves to the light of nature?

Reason proves as satisfactorily the resurrection of the dead, as the immortality of the soul. But seek we the will of God in Revelation? Here the proof of our doctrine is more abundant still. The language of our Saviour is, "Marvel not at this; for the hour is coming in the which all that are in their graves shall hear his voice, and come forth."—John v. 28. And corresponding to this is another passage, "Many that sleep in the dust shall awake; some to everlasting life, some to everlasting shame and contempt.—Dan. xii. 2. Paul said that he had a hope toward God, that there shall be a resurrection of the dead, both of the just and unjust.—Acts xxiv. 15. And he asks why it should be thought a thing incredible that God should raise the dead.—Acts xxvi. 8. He tells us that "the trumpet shall sound, and the dead shall be raised incorruptible, and we shall be changed. For this corruption must put on incorruption, and this mortal must put on immortality."

37.—RESURRECTION OF THE CHRISTIAN.

J. M. PENDLETON.

The term sleep, necessarily implies an awaking. When we see an individual asleep, we expect him to awake. As deceased Christians, therefore, are said to be asleep, the language implies that they will awake. The application of this phraseology to the dead teaches, by implication, the doctrine of the resurrection. The sacred writers would not have used the phrases "to die" and to "fall asleep" as synonymous in signification, had they not anticipated a resurrection day. But looking forward through the intervening years of time to such a day, they represented the dying saint as falling asleep, intending to convey the idea of an eventual interruption of his slumbers. To the Christian it is not a thing incredible that God should raise the dead. Indeed this is one of the most consoling articles in his creed. This doctrine, which bears the stamp of Divinity, alleviates his sorrows under the loss of friends. He sees his fellow-Christians fall around him like the withered leaves of autumn; but he says, "though they fall they shall rise again." This consideration was to the author of our text a transporting one, and he presented it to his Thessalonian brethren as well adapted to cheer them amid their painful bereavements. He wished them not to be unacquainted with the prospects of their pious friends, who had died in the faith of the gospel. "I would not have you ignorant," says he, "concerning them who are asleep, that ye sorrow not even as others who have no hope." It is natural for us to lament and weep when our relatives and acquaintances are taken from us by the hand of death. Hence unenlightened heathen, who are to a considerable extent destitute of those refined social sensibilities and attachments which characterize civilized nations, express their unavailing grief in a variety of ways when their friends die. The apostle, in the text, alludes to those who in his day mourned immoderately when they saw those they loved lying cold in death. He represents them as having no hope. Greece was at that time only partially illuminated with gospel light. The most of her cities, and indeed most of the provinces of the Roman empire, were enveloped in the darkness of heathenism. The wisest philosophers of those days contemplated the grave as the eternal habitation of the dead. They entertained some unsatisfactory conceptions of the soul's immortality, but of the resurrection of the body they had no idea, and consequently no hope. They never imagined that even their favorite Jupiter could bring into requisition power competent to dispel the darkness of the tomb, and raise the dust of mortality from its cold embraces.

The poets of Greece and Rome complain in verse touchingly eloquent and mournful that the sun and moon could set and rise again, but as for man, said they, when the lamp of life is extinguished in death, it cannot, it will not be rekindled. They saw that the stars, though concealed during the hours of day from human vision, paid their nocturnal visits to earth, and they wept that man, when once he disappeared from the walks of mortal life, returned not to those walks again. Leaving the sun, moon, and stars in all the grandeur of silent majesty, they fixed their contemplations on the various tribes of flowers, which, though destroyed by winter, develope their beauty when spring returns. Then exclaimed one of their number, in language which has been thus translated:—

> "Alas, the tender herbs and flowery tribes!
> Though crushed by winter's unrelenting hand,
> Revive and bloom when vernal zephyrs call;
> But we, the brave, the mighty, and the wise,
> Bloom, flourish, fade, and fall:
> And then succeeds a long, long, dark, oblivious night—
> A night which no propitious power dispels,
> Nor changing seasons nor revolving years."

Thus gloomy and dark did the grave appear to the ancient heathen. They knew not that a revelation from Heaven had poured its holy light on the territories of death. They knew not that life and immortality had been disclosed through the gospel. They were ignorant of the enrapturing fact that Christianity had made provision for dispossessing every tomb of its occupant, and for opening a highway from the realms of corruption. Hence, when their friends died, they sorrowed, having no hope; no hope of seeing them again, no hope of a resurrection. But Paul exhorts the bereaved Thessalonians not to sorrow as those without hope. The passage may be paraphrased thus:—"You, Thessalonian brethren, believe that the dead will rise, that your separation from your deceased friends will be only temporary, that you will soon be reunited to them by ties which can never be sundered; therefore, extravagant and unsuppressed lamentation, such as your heathen neighbors indulge when they follow *their friends* to the grave, would be highly inappropriate, and absolutely unjustifiable. You may mourn and weep in moderation. Affection for the dead dictates and authorizes this; your hope of a resurrection forbids more than this." Moderate sorrow—sorrow kept within appropriate limits—when those we love die, is justifiable, and even commendable. The example of devout men who carried Stephen to his burial, and made great lamentation over him, justifies it. The tears which Jesus shed when the beloved Lazarus lay in the grave justify it; for we are told that "Jesus wept." But, thanks be to God, we have hope. The dead will rise. Christians will assume immortality. Glorious hope! the kind alleviator of our griefs, the diminisher of our sorrows, the solace of our perturbed spirits!

38.—THE FINAL JUDGMENT.

SAMUEL STILLMAN.

The scriptures assure us, in language calculated to awaken our attention, that Jesus Christ will descend from heaven with a shout, the voice of the archangel, and the trump of God: that the heavens being on fire shall be dissolved, and the elements shall melt with fervent heat; the earth and all that is therein shall be burnt up. Then they who have done good shall come forth to the resurrection of life; and they who have done evil to the resurrection of damnation. O how solemn will be this concluding scene! The last trump will awake the sleeping millions; the sea give up the dead that are in it; death and hell give up the dead that are in them; and all crowd around that throne on which the Judge is seated, from whose sentence there will be no appeal! Amazement all!

The different characters of men are marked; all carry their destination in their countenances. The righteous fly to meet their glorious Judge, their Saviour and their friend, and bid him welcome ten thousand times. Their hearts beat high with joy and praise. Each eye beams peace, and all the innumerable multitude of redeemed sinners sing, "Lo, this is our God, we have waited for him; we will rejoice and be glad in his salvation." These he shall place on his right hand.

But the ungodly approach with horror and despair; for their conscience at this fatal moment, more than ever, anticipates their doom. Hence they say to the mountains and rocks, Fall on us, and hide us from the face of Him that sitteth upon the throne, and from the wrath of the Lamb; for the great day of his wrath is come, and who shall be able to stand? These the Judge shall place on his left hand. The critical and decisive moment has arrived—all nations are before him: they are separated the one from the other, as the shepherd divideth the sheep from the goats. To them on his right hand he will say, "Come, ye blessed of my Father, inherit the kingdom prepared for you from the foundation of the world. For I was an hungered, and ye gave me meat: I was thirsty, and ye gave me drink: I was a stranger, and ye took me in: naked, and ye clothed me: I was sick, and ye visited me: I was in prison, and ye came unto me." Then shall he say also unto them on his left hand, "Depart from me, ye cursed, into everlasting fire, prepared for the devil and his angels: for I was an hungered, and ye gave me no meat: I was thirsty, and ye gave me no drink: I was a stranger, and ye took me not in: naked, and ye clothed me not: sick, and in prison, and ye visited me not." "And these shall go away into everlasting punishment; but the righteous into life eternal. Thus the solemn scene is closed. "They that were ready went with him to the marriage, and *the door was shut.*"

39.—NECESSITY OF THE SINNER'S DESTRUCTION.

W. H. JORDAN.

THERE is a necessity for the destruction of those who reject the gospel, resulting from the moral character of such persons. There is no fitness in them for the enjoyment of heaven. *They are fit only for destruction.* What employment will they find in heaven adapted to their taste? The angels of God are engaged in studying the eternal and unsearchable mysteries of redemption. *They* are singing the praises of Jesus. The pillars of heaven are trembling, and its vault resounding, with the mighty song of the great congregation, "Unto Him that loved us, and washed us from our sins in his own blood, and hath made us kings and priests unto God and his Father, to him be glory and dominion for ever and ever." Patriarchs, prophets, apostles, and martyrs, are gathering around the throne, in joyful acclamation, to put the crown upon the head of Him who has been despised, rejected, and crucified by the gospel-slighter. *He* cannot lift his song, *he* cannot bend his knee, amid that glorious multitude. *He* does not love the Saviour. The guilt of his blood is upon his soul. *Where* will he find society? If he go to Abraham, *he* has no heart for any other song than the praises of that Redeemer, even whose distant day gladdened his heart. If he turn to Moses, *his* face is shining with a brighter glory than on that eventful day when he returned from communion with God in the holy mount, as he *now* looks upon the face of Him of whom he once "did write." The strains of seraphic animation and profound adoration, breaking from the harp of Paul, in the praises of Him who came into the world to save the chief of sinners' rebuke the hope of any companionship with him. He has already pronounced, with what he saw of the Redeemer's glory, even amid the impurities of this mortal state—"If any man love not our Lord Jesus Christ, let him be accursed." Where will he seek repose for his guilty heart and his unblessed feet? Every place is fragrant with the love of Christ, resplendent with the beauties of holiness, and perfumed with the breath of the Lord. The unsullied flowers of paradise strike an awe upon his guilty soul, and remind him that this is no place for the enemy of God and the despiser of the Lamb. *Where* will he find companionship? Not until he sinks into that dark abyss, where are to be found, "weeping, and wailing and gnashing their teeth," the enemies of God and the despisers of Christ. Ah! little does the sinner know what he is doing, when he is rejecting a crucified Saviour. If there be such a thing as responsibility—if men be not above it as gods, or below it as brutes—the rejection of the gospel must involve a fearful responsibility.

But, after all, objects, perhaps, the unwilling sinner—seeking rather to justify himself in his sins than to be saved from them—it is severe, it is hard, it is *unjust*, to condemn a creature to eternal misery for the sins of this short life. Hard and severe I will acknowledge it to be. Such it will be found—to a degree of which, at present, we can form no adequate conception—by all who shall unhappily fall under so disastrous a doom. But that it is not *unjust*, I think, all that has been said is calculated to show. Let it, furthermore, be asked, is the condemned criminal a proper judge, either of the nature of his crime, or the degree of its criminality? Sin, let it be remembered, consists, not so much in action as in principle. It needs not years for a man to prove whether he be a thief, a liar, a traitor, or a murderer. Let principle display itself in one single characteristic act, and his character is confessed, his doom pronounced. He is just then what, without an entire revolution in the moral elements of his character, he will *for ever* be. By one single act—indeed, by one unholy thought—as well as by years of protracted profligacy, may a creature expose himself to eternal damnation.

This view agrees, too, with all the analogy with which we are conversant. By *one* false leap, may a man precipitate himself into a bottomless abyss. It requires not many—nor does the nature of the case admit of it—but by *one* false step, he falls from the greatest height to the lowest depth. Such has been the unhappy fall of man. Such the depth from which the Son of God came to rescue him.

As in the natural, so also in the moral aspect of the subject, we are supplied with analogy illustrative of the *decisive* character of a single act. Who would acknowledge any force in the complaints of the condemned criminal, with his hands bloody with the murder of his brother, and ready, when freed from their manacles, to repeat his crime, arguing the injustice of depriving him—for one single act—of his life, which can never be restored to him? What shall redeem lost character, or brighten tarnished reputation?—reputation lost by one *foul*, one damning act? How many, by *one* false, *one* fatal step, stamp upon their character indelible disgrace? It will be in vain to complain that it is hard. Such is the natural course of things. There is no remedy for it.

But, says the sinner, I cannot *understand* how men should deserve to be damned for the sins they commit in this world. What then? is it, therefore, not true? Is the proposition to be admitted, that nothing is true—in physics, in morals, in religion—which men do not understand? Is our understanding the rule by which to ascertain the dimensions, the line by which to sound the depths of all truth. Can we see no necessity, with our very limited faculties—blinded and depraved as they are by sin—for an infallible revelation, that we may both know and do our duty? Alas! how great is the folly—how great, too, the danger, rejecting the sure word of God—of betaking ourselves to the bewildering and delusive glare of human reason! God has mercifully given us a light, to which, if we take heed, we shall do well. If we neglect it, we shall stumble in darkness.

It only remains, my friends, that I press upon your minds the solemn subject of this discourse—*the certain and just destruction of those who refuse submission to the gospel of Christ.* If you reject "the glad tidings of great joy," the publication of peace and love from God to man—upon the authority of that Saviour who came to redeem you from hell, and who will judge us all in the last great day, you will be damned. Oh! fearful doom of the impenitent sinner! Think of it *now*, before it is too late! Think of your souls! Think of the love and blood of Christ! Think of the terrors of an avenging God! What will become of the sinner, if he shall despise the grace of the gospel? Soon will he be ripe for the sickle of avenging justice! *Soon* the Spirit of God will be gone, and all holy influence have forsaken him! The measure of his iniquity now full—the willing and fast-bound captive of the devil—he stands for a time to attract upon his guilty head the lightning of the Divine wrath! Miserable man! He has rejected Christ! Such is his awful doom! May God, of his infinite mercy, save us from such a guilt, and from such a doom. Amen.

40.—MEMORY INCREASING THE MISERIES OF HELL.

L. A. ALDERSON.

MEMORY, in the world to come, will tend to aggravate the torment of the wicked.—"Son, *remember*, that thou in thy life-time receivedst thy good things."

The wicked will remember the sins they committed. Transgressors frequently violate the laws of God without feeling the pain of guilt. For most offences, however, their consciences condemn them, and for a while they are miserable. But time too often heals these painful wounds. It will not be so with the ungodly in the world of misery. There, their sins will ever appear before their eyes, written in living characters. They will have a painful view of all their wicked deeds—their fraud, their treachery, their intrigues, and their unholy indulgences. There, too, will be written their profane oaths and their blasphemous expressions. Their envy, their malice, their wicked desires, and all their unhallowed thoughts, will also be recorded, never to be blotted out. O, what a fearful catalogue! If, my ungodly friend, all the secret workings of your wicked heart, even for one day, were recorded, would it not present a dark page from which you would turn away with horror? But think, O think, if you continue an enemy to God, in that prison of wo, a similar record for every day of your life will be presented before you, and, in the bitter anguish of your soul, you will have to gaze upon it to all eternity.

They will remember the character of the Being against whom they have sinned. If such laws were now in force as existed under our colonial government, and we, by those laws, were thrust into prison for preaching the gospel, we should be convinced that the laws were oppressive, and that the sentence pronounced upon us was unjust. Hence, we should be enabled to bear our sufferings with some degree of patience and resignation. The transgressor of the laws of God, who is condemned to writhe in torment, will have no such consoling reflections as these. He will remember that God was represented to him as a God of justice, and now he will be convinced of the fact. He will consider that the sentence pronounced upon him is just, and that he is receiving the due reward of his deeds. Again, his sins were committed, not against a Being who took pleasure in inflicting punishment, but against Him whose name is Love, and whose dealings towards him were dealings of mercy; who watched over him with more than a parent's tenderness; who ministered to him all his earthly comforts; who often delivered him from impending danger; and who even provided a Saviour that he might live. Will not the reflection of having sinned against such a Being increase the pangs of his torment?

Sinners in hell will remember that they were often urged to turn and live. The Bible, ah! the Bible, which is here so much forgotten, will there be remembered. Hear the lamentations of a condemned sinner, destined to spend an eternity in misery: "That book, which I so much slighted, was my best friend. It pointed out my sins; it told me of a Saviour; and it bade me seek that I might find, and knock that it might be opened unto me. There, too, was the faithful minister, who portrayed to me the glory of heaven, and the awfulness of perdition; who pointed me to Jesus, 'the way, the truth, and the life;' and who, in his melting appeals, called upon me to escape for my life. There, too, were my parents, now with angels before the throne of God. O, that I could blot out from my recollection their affectionate counsel, and their oft-repeated prayers that ascended up in my behalf! As if God, too, would hedge up my way, he warned me by his providences, and drew me by his Spirit.

Then I was 'almost persuaded;' but my deceitful heart whispered, 'there was time enough;' and now my doom is eternally fixed."

Nor can he forget, that the way to heaven was once plain, and the requirements reasonable, but now that way is closed for ever. If the sinner had been destined to a life of wickedness, and his condition unalterably fixed, without any provision whatever for his escape, his pain would be more tolerable. Christ, however, was presented to him as an all-sufficient Saviour, and all that was required of him, was to renounce his sins and accept of him as his Saviour. But he wilfully rejected the Son of God, choosing the pleasures of sin for a season, and, in the end, eternal destruction, rather than the mild sceptre of the Prince of peace, and that endless joy which is unspeakable and full of glory. Having refused the plan of salvation, which was offered to him on such reasonable terms, his destiny is now for ever fixed. Between him and heaven, there is a great gulf, across which none can pass. No invitations to turn and live, will again salute his ear.

> "In that lone land of deep despair,
> No gospel's heavenly light shall rise;
> No God regard *his* bitter prayer,
> No Saviour call *him* to the skies."

The gates of heaven now barred against him for ever, hope, that sustains us amid the trials of life, and that cheers us in our final separation from friends and kindred—hope, that sheds a light around the dark walls of the prisoner's cell, and that even casts a smile upon the pale countenance of death, takes her everlasting departure, and leaves him in the blackness of darkness to brood over his melancholy condition.

Sinners, in that awful world will remember, that having rejected the gospel plan of salvation, and persisted in sin, they were their own destroyers. That man who, by a life of dissipation, has brought upon himself some mortal disease, as he lies upon his bed contemplating his wretched condition, and the speedy termination of his present existence, must be miserable beyond description. There is no one that he can blame for his misfortune. His miserable end is the result of his own imprudence. If he had contracted a lingering disease from an exposure to an unfriendly climate while disseminating the truths of the gospel, or even while engaged in patriotic services to his country, he could endure it with fortitude. Can you imagine the anguish of the miserable sinner in perdition, when he reflects that there are none upon whom he can charge the guilt of his destruction ?—that they were his own sins that closed the door of mercy—that dug the pit of hell—that reared its walls, and that kindled its flames ?

Moreover, they will remember, that they not only ruined themselves, but aided in the destruction of others. It has been justly observed, by Andrew Fuller, "that we are so linked together in society, that we almost necessarily communicate our dispositions one to another. We draw, and are drawn, both in good and evil. If we go to heaven, we are commonly instrumental in drawing some others along with us ; and it is the same if we go to hell." How painful must be the reflections of that accomplished sinner, who, in his career of wickedness, beguiled the innocent and unsuspecting youth, and led him into the vortex of destruction ! There, too, the Universalist, the infidel, and the atheist, will remember that they did not only close their own eyes to the truth, but blinded the eyes of others. Behold the ungodly parent withering under the hot indignation of God, and surrounded by his offspring, who reprove him for his wicked example, and for having withheld from them the light of truth. Hear them exclaim :—"You were an indulgent parent—you loved us, and were concerned for our happiness : why did you not tell us of Jesus ? You taught us the value of riches: why did you not tell us of a treasure in heaven? You relieved us when in distress, and guarded us against danger: why did you not warn us of the pit of destruction?"

Finally, the wicked in torment will remember with pain their enjoyments in this life. "Son, remember that thou in thy life-time receivedst thy good things." The Siberian exile, as he wanders alone amidst the dreariness of almost perpetual snow, thinks of the sunny plains of his own native country—he thinks of the friends whose society he once enjoyed—above all, he thinks of his beloved children, and her to whom he pledged his vows, and whose smiles so often cheered him in the hour of despondency. Can you conceive the anguish that rends his soul? Much less can you conceive the pain endured by the exile from heaven, when he reflects upon the comforts he was once permitted to enjoy. Once, when afflicted and distressed, he had friends to share his sorrows; but now, not a single tear of sympathy is to be found in all the regions of despair. Once, he could quench his thirst with the cool and refreshing draught just from the fountain; but now, even a drop of water is denied him to cool his tongue. When he returned home, wearied with the toils of the day, he was welcomed around the domestic hearth, and was permitted to rest in quietness upon his pillow; but now, his troubled soul finds no rest, day nor night.

THE BAPTIST PULPIT.

IV.

THE CHARACTER, HAPPINESS, AND PROSPECTS OF THE CHRISTIAN.

1.—SALVATION NOT BY THE LAW.

T. D. HERNDON.

SALVATION for sinners, by the deeds of the law, is utterly impossible. To be ignorant on this point is fatal. To be zealous to establish our own righteousness by a law already transgressed, is but a fair index to our ignorance of the purport and design of law. A law which will forgive the transgressor, cannot be viewed as an infallible rule of action; and if its letter and spirit be not relied on, as affecting every individual case, under every possible exigency, then those designed to be governed cannot possibly make any just calculation as to the effect of disobedience in any given case.

The moral law of God has been, and ever must be relied on, as the only perfect and unchanging standard of moral actions. An abandonment of the penal enactment of the law, in one case, without a suitable satisfaction, would open the door for its abandonment in another; and the principle which would admit one sinner into favor with the lawgiver, would, other things being equal, admit any and every other. Surely if the expression of *regret* on the part of a rebel, would render satisfaction to the law he had violated, the expression of regret in a suitable degree and manner on the part of any and every other rebel, might be received on the same principle.

But, as we have intimated, the law has gone forth, and cannot be reversed either in its precept or its penalty. To love God with all our heart, soul, mind, and strength, was always right. To fail in this, in any case, was palpably wrong, and had a tendency to deny *his right* to supremacy, and *our duty* to submission. The indulgence of a *thought* contrary to the harmonious government of God, is the violation of a law whose penalty is death. How inadequate are we, therefore, to make an atonement for the *least* crime, since the law requires unabated love and devotion to God, from our earliest breath to the last gasp of life. How especially is atonement by us impossible, since the penalty of the law is eternal death for *any* and for *every* transgression. Will you not then, my dear hearers, cordially unite with the apostle in his declaration, that "by the deeds of the law no flesh shall be justified?" And will you not, each and every one, become a candid inquirer, this day, "How shall man be just with God?"

2.—NATURE OF REGENERATION.

J. OGILVIE.

The new birth is the production of something in the soul which did not exist there before. This is fairly implied in the language "born again;" as also in the terms employed in other portions of the scripture, where the same subject is spoken of, such as "you hath he quickened, who were dead in trespasses and sins"—"According to his mercy he has saved us, through the washing of regeneration, and the renewal of the Holy Ghost"—"Created in Christ Jesus unto good works;" with many other texts of like character. It is altogether spiritual in its nature. Nothing of matter pertains to it. This appears from the words of the Saviour, "That which is born of the flesh, is flesh; but that which is born of the Spirit, is spirit." It was the spiritual or immaterial part of man, which God created originally in his own likeness; and it is this same part of man which must be operated on in the great work, which prepares him for the everlasting enjoyment of his Maker, and meetens him for the kingdom of glory. It is not the production of any new faculty in the soul, or intellectual part of man. All these faculties exist in him, as well before as after regeneration. They are the same in number, in kind, and in vigor. The unconverted sinner thinks, investigates, compares, combines, and deduces—loves, hates, hopes, fears, loathes, desires, desponds, and rejoices, as well as the converted man, showing that these and all other faculties exist in him by the Almighty fiat, which made him man, and not by that act of power which made him "a new creature." The possession of these faculties constitutes the basis of his accountability. Let him be destitute of such of these as entitle him to the appellation of a rational being, and we hold him no longer accountable to us for his conduct, and we do not consider that his Maker holds him accountable for his actions unless in such cases as those in which the rational faculties have been destroyed by vicious habits, and in which mental privation his Maker has had no agency. In this case his inability to comply is no reason why God should not demand. The Saviour teaches the doctrine of man's accountability and ability bearing just proportion, in the language, "From him to whom much is given, much is required; and from him to whom little is given, little is required." Then where nothing is given, nothing is required. There all accountability must cease.

Our previous remarks having cleared the way for

the introduction of what the new birth is, we state that it is the production of new dispositions and new affections. As it regards these, old things are passed away, and all things are become new." The work of regeneration has its seat in the heart. It is there the seed is sown—it is there the plant germinates. It is this which the word of God, as a hammer, breaks to pieces. It is this which the Spirit of God cleanses, and makes right, and turns to himself. By the work of regeneration, the native enmity of the heart is slain, and reconciliation produced. Hatred to God and man is expelled, and love takes its place. Unholiness is dislodged from the affections, and holiness is planted therein. In short, the whole current of the affections is changed; the passions are controlled; the subject "is made free from sin, and has his fruit unto holiness; and the end is everlasting life."

3.—THE INFLUENCE OF FAITH.

D. H. GILLETTE.

Sustained by faith, the ancient people of God eagerly looked for the rising of the gospel-sun, which by his purpose, was to beam on the darkened east—to throw light over the distant west—to encircle the world with its rays, and shine with more than noon-tide effulgence on all the nations of the earth. Though the religious ceremonies of that ancient economy were but dim shadows of living realities, nevertheless, they became vast sublimities by revealing what is profound and terrible in invisible power, and, by the ardor of the suppliants, seemed about equally blended with beauty and loveliness. So firmly was their confidence fixed in the unseen reality, while they enjoyed the deep luxuriant shadow, that no earthly power could move them. The patriarch could leave his home and

ENGRAVED BY [illegible]

kindred, sever all ties of consanguinity, and journey to a distant, unexplored land, led only by the promptings of an unseen hand—and with equal readiness would he have bathed the dreadful knife in the vitals of his son, had it pleased the mind of the Lord. Time would fail us to observe the many striking examples in which the power of faith is seen equalled by no human strength. But let us take one more, as seen in the rites of the temple-worship, than which, nothing can be conceived more imposing and sublime; that the suppliants, while won by the attractions of the scene, might be awed into contrition, humility, and adoration. There were the priests ministering before the Lord in their splendid livery—victims burning upon the altar, from which a hallowed vapor floated off upon the breezes, skirting the brow of the neighboring mountains with beautiful festoons. The sound of the golden bells fastened to the high priest's robes, as he entered the holy of holies—mingled with the half-uttered and half-suppressed ejaculations of ten thousand hearts, pleading with God that their offerings might be accepted and their sins forgiven. The vast concourse filling the temple, and stretching off in the distance like a forest of moving trees. These are the brief outlines of a scene that was yearly repeated before the enraptured view of God's ancient people. But their faith only made their worship acceptable—enabled them to wait patiently for the coming Messiah, and disclosed to their minds a much sublimer scene beyond. They listened to the stirring melody of the prophetic muse, and it seemed as the voice of angels. The abrupt and broken, but mighty accents of the rapt seer, were equally cheering; for they proclaimed liberty to the captives, the opening of prisons to them that are bound, the ultimate destruction of sin, and the universal triumph of peace. All this they firmly believed; and though they little expected to see it, yet they knew that such would be the condition of the world, and that all ntions would enjoy peace like a river of righteousness—like the waves of the sea.

4.—ILLUSTRATIONS OF FAITH.

I. S. TINSLEY.

It has pleased God, for purposes of his own wisdom and glory, to accomplish, through the agency of his servants, under the influence of faith in his name, in different dispensations of the church, a train of stupendous achievements, at which the puny theories and ambitions of this world may gaze with surprise and wonder. I speak not of conquered realms—of gory fields—of slaughtered nations—and vanquished heroes. These are not the peculiar triumphs of which it boasts. On the bloodless folds of the white waving banner of faith are inscribed, in letters of living beauty, this motto—"ON EARTH PEACE, GOOD WILL TOWARD MEN."

Every revolution which, through the instrumentality of faith, has been accomplished, whether among nations or in the condition of individuals, has been for the glory of God, and the eternal happiness of mankind. Dark and mysterious have been the trials through which many of the subjects of faith have been led, but bright and glorious are the honors which they have won.

We are referred to Abraham, who, in obedience to the Divine will, did not hestitate to sunder all the early attachments of life, and to surrender all the sacred associations and endearments connected with the home of his youth and the land of his nativity, and became a houseless wanderer in a strange land, "not knowing whither he went," because God had said to him, "Get thee from thy country, and from thy kindred, and from thy father's house, unto a land that I will show thee." And yet these trials of his faith, and these personal privations, were trifling, in comparison with the glory which followed. He became the special friend of God, and the father of the faithful.

We are referred to the history of Moses as an illustration of the triumphs of faith on earth. Moses was the appointed instrument of Heaven, through whose agency God designed to deliver his people from suffering and oppression. Under the influence of that faith which sheds the light of an eternal world over the prospects of the righteous, and brings the rewards of the faithful into view, Moses, when he came to years of discretion, did not hesitate to relinquish the respective pleasures and glories of an Egyptian crown for a life of suffering and affliction among the people of God. But the particular work for which he had been designated as the champion of Israel, required a still greater degree of confidence; and it was not without unfeigned diffidence and fear, that he was made willing to encounter the stern decrees and the unrelenting despotism of Egypt's haughty monarch. "Who am I, that I should go unto Pharaoh, and that I should bring forth the children of Israel out of Egypt?" he exclaimed. But the Lord said unto him, "I will be with thee;" and Moses went. He contended with Pharaoh long and earnestly, concerning the people of God; but such was the hardness and stupidity of Pharaoh's heart, that he would not let them go, until the Lord, as by sovereign command, bid them depart from his dominions. They had journeyed as far as the Red Sea, a place which in the dispensations of Providence seems to have been reserved for the greatest trial of Moses' faith. The sea, with its extended waste of waves, was rolling before them, and Pharaoh with his armed legions was pressing close in the rear. At this moment the armies of Israel stand in awful suspense, as they look upon the fearfulness of the one, and think of the threatening dangers of the other. Already I hear the voice of complaint uttered from a thousand lips at once, "Because there were no graves in Egypt, hast thou taken us away to die in the wilderness?" But the man of God is unshaken in his confidence, and firm to his purpose. He lifts the mystic wand to heaven, the ensign of his power, and as he stretches it over the deep, the murmuring floods roll back upon themselves in wild confusion, and stand like a wall on either hand; the armies of Israel pass through in safety, but Pharaoh and his hosts perish in the waters. On the distant shore I see them standing, with faces gleaming with joy, and hearts of overflowing gratitude, while with songs of praise and triumph they

"Sound the loud timbrel o'er Egypt's dark sea."

Little did the proud and cruel king of Egypt think, while he was reveling in wickedness, and while his bloody mandates were tearing the screaming infants from the heaving bosoms of their defenceless Hebrew mothers, that in a slender ark of bulrushes, the work of woman's delicate fingers, and entwined with the tenderest solicitude of a woman's heart, there lay a little helpless babe upon the banks of the Nile, that should one day rival his power, and lead the armies of Israel forth to their promised inheritance, while his horsemen and chariots were sunk in the bosom of the deep.

We are referred to Gideon and Barak, to Samson and Jephthah, to David, Samuel, and the prophets, "who through faith subdued kingdoms, wrought righteousness, obtained promises, stopped the mouths of lions, quenched the violence of fire, escaped the edge of the sword." And what are the boasted advantages of the worldly mind, in view of such achievements as these? How do the bays of intellectual chieftainship, or the laurels of military conquests, sink into insignificance, when brought into such comparison!

Nor is the present world the only theatre on which the wonders of faith shall be displayed. As over the broken waves, and through the stormy elements of time it guides our bark, we are steering for eternal worlds. And often as the mist and darkness around us are cleared away, we are enabled to look far beyond the dim circle which bounds the dark valley of the shadow of death ; as the hills of our heavenly Canaan rise before us in an ever-blooming prospect and undecaying beauty. Nor will the work of faith be accomplished, until we shall have been conducted to the haven of eternal repose ; and shall, with the father of the faithful, and all the heirs of promise, have obtained an ever-enduring inheritance on the cloudless continent of immortality.

O that each of us present may have that faith which will qualify us to live, and prepare us to die ! With it, and the attendant graces of the Divine Spirit, we shall be blessed on earth, and happy in heaven. Without it, we must remain strangers to God in this world, and be lost for ever in the world to come.

5.—TRUST IN GOD.

J. DU PRE.

Trust in God is inconsistent with a departure from any known or obvious duty. He has nowhere promised protection, deliverance, support in trouble, or any blessing whatever, to those who wilfully depart from the path of duty ; or use, when involved in difficulty of any kind, unlawful means to extricate themselves. Had not Daniel been in the path of duty, when he was arrested and thrown into the den of lions, he could not have expected the Divine interposition in his behalf. It would have been presumption to have done so. There is on record no promise to meet our exigencies, if we go beyond the limit of duty, or pursue a course contrary to the plainly revealed will of God.

Trust in God is equally inconsistent with a careless and inconsiderate course. The language of the Saviour, (Matt. vi. 25—30,) has been greatly perverted to this purpose. The meaning attached by some to these words, is that they authorize the utmost indifference to our future temporal condition and welfare. But this is not the meaning of the Divine teacher. The expression, "take no thought," means literally, "be not over anxious"—indulge no such painful anxiety about your future safety, as will paralyze your efforts, and induce a distrust of the promised protection and care of God. But the counsel of Christ in this passage is capable of a *practical* test. Let an individual interpret it literally, and actually "take no thought" for his life, and see what his condition will be; see whether he will have food to eat, and raiment to put on; see whether he will be miraculously delivered from dangers and difficulties, which common prudence would have enabled him to avoid. We should be exceedingly careful how we misapply and torture scripture. We are encouraged to trust in God, yet it is only in the use of the means of his own appointment. In other words, having made every necessary effort to procure the means of support, or to shield ourselves from evils to which we may be exposed, *then*, and not till then, are we warranted to cast our care upon the Lord; and then too, and not before, will he care for us. (1 Pet. v. 7.)

Trust in God is inconsistent with all apprehension of future evil. Both these states of mind cannot exist at the same time, in the same bosom—the one is destructive of the other. If we *truly* confide in an Almighty arm for protection and safety, we shall feel as secure in his keeping, as if we were effectually removed from all evil. We have a remarkable illustration of this remark in the case of the apostle Paul. Though assured that "bonds and afflictions" awaited him, wherever he went as the minister of Christ, yet, what were his emotions, in this gloomy prospect? Was he deterred from the course of duty? Was his attachment for Christ and his cause lessened? By no means. But hear his own composed and cheerful language:—"None of these things move me; neither count I my life dear unto me, so that I might finish my course with joy." (Acts xx. 24.) This is the language of strong confidence in God; and under its sustaining influence, he felt persuaded of his ultimate, perfect security. Such a state of mind, argues the present attainment of an elevated standard of piety; but one, however, which all Christians may reach.

6.—EVANGELICAL REPENTANCE.

J. G. OGILVIE.

Repentance, in general, is sorrow for any thing past. In theology, it signifies that sorrow for sin which produces newness of life. It is a doctrine abundantly taught in the scriptures; and is always exhibited as of the utmost importance. It is an absolutely necessary prerequisite in every sinner, in order to his obtaining pardon and acceptance with God. Notwithstanding the atonement of Jesus, and the satisfaction he made by his obedience to the law and justice of the great Supreme; by the constitution of the gospel, none can be saved but in the way of repentance. The gospel offers no salvation for impenitent sinners, any more than the law. Hence repentance is a gospel doctrine; and to this, the believers and friends of the Christian revelation ought to attend.

There are different kinds of repentance, and among

them are legal and evangelical repentance. The former is only a partial and external reformation of life; but the latter is a total change of heart. This is the repentance which the apostle Peter recommended to the Jews on the day of Pentecost. Its author is the Spirit of God—it causes a true, sincere, and sorrowful sense of sin—it makes us feel towards sin as we ought to feel, and to contemplate it as the most odious thing in the universe—it makes us acknowledge ourselves as altogether to blame, acquitting the throne of God, justifying his justice, and indicating his law as perfect, holy and good. In this view of sin, under the sight of the glory of God, we abhor ourselves, the baseness of our hearts, the irregularities of our lives, and repent in bitterness of soul. We are now disposed from the heart to renounce our iniquities, and to discard all hopes of acceptance with Jehovah by any possible performances of our own. We now, with Job, abhor ourselves; with the psalmist, acknowledge that we have sinned against Heaven, and our only cry is, "For the sake of Jesus, O Lord, have mercy upon us!"

7.—CHRIST AND SINNERS.

B. HARVEY.

[Delivered in New York, 1846, the preacher being in his 111th year. He died in 1847.]

WHO of this congregation has reason to rejoice and give honor to Christ? It is all his servants; all who love him. No matter whether rich or poor, young or old, black or white. God delights in having all his servants rejoice and be glad, for this gives honor to him. Whenever a congregation, or class, or people is called upon to give honor to him, what is it? "The marriage of the Lamb is come, and his wife hath made herself ready." And what does this suppose? Why, that there was a time when she was not ready. What is necessary? Why, to put off the clothes of sin and shame, with all the beggarly elements that belong to a state of nature; and it shall be granted to her to be clothed in fine linen, clean and white; for the fine linen is the righteousness of the saints.

A deceitful, wicked man is not fit to serve either God, man, or the devil. I'll tell you why. He is not fit to serve God, because he is unholy; he is not fit to serve man, because he is deceitful; and he is not fit to serve the devil, because he is not content with his wages. I once saw a rogue of a soldier, for some crime that he had done, tied up and flogged with forty lashes, well laid on; and while he was taking his wages, he made all sorts of noises, but he never once said that he liked it. No, no, my friends, the sinner is not satisfied with the wages which the devil gives, and he never will be—for "the wages of sin is death!"

Behold the Lamb of God! And where shall we behold him? Shall we behold him, when he pushed space apart, and dropped into this little system? when the morning stars sang together, and all the sons of God shouted for joy? Shall we behold him when he takes from his bride her robes of shame and sin? "As many as received him, to them gave he power to become the sons of God, even to them that believe on his name." "The word was made flesh!" O, there was life in that nature! God and man! Jesus was as much man, as if he had not been God. O, there is one Mediator, the man, Christ Jesus! That human nature he laid down as the purchase of his bride. So any one who has human nature has a right to plead the promises and love of God. O the love of God and of Christ! The Son came as a volunteer. What does he say? "In the volume of the book, it is written of me, I delight to do thy will, O God."

Who am I inviting? Why, the poor sinner—the

poor prodigal. O return, return to your father's house! And when the poor prodigal returned, what did he do? O, he fell upon his neck and kissed him. And what then? O, he tells the servants to bring the best robe and put it on him. Return then, prodigal, you shall have the best robe there is in the kingdom of heaven. O, the good will of God! O, I cannot get words to express it just as I could wish, but it shall be a durable covenant. Jesus shall say at last, "Well done, good and faithful servants." O what an applause that will be! O, if my soul can only hear that applause! All that have done good shall come forth to the resurrection of life; but O! they that have done evil—shall I speak the word?—"to the resurrection of damnation."

8.—SINNERS DIRECTED TO THE ATONEMENT.

B. I. LANE.

THREATENING may awaken fear and force submission, but it cannot beget love—it cannot reconcile the heart to that from which it has been estranged. It is not in its nature to do so. We repeat, that we are not speaking against alarming the sinner, and pointing him to the coming wrath. It is important that we do so. The doctrine of man's total depravity, the sovereignty of Divine grace, the resurrection from the dead, and the final judgment, together with other great truths, must be often and carefully insisted upon. But we must go further. And the point on which we are insisting, does not, it appears to us, hold that prominent place in the ministry of most preachers, that it does in the Bible. It may be coldly stated, and a few passages of scripture in relation to it indifferently repeated; but it is not earnestly and affectingly dwelt upon in its place. When the sinner stands trembling upon the brink of wo, when he is appalled in view of the fearful miseries that await the wicked, it is not the time to point him to Sinai's lightning, or to a burning hell; but the love and compassion of God in the atonement should be exhibited, as the arm of God stretched over the pit of ruin to catch the helpless penitent. This is the top-stone of the spiritual temple, "brought forth with shouting, crying grace! grace unto it!" This truth clearly stated, understood and embraced, will complete the work of truth, and reconcile the sinner to God. He may be awakened, he may be convicted, but he will not, he cannot be converted—the affections of his heart cannot be won to the love of God by any other means than the melting tenderness of the gospel. "God was in Christ, reconciling the world unto himself, not imputing their trespasses unto them;" this is the word of reconciliation committed to us. In this word, illustrated and enforced in ten thousand ways, we have the grand instrument of genuine *revivals*. With this word, you may successfully assail the citadel of the "strong men armed."

When, my brethren, every thing else fails to change the affections of sinners, and bring them to a cordial love and obedience of the gospel; when the ordnance of reason fails to make any impression; when the weapons of terror fall upon sinners' hearts, as pebbles upon the shield of Achilles; when the battery of a coming wrath fails to bring one sinner upon his face, then, in "burning thought and breathing words," charge upon them from the humiliation of Bethlehem, the groans of Gethsemane and the deeper agonies of Calvary. Let

> "It come o'er their ears like the sweet breath of heaven,
> That breathes upon the flowers of Paradise,
> Gathering and giving odor,"

"that God was in Christ, reconciling the world unto himself, not imputing their trespasses unto them," and you shall presently see the mighty effect of it in the inquiry, "Men and brethren, what shall we do?"

A company of missionaries had labored many years without witnessing any saving results. They consulted together. In reviewing their course, they found that, though they had dwelt much and strongly upon the doctrine of man's depravity, Divine sovereignty and a coming judgment, they had failed in the story of the love of God in Christ Jesus. They went anew to their work, and as soon as they dipped their arrows in atoning blood, the enemy began to yield. The very first Sabbath, they witnessed some fruit of their labor.

9.—THE POWER OF GOD IN SALVATION.

T. WINTER.

In the formation and support of the Christian character, there is a necessary exertion of the power of God. This doctrine is set forth by the apostle Paul, in his epistle to the Ephesians, with peculiar energy. "And what is the exceeding greatness of his power to us-ward who believe, according to the working of his mighty power, which he wrought in Christ when he raised him from the dead, and set him at his own right hand in the heavenly places."—Ephes. i. 19, 20. The apostle's mind seems to labor with the greatness of the idea, and he adds expression to expression to give full utterance to his conceptions on the subject. This great work accomplished for fallen man, requires the power of God—the greatness, yea, the exceeding greatness of his power—yea, it is according to the working of that mighty power which he wrought in Christ, when he raised him from the dead, and set him at his own right hand in the heavenly places. This power is employed to effect what is elsewhere called quickening those who were dead in trespasses and sins, translating them out of the kingdom of darkness, into the kingdom of his dear Son. That this is the reference of the apostle, I think there can be no just ground to doubt; and to apply this passage to the resurrection of the dead, or to interpret it with an exclusive view to this solemn event, is to evince an utter ignorance of its true meaning, or to be guilty of a wilful perversion of its true design. The apostle speaks not of a power to be exercised at a future day, but of his mighty power to us-ward who believe. It is an energy in actual operation. Let us then consider the point, that in beginning and carrying forward the work of human salvation or of the soul's sanctification, the mighty power of God is indispensable.

In bringing over the primitive Christians to discipleship to Christ, there was doubtless a peculiar manifestation of this divine power. These were not only immerged in that stagnant sea of depravity which has swallowed up the whole of our race, but they were also under the active influence of religious prejudices, with which the religion of Christ was at variance. The Jew was subject to the influence of every worldly consideration to retain his fellowship with the rites and worship of his nation. From his youth he was taught with the strictest truth to observe and venerate these as divinely appointed, and as forming a glorious and broad line of separation between himself and a world immersed in the degradation of abominable idolatries. In a faithful adherence to the religion of his nation, he has before him the common chance of rising to honor, to wealth, and influence. But in departing from this religion, he saw before him nothing but reproach and poverty. The attachment of the Gentiles to their respective modes of idolatry, was cherished by motives equally strong. Now it was to such persons that the gospel had to be preached, to such its doctrines were to be proposed, and its invitations and promises addressed. And of such was the Church of God to be composed, if at all established. But what external inducements has Christianity to hold forth to overcome the natural and educational prejudices of those to whom it was proclaimed? What worldly advantages could it promise, to counterbalance those which must be relinquished by all that would forsake their former systems, and live godly in Christ Jesus? It had none to promise, and it promised none. It rather announced at the very threshold, that every candidate for Christian discipleship must be willing to forsake all that he had; father, mother, and house, and friends; yea, and to lay down his life also, if he would share in the redemption of Christ Jesus. And it taught that he who was not thus willing, could not be admitted into the household of faith.

Now, reasoning on the known and common principles of human nature, as to the result of the gospel ministry, would any man have concluded that the least degree of success could attend that ministry? Would he not rather have confidently concluded, that a religion so novel in its appearance, so repulsive to the reigning prejudices and usages of the whole world, so austere in its requisitions and prohibitions, and withal so utterly destitute of human patronage and human glory—I say, would he not rather have concluded that every hand would be raised to its total extermination from the earth, or that it would of itself sink into contempt and perpetual oblivion? But we all know, that if such was the reasoning, and such were the conclusions of any, the event showed how much they were mistaken. "As it is written, I will destroy the wisdom of the wise, and will bring to nothing the understanding of the prudent; because the foolishness of God is wiser than men, and the weakness of God is stronger than men." Instead of the cause of Christianity being exterminated from the earth, or sinking into neglect and oblivion, it rather extended its empire far and wide, and speedily numbered among its devoted adherents thousands and tens of thousands of many different nations and tribes. And why? we cannot consistently account for the extensive prevalence of gospel truth, and for the vast accessions made to the Church of God, without admitting the accompanying and almighty energy of God in producing these results. Those, whether Jews or Gentiles, who renounced their former religious prejudices, and their sins, and became the humble, self-denying, devoted, and happy followers of the Lamb, could ascribe their glorious change of mind, and heart, and life, only to the exceeding greatness of God's power, according to the working of his mighty power, which he wrought in Christ when he raised him from the dead, and set him at his own right hand in the heavenly places. To this the apostles uniformly and distinctly referred all the success which attended their labors. Among these distinguished men, and others associated with them in the sacred ministry, there were doubtless many of good natural parts, and others of commanding scientific attainments. They could apply the force of clear reasoning, and the charms of moving eloquence to defend and promote the holy cause of Christianity. But they claimed for none of these means power sufficient to carry saving conviction to the minds of their hearers, or to win over their hearts to the side of God and truth. But hear their own language:—"Who then is Paul, and who is Apollos, but ministers by whom ye believed, even as the Lord gave to every man? I have planted, Apollos watered, but God gave the increase. So then, neither is he that planteth any thing, neither he that watereth, but God that giveth the increase."—1 Cor. iii. 5—7. They claimed the honor of being "laborers together with God;" but they said, "Ye are God's husbandry, ye are God's building." They knew it was their duty to preach Christ, warning every man, and teaching every man in all wisdom; and they knew and insisted that it was the imperious duty of every man thus taught and thus warned, to flee from the wrath to come, and to lay hold on the hope set forth in the gospel, yet they equally knew that no power short of that which raised up Christ from the dead, could give their labors saving efficacy on the hearts of any. Without this they knew the Jew would still cleave to the covenant of works, and reject the Messiah, the only hope of Israel, and the gentile would still bow down to his dumb idols, and blaspheme the only living and true God.

10.—CHRISTIANS THE PROPERTY OF CHRIST.

R. B. C. HOWELL.

WHAT do we mean when we say that what we hold is not our own but another's? We mean that we have no *right* to use it as our own. We must be governed in our use of it, simply by the direction of the owner. If we appropriate it to our own use, we are dishonest. We are guilty of robbery. Or, if he allows us to use it, or any part of it, for ourselves, we must be governed in all respects by his will. If a man commit his property into my hands for a term of time, I must surely do with it just what he prescribes.

And, again, we must give up what is not our own, whenever the owner calls for it. If we refuse, we are dishonest. We have no right to retain the whole, or any part of it. It is all the owner's, and he is the only rightful proprietor. If you lend a man a hundred dollars, and when you call upon him for it, he declines to surrender your property, or puts you off with a shilling, you would never trust him again. Now this is precisely what is meant, when, in our text, it is said, "Ye are not your own." Whatever we possess is not our own, but Christ's. A certain nobleman delivered to his servants talents, and said, "Occupy till I come."

You are called by the name of Christ. You profess to be his. You say you are not your own. But have you ever reflected on the meaning of this confession? You are a professional man; your learning, and talent, and influence are Christ's. What right have you to use them for the purpose of fostering your own ambition, or in any respect ministering to yourself? If you thus use them, you rob Christ.

You are a minister of the Gospel. You have been in a peculiar manner set apart to the service of the Saviour. You have, by your own will, laid yourself upon his altar. Have you then a right to live as other men live? Have you a right to shrink from hardship, and reproach, and inconvenience, and toil, and declare that you will serve Christ, but it must be in a comfortable settlement? Have you a right to pursue what studies you please, to read what books you please, engage in what enterprises you please, for the sake of reputation, or honor, or power; or, in a word, to make your calling as an ambassador for Christ, an instrument for attaining to temporal ease, or honor, or emolument? Christ had infinitely greater facilities than you for doing this; did *he* use them thus? Paul was an abler and more learned man than you; *he* rejoiced in being made the offscouring of all things for Christ.

You are a merchant or mechanic. You are by industry and skill acquiring property and standing. But you say that these are not your own. By what right, then, do you use them as you do? In your arrangements at home and abroad, in your expenditures for pleasure or amusement, for yourselves or your children, in your principles of accumulation, I do not see that you even profess to differ from honest worldly men around you, who never profess that they are not their own.

11.—THE CONTEMPLATION OF MORAL BEAUTY.

C. TRAIN.

It is much to be regretted, that so many possess a just and discriminating taste in regard to the beauties of Nature and Art, are progressing in intellectual improvement, and all the embellishments of social life; and that so few, comparatively, manifest a relish for moral and religious attainments. Natural and artificial beauties are enjoyed no less by the religious than by the irreligious. Humble and fervent piety has a double advantage. How much more numerous, soothing, and joyful, are the emotions of the Christian, who perceives himself surrounded by the beauties of both worlds. He looks upon the works of Nature as the works of God, bearing the impress of infinite power, wisdom, and goodness. He is charmed with the beauties of moral excellence, wherever he beholds them. His faith, being the substance of things hoped for, and the evidence of things not seen, looks beyond the confines of this short life, and yields him the delightful prospect of a state of perfection. Under the purifying influence of faith in the Redeemer, he finds his capacity for discrimination and enjoyment gradually improving, and his heart as gradually transformed into the image of Him who is altogether lovely. Christ, and him crucified, is the sole foundation of his hope, and the joy of his heart. At the recollection of Calvary, he dissolves into contrition, warms with affection, and like the good Samaritan, he becomes obedient, from evangelical principles, to the calls of suffering humanity. Having obtained mercy, he becomes himself merciful. Having received the benefits resulting from the patience and sufferings of Christ, he feels happy in extending, to the utmost of his power, the same benefits to others. Every duty is easy, and every burden light. Although he counts not himself to have apprehended that for which he was apprehended of the Lord Jesus, yet, forgetting the things that are behind, and reaching forth unto those things that are before, he presses toward the mark for the prize of the high calling of God. Let any one who has neglected this great salvation, receive with meekness the ingrafted word, and walk by faith, as he is bound to do, and a great moral change becomes perceivable. The works of grace, like those of nature, not unfrequently present sudden and magnificent displays of mercy, subjugating the whole man, and bringing the soul into cheerful obedience to the law of Christ. However gradual, or however sudden, the change apparently may be, it is of grace, and effected by the Spirit of truth. Without this surrender to religious principle, in vain do we look for great moral worth, such as will be approved by Him who trieth the heart. Without this ardent love to Christ and the souls of men, neither Peter nor Paul would have poured forth such strains of Christian eloquence, as disarmed the enemies of Christianity, and changed the tigers to lambs. Without this love to Him who redeemed us by his blood, the poor widow would not have cast all her living into the treasury of the Lord, Aquila and his wife Priscilla would not have laid down their necks for the gospel's sake. But they cheerfully suffered the loss of all things, that they might win Christ, and be found in him, not having their own righteousness which is of the law, but that which is through the faith of Christ, the righteousness which is of God by faith. The beauty of the Lord was upon them, and they were blest in their deed. It was the very spirit of Him who was rich, but became poor, that we through his poverty might be rich. It was this holy, this dauntless spirit, which feared no danger, quailed at no toil, no sacrifice, that first spread the gospel among the nations. Howard, and Raikes, and multitudes whose name never met the public eye, have drunk deep at the same perennial fountain. On their hearts was written the law of kindness, and their lives adorned the doctrine of God, the Saviour.

12.—ESTABLISHMENT IN THE DOCTRINES OF GRACE.

ELIJAH HUTCHINSON.

By doctrines of grace, we mean the great foundation doctrines of Christianity—those which are essential to its very existence, such as Divine Sovereignty, Total Depravity of Man, the Necessity of Regeneration, the Work of the Holy Spirit, the Atonement, and others of kindred character. To be established in the doctrines of grace, supposes a deep and thorough knowledge of them, a strong and growing affection for them, and a firmness and fixedness of belief, which cannot be shaken. Allow us to suggest a few considerations to enforce this subject.

1. Establishment in the doctrines of grace, is indispensable to constant progress in the divine life. Divine knowledge is the natural and proper food for the renewed soul, and permanent religious prosperity cannot be secured without it; growth in grace necessarily implies growth in knowledge also. The young convert lives for a time upon emotion—his feelings are strongly excited, and his zeal is far greater than his knowledge. While the external excitement continues, and his heart is warm, he runs well; but let the excitement cease—let the ardor of his feelings abate, and if his mind has not been furnished with religious knowledge, there will be a sad reaction, if not

an entire apostacy. May we not in this way account for many painful departures from Christ, which often immediately follow revivals? On the contrary, let the young Christian be early led, step by step, into the great field of doctrinal knowledge, let his religious belief be firmly fixed and his mind be fortified with truth, and there will be constant growth in grace, and in knowledge, and a great security against backsliding. Look at the members of our churches. Who, among them, have for years been most distinguished for their deep and solid piety? Who are making most rapid advances in the Divine life? Uniformly those who are worthily called doctrinal Christians, those who take great delight in studying the good old doctrines of grace, those who are established in the faith.

2. Those who are established in Christian doctrine rightly estimate the ordinary means of grace; they recognize them as of Divine appointment. Hence they prize the Bible above all other books, and make it their sole manual of doctrine and duty; they will not allow the best religious volume, much less the book of questionable character, to crowd aside the word of God. They value the duties of the closet so highly that they will not permit the holiest public devotions to be substituted for them. They delight in the courts of the Lord's house. They love the worship of God in their own sanctuary, and the simple preaching of the cross from their own pastor. They expect the divine blessing, not upon the preacher, but upon the preaching. They have confidence, therefore, in the regular ministrations of the sanctuary, accompanied by the prayers and activities of the church, as the divinely appointed means to secure the salvation of men.

3. A universal establishment in the faith would rid the church of periodical professors. By periodical professors, we mean those who are controlled entirely

by impulse, and never act unless they have a certain undefinable feeling. This class are an intolerable burden to any church. They always have far more feeling than wisdom, and their zeal is ever in advance of their knowledge. To-day they drive forward with the zeal of Jehu; to-morrow they are twice dead. At one time their engagedness runs into the wildest enthusiasm, at another time their deadness leads to the most painful backsliding. When their feelings are aroused, they are almost ready to offer themselves as missionaries, but wait a few days, and they would see missionaries called home for want of support before they would give a farthing. Appoint a meeting of days, and they will attend day and night for many weeks; at the same time they will neglect the weekly prayer-meetings for a whole year. How easy to see that such, if their hearts were ever changed, were never established in the doctrines of grace. Indeed they were never established in any thing. They have no fixed belief—no settled principles of action. Let the whole church, therefore, be established in the faith, and how soon this spasmodic action would be done away; how soon should we see a readiness for every work of faith, and labor of love. Is the gospel to be sustained at home? There will be no covetous excuses, no hanging back, but a cordial coming up to the work, and a willingness to have an equality, that no one be burdened. Does the Macedonian cry come from the destitute in this or other lands? Like faithful stewards, they cheerfully make the needed offering. Is direct effort demanded for the salvation of souls? Those who have long loved the doctrines of the gospel are ready for the work. Hence this establishment in doctrinal knowledge lays the foundation of all the effective labors of the church.

4. Establishment in the doctrines is needful to prepare the church for days of trial. The history of the Christian church, in all ages, shows that her days of

trial have been many. Scarcely does she rejoice over the fruits of the revival, ere she mourns over the declension, when few come to her solemn feasts. Then comes the discipline, separating from her fellowship some who have been among her most active and promising members. Again, the storms of fanaticism and heresy sweep, like a tornado, through the land, trying the faith of all, and deceiving, if possible, the very elect. Who are the disciples who stand firmly amid such days of trial? Who compose that precious few, whose seats are seldom vacated in the solemn meetings of Zion, and who, like Aaron and Hur, are holding up their pastor's hands? Who adhere to the church in her darkest days of trial, and never shrink from the most painful cases of discipline? Who stand like the unbending oak, amid the fiercest tempests of heresy? Not those who are as light and as changeable as the wind, but those who are "rooted and built up in Christ"—"stablished in the faith;" those who know in whom they have believed, and are immovably fixed in the great doctrines of grace. They are the pillars in the church, standing firmly when all others forsake her. They are the defenders of the faith, and the bearers of the oracles of God. And they will compose "the general assembly and church of the first-born which are written in heaven."

13.—THE FLOCK OF CHRIST.

T. F. CURTIS.

WHO now are Christ's "little flock?" Surely this endearing appellation, or the assurance that accompanies it, is not to be confined to the little handful of disciples which first flocked round the Son of God. Equally sure is it, that if all nominally Christian nations are to be included, it is now no longer a "little flock." We are not left to conjecture on this subject, since in many other places Jesus makes use of the same figure of a flock of sheep, in describing his disciples. Thus in the tenth chapter of John, he says, "I am the good shepherd, and know my sheep, and am known of mine; and other sheep I have, which are not of this fold, them also I must bring, and they shall hear my voice; and there shall be one fold and one shepherd." Since this latter clause plainly alludes to the call of the Gentiles into the fold of Christ, it shows that whether Gentiles or Jews, *we may* be included in this little flock. It does not, however, intimate that all the Jews or all the Gentiles who are called by his name are thus included. Indeed, even to many of those who attended on his own personal ministry he said:—"Ye are not of my sheep; my sheep hear my voice, and I know them, and they follow me. They "hear his voice" then, and they "follow him," as the worldly do not. Providence, the word of God, the means of grace, speak to them with authority, in the name of Jesus—a voice which they receive as his.

When lost in the thick, dark woods, or wandering in a strange city, how cheering to hear the voice of a well-known friend! You recognize his voice at once from a thousand other sounds—amidst—above them all you hear him—him alone. Though you see him not, you know him, and his voice directs your course. And thus is it with the disciples of Jesus, bewildered and astray amid the entanglements of this world. There is still always a spiritual perception, that enables them to recognize the Saviour. They know his voice, and a stranger will they not follow. By means which the worldly man can neither see nor appreciate, he manifests himself unto them—comforts and directs them.

"They find access at every hour,
To God within the veil;
Thence they derive a quickening power,
And joys that never fail."

They are thus spiritually intimate with him as a friend, and they also "follow" him as a *teacher*, by listening to his doctrines. In their *imaginations* they follow him personally, delighting in spirit to retrace all his course while on earth:—to Gethsemane, where he prays and is betrayed—to Herod's palace, the scene of mockery and buffeting—to Calvary and the cross—from the cross to the tomb—that wondrous sepulchre, *for a while*, of his dear body—*for ever* of our sins. They trace his glorious pathway to the skies, the right hand of the Father. They follow him *in heart*, embracing him as their surety, their advocate, their intercessor, their friend. They follow him *in their lives*, by imitating his virtues, and in preference to dear friends, strongest interests, father or mother, yea "through much tribulation;" so as to justify the description of them given by the angel, "These are they that follow the Lamb whithersoever he goeth."

Not only do they thus recognize and follow him; he, in like manner, recognizes them. "I *know* my sheep," he says; so that no one of them is overlooked—though extending over every "kingdom, and nation, and tongue"—over hundreds of generations—not one, however poor, despised, friendless, but he marks and knows individually. "He calleth his own sheep by name." There is a holy *intimacy* between the true sheep and Christ indicated, when it is said, "I know my sheep, and am known of mine;" and it is this high and spiritual intimacy which characterizes the flock of Christ.

We have then, here, but to inquire further, how this can now be truly described as a *little* flock. Doubtless it was so when it consisted but of the twelve and the seventy; and it is but a *little* flock still. We do not here take in, you perceive, the *number of nominal Christians* through the world, and compare it with that of pagans and Mahometans; though that would leave us but a sad minority. Christ's flock is small.

compared with the number of nominal Christians. Even among Protestants, how small a portion pretend to any thing like an experimental knowledge of Christ, and how many that do, will not at last be found among his true followers! Truly, then, does the text still denominate the band of Christ's disciples, "a little flock."

14.—GRATITUDE TO CHRIST.

C. TYREE.

JESUS CHRIST has, upon his followers, a thousand claims—claims not merely derived from creation and providence, but from redeeming love. It is neither a rhetorical nor a figurative, but an actual historical truth, that each Christian has been redeemed by Christ's blood. Our familiarity with this great subject may have diminished its freshness and fire; it is nevertheless true, that the claims of Christ are just as binding, as if the price had just been paid, and the wonderful scenes of Calvary had just transpired.

Let us, then, approach near the cross. Look at that streaming blood, hear those death groans, and compute, if you can, the sacrifices Jesus Christ once made for you. It was for you he exchanged the bliss of heaven for the agonies of Gethsemane—the adoration of admiring angels for the spitting of Roman soldiers—the diadem of glory for a crown of thorns—a robe of light for Pilate's faded garment—the palace of the universe for the judgment hall—his body guard of holy and mighty angels for the cruel mockings of puny mortals—the honors of the great white throne for the shameful death of the cross. He stooped from the height of his throne, to snatch you from eternal flames to the transports of immortal life; from everlasting contempt, to be kings and priests unto God; to raise you from the turpitude of sin to the purity of the Divine image—from a dungeon to the radiance of his throne—from the society of devils, to commune with angels—from the blasphemies of hell to the songs of paradise—from universal destruction to infinite riches—from contraction and degradation, to expand for ever in the regions of light. He died the death of the cross, that you might not die the second death. He suffered the penalties of the law in this world, that you might not suffer its penalties in the world to come. He toiled and wept on earth, that you might rest and sing in heaven. He was clothed with a mock-robe and crowned with thorns in this world, that in his Father's kingdom, you might be clad in the white raiment of his righteousness, and wear a crown that fadeth not away. In a word, from his bleeding cross you derive your repentance, your pardon, your regeneration, your justification, your faith, your sanctification, your hope, your joy, and your home on high. He is your help for the past, and your hope for the future.

Now, can you live unto yourself in view of all the benefits you have received from Him who gave you these blessings? Can Heaven wield a stronger motive to incite you to deeds of goodness, than this? The author of the commission to preach the gospel to every creature is the Being who loved you, and gave himself for you. He who commands you to exert yourself in giving the gospel to the world, is the Being through whom you are delivered from hell and elevated to heaven. O, where is the Christian that can resist this appeal?

15.—CONNECTION OF CHRISTIAN DUTY WITH CHRIST.

J. FIFE.

Christ is all in the duties which Christians have to perform. In the sacrifice he has offered—in the example he has set—in the institutions he has established—in the commands he has given, supported by surpassing kindness, blended with Divine authority, Christ is the theme of the Christian ministry. "We preach not ourselves, but Christ Jesus, the Lord, and ourselves your servants for Jesus' sake." "For none of us liveth to himself, and no man dieth to himself. For whether we live, we live unto the Lord, or whether we die, we die unto the Lord: whether we live, therefore, or die, we are the Lord's. For to this end, Christ both died, and rose, and revived, that he might be Lord, both of the dead and the living." Not an instance can occur in all the vicissitudes of man's history, in which duty cannot be learned or inferred from the precepts or example of Christ. "Tribute to whom tribute, custom to whom custom, honor to whom honor, fear to whom fear" is due. To render to all their dues is the practical spirit of the Gospel. These principles our Lord enforced by his example as well as by his precepts. Although as one of the royal family, and not a stranger or mere citizen, he was under no obligation to contribute money to the support, either of government or of the temple, yet when called upon by the collector at Capernaum, he instructed his apostle, Peter, to repair to the water and cast out his line. The first fish that came contained the didrachma, the precise sum requisite to pay the tax for both Peter and himself.

It is deeply interesting to see how the commonest duties of life which seem to be taught by natural affection, are sanctified and made spiritual by being performed with a view to the authority of the great lawgiver. Take, for example, the duties of husbands and wives. "Wives, submit yourselves to your own husbands as unto the Lord. For the husband is the head of the wife, even as Christ is the head of the church, and he is the savior of the body. Therefore as the church is subject unto Christ; so let the wives be to their own husbands in every thing." So on the other hand, it is enjoined, "Husbands, love your wives, even as Christ loved the church, and gave himself for it. So ought men to love their wives as their own bodies, for he that loveth his wife, loveth himself; for no man ever yet hated his own flesh, but nourisheth and cherisheth it even as the Lord the church." The duties of parents and children are urged upon the same principle. "Children, obey your parents in the Lord, for this is right—well pleasing unto the Lord." And to parents it is said, "And ye, fathers, provoke not your children to wrath, lest they be discouraged, but bring them up in the nurture and admonition of the Lord." The duties of masters and servants, "Servants, be obedient to your masters according to the flesh—not only to the good and gentle, but also to the froward—with fear and trembling, in singleness of your heart as unto Christ, doing the will of God from the heart, with good will doing service as unto the Lord, and not to men; knowing that of the Lord ye shall receive the reward of the inheritance, for ye serve the Lord Christ." The exhortation to masters is, "And ye masters, do the same things unto them—give unto your servants that which is just and equal—forbearing threatening, knowing that your Master also is in heaven, neither is there respect of persons with him."

Let us, then, dear brethren, count all things but loss, for the excellency of the knowledge of Christ Jesus our Lord. "I have," says the psalmist, "set the Lord always before me; he is at my right hand, therefore I shall not be moved." And we beseech such of you as have no interest in Christ, and live regardless of his authority, to reflect on your criminality in treating the Lord of glory with neglect. Are you esteeming the world your "all in all," instead of Christ? How uncertain in continuance is such a portion, and how unsatisfactory, if you had even all that Solomon possessed. Christ Jesus has durable riches with righteousness, and he counsels you to come to him, and buy of him fine gold, that you may be rich. To him be glory and dominion now and evermore. Amen.

16.—HUMILIATION BEFORE GOD.

J. B. MEACHUM.

WHEN Mordecai perceived all that was done, he rent his clothes, and put on sackcloth with ashes, and went into the midst of the city, and cried with a loud and a bitter cry, for he knew that they were in a dreadful condition, from the decree that had gone out from the king, that every Jew should be destroyed. This went through all the province wheresoever the king had command. Surely, this rested heavy on the minds of the Jews—they proclaimed a day of fasting and prayer. It seems that every Jew was in the same condition, that lived in the king's provinces. Well, they cried with Mordecai, and united their cries to the Lord, the God of heaven and earth; and this cry came to the queen, and she was a Jewess; and when Mordecai brought it to her understanding, that though she was queen Esther, she was a Jewess, and had to die with her people, then she increased the fasting and praying threefold; for she and her maidens fasted and prayed three days and three nights. Although it was death to enter the king's inner court, yet she arose and said, "If I perish, I perish;" and she dressed herself in royal apparel, and went into the inner court, and the king held out the sceptre to her. Thus was she made instrumental, in the hands of God, of turning the king's fury, and granting liberty to the Jews. O, can we not trust God for all things, and go to work like men that belong to the Lord our God? You see this great deliverance that the Lord our God hath wrought for the Jews. He is no respecter of persons, of those that put their trust in him. Let us take God at his word; watch and pray, that ye enter not into temptation. You will recollect that Jonah was not delivered from the whale's belly, until he had prayed and entered into covenant with God, and agreed to do that thing which the Lord had commanded him to do; then the God of the sea and land commanded the fish to take him to shore. It seems there must be an unwillingness in man to do what God intends he shall do; and if he still hardens his heart, he has great reason to fear the judgments of the Almighty. It becomes us to ask of God what he will have us to do. Let all ask, and not only ask, but let us mend our ways while we are asking of our heavenly Father. I find, while Jonah prayed, his heart became more humble; he says he was in pain. When God Almighty threatened Nineveh with an overthrow for their transgressions, did they stand idle after they got the word from the man of God? No! but they came down immediately, even in dust and ashes before God; fasted, prayed, and God's wrath was appeased. Ask, and it shall be given you.

17.—THE EXCELLENCE OF HUMILITY.

H. HOLCOMBE.

ALL must allow that humility tends, in a high degree, to maintain and promote personal peace and tranquillity.

Pride threw Naaman into a fit of wrath, when he was refused by a prophet the attention commonly paid to rank and consequence. Had the Assyrian captain known himself, it would have prevented this painful emotion of disappointed pride. Haman could enjoy nothing, though loaded with royal favors, because he was not bowed to by Mordecai, the Jew. If that haughty minion had been clothed with humility, without noticing a poor captive's uncourteousness, half his wealth and honors would have strongly excited his gratitude. The humble sleep quietly, as Henry observes, under what would break a proud man's heart. Humility divests our enemies of their chief power to injure us, and extracts from all evils their poisonous qualities. It renders us easy and happy, however exceeded and eclipsed by others, and greatly magnifies all our blessings and privileges. It may be justly observed, too, that this grace is essential to the peace of all communities. The proud, only, and always, are contentious. They proclaim their own imaginary goodness, exact incessant attention to their own affairs, and extol themselves till they provoke one another to emulation, wrath, and strife. Among the humble, each claims to be the most indebted to grace, and strives to take the lowest seat. Were all clothed with humility, wranglings, duels, and wars, would be impossible; for they cannot exist, much less flourish and abound, without pride.

To all the other excellences of humility may be added, the happy influence it exerts on every species of improvement. With humility, all the useful branches of knowledge, virtue, and piety, are as the vine in a fertile vale. Instead of gazing on their present attainments, the humble, like Moses, however they may shine, are not apprized of it; but under a painful sense of their deficiencies, press forward. To them "the words of the wise are as goads." They readily admit the light, from whatever quarter it may break, and practise what they receive. God himself condescends to guide the meek in judgment, and with the lowly is wisdom. Of course, humility is conducive to usefulness. It condescends to men of low estate; stimulates to diligence; engages in all the offices of kindness; extends its genial influence to the most solitary recesses of society; and soothes the anguish of neglected sufferers. The proud seldom appear on other than distinguished occasions; owe all their zeal to the magic eye; and are rewarded by the admiration of fools. But the humble are useful in all their circles, on all occasions. They act from principle, are well advised with respect to rules of conduct, and look for their reward in the pleasures of an approving conscience, and the resurrection of the just.

Again—nothing more enjoys the presence, and coincides with the designs of God, than humility. "The Lord is nigh to them that are of an humble heart, and saveth such as be of a contrite spirit." Though the Lord be high, yet hath he respect unto the lowly. "Thus saith the High and Lofty One, I dwell in the high and holy place; with him also who is of a contrite and humble spirit, to revive the spirit of the humble." Humility is one of the discriminating badges of the elect of God. "Put on, as the elect of God, humbleness of mind;" or as the same charge is expressed in our text, "Be clothed with humility." No duty or grace is oftener required, or more encouraged in the word of God, than that of humility. The whole scheme and every doctrine of grace is calculated to abase man; that no flesh should glory in the Divine presence. "He that humbleth himself shall be exalted," and the contrary, were observations very frequently made by our Saviour, who humbled himself to astonishment, and commands us to learn of him, as meek and lowly, that we may find rest to our souls. Humble yourselves, therefore, in the sight of God, and he shall lift you up; he shall exalt you in due time. "Let this mind be in you, which was also in Christ Jesus; who, being in the form of God, thought it not robbery to be equal with God; but made himself of no reputation, and took upon him the form of a servant, and was made in the likeness of man, and being found in fashion as a man, he humbled himself, and became obedient unto death, even the death of the cross; wherefore God also hath highly exalted him, and given him a name which is above every name; that at the name of Jesus every knee should bow, of things in heaven, and things in earth, and things under the earth; and that every tongue should confess that Jesus Christ is Lord, to the glory of God the Father." This, Christians, is the Captain of our salvation—setting us an example, that we should bear his likeness, wear his uniform, follow his steps, and fight manfully under his banners. Wherefore, instead of spending, with some, your substance on the pride of life, and your zeal, with others, in making sinners easy in sin, by saying to them in the very words of Satan, "Ye shall not surely die;" be ye followers of the apostles, as they were of Christ, in bearing both a verbal and a practical testimony against conformity to the world that lies in every species of delusion and wickedness.

18.—HUMILITY CHERISHED BY AFFLICTION.

J. CLARKE.

Divine chastening, duly sanctified, makes us truly humble. No man is fully acquainted with his true character. Much evil lies concealed; and self-love makes him partial in judging of what he perceives. Few, indeed, can analyze themselves. Hence the great study of *man* has always been neglected. Still, honest endeavors are richly rewarded. Self-knowledge, to a certain extent, is attainable by all; and the person who has neglected to obtain a reasonable portion of it, is liable to mortifying mistakes. If a young man, he will perhaps aspire to high literary distinction; while, on testing his capacity for improvement, he finds himself unable to obtain a respectable standing, even among scholars of an inferior grade. But his object may be the ministry, and his natural talents tolerably good. He begins to exhort; and he is abundantly satisfied with his performances; and he thinks it would be absurd for him to pursue the usual course of education. He is at length, however, prevailed on to enter an institution; but considering himself already prepared for the sacred office to which he aspires, he leaves about as learned as he went. Still, from the fact of his having been several years under the care of eminent men, he enters the field with high expectation. His learning is not suspected; and his clamor strikes the attention of the multitude, and fills them with wonder. But, on his becoming the subject of judicious criticism, he is pronounced an object of pity; and is compelled to relinquish his post. These, and similar evils, always attend the want of self-knowledge, or true humility. Let a man only possess this spirit, and all will be well. If his talents be inferior, he will know it; if respectable, he will think them by no means remarkable. If young, he will submit to the aged; if old, he will recollect that age and wisdom are not always associated. If his station be private he will be perfectly contented; if public, he will feel its importance, and try to be prudent and faithful. Humility is a peculiar excellence. It excites no envy—no self-congratulation: it is true dignity, happiness, and glory; rarely possessed, always admired. That past chastening, duly sanctified, produces this true humility, is evident from the very reasons which render it, for a season, "not joyous, but grievous."

19.—CONFIDENCE IN THE DIVINE RECTITUDE.

J. L. REYNOLDS.

A CONFIDENCE in the rectitude of the Divine government will reconcile the mind to the unexplained difficulties which encumber it. Many pious persons have suffered themselves to be perplexed with the mysteries of providence and the economy of grace. There has been much speculation about the existence of natural and moral evil; the consistency of Divine sovereignty with human responsibility; the eternal duration of future punishment; and many other questions which are but little helped by the most refined and attenuated speculation. These truths are plainly taught in the scriptures; and they demand our unqualified assent. Let us not vainly quarrel with the dispensations of God's providence, or the methods of his grace; but rather adore a wisdom which we cannot comprehend, and bow before a power which it would be folly to resist.

A conviction of our ignorance should induce us to pronounce with caution and modest reserve upon the measures of the Divine government. "We are of yesterday, and know nothing." Our faculties are too limited in their range to compass the extent of God's moral government, and detect the motives which determine his procedures. His way is doubtless perfect. Although "clouds and darkness are round about him, justice and judgment are the habitation of his throne." If we fail to apprehend this truth, it is solely in consequence of the feebleness of our minds, the imperfection which attaches to all finite beings.

"All nature is but art unknown to thee,
All chance direction which thou canst not see,
All discord harmony not understood,
All partial evil universal good;
In spite of pride, in erring reasons spite,
One truth is clear—whatever is, is right."

The truth which I have endeavored to establish, so fruitful of good to the believer, speaks no comfort to the sinner. It will fearfully augment the doom of the impenitent, that it is denounced injustice. Caprice may yield to circumstances, but principle, never. Passion may be calmed; malevolence may be appeased; mercy may be moved; but justice is inflexible. It should be a most alarming consideration to every impenitent sinner, that the Judge of all the earth will do right. May the truth strike every such person with salutary terror, and induce him to flee at once for refuge to that glorious gospel which, blending mercy with jnstice, affords the only means of deliverance from the wrath to come.

20.—INFLUENCE OF HOLY CHEERFULNESS.

J. CHAPLIN.

THE members of a church, if eminently spiritual, will do much to promote the success of the gospel among themselves by the holy cheerfulness which they will manifest both in the duties of religion, and in their daily deportment. It will, indeed, be admitted that some professors of religion who enjoy good health, and a great flow of animal spirits, are commonly cheerful, although they manifest little or nothing of the spirit of Christ. It will also be admitted that men of eminent piety are sometimes greatly depressed in consequence of nervous debility, or of the sore conflicts which they have with their spiritual enemies, or of the afflicted state of the church of God, or of the general prevalence of error and sin in the world around them. It is certain, however, that the tendency of true religion is to render its possessor happy, and, of course, that one principal reason why some pious men enjoy themselves so little, is that they are not habitually and eminently spiritual. They have, indeed, tasted that the Lord is gracious, and have chosen that good part which cannot be taken from them. But the spirit of the world has still great influence over them. They do not maintain a close and steady walk with God. They frequently quench and grieve his Holy Spirit. Hence they enjoy but a small share of that consolation which he affords his people. They are seldom blessed for any considerable length of time with the light of his countenance. They pass days, and weeks, and sometimes months, with little or no comfort. If we would possess an abundant measure of holy joy, we must be eminently spiritual. And from those who are eminently spiritual, this exalted privilege will not, in general, be withheld. The primitive Christians "walked in the fear of the Lord," and they were blessed with "the comfort of the Holy Ghost." They had a constant and rich supply of spiritual consolation. The same will be the effect of eminent piety at the present day. The holiest man will, ordinarily, be the most cheerful.

Now, it is easy to see that the exhibition of holy cheerfulness by the members of a Christian church must tend greatly to promote the conversion of sinners. No mistake which the latter entertain respecting the nature of religion is a greater obstacle in the way of their embracing it than the opinion that it is adapted to make them unhappy. A thirst for happiness is one of the most powerful principles of our nature. It manifests itself at the very dawn of our existence, and continues to exert a mighty influence over us as long as we live. Hence, we can hardly be prevailed on to betake ourselves to any course of life which must preclude, or greatly diminish, the enjoyment of this most desirable object. Nor will it suffice us to be assured that the course recommended will result in a happy existence beyond the grave. We cannot, willingly, abandon the prospect of happiness in the present world. The idea of passing months and years without comfort is extremely appalling to the mind of man. Of future happiness he can form but a very faint and indistinct idea. It is a far distant object, resembling one of those twinkling stars which, though perhaps as large and luminous as our sun, appears extremely small, and affords us less light than the blaze of a candle. On the contrary, the happiness of this life is near, and is seen in its full dimensions. Nothing, therefore, tends more powerfully to reconcile men to the thought of becoming religious, than an assurance that religion is adapted to promote their present happiness. Only convince them that wisdom's ways are ways of pleasantness, and all her paths peace, and you remove a principal hindrance to their entrance on a religious course. Now, you will do this most effectually by pointing them to persons who, while they maintain a holy life, are evidently happy. Nothing convinces men like facts of this kind. A preacher may discourse as ably and eloquently as he will on the pleasures of religion, and produce very little effect. His unconverted hearers will strongly suspect that there is, after all, a latent fallacy in his reasoning. But if he can point them to the members of his church, as evidences of the truth of his doctrine, he will do something to the purpose. If, while his brethren are strict in the performance of moral and religious duties, they are evidently the happiest persons in the neighborhood, they furnish the most satisfactory proof—proof which unconverted men cannot resist—that religion is no enemy to their present happiness. This holy cheerfulness will, besides, go far toward convincing them that the gospel, producing as it does such happy fruits, must be from God; and that all its promises and threats, in relation to the future world, will be fulfilled.

21.—PRAYER.

G. SEYMOUR.

PRAYER *is the desire of the soul uttered in words.* I conceive it so deduced from the many accounts given in the Bible of persons who prayed and whose prayers are recorded or spoken of.

But words only, however appropriate or well spoken, do not constitute prayer. And the complaint of God of his own Israel is, that "they honor me with their lips, but their hearts are far from me." And also the lesson given by the Saviour in his account of the Pharisee, Luke 18, 11, "The Pharisee stood and prayed thus with himself," plainly indicates that the *desires* of the soul must accompany the words; or rather the words must embody the desires of the soul—must harmonize. Another requisite in prayer is a proper conception of our relation to the Great Being whom we address; he is our Maker—our Preserver—our merciful Redeemer. Improper conceptions of his character have led to the supplications to Saints and to Angels. We should consider ourselves as his creatures; accountable to him for every emotion of the soul that arises, and for every word we utter; and that he is independent of us, but that we are entirely dependent upon him: that it is indeed "in him that we live, and move, and have our being." I am led to these remarks because of the prevalence of two extremes that characterize many prayers that are offered to the Almighty. The one is a low and mean style which abounds with images and saucy familiarities with the ever blessed God; the other is a pompous style, betraying a mind full of *self* and too little affected with the sense of divine things, and abounding with splendid borrowed expressions. Prayers should be grave and simple, consisting of the outpourings of the soul before God in the genuine language of an humble and devout temper.

22.—IMPORTANCE OF PRAYER.

E. M. LEVY.

THIS is the duty which precedes all others; with it all religion originates, and in its neglect all religion expires. You need not wonder, then, my dear friends, that I am anxious upon this point. It is every thing to you; it is your life! The Christian is only safe when he is watching unto prayer. Prayer is well calculated to strengthen the soul for its spiritual conflicts. It calms the troubled spirit—it elevates the grovelling affections—it loosens the bonds of sin by which we are enchained—it overcomes the attraction of earth, and draws the soul upward to heaven. A praying Christian is in an attitude of defence, clothed in the whole armor of God; and "praying always with all prayer," he is able "to withstand in the evil day." The powers of hell may rage against him, the great enemy may assail him with all his fiery darts, but prayer makes him invincible.

Prayer should be *daily*. We have daily wants to be supplied, daily dangers to surmount, daily enemies to encounter, daily temptations to overcome, daily blessings to acknowledge, and therefore daily calls to the throne of grace. And until the day comes in which the Christian is sure he will meet with no trial of mind or body; no temptation from the world, the flesh, or the devil; nothing that tends to stir up the corruptions of the heart; no difficulty to encounter, and no opportunity to call into exercise the gifts of grace, he must enter his closet, and pray to his Father who is in secret, and daily with his household surround the family altar.

David, notwithstanding his numerous engagements, found time to worship God three times a day. "Evening, and morning, and at noon, will I pray and cry aloud."—Ps. lv. 17. And so did Daniel, when first president of the vast kingdom of Babylon.—Dan. vi. 10.

While the Christian remains in the scene of his pilgrimage, encompassed with wants, and privileged to make his requests known unto God, so long, Elijah-like, must he often be found in the posture of fervent supplication. Yes, at every step of his progress through time, he must be a *suppliant.* And up to the very moment when he crosses the threshold of eternity, he has not escaped the necessity of soliciting blessings. In the dark valley of the shadow of death, he has still the Divine succor, and presence, and countenance, to entreat. And in the dismal recesses of that dark valley, he may be destined to experience the aids of that rod and staff of the Lord, enjoying which he shall advance to eternity, fearless of evil. Yes, brethren, to pray is matter of necessity with him; for he has many wants to be supplied. It is matter of choice with him; for some of his finest enjoyments are derived from his hours of child-like converse with his Father in heaven. To pray, is his watch-word for his hour of prosperity; for it sanctifies its joys. To pray, is his privilege in the moments of temptation; for it baffles its power. To pray, is what sustains his soul when perplexities beset it. To pray, is what quickens his transports when faith and hope are on the wing. To pray, is what infuses a charm into his seasons of retirement. To pray, is what gives an elevation to his busier hours. To pray, is the exercise which sheds sunshine on the daily path of life. To pray, is the vocation which gilds with celestial lustre the course of his declining years. To pray, is the closest symbol of heaven before the Christian attains it. And to pray, transmits its echoes to heaven when once he has arrived there. Or, to express all in the fine language of the poet,

"Prayer is the Christian's vital breath,
The Christian's native air;
His watch-word at the gates of death;—
He enters Heaven by prayer."

23.—SOCIAL PRAYER.

J. T. RAYMOND.

Our covenant God and Father has ordained prayer to be both the duty and interest of his spiritual family on earth. It is intended not only to express our wants, represent our weaknesses, discover our temptations, and seek the pardon of our unfaithfulness, but also our confidence in God, without which we cannot pray in faith. Prayer is a duty which involves the whole compass of our intercourse with God. It is in the most emphatic sense the dialect of the broken in heart, and the contrite in spirit, in behalf of Zion in general, that she may become enlarged, edified, and established in her most holy faith, looking forth as the morning, fair as the moon, clear as the sun, and terrible as an army with banners. And then prayer extends to the church in particular. It is natural to feel a peculiar attachment to that branch of God's Zion, with which we have been agreeably and profitably connected. Hence prayers are mutually offered up to God, for the increase and perpetuation of her peace, union, and prosperity—that a blessing may rest upon her officers, that they may be distinguished for wisdom and grace—that the sick and afflicted may be comforted, and prepared for death, or for further usefulness in the cause of Immanuel—that backsliders may be returned to the fold—and that the impenitent may be converted to God. It is impossible fully to enumerate the blessings accruing from mutual prayers on the part of holy brethren determined to agree.

24.—FERVOR IN PRAYER.

E. ESTIS.

WHEN our supplications are really spiritual and for specially Christian objects, they will be fervent and importunate. That we shall be fervent when we pray "according to the will of God," cannot be reasonably questioned; for then, that desire predominates, the accomplishment of which is certain. We do not desire, fervently, at the same time, every good gift—or even many dissimilar and unconnected favors—but upon one all-absorbing good, may the suppliant say, "My heart is fixed, O God, my heart is fixed." The groanings which cannot be uttered, have a meaning, which is simple and exclusive, and a fervency which is as inimitable as it is peculiar. And he, who thus orders his course before God, is truly importunate. When the object of his fervent prayer is, that the Lord may appear in Zion and revive his work in the earth, his sympathies and affections in relation to it become tender and ardent. He travails in birth for souls, and his prayer that Christ may be formed in them, as holy incense ascends up to the throne of God. And the Lord hears his own elect, who cry day and night unto him, in regard to this or any other matter of prayer which he indites; for fervent prayer avails much. Jacob was certainly fervent and importunate when he said, "I will not let thee go, except thou bless me;" and of the same qualities do our supplications now partake, when in truth we have hearts to seek the God of Jacob. "I am the Lord thy God, who brought thee out of the land of Egypt; open thy mouth wide, and I will fill it." But instead of believing the promise, and waiting with fervent desire before the mercy-seat, we neither hunger nor thirst after righteousness, nor ask aright, until he, in pursuance of his fixed intention to give, prepares our hearts by the spirit of supplication and grace to receive.

We may indeed be both fervent and importunate without the special influences of the Spirit, but our prayer in such cases will certainly be ineffectual. Spiritual fervor is very different from self-moved or sympathetic fervor. And it is very possible, nay, a case that frequently occurs, that the fervent desire, directed by the Spirit towards a particular object, instead of being fully indulged in the pursuit of the good thus wisely and graciously selected, is incautiously expended in endeavors to encircle other objects intrinsically desirable. Here is fervency, truly proceeding too from the Spirit of life; but it is presumptuously diverted from the proper channel. The selfish worshipper, however, in view of the sensibility which appears in his exercise, improperly concludes that his prayer is decidedly spiritual.

But, while we regard the duty of "praying always, with all prayer and supplication in the Spirit;" let us not be unmindful of the "watching thereunto," suggested by experience, and enjoined by the word of truth. For to pray acceptably, we must not only have the Divine influence in the origination of our desires, but be watchful against that immodest, self-confiding disposition, which, if it does not at once oppose, is too ready to blend with the motions of the Spirit the wishes of the flesh. O let us not, in this sacred employment, lean to our own understanding; nor, in the neglect of it, impoverish ourselves, slight others, or sin against God. And the pain that he must suffer who has once tasted that the Lord is gracious, but has now no cause to order before him—no particular business at the posts of his doors—can be exceeded only by that which *they* endure, whose knowledge of God commences in eternity. Let us not suppose, then, that we pray spiritually when, like Saul, we force ourselves to the offering; nor that the sacrifice will be acceptable without fervency of spirit. But genuine prayer is always efficacious. For "the Lord is nigh unto all them that call upon him, to all that call upon him in truth. He will fulfil the desire of them that fear him." In the full assurance of faith, then, may we draw nigh unto him, knowing that what he hath promised he will certainly do; for his mercy endureth for ever. "Ye have not, because ye ask not. Ye ask, and receive not, because ye ask amiss." But blessed be God, an unfailing promise encourages him who asks aright. That he may indeed do so, he must be spiritual and fervent; and then the happy consequences follow with indubitable certainty. "For every one that asketh receiveth; and he that seeketh findeth; and to him that knocketh it shall be opened."

25.—INFLUENCE OF A PIOUS WIFE.

R. FLEMING.

THAT she who is "bone of our bone," and "flesh of our flesh," should have a greater influence over us than any one else, is a point settled by the word of God. "Wherefore shall a man leave his father and his mother, and cleave unto his wife, and they shall be one flesh."—Gen. ii. 24. The tender chords which bind the affectionate son to his kind father and amiable mother, are loose when compared with those which now bind him to the wife of his virtuous choice. It is true, he does not cease to love his father and mother, but he loves his wife more. This is one of the laws of Heaven, stamped upon our existence for purposes wise and good. Thus the affections of the son and his wife, as they do not flow back to the parent, are concentrated and thrown forward upon each other and upon their mutual offspring, from age to age, through all coming time.

The husband is destined to feel the influence of his wife, either for weal or for wo. The inspired penman has written, "It is better to dwell in the wilderness, than with a contentious and angry woman." But it is again written, "The unbelieving husband is sanctified by the wife," the believing wife.—1 Cor. vii. 14. Who can estimate the amount of holy influence which the prayers and godly conversation of a Christian wife may have over her impenitent husband? God has said, "It is not good that man should be alone." The wife was not created merely to help him to make money—to help him to decorate the frail body, which is so soon to fall a prey to the greedy worms of the grave. No; more valuable purposes were to be accomplished in bestowing upon man a help-meet. She is eminently qualified, by piety, to help him to make his calling and his election sure. What pious husband, who is blest with an intelligently pious wife, has not felt the force of this declaration? How pleasant the family altar, where hearts united in fearing the Lord meet to implore his blessing upon their undying spirits! The Almighty himself has fixed, unchangeably, a price upon the virtuous, sensible, pious woman. We repeat it. "Her price is far above rubies." "The heart of her husband doth safely trust in her." "She will do him good and not evil, all the days of her life." "*She will do him good*"—it will not be an attempt followed by a failure. The man who can lightly esteem such a woman, offers insult to the God that made him. And he who makes piety a secondary consideration in the selection of a wife, makes religion a secondary object in his own soul. Such an individual seems to say, "Give me a wife with plenty of money, and money's pleasures; and religion, and religion's pleasures you may give to the winds."

It sometimes occurs, that the wife is religious and the husband an *unbeliever*. How can she exercise, to the best advantage, an influence over him? She may do this by her pious *deportment;* but there is nothing in the word of God, nor in the feelings of a *kind* husband, which forbids her praying in his presence in the family.

But the devotions of the *Christian husband* are aided by the religious wife. He may be "cast down," and feel—deeply feel—the need of spiritual help. How seasonable! how pleasant are the prayers of the wife on such occasions at the family altar! Again, he may be confined to his chamber on a bed of affliction. O, who can come around his pillow—who can offer supplication so sincere, so moving, and so availing, as the wife whose holy life has been to him a "crown of rejoicing" in his healthful days?

26.—FRAMES AND FEELINGS.

J. S. LAW.

How often are Christians heard complaining of coldness—want of joy and feeling; but how seldom are they heard lamenting their want of increased and increasing knowledge of Christ, and confidence in him as a Saviour, which is the true fountain of spiritual joy. They seem to take it for granted, they know Christ and have faith in him, and all they want is feeling, joy; forgetting that it is the peculiar property of faith, to impart consolation—"believing in Christ, we rejoice with joy unspeakable and full of glory"—and also forgetting that that very comfortable feeling after which they are seeking, is absent, because faith which works by love, and purifies the heart, and overcomes the world, is not in exercise.

Did the apostle Paul ever take it for granted, that he knew Christ and his salvation so well, that nothing remained to him but to spend his days in seeking, so far as personal religion was concerned, after comfortable frames of mind? Hear him in his own impassioned and soul-thrilling language—"I count all things but loss, for *the excellency of the knowledge* of Christ Jesus my Lord; for whom I have suffered the loss of all things, and do count them but dung, that I may win Christ, and be found in him, not having my own righteousness, which is of the law, but that which is through the faith of Christ, the righteousness which is of God by faith; that I might *know* him and the power of his resurrection, and the fellowship of his sufferings, being made conformable to his death; if by any means I might attain unto the resurrection of the dead." That knowledge of Christ which is eternal life, was the grand absorbing object of the apostle's soul. To this he bent all the energies of his great mind, and to this he consecrated all the affections of a heart in love with Jesus. They who will follow him in this, will never want for joy in the Holy Ghost; will never mourn the absence of a Saviour's love.

But why do Christians desire feeling so much more than knowledge? I know not, unless it is because they are disposed to regard a personal interest in Christ, as one of the objects of saving faith, and feeling, as one of the best evidences of such a state, and therefore good evidence of their possessing saving faith; consequently, they desire the peace and joy of justification without keeping the faith in exercise that justifies. They want peace without believing; they want life, spiritual life, without acquiring that knowledge of Jesus Christ that imparts life; they would enjoy peace with God, but will not acquaint themselves with him. Let me reprove such, by again referring them to the example of the Apostle Paul. In continuation of my last quotation from him, he says, "Not as though I had already attained or were already perfect; but I *follow* after, if that I may apprehend that for which also I am apprehended of Christ Jesus. Brethren, I count not myself to have apprehended; but this one thing I do, forgetting those things which are behind, and reaching forth unto those things that are before, I press towards the mark for the prize of the high calling of God in Christ Jesus." He tells his brethren not to understand him, from what he had said, to mean that he had reached the goal as victor—no, he did not so account himself; but this he did, unheedful of all his past attainments and services in the gospel, he pressed, in allusion to the racer, he stretched his head and hands towards the goal—thus exhibiting his earnestness and deep anxiety to reach it. Oh! what bright visions of coming glory were spread out before the apostle's mind! He stopped not to inquire after the imperfect joys of his present state, but abounding in hope through the Holy Spirit, his present joy and consolation consisted in his holy, fervent desires and self-sacrificing labors to gain the prize, eternal life. Having obtained like precious faith with him, let all our joy and comfort from religion arise from like holy diligence and perseverance to obtain the same blessed reward. Let faith gaze into the depths of the riches of God's grace—let it be firmly fixed upon the glory and dignity of Jesus Christ; and let hope lay hold upon all that faith sees, and the soul shall be filled with unspeakable joy in anticipation of an exceeding weight of glory.

27.—INFLUENCE OF BENEFICENCE.

J. B. JETER.

Beneficence is ennobling. Selfishness is mean and despicable. Who ever venerated a miser? He possesses no sympathy with the world in which he lives. He is a blank—a blot in creation. He lives without usefulness, and dying, goes down to the vile dust, "unwept, unhonored, and unsung." But goodness exalts its possessor. The patriot, who perils his life, fortune and sacred honor, to procure the liberty or

J. B. JETER.
St Louis Mo.

Edwd. H. Fletcher, Publisher.
Lith of Michelin 180 Fulton

to promote the prosperity of his country, deserves the praise of his fellow-citizens. Washington acquired a fame which must endure to latest time; but it is not so much as a warrior, or as a statesman, but as a patriot that he receives his highest honor. The philanthropist, who, spurning the narrow bounds of tribe or kingdom, nobly seeks the welfare of his race, is entitled to still higher praise. Who has not heard of the name of John Howard? It is identified with all that is lovely, and generous, and noble in humanity. He spent his life, and embarked his ample fortune, in an enterprise of benevolence. He visited and minutely inspected the prisons of his own country, and of the continent, in the beautiful language of Burke, "to remember the forgotten, to attend to the neglected, to visit the forsaken, and to compare and collate the distresses of all men in all countries." But the Christian benefactor, who, taking enlarged views of the destiny and interests of his race, and with a benevolence inspired from above, goes forth with the priceless treasures of salvation, to enrich a world impoverished and ruined by sin—and willing, if God require it, to lay down his life for the gospel's sake—earns, and sooner or later, must receive the highest honor. Such a man was Paul the apostle, who counted not his life dear to himself, so that he might finish his course with joy, and the ministry which he had received of the Lord Jesus, to testify the gospel of the grace of God.

Beneficence assimilates us to Christ. He is love incarnate. Love brought him from the skies, animated him in the self-denying labors of life, and nailed him to the cross. His history is written in a few words, "he went about doing good." Having ascended to heaven, and taken his seat at the right hand of the Father, he receives the ceaseless and grateful homage of all the hosts of heaven. But it is not so much his power, or the miracles which he performed, as his disinterested and self-sacrificing love, that renders him an object of intense interest, and supreme adoration to the celestial inhabitants. They cry, "Worthy is the Lamb that *was slain* to receive power, and riches, and wisdom, and strength, and honor, and glory, and blessing." If we imbibe the spirit and imitate the example of the Redeemer, we shall partake of his glory. In proportion as we desire, and unostentatiously seek the happiness of mankind, shall we be elevated in the scale of moral being, gain the confidence, esteem, and homage of our fellow-men, and approximate those orders of intelligences, which dwelling in the presence of God, are "sent forth to minister for them who shall be heirs of salvation."

Beneficence glorifies God. Every sincere Christian supremely desires to glorify the Lord. For this purpose he was redeemed, enlightened, renewed; for this purpose he is constantly guided, strengthened, comforted; for this purpose he lives; and for this purpose he is ready to suffer, and if need be, to die. God is peculiarly honored by acts of beneficence. Veracity, justice, and temperance are virtues, imperiously demanded by the very constitution of society. It could not exist without these virtues; at least, without the semblance of them. They are enforced by human legislation. Men are impelled to practise them by sheer selfishness. It is easy to find men of strict veracity, honorable in their business, and temperate in their habits, who neither fear God nor regard their fellow-men, except so far as they may be made subservient to their own interests. Beneficence, from necessity, must be voluntary. It may be counterfeited—it may spring, as I have shown, from wrong motives; but in general, the discerning will distinguish between the false and the true.

Contemplate the character of the Christian benefactor. He was once like other men, selfish, proud, envious and despiteful. Wrapt up in the mantle of self-interest, he felt not the chilling blast of poverty which swept over the land. Intent on the prosecution of his own business, he heard not the cries of the needy and suffering. To live in wealth, and splendor, and luxury, was his highest ambition. But a great change has passed upon him. His self-love has been displaced by love to men. Now to do good is his desire, and study, and constant aim. He serves his generation by the will of God. He pursues his business with diligence and economy, that his means of usefulness may be increased. Now you may find him, not at the gaming board, but in the sick chamber—and now you may hear his voice, not in profanity, but ministering consolation to the afflicted. To every charitable and religious purpose he contributes with a liberality and cheerfulness equalled only by his modesty. He honors the Lord with his substance, and with the first-fruits of all his increase. What wrought this wonderful change?—by what mysterious and potent influence was the native current of this man's life turned? Who melted the selfishness of his heart? Who opened in his bosom the living fountain of benevolence? Who impressed upon his character the lovliest features of Him, who is the brightness of the Father's glory? The hand of God is visible in the change. Grace, divine, free, rich and efficacious, wrought the pleasing, wonderful transformation. To God be all the praise.

28.—THE CHRISTIAN'S REVIEW OF THE PAST.

J. L. BURROWS.

As travellers toiling up the rugged mountain of life, on our journey to the skies, let us pause a little and look back. From the past we may gather lessons of wisdom for the future. If you trace your individual paths, my brethren, can you not see the miry marshes of temptation in which your feet were clogged in worldliness? Have you not passed over some rough rocks where you stumbled and almost fell? Have not the cares of the world, or the deceitfulness of riches, like the dense thicket or thorny underbrush, almost at times choked the seed of the word? Have you not heard, too, the hiss of the serpent, and the growl of the roaring lion, seeking to drive you from the right way? Can you not, in looking back along the path, say, there I buffeted a storm of trials; there I was engaged in a conflict with temptation; there my heart sunk in fear and despondency because of foes; and there, too, is the spot on which I was refreshed with manna from heaven, or with a cooling and stimulating draught from the well of salvation. There I enjoyed sweet communion with the companions of my pilgrimage, and obtained a glimpse of the smiling countenance of my Saviour, and saw the clear sky through a rift in the clouds. Sadness and satisfaction, miseries and mercies, pleasures and pains, adverses and advantages have been strangely interblended in the history of our lives. A bright warp has been interwoven with a dark woof, sadly variegating the drapery of life.

How powerful is the attraction of Eternity! Time seems to fly with greater velocity, in proportion as the squares of the distance between us and the grave decrease. Each successive year appears to wing its flight past us with greater rapidity. It is a remark often made, the truth of which all experience, that the longer we live, the shorter seem the passing hours and years. The nearer the grave, the more rapid the motion toward it. "Whatsoever thy hand findeth to do, do it with thy might, for there is no work in the grave whither thou goest."

29.—SAFETY OF BELIEVERS IN JESUS.

T. W. SYDNOR.

THE peculiar spiritual union between Christ and his people, ensures their eternal salvation. They are represented as the possession, the property of Christ, his peculiar people, given to him by the Father—his purchased people, bought at an infinite price, redeemed with his own blood. Will he fail to take care of his own property, especially that which he has secured at such immense cost? They are spoken of as the members of his body. Will he allow his own body to be maimed? Will he suffer any of its members to be severed and destroyed? They are represented as his spiritual seed, his sons and daughters. Will he be so negligent of his own offspring, as to allow any of them to be torn from his family, and to be made the children of the wicked one? It cannot be. The relation of parent and child is indissoluble. The believer is a child of the Most High by a two-fold title, that of regeneration and adoption, and can never cease to be a child. "Being born again, not of corruptible seed, but of incorruptible by the word of God, which liveth and abideth for ever."—1 Peter i. 23. "God sent forth his Son, made of a woman, made under the law, that he might redeem them that were under the law, that we might receive the adoption of sons."—Gal. iv. 5, 6. Regeneration gives us the nature of sons; adoption the privilege of sons. Nor is it possible, as in the case of earthly parents, for the love between Christ and his children ever to cease. His is unchanging love. Having loved his own, he will love them unto the end. And he sends forth his Spirit into the hearts of his children, crying Abba, Father; and puts his fear into their hearts, that they shall not depart from him. They are represented as his *brethren* also. "Both he that sanctifieth and they who are sanctified are all of one, for which cause he is not ashamed to call them brethren."—Heb. ii. 14. And as his brethren, they are heirs of the same inheritance, "heirs of God, and joint heirs with Christ." Jesus, our elder brother, has already passed into the heavens, and taken possession of this inheritance, to hold it and keep it in readiness for us who are to come after him. They are represented as his *spouse* to whom he is betrothed, his *bride*, his beloved, over whom he rejoices. Can it be supposed that he will suffer these objects of his tenderest love to perish? This union of believers with Christ ensures their perseverance. They are one with him. Their life and interest are identified with his. "Their life is hid with Christ in God." Whilst there is life in him, there must be life in them. He is the vine, they are branches. He diffuses his virtues to them as naturally and as freely as the vine sends forth its sap into its own branches. Now who can sever this bond of union? "Who shall separate us from the love of Christ? Shall tribulation, or distress, or persecution, or famine, or nakedness, or peril, or sword? Nay, in all these things we are more than conquerors through him that loved us. For I am persuaded that neither death, nor life, nor angels, nor principalities, nor powers, nor things present, nor things to come, nor height, nor depth, nor any other creature, shall be able to separate us from the love of God, which is in Christ Jesus our Lord."—Rom. viii. 25—39.

30.—SOURCE OF THE CHRISTIAN'S COMFORT.

A. BROADDUS.

FAITH is the sovereign remedy for heart troubles. "Let not your heart be troubled; ye believe in God, believe also in me." But here I would caution you against a mistaken view with respect to this point.

Let it not be thought that we are to consider *faith in itself* as possessing this virtue. No, brethren; here, as in other cases, where the most interesting and important results are ascribed to faith, the *efficient* cause is to be found in the *object*, not in the *act* of faith. It was thus in regard to the healing of bodily diseases: "thy faith hath saved thee; go in peace." In all such *cases*, the result is ascribed to faith as the *instrument*, and as, in that character, taking hold on the object, and receiving and appropriating the benefit. A wonderful instrument indeed is faith! capable of achieving wonders, through the efficacy of the object on which it acts! In this sense, then, is this faith to be considered, when we speak of it as the sovereign remedy for the troubles of the heart.

Well, brethren, we have our songs in the house of our pilgrimage; and here too we have our troubles; for this is not our rest. And we are now to see how the remedy provided by our heavenly Physician may be brought to bear upon those afflictions. I am aware, brethren, how much easier it is calmly to present the remedy for the evils and afflictions of life, and earnestly to press the advice that we should appropriate and apply that remedy, than it is to put this advice into actual practice for our own benefit. But trusting in that grace that can give effect to our feeble efforts—remembering that we ought to bear one another's burdens," and having a common interest with you in this case, I am encouraged cheerfully to proceed with this part of our subject.

"Many are the afflictions of the righteous." To attempt an enumeration of them in detail, would be a task which we cannot undertake, nor is it necessary. There are *classes* of affliction, including all the particular cases to which we may be subject, and if the remedy provided by Infinite Goodness should be found to cover all these classes of human evil, then may we feel assured that it is sufficient for all particular cases, whether specified or not—whether appertaining to mind or body—whether of a spiritual or an earthly character. Be not discouraged. If "many are the afflictions of the righteous," remember, "the Lord delivereth them out of them all."

These classes of affliction may arise at different times from different quarters, as the storm arises sometimes from one point of the horizon, and sometimes from another. And I may add, that as in the case of a storm, so here; the clouds of trouble may gather from different quarters at the same time, and meeting and mingling in conflict, what a tempest threatens to crush the sufferer! See Paul "in heaviness through manifold temptations!" and hear the old patriarch exclaim—"All these things are against me!" Brethren, if amidst your trials you have been spared from the severity of the tempest, you have reason to bless the hand divine for milder dealings: and if ever *that* should be your lot, remember that He who rides in the whirlwind has promised, "as thy days, so shall thy strength be."

Shall we undertake, by dressing it in pompous words, to adorn the promise of the Redeemer that he will come again and conduct his disciples to the mansions in his Father's house? This would be "to varnish the gold, or paint the diamond." The mind cannot imagine any thing more perfectly finished; and it only requires that our attention be directed to it, in all its bearings, to see its beauty and to feel its influence.

"In my Father's house are many mansions." "My Father's *house.*" How familiar the expression! like that of a prince brought up in a palace, and undazzled by the splendors of royalty. "My *Father's* house." Then *you* have an interest in it; for you belong to my family. "Many mansions." *Here* you may be slighted, uninvited, cast out, as unworthy of a place among the children of this world; but be of good cheer; there is room for you in the mansions above. "If it were not so I would have told you;" so that you should not have been tantalized with the vain hope of a place among the blessed, and then shut out as unwelcome intruders. "I go to prepare a place for you,"—to bespeak your future habitation, and see that all is in readiness for your reception. "And if I go and prepare a place for you, I will come again and receive you unto myself; that where I am, there you may be also." Count upon my return, as certainly as on my departure. "That where I am, there you may be also." Christians, are you not ready to say, "Lord, it is enough! Let me be where Jesus is, and I shall be with God, who is the fountain of bliss; for in his presence there is fulness of joy; at his right hand there are pleasures for evermore. *There* the turmoil of life is hushed in perfect repose, and peace and joy take the place of sorrow and affliction. Where is the believer who, in view of such a prospect, will not subscribe to the apostle's estimate, "I reckon that the sufferings of this present time are not worthy to be compared with the glory which shall be revealed in us?"

31.—HOLINESS OF CHRISTIAN DOCTRINES.

SPENCER H. CONE.

We hope, dear brethren, that you have never, by your conduct, armed our adversaries with plausible objections against the distinguishing and glorious doctrines of salvation by *free grace alone*. If you have, remember the reproach belongs to you, and not to the "words of truth and soberness." Brethren, suffer the word o fexhortation. "Let every man prove his own work, and then shall he have rejoicing in himself alone, and not in another." Remember that "to be carnally-minded is death, but to be spiritually-minded is life and peace." Examine yourselves, therefore, whether ye be in the faith, and give diligence to make your calling and election sure. "Add to your faith, virtue; and to virtue, knowledge; and to knowledge, temperance; and to temperance, patience; and to patience, godliness; and to godliness, brotherly kindness; and to brotherly kindness, charity? for if these things be in you and abound, they make you that ye shall neither be barren nor unfruitful in the knowledge of our Lord Jesus Christ." Ye followers of the Lamb, we are deeply interested in your spiritual welfare; "our mouth is opened unto you, our heart is enlarged." We profess to know that we are of God by his Spirit which he hath given us. If the Spirit itself beareth witness with our spirit that we are the children of God, then He is the spirit of adoption by which we cry Abba Father; and with childlike simplicity and godly sincerity, we desire to do the will of our Father who is in heaven. Because we are sons, he hath sent forth the Spirit of his Son into our hearts? and having predestinated us to the adoption of children by Christ Jesus to himself, according to the good pleasure of his will, we should follow after peace with all men, and holiness, the only satisfying evidence of our adoption into the family of God.

If we have the witness in ourselves, He is the Spirit of grace and of supplications. We acknowledge that salvation is all of grace—that if we differ from others, or from our former selves, it is God who hath made us to differ. If we have a hope full of immortality and everlasting life, it is only a good hope through grace; and we may know that the Spirit of grace dwelleth in us, by his being a Spirit of prayer. He hath taught us our need. He hath led us to Christ, the fountain of supplies, in whom it hath pleased the Father that all fulness should dwell. He helpeth our infirmities, for we know not what to pray for as we ought, but the Spirit itself maketh intercession for us with groanings which cannot be uttered. And while this Spirit of grace and of supplications leads us to cry mightily unto God to work in us both to will and to do of his good pleasure, may we constantly bear upon our hearts to the throne of grace the sad condition of our perishing fellow-creatures, " until the Spirit shall be poured upon them from on high, and the wilder ness be a fruitful field."

32.—TENDENCY OF THE DOCTRINE OF ELECTION.

C. F. BURNLEY.

THE most weighty objections to the doctrine of election are based upon its tendency. They are such as these; that it drives sinners to despair—that it is unfriendly to good works—and that it encourages licentiousness. These are grave charges, and could they be established, would set aside the doctrine. But in the view of Paul, Election redounds "to the praise of the glory of Divine grace." And if, as all admit, God is glorious in saving sinners, what argument is needed to prove that he is equally glorious in doing this according to an eternal purpose? To determine to do that which is right cannot be wrong. Let me here ask what is there so horrible in this doctrine? According to this view of truth, all who repent and believe will be saved; and according to the opposite view, no more will be saved; so that it does not close the gates of heaven against any. Again, according to Election, all the impenitent and unbelieving will be lost; and according to the opposite doctrine, the same persons will be lost. Election does not, therefore, consign any over to perdition.

1. As an antidote to errors of pride and presumption, Election exerts an influence salutary to man and worthy of God. Almost every radical error is distinguished by some or all of these characteristics. It has

its origin in the pride of the heart; it proceeds upon an incorrect view of human depravity; it lays an undue stress upon good works, as constituting, wholly or in part, the grounds of justification; and its ultimate tendency is to derogate from the glory of God.

Thus, Arminianism represents the conversion and salvation of the sinner, as the result of the volitions of his own will. According to this doctrine, the sinner who believes and is finally saved, having made a better improvement of the grace given equally to all, has caused himself to be better than others. And the only answer an Arminian can return to the apostolic question, "who maketh thee to differ from another?" (1 Cor. vi. 7,) is, I myself. A different answer involves an abandonment of his creed. He, therefore, cannot praise the riches of God's grace that he is better than an infidel, but for this he must commend the wisdom of his own choice. And Deism, Arianism, and Socinianism—those three Antichrists, which make repentance and sincerity the grounds of the sinner's hope—administer food to the pride of the carnal mind, and exalt the sinner in his own eyes, instead of the Saviour. Rationalism assumes that the scriptures abound with absurdities, which are to be corrected by the suggestions of reason; thus making reason more unerring than the word of God, and bestowing a compliment upon human intellect at the expense of Revelation. And the self-styled Reformation of the present age also magnifies the merit of works; and teaching that men need no spiritual influence to change their hearts, inspires them with a very satisfactory opinion of themselves. Now is it not to be desired that some grand truth, involving other leading truths, shall be presented to the mind as a barrier to the inroads of these and similar errors? Such a doctrine is found in Election. It pre-supposes the desperate wickedness of the heart; it clothes the sinner with sackcloth and ashes; it represents salvation from first to last as being all of grace; and it throws around the amazing love of God the brightest lustre. It contemplates Christ as the author and finisher not only of our faith, but of every grace within us; and before we can maintain the sufficiency of reason unenlightened to correct the oracles of God; before we can suspend the salvation of the soul upon the uncertain volitions of the human will; before we can deny the doctrine of native depravity, or the divinity of Christ; and before we can in any sense depend upon works as the procuring cause of justification, every vestige of this truth must be obliterated from the mind. Election is a lofty and holy elevation, upon which we may stand erect and secure; but leaning on either side, down we go, like the stone detached from the mountain's top, with speed and violence continually accumulating. And the stopping-place none can predict. Witness Dr. Priestley. His first position was Calvinism; thence he descended to Arminianism; thence to High Arianism; and thence to Socinianism.

During revivals of religion, this subject prudently discussed, might effect incalculable good, in preventing false hopes. As a test of character, it scarcely ever fails, either by angering or humbling the sinner, to develope the principles of the inner man. It strips from his soul the filthy rags of his own righteousness, and lays his sins bare in all their blackness and guilt before his own eyes, and the eyes of God. This always makes the sinner ashamed and humble, or it makes him mad. It asserts, too, his guilt and dependence, and the righteous sovereignty of God—other truths which unsanctified hearts do not relish. By teaching a doctrine nearly akin to this, our Saviour once unmasked a number of professed friends, and sent them back to the world.—John vi. 65. Brethren, would you ascertain whether men have the love of God in them? you may tell them of his amazing love to them, and inquire if they love this exhibition of his character. But let not this suffice. "Sinners love those that love them." Present God to their contemplation in his unspotted holiness, in his inflexible justice, and in his absolute sovereignty, and inquire of them if they love these perfections of Deity.

It is by explaining away or lowering down the doctrines of the cross, that unsubdued and unsanctified hearts are brought into the church. Sinners are generally presumptuous, and while encouragement is to be given to some, in most cases, something is to be done to prevent them from becoming mere professors of religion. They should be met at the threshold of the church with such declarations as these—"No man can come unto me except the Father who hath sent me draw him;" "If any man will come after me, let him deny himself, and take up his cross and follow me;" "The foxes have holes, and the birds of the air have nests, but the Son of man hath not where to lay his head." These were touch-stones in the hands of Christ; and they may be thus employed by us. If men receive these sayings, they are humbled, they are in earnest, and they are prepared to encounter trials for Christ's sake.

The number of spurious conversions seen at the present day, may be partly ascribed to the silence of ministers upon this subject. And why are brethren so much afraid of this doctrine? "Oh, it will kill the revival, it will put out the fire," is the reply always at hand when this subject is named. But it is not so. If the revival be of God, his truth will not bring it to nought; if the fire be sent down from heaven, it will not go out. But if the fire be kindled by human means alone, such as pompous declamation and irresistible bursts of oratory, or by the more common though not less effectual means of stamping the feet, clapping the hands, vociferating and shouting—beware of Election; it will be as cold water upon it. Yes, Election faithfully preached, will put out the fire of mere human excitement; and if it die, let it die. In a revival, however, effected by God's Spirit, this doctrine will be useful. Where, since the days of Paul, shall we find one who more fearlessly and earnestly proclaimed Election, than the evangelical Whitefield? And who has had more seals to his ministry? Who, laboring under as many obstacles, have been more successful in winning souls to Christ, than the pioneers of the Baptist cause in these States? and they generally held and inculcated this truth.

2. Election promotes the holiness of believers. Holiness is one of the objects contemplated in this doctrine. God hath chosen us, that we should be holy: "Whom he did foreknow, he did predestinate to be conformed to the image of his Son." Every one, therefore, who keeps before his mind the design of this truth, and conforms to it, will purify himself even as God is pure. Were the doctrine what it is represented by its enemies, it would encourage licentiousness; and some of its professed friends, holding views of election not taught in the Bible, have led disorderly lives, while they have flattered themselves that they were the subjects of God's electing love. Men without charity, self-willed, heady, proud, in their spirits unmercifully censorious, in their creed Antinomian, and in their lives not "without blame," have maintained an election of their own, and their error contributed to the deformity of their character. But this constitutes no objection to the truth. The doctrine of salvation by grace has been abused: men, turning the grace of God into lasciviousness, have said, "Let us sin that grace may abound." But who, on this account, would contend that we are saved by works of righteousness which we can do, and object that the contrary opinion promotes licentiousness? Brethren, let us, who hold the doctrine of election, exemplify in our lives the holiness of its tendency, as

the best answer to gainsayers, and as the most conclusive proof of its truth.

3. Our doctrine tends to the praise of the grace of God, by presenting encouragement to Christians to labor for the salvation of sinners. Its influence in this respect is beautifully illustrated in the labors and sacrifices of Paul. "Are they ministers of Christ," said he, "I am more: in labors more abundant, in stripes above measure, in prisons more frequent, in deaths oft." None ever made greater sacrifices or performed more arduous labors for Christ than Paul, and the secret of his exertions and sufferings is found in his confidence in the purpose of God to save sinners. His own testimony upon this point is, "I endure all things for the elect's sake." Hence he endured opposition and blasphemy at Corinth that might have otherwise dispirited him. God encouraged him with this assurance: "I have much people in this city."

Brethren, you who labor in word and doctrine, have been often cheered in a similar way. More blessed than his brethren is that servant who has never been called to labor in some part of the Lord's vineyard which under his culture has yielded but little fruit. Many of you, with desponding Simon on a different occasion, have often confessed, "Master, we have toiled all the night and taken nothing." Well, brethren, when retrospecting a long night of patient but unsuccessful toil, you have inquired with deep sorrow, "Who hath believed our report? and to whom is the arm of the Lord revealed?" have you in despair abandoned the work? No, no, this precious doctrine has sustained you. "My arguments have failed, and all my strength has been spent in vain. But God has among men a people in whose salvation he will glorify his Son. I may not see it, I may not be the instrument in turning them to God, yet they will be saved; the Redeemer's crown will not want gems heaven's many mansions will not want inhabitants." With these or similar reflections, you have fortified your hearts against despair, and again you have gone forth into the field weeping and bearing precious seed.

From this source too, brethren, we have been inspired with hope when we have witnessed the progress of heresies, and the apostacy of professed believers. Every one knows how under these disasters the heart sinks, and with what dread we anticipate the developments of the dark future. The more timid are heard with portentous countenance predicting appalling evils; "churches will be rent; schisms and errors will prevail; iniquity will abound, and the love of many wax cold; the ungodly will be confirmed in unbelief and sin." Such are their fears. But the believer in this doctrine of blessed influence, responds to these predictions; "Should God, for wise purposes permit these things, he shall so overrule them that they shall work together for good to them that love God, to them who are the called according to his purpose. Alexander may do us much harm; Hymeneus and Philetus may overthrow the faith of some; nevertheless, the foundation of God standeth sure, having this seal, the Lord knoweth them that are his."

4. Election redounds "to the praise of the glory of God's grace," as it secures the salvation of a multitude which no man can number. Let this doctrine, with those kindred truths which lend their aid to its support, be blotted from God's book, and this glorious event is of all possibilities the most improbable. Hence, from the denial of this doctrine, is always derived the awful fear of being finally cast away; for if Election be not true, however assured the believer may be at the time that his sins are forgiven, he cannot say that to-morrow he will not be engulfed in bottomless perdition. How a rational being with such a contingency before him, can be otherwise than perfectly miserable, I cannot see. But established in the belief of this truth,

we can say with Paul, "Who shall separate us from the love of Christ? Shall tribulation, or distress, or persecution, or famine, or nakedness, or peril, or sword? Nay, in all these things we are more than conquerors, through him that loved us. For I am persuaded that neither death, nor life, nor angels, nor principalities, nor powers, nor things present, nor things to come, nor height, nor depth, nor any other creature shall be able to separate us from the love of God which is in Christ Jesus our Lord."

And while Election secures the salvation of countless multitudes, it ascribes all the glory of their salvation to God. This to the Christian is the most endearing feature of the whole subject, and it constitutes one of the many proofs that the doctrine is divine. Hence just views of Election heighten in the minds of believers the conviction of their obligations to glorify God. We are bound to render thanks to our heavenly Father for the gift of his Son, for the influences of his Spirit, and for his word. But this is not all. We are bound to render him special thanks for the additional expression of his love towards us in the conversion of our souls. Had God left us to the inclination of our own wills, we should have lived and died in sin, in full view of the atonement of Christ; but when we were rejecting the offers of mercy, and going further and yet further from heaven, he pitied us, and turned our feet from the way that leads to death. We must adore and praise the goodness of God, brethren, for the provisions of grace, for invitations given us to seek them, and especially for the disposition, imparted by Divine influence, to comply with these invitations. By the grace of God we are what we are; and in eternity, if we should be found among the redeemed of the Lord, we shall most willingly cast our crowns at the feet of Christ, and ascribe "Blessings, and honor, and glory, and power, unto him that sitteth upon the throne, and unto the Lamb for ever and ever."

Unconverted friends, let me entreat you not to pervert the doctrine which I have advanced. The scriptural doctrine of Election furnishes no excuse for your continuance in sin. If anything said by me has this tendency, reject it, it is not of God. But that it should *appear* to some to have this tendency is rather a proof that it is in accordance with what Paul taught. He anticipated this perversion of the truth inculcated by him. —Rom. ix. 19. The purposes of God neither excuse sin, nor supersede exertion.—Acts ii. 23; 2 Pet. i. 10. You know that you are under no constraint to sin against God; it is your own wilful and deliberate act, and God holds you responsible for it. May he grant you repentance to the acknowledging of the truth, for Christ's sake.

33.—CALL TO CHRISTIAN ACTIVITY.

IRAH CHASE.

O, MY brethren, it is indeed time to awake. Amidst all the prosperity of our churches, and all the spread of Christian truth, we have, certainly, much cause for gratitude and encouragement. But let us not be deceived into the opinion that a tenth, or a hundredth, or a thousandth part of what is attainable, has already been attained. Onward, our Saviour bids us onward, at every remembrance of our baptism. The Holy Scriptures, by which only we should be content to estimate our attainments, bid us onward. Our consciences this day condemn us, even the best of us, the most active and exemplary. Truly, we have but just begun to see and to feel what devolves upon us. The zeal and enterprise of others tell us it is no time for us to recline at our ease. The signal events of the times in which we live, bid us up and be doing. From the forests of the West to these shores of the Atlantic, and from Halifax to New Orleans, the startling cry is heard—Awake, thou that sleepest! It is echoed from the mountains and valleys of South America—Awake, thou that sleepest! Africa utters her groans, and beseeches us. Burmah—all Asia implores us by the whitening bones of the deluded pilgrims; by the unuttered anguish of the widows perishing on the funeral piles of their deceased husbands; in a word, by all the temporal woes of idolatry and superstition; and by the millions plunging, year after year, into the abyss of a dark eternity. Europe, with all her refinement and elevation, urges us by all that is impressive in human condition and human prospects. The souls of thousands around us, of friends and kindred, of members of our own families, in danger of perishing, call us to a holy circumspection and a life of prayer. The voice of our departed fathers and brethren, charges us to live to God; to remember that our time is short; and to think constantly of the example and sufferings of Him who for us "humbled himself and became obedient unto death, even the death of the cross."

34.—REASONS FOR HOLY ACTIVITY.

W. A. WHITSITT.

THE reasons why we should not lie at ease in Zion will now claim our attention.

1. *We are surrounded by enemies;* and are far distant from home. These enemies are very numerous, and very powerful; and they are determined not to yield without a mighty struggle. But we are weak, O very weak! How then may we hope to gain the victory? Shall we gain it by folding our arms, and saying, "A little more sleep, and a little more slumber?" Never, no, never. We must put on the whole

armor of God, resolved to endure hardness as good soldiers, and go forth in the strength of the Lord of hosts, determined to conquer or to die.

2. *Satan, our great inveterate enemy, never sleeps.* He is ever on the watchtower. "As a roaring lion he goeth about, seeking whom he may devour." Already has he dragged down to perdition thousands who had taken upon themselves the hallowed name of Christian. He knows the most accessible avenue to every heart. He knows the besetting sin of each. And he is sure to make his most vigorous attack at the weakest and most assailable point. O, then, "let us not sleep as do others;" but let us "watch and pray." For if we résist him successfully we have no time to be idle.

3. *The world is to be converted.* The adorable Redeemer having given himself a ransom for all, and having arisen triumphantly over death and the grave, assembled his disciples together, that he might give them his last parting command. "Go," said he unto them, "and preach the gospel to every creature." He might have called forth the archangels to have embarked in this glorious work, and the heavenly messengers would have gone forth on the wings of speed to earth's remotest bounds, publishing the glad tidings of salvation. But no; He has seen proper to work through the instrumentality of the church. This command is just as obligatory upon the church now as it was eighteen hundreds years ago; and doubtless the Son of God feels now as deep an interest in the welfare of the perishing millions, as when first he shed his blood for the healing of the nations. The fields are already white unto harvest. Yea, more. Long ere this has the Macedonian cry for help been heard from Europe, Asia, Africa, America, and the isles of the sea. Well may we exclaim, "The harvest truly is great;" for "the field is the world." But the laborers are few and feeble. Now I ask, if this great

commission be faithfully observed, when will we find any time for slothful ease? Every Christian may do something—*must* do something in this great work. All can aid by their prayers; and few, *very few* are there who cannot aid by their contributions. All who have the *will* to assist can find a *way*.

4. *Souls are perishing.* Oh! who can tell the value of the soul? That deathless principle that will live on when time shall be no longer—more priceless than the cattle on a thousand hills, than the mines of Peru, or the gold of Ophir. Now "he that converteth a sinner from the error of his ways shall save a soul from death." Many a pious mother has been the means of leading her children to the Saviour. Many Christians have been the honored instruments in the hands of the Lord of rescuing their neighbors from that dread death that never dies. Great is the encouragement to labor in the vineyard of the Lord; for Jesus has promised to be with us while thus engaged. My Christian friends, many of our beloved associates and dearest relatives are yet without God and without hope. If they were groaning under the influence of some painful bodily disease, how willingly would we assist them. But their *souls* are diseased. And I greatly fear the fault is in a measure ours. We have not let our light so shine as to constrain them to glorify our Heavenly Father. We have not prayed for and with them as often and as fervently as we should. We have not warned them time and again of this awful danger with that affection, earnestness, and engagedness of soul, which the great importance of the subject so imperatively demands. Their precious souls are perishing while we are slumbering at our posts.

5. *The time for action is short.* The Lord is continually calling his laborers home, and very soon he will send his messengers for us. Our work will have been accomplished, and we shall have entered into

rest. The places which know us now will soon know us no more. Mothers, you will soon have done praying for your children. Fathers, you will soon cease to warn your beloved offspring. Ministers, you will soon cease to go forth weeping, bearing precious seed. Brethren, the blessed privilege you now enjoy of inviting those you love to the Lamb of God, will soon be over. Many of us, no doubt, will cease from our labors during the present year. Away, then, with slothfulness! What our hands find to do, let us do with our might; for there is no work, nor knowledge, nor wisdom in the grave; and we shall all soon be there.

35.—TOKENS OF DIVINE FAVOR.

W. T. BRANTLY.

WHILST we allow that success is not an invariable criterion of merit in any cause, we must maintain that a cause wholly without success would encounter a very practical argument against its worth. We can never be surprised at the prevalence of a plan which accommodates its requirements to the taste, habits, and fashion of its supporters; which enforces no expedients adverse to their temper, and courts them by a supple compliance with their native desires. But we may be reasonably surprised at the advancement of a system which throws innumerable obstacles in the way of nature's regular course; which meets every heedless impulse with a veto; which glories in nothing more than in being at war with our inclinations. Yet, through all this opposition, does the truth of God make its way. Its success, though not uniform, has been certain, and in the majesty of its march has it conquered inveterate foes. Its mildness made it appear an unfit instrument to subdue the daring ferocity of pagan errors; and that it should have been victorious in the struggle, is a manifest token of protection and favor from Heaven. Such tokens the Church of Christ has experienced in successive ages; not only when it had to contend with the iron obstinacy of heathen hate and animosity, and pour out its best blood as the seal of its faith; but when, groaning under the oppressions of papal tyranny, its martyrs resisted the encroachments of a polluted hierarchy, and contended against an apostate church for the faith once delivered to the saints. God was in the midst of his faithful people, and preserved for himself a devoted remnant. Even throughout the dark ages, when defection from the pristine purity of doctrine became general, we trace the vestiges of an uncorrupt church like stars that twinkle in the midnight gloom. Through the enormous addition of human rites and observances, we can see the current of an unadulterated doctrine, running like the limpid stream through swamps and marshes. To suppose that this rectitude of doctrine and discipline could have existed without Divine help, would be as absurd as to think that a spark could live in the raging ocean.

In forming a scheme for the conversion of mankind, what mind would ever have devised one so improbable as the cross of Christ? To human wisdom it would have appeared an idle frenzy, to think of reducing a rebellious people to allegiance by the unmixed scandal of an ignominious crucifixion. Of all improbable plans, this might have seemed the most unpromising. Yet, behold what wonders were accomplished by the unvarnished majesty of this simple fact. Without any of the aids of learning, of authority, or eloquence; with none of the ingenious sophistries of the schools; without any elaborate discussions, or studied appeals to the passions, we see humble, unassuming men carrying in triumph a religion obnoxious to the repulsive spirit of human pride and ambition. They had the approving tokens of Divine regard. Their gospel became the power of God and the wisdom of God to them that believed; and their work, which in itself would have been the derision of every idler, when confirmed by the hand of the Lord, applied to thousands the elements of a new life; struck terror into the opposing ranks of sin; subverted the rites which antiquity had consecrated; and organized communities for the worship of one God and one Mediator. Nor has their case been one of uncommon occurrence. The effects of that preaching in which Christ crucified is the leading theme, are still stupendous. It contains the power of a mysterious attraction. The solemn echo from groaning Calvary, is the eloquence which persuades men. Here shines the true morality—here virtue improves into devotion; here the soul catches the fire of holy inspiration, and rises to assert its kindred with the spirits of the just.

In memorable instances the Lord has visited his people with times of refreshing from his presence. No tokens are more grateful than those which evince the Spirit's power in giving life and energy to the world. Whatever may be the sneers of the unbelieving, or the more formal cavillings of those who are contented with the mere prose of piety, it must be admitted that an accountable religious excitement does often prevail in places where the means of grace are observed. In these cases, the young and the old, the enlightened and the ignorant, have been equally affected. A surprising influence has turned to the exulting ways of Zion those who were wandering in the devious paths of sin. The impetuosity of youthful guilt has been stayed, and the hoary veteran in the world's service has been brought to a temper soft and relenting. Songs of deliverance have succeeded the clamor of unsanctified revelry, and many have met us on the way with that cheering declaration, "We will go with you, because we have heard that God is with you." These are the festive scenes, my brethren, which impart a holy aspect to our earthly temples. Neither corn, nor wine, nor oil, can afford such joy. There is a heaven-born melody in the songs of redeemed souls. Their music floats along the lengthened desolations of Jerusalem, and the wilderness rejoices. The chorus which they swell, falls in melting extasies on the pensive bosom of mourning Zion. It is the joy of saints.

The preservation of personal religion in the heart, can be the effect only of Divine agency, and therefore is an approving manifestation of Divine regard. We have a natural reluctance to comply with the self-denying restrictions and exercises of religion. If any progress is made, it must be in spite of a counter-influence. Like the tide which beats upon the margin of the ocean, we appear to lose by frequent recessions what we had gained in progress, and by many deviations from the direct course of our journey, seem to have made no advancement. Yet, in all these variations and wanderings, we are held by the power of God, and the good work is going on in our heart. God holds up our soul, and through the retarding power of sin, like the force of gravitation acting upon an ascending body, would cause us to relapse to our original state, yet the impulsive energy continues to act, and we are sustained in our flight for heaven by the invisible agency of the Holy Spirit. How much reason have we then to live and act in the spirit of the Psalmist's prayer, "Hold thou me up, and I shall be safe."

36.—ANGELIC KNOWLEDGE OF CHRISTIANS.

J. BACKUS.

The law of God, as it was first given to man, required perfect and perpetual obedience as the condition of life, and declared death as the wages of sin; and spiritual death immediately came upon our first parents when they ate of the forbidden fruit, and spiritual and natural death have reigned over their posterity ever since. And though God early revealed his design of salvation to men, and gave increasing light concerning it afterwards, yet when the Son of God was manifested in the flesh, he was seen of angels. The angels of light saw more of God than they ever did before, as appears by various scriptures; which should teach us always to take our ideas from revelation, concerning the entire depravity of man, the obedience and atonement of Christ, the sovereignty and efficacy of his grace, regeneration, justification by faith in his perfect righteousness, and the final perseverance of true believers in holiness to eternal happiness.

THE BAPTIST PULPIT.

V.

THE CHURCH AND THE MINISTRY.

1.—THE KINGDOM OF HEAVEN.

D. MERRILL.

THE kingdom of Heaven is, in its beginning, progress, and extension, like to a grain of mustard seed, which a man took and sowed in his field. This is indeed the least of all seeds, which men sow in their fields, for the purpose of gathering a harvest of seed. But when it is grown, it is the greatest among herbs, and becometh a tree. So this kingdom, in its origin, was indeed the least of all kingdoms, but it is now spreading like the thousand branches of the mustard tree, and will increase, till it shall be the greatest of all kingdoms, and fill the world.

This kingdom is also like unto leaven, which a woman took and hid in three measures of meal, till the whole was leavened. The doctrine, spirit, and power attending this kingdom, are like leaven put into meal, which will ferment and leaven the whole. No opposition shall be able to stop their fermenting, till all kings shall bow down before the Lord, and all nations shall serve him. This kingdom, in value, is like unto an inestimable treasure, and an invaluable pearl, for which men will sell all that they have. There is no other way to possess the kingdom, but to forsake or sell all for it. This kingdom is also like a net, that was cast into the sea, and gathered of every kind. Hypocrites have, and probably will, for the present, work themselves into this kingdom, notwithstanding all its members profess to be born of God—to have repentance towards God, and faith towards our Lord Jesus Christ, and upon this profession, have every one of them put on Christ, by being baptized into him.

The subjects of this kingdom are carefully submissive, in civil things, to kings, to governors, and to all in authority: but in religious matters they, of right, acknowledge no other Legislator but Jesus Christ the Lord, and will submit to none other. In this the kingdom is distinct from all other religious societies which observe religious ordinances.

In one thing this kingdom is similar to other kingdoms—it has in its code a law for naturalizing foreigners, by which its members may be augmented. But then, it is a law of which its enemies have been accustomed to complain, and is unlike to that of other kingdoms. It requires that every person to be naturalized, should heartily condemn himself for his former course of sinning; and confess that he is totally unable to help himself, and not worthy that any should help him; that it would be mere grace should he be helped at all. It also requires, that the person should exhibit a willingness to be pardoned and received to favor, through the righteousness of another. It further enjoins, that any one making the above profession, whether male or female, should be buried and raised again in baptism; denoting that he had died to all hope in himself, and was now willing to follow Jesus, the only Saviour of sinners, to death, the burial, and the resurrection, and to hope in him, and in him only, for salvation. This law, by which subjects are naturalized into the kingdom of God, has long been to the Jews a stumbling-block, and to the Greeks foolishness. But it is still in force, and it is still true, "that as many of you as have been baptized into

Christ, have put on Christ." There is no naturalizing law to be found in the records of the kingdom aside from this; nor is there any other way of obtaining citizenship in this kingdom of God, but by submitting to it. Such as do not submit, whatever may be their moral character, are yet foreigners. They may be Hebrews in the camp of the Philistines, or God's people in Babylon, but they are not citizens of that kingdom which the God of heaven hath set up.

This definition agrees with Moses and the prophets; with that Elias who was to precede the Messiah, and prepare the way before him; and with Christ Jesus and his apostles. Moses and the prophets thus define the moral character of the people of this kingdom. That they shall all hear Jesus Christ; that they shall be all taught of God; and that they shall all know the Lord, from the least of them to the greatest of them.

John the Baptist, whose express business was to make ready a people prepared for the Lord, preached to the people repentance, faith, the baptism of repentance, and baptized the people who confessed their sins, and reproved with great severity, those who came for baptism on their father Abraham's account. Christ Jesus made and baptized more disciples than John, though *personally* he baptized not. He sent his disciples to teach the nations, and to baptize the taught. The apostles preached to the people, that they should repent and be baptized in the name of Jesus Christ, for the remission of sins. Such as received the word gladly, were baptized. As many as were baptized into Christ put on Christ, or were naturalized into his kingdom; and the Lord added to the church daily such as should be saved. He added them from the Jewish church or nation; as he did afterwards from the Gentile nations. A full proof that the kingdom of God is no more the Jewish church continued, than it is a continuation of the heathen Roman empire.

2.—THE DIGNITY OF THE CHURCH.

G. B. IDE.

THE church of Christ needs to be elevated in the grandeur and universality of her plans of benevolence. The spectator, who occupies the mountain-top, has a more extensive and commanding prospect than he who dwells at its base. In like manner should the Christians of our day ascend into the "Mount of vision," that they may survey the wide moral landscape, and take the dimensions of the whole mighty territory which they are summoned to invade and conquer. While remaining at a low point, we are apt to confine our aims and efforts within a narrow circle, and to think little of the far-spreading fields which distance and interposing heights shut out from our view. It is, therefore, necessary that we should obtain a loftier post of observation, whence our eye may range over a broader compass, and where we may enlarge our calculations in proportion to the enterprise to be achieved. Planting our feet on the bright eminence which has been described, let us throw our glance over the immense regions that lie beneath, stretching away in illimitable perspective. A *world* is before us, with all its peopled continents, its crowding millions, its darkness and wo. Upon the whole boundless expanse, guilt and death, with raven wings, "sit brooding." Here, close at hand, we see our own favored country—where the free word of God, proscribed or trammelled in all other lands, has found its refuge, and wrought its most signal results—sinking into the gulf of degeneracy ; menaced with the fearful domination of the Man of Sin ; "sapped and convulsed by giant vices ; its rulers, its politicians, and its insane population casting off the laws of Jehovah ; while the church is at ease, her sentinels asleep, and the beacon-ights burning dimly on her towers. Yonder we see

Europe, the proud home of arts and civilization—one half of it shrouded in the blackness of Papal night, and the other, a solitary kingdom excepted, covered with the huge corpse of a dead Protestantism, and its monstrous emanation, a baptized Infidelity. And even in that single nation where vital Christianity still lives, we witness a concerted and vigorous attempt to pollute or destroy it, and substitute in its room the exploded mummeries of a darker age. On this side, we behold Africa—wronged, bleeding Africa—sitting in the dust, and mantled with one wide pall of barbarism. We see her vast interior thronged with savage hordes, scarce raised above the level of the brute, and given up to the most degrading idolatry. We see the slave-ship hovering on her coasts, and hear the clanking of her fetters, the shrieks of her children, the shouts of rapine and violence, echoing along her plundered shores. And then, far in the dim and ancient East—the hoary cradle of the world—we look on the unnumbered myriads of Asia, plunged in heathenism, a prey to debasing passions, strangers to hope, and hurrying blindly into the abyss. Everywhere we perceive the presence and the power of that relentless enemy of God and man, whose throne is on the high places of the earth, and whose trophies are murdered souls. We see Romanism deluding its countless votaries; Paganism enthralling two-thirds of our species; and the fell imposture of Mahomet blasting the fairest portions of the globe, and even lifting its foul crescent above the hallowed scenes which the Redeemer trod. We see government, laws, society, both in lands benighted and civilized, constructed on principles alien to the Gospel; and the spirit of ungodliness diffused through all ranks and classes of mankind; while the few, who cleave to the cause of truth and Heaven, are, in comparison, but as the three bands of Gideon to the dense host of the Midianites, or as the lonely spots of verdure that gem an otherwise unbroken desert.

Such is the spectacle which from the "high mountain" presents itself below and around us. The work which we are called to accomplish, is the moral renovation of this entire extent of sin and misery, its complete subjection to the authority of Christ, and its universal transformation into beauty and holiness. Not a corner of it is to be left unreclaimed; not a dark recess forgotten; not a remote isle of the sea unevangelized; not a wanderer of the wilderness unillumined; not a solitary child of Adam unblessed with the tidings of peace and pardon. Over all, the loveliness and purity of Eden are again to return. Over all, Christ is to reign, and to reign through the instrumentality of his people. Here, then, let us stand, and devise our plans, and form our resolves, with a vigor and a scope commensurate with the greatness of the undertaking which devolves upon us. To this all-viewing height, let the whole church come up, and estimate the task to be performed, the evils to be removed, the obstacles to be encountered, and lay out her schemes of effort with an amplitude that shall embrace the world.

3.—THE IMPORT OF BAPTISM.

S. W. LYND.

BAPTISM exhibits in emblem the resurrection of the Lord Jesus Christ, a fundamental fact in the Christian institution. Paul says, "If Christ be not risen, then is our preaching vain, and your faith is also vain." The resurrection of Christ was the confirmation of his doctrine, the proof of his finished work. This was a leading theme in the ministry of the apostles. Are we asked for evidence that the rite of Baptism symbolized this fact?

We have it clear and strong. The apostle Peter, speaking of the family of Noah, saved by water, makes a transition to Baptism, and says that this rite, in a like figure, saves us by the resurrection of Jesus Christ. Here Baptism *figuratively* saves us, as a memorial of the resurrection of Jesus, by which we are *really* saved. Noah and his family were *saved by water*, emerging, as it were, from a grave of water, in which all the world besides was buried. Believers are saved by the resurrection of Jesus Christ. But his resurrection is symbolized in the act of Baptism, and hence, in like manner, that is *by water*, we are, *in figure*, saved. Neither sprinkling nor pouring can symbolize this fact. Immersion is the only proper memorial, and this gives to the ordinance beauty, force, and value.

Baptism is a rite, emblematic, at the same time, of our own resurrection from the dead, because believers are represented as dying, rising, and reigning with Christ, in his death, resurrection, and ascension to glory. Some of the Christians at Corinth denied the resurrection of the dead. The apostle Paul, in his first letter, proves that a day is coming when all shall be raised out of their graves. Among the considerations, he appeals strongly to their own Baptism. "Else, what shall they do who are baptized for the dead; if the dead rise not, why are these baptized for the dead?" The expression "for the dead," is obviously elliptical—something is understood; and the connection teaches us that the word "resurrection" is to be supplied. Properly translated and pointed, this will be apparent to every reader. "What shall they do who are immersed for the resurrection of the dead, if the dead rise not at all? And why are they immersed for the resurrection of the dead?" If there be no resurrection of the dead, why is our resurrection symbolized in the ordinance of baptism? Here you perceive the adaptedness of the emblem to the apostle's design. But this is entirely lost, if Baptism is not immersion.

In connection with this train of thought we may remark that Baptism was designed to symbolize death and resurrection spiritually, that is, our death and burial to sin, and our resurrection to a life of holiness. On this ground some of the strongest appeals are made to the consciences of believers; as to the Colossians: "Buried with him in baptism, wherein also ye are risen with him, through the faith of the operation of God, who hath raised him from the dead. If ye then be risen with Christ, seek those things which are above." And thus did Paul write to the Christians at Rome—"Know ye not that so many of us as were baptized into Jesus Christ, were baptized into his death? Therefore, we are buried with him by baptism into death; that like as Christ was raised up from the dead by the glory of the Father, even so we also should walk in newness of life."

4.—DIFFERENT VIEWS OF BAPTISM.

I. ORCHARD.

THAT baptism is commanded, cannot be denied; and the very fact of its being commanded proves it to be more than an unmeaning ceremony. It must have a meaning, and he who would be benefited by it should understand that meaning. But what is its meaning? It has been announced to the world by a popular minister of another denomination, as "the rite of initiation into all the benefits of the crucifixion, death, burial, and resurrection of Christ." But is this definition correct? If it be so, then all who die unbaptized, must die without the benefit of the work of Christ, and consequently must perish; while all baptized persons must be partakers of those benefits, and consequently must be saved. The Bible supports no such sentiments—this statement of the signification of baptism must therefore be false; and yet it harmonizes with much of what is written in favor of the prevailing practice. It is a delusive error—the immediate offspring of its parent heresy, that baptism is regeneration: a heresy which makes man the Saviour and not God, and puts an outward act performed upon an unconscious subject, and often by persons who are strangers to godliness, in the place of the operations of the Holy Spirit. Let us turn then from such notions, and go to the sacred scriptures to learn the import of baptism. The apostle Peter calls it "the answer of a good conscience towards God;" setting forth not merely amendment of life, but consciousness of being saved in Christ. He says, "the answer of a *good* conscience;" if good, it must have been purified, and a previous work of grace must have been wrought upon it. It is the answer of such a conscience towards God—that is, to the claims of God. The gospel being presented to attention by the Holy Spirit, the purified conscience thus testifies its reception of, and acquiescence, and participation in the gospel, by preaching in a figure that same gospel before heaven and earth. Such I understand to be the signification of baptism; and thus understood, it is an avowal of faith, a declaration of experience, and a conformity of practice.

5.—INFANT BAPTISM.

ADONIRAM JUDSON.

NOTWITHSTANDING the obvious import of the law of baptism, the greater part of the Christian world baptize the children of believers, on the faith of their parents, or the profession of their sponsors, and refuse baptism to believers, if they have been baptized in infancy. Does their practice appear consistent with the command of Christ? Christ commands those who believe to be baptized. Pedobaptists adopt a system which tends to preclude the baptism of believers. They baptize the involuntary infant, and deprive him of the privilege of ever professing his faith in the appointed way. If this system were universally adopted, it would banish believer's baptism out of the world. But leaving the evident discordance between the system of the Pedobaptists and the command of Christ, let us inquire whether infant baptism has any just support, either direct or inferential.

When any practice is proposed and enforced as a binding duty, we have a right to examine the grounds of the alleged obligation. It is not sufficient for the purpose, to show that the practice is innocent, and even compatible with every other duty; it is requisite that he prove it binding. If one should enforce the ancient custom of dressing in white, for several days after baptism, as the duty of every Christian, it would not be necessary for us to urge one argument against it; nor would it be sufficient for him to prove it innocent, and even compatible with every other duty. We might reasonably refuse compliance, until he should prove that we are bound to comply. So, in the case of infant baptism, it is not necessary for us to urge one argument against it; nor is it sufficient for the proposer to prove that every objection is groundless. It is necessary for him to prove that it is obligatory. The question with every parent ought to be, "Am I under obligation to have my children baptized?" Now, on what grounds is this obligation predicated?

We should naturally expect, that the baptism of infants, if enjoined at all, would have been enjoined in the law which instituted the ordinance of Christian baptism. But this law is silent on the subject of infants. Has not Christ, however, left some other command enjoining infant baptism? Not one. Have not the apostles who were entrusted with farther communications of the will of Christ, left some command on this subject? Not one. Have they not left us some example of infant baptism? Not one. Have they not spoken of baptized infants, and thus given undeniable intimations of this practice? No, in no instance. On the contrary, whenever they have spoken of baptism, or of those to whom it was administered, their language implies that baptism was a voluntary act of worship, and the baptized, professing believers. "As many of you," says Paul to the Galatians, "as have been baptized into Christ, have put on Christ."

6.—FOLLOWING CHRIST IN BAPTISM.

JOSEPH FREEMAN.

Once convinced that our Saviour was immersed, and the devoted Christian, at times, at least, and those times, too, the sweetest, the happiest and the holiest of his earthly being, will look towards the baptismal waters with feelings of inexpressible interest and complacency. Whatever of gratitude for the bestowment of the richest blessings, purchased at a most extraordinary and awful sacrifice; whatever of admiration for the most singular and unparalleled manifestation of disinterested benevolence; whatever of love for the most exalted worth, embodied and personified in a Being sustaining towards us the most interesting and endearing relationship possible; whatever of veneration for a character of the greatest richness, elevation and majesty, joined with the greatest simplicity, humility and plainness; whatever of all these feelings the Christian possesses, in his purest and most heavenly moments, will prompt him, in this, as well as other duties, to walk in the footsteps of his Master, and seek the place where Jesus lay. Talk to him of the inconveniences of this ordinance! You do but remind him of the trials and sufferings of his

M. P. Jewett

Principal of Judson Female Institute, Marion, Ala.

Lord, and lead him the more joyfully to embrace an opportunity of testifying his gratitude to him who patiently endured the infinitely greater *inconveniences* of the *garden* and the *cross*. "Inconveniences!" he will exclaim, "inconveniences. Indulgent God! the disciples of a crucified Saviour talk of the inconveniences of being buried *with him* in baptism! No, let me, even in this particular, endeavor to be like him. Was Christ immersed? In vain, then, do you seek to persuade me that some other way will do as well. I want no other way. Since this has been honored and adorned by the footsteps of my Master, it is the way I choose. If, as you say, it is not required, it is at least permitted. And thanks to thy name, thou once crucified, but now exalted and glorious High-Priest of my profession, that one so low, so deeply indebted, so insignificant and unworthy, in token of the love he bears thee, is permitted to descend into thy emblematic grave! that I am suffered thus to testify to the world which crucified thee that I am dead to it for ever. And as I arise from my emblematic burial, grant me strength to enter upon a life, of which thou shalt be the end and the inspiration."

7.—RESPONSIBILITY OF BAPTIZED CHRISTIANS.

MILO P. JEWETT.

THE significancy of baptism, and the obligation under which its reception lays its subjects, afford conclusive proof that it should be applied only to believers. On examining the Acts of the Apostles, we find baptism everywhere regarded as a public profession of faith in the Lord Jesus Christ. Those "who gladly received the word were baptized." So Crispus and many of the Corinthians hearing, "believed and were baptized." Hence, baptism is considered the solemn initiatory rite of admission into the Christian church. As soon as a person was baptized, he was called a "saint," a "disciple," a "believer." So, by baptism, we sacredly bind ourselves to believe the doctrines of the Saviour, to obey his precepts, to lead pious and godly lives, after his example. Paul says, "As many of you as have been baptized into Christ, *have put on Christ;*" that is, are Christians, and are therefore bound to confess him for your Lord and Master, to obey him, and to follow his example. Peter calls baptism "*the answer of a good conscience towards God.*" The meaning of the word here rendered "answer," is, engagement, pledge, or promise, and so denotes any solemn obligation which one assumes before God. The idea of the apostle is, by baptism we take upon ourselves the sacred obligation, in the presence of God, to maintain a good conscience, to be watchful against sin, and to strive after holiness. As the Israelites, being baptized unto Moses in the cloud and in the sea, submitted themselves to his authority and guidance; so baptism into the name of Christ is an oath of allegiance to him as a Sovereign; it is a *devotement* to him, a voluntary yielding up of the whole body and spirit a "living sacrifice" to his glory. It gives a beautiful and strong expression to the feelings of the Christian, who can say :—

"Were the whole realm of nature mine,
That were a present far too small;
Love so amazing, so divine,
Demands my soul, my life, my all."

But nothing but the baptism of holiness can meet the representations here given. Infants cannot profess their faith, or put on Christ, or acknowledge their obligations to maintain the answer of a good conscience, or practise the self-devotement, which is required of the baptized. And yet all these are exhibited in the New Testament as essential to the nature of baptism.

The New Testament also represents baptism to be emblematical of the death and resurrection of Christ. "Know ye not that so many of us as were baptized into Jesus Christ, were baptized into his *death?*" or did, by our baptism, acknowledge his death, as declared in the gospel? "Buried with him in baptism, wherein," or, in which emblem, "also ye are risen with him, through faith of the operation of God, who hath raised him from the dead." Here the apostle associates our being quickened or rising to a holy life, with Christ's rising from the grave. And he reminds us of the source of all our hopes, "having forgiven your trespasses," by reminding us of the significant and solemn act by which we publicly devote ourselves to the Saviour, "being buried with him in baptism."

Baptism is also significant of the belief of the subject of it in the resurrection of the body. "Else, what shall they do who are baptized for the dead? If the dead rise not, why are they then baptized for the dead?"—1 Cor. xv. 29. That is, if there shall be no resurrection, why do the followers of Christ, by their very baptism, profess their belief in the doctrine of the resurrection? And why is baptism so significant a sign of our dying and rising again?

But what avails all this fulness of meaning, this richness and preciousness of instruction in the gospel ordinance, if it is to be thrown away upon unconscious infancy? But if only those who believe are proper recipients of the ordinance, then indeed can we perceive it to be instructive, impressive, and delightful.

8.—THE MANIFESTATIONS OF RELIGION.

G. KEELY.

A RENEWED heart is the germ of a righteous life. Many form inaccurate opinions of this subject. It is generally supposed by unbelievers that those who enforce the doctrines of grace, understand faith as a kind of prospect, which secures the passage of him who possesses it, irrespective of any thing else, safe to heaven; and hence they say, tell us no more of this faith, but urge good works! Such individuals, whatever else they know, are ignorant of even the rudiments of Christianity. Allow us a fair comparison, and we will hazard every thing upon the result. Take, for instance, the best on each side—or the worst if you please—and if the conviction, upon comparison of their lives, be not in favor of those who hold the doctrine of salvation by grace, through faith, we are silent. The fact is, and it has been conceded by competent judges, that faith is the most powerful and most operative principle that can influence man. "The grace of God, which bringeth salvation, hath appeared unto all men, teaching us that, denying ungodly and worldly lusts, we should live soberly, righteously, and godly in this present world." Men frequently refer us, with seeming confidence, to those amiable persons who, by the influence of moral training, or the mild temperature of their fluids, practise, with great punctuality, the social virtues, but who live unmoved by the love and grace of the gospel, and uninfluenced by religious institutions, and ask, "What can Christianity do for them. Are they not every thing we could wish? They need no conversion nor other influence than they possess." I reply, while such persons claim our esteem and regard we are not backward to give our opinion of their state. What are the social virtues as to importance, when com-pained with love to God, and devotedness of heart and life to his service? The inequality between our duty to him, and what we owe to our fellow-men, is as great as the difference between his nature and theirs. These amiable moralists must live without God in the world, or they could not be indifferent to his revealed will. Nor is this all. Our actions take their character, in the estimation of God, from our motives. An action, beneficial to men, may be offensive to God. A man may relieve an object in distress, while he feels no charity or compassion, but only wishes to obtain a reputation for liberality. You will not say God approves the act; you will not say the gift is not beneficial. The alternative supports the position—an action beneficial to man may be offensive to God. Again; you have a son; he is obedient; but you hear him interrogated, Why are you so punctual to do all your father's commands? He replies, I have no great respect for my father, but it is in his power to do me much good, or much injury, and I serve him for the good he may do me. Will his service secure your cordial approbation? Thus those who obey merely from a fear of future punishment, or from a mere expectation of meriting a reward; or practise the social virtues from a dislike of prostrating their moral reputation, though obedience from a base motive is preferable to vice, yet fall short of what God requires of man. If Christianity do not much for them, they are undone for ever. They need, and so do all, to be renewed in the spirit of their minds. But where love to God, and a sense of obligation to holy obedience, are inspired by a view of the riches of redeeming mercy, there God looks with approbation. "The love of Christ constraineth us; because we thus judge, that if one died for all, then were all dead, and that he died, that those who live should not henceforth live unto themselves, but unto him who died for them and rose again." Morality, without the sanctions and motives of revealed religion, is like a body from whence the spirit has taken its flight; it may retain its external form for a time, but it has the coldness of death, and nature will hasten its dissolution, and transform it into visible and palpable corruption. But he who is renewed in the spirit of his mind, feels the influence of holy motive, and cheerfully obeys from an ardent love to the moral character of God, a feeling of tender gratitude for redeeming mercy, and a conviction of the Divine right to challenge the obedience of the whole heart and mind. His life is like "a city set upon a hill, which cannot be hid." The congruity between his obligations and a free offering of all he is and can command, is felt in all its pervading influence as the ruling principle of the heart, and the prevailing habit of the life. "I thought," says he, "upon my ways, and turned my feet to thy testimonies. I made haste and delayed not to keep all thy commandments."

9.—GOD ACTING FOR HIS CHURCH.

E. E. T. TAYLOR.

A DISPOSITION and a delight to record the merciful dealings of the Lord, and to refresh the mind often with their remembrance by a frequent rehearsal, is a prominent feature of genuine piety. In this spirit Jacob erected his pillar at Bethel, and Samuel set up his Ebenezer at Mizpeh. With the same pious design, Moses composed his song on the passage of the Red Sea; and many of the Psalms were composed to keep in remembrance and perpetuate God's merciful dealings with his church. So at Antioch the church were gathered together to hear how God had prospered Paul and Barnabas in their mission.

Great things have been done for the church, the author of which is God himself, to whom is to be ascribed all the praise for them. It has sometimes been said that there is an improvement in man's moral nature, on account of which less divine power is required to bring it into subjection to the cross than was requisite in the days of the apostles. But it is true, and always will be, "the carnal mind is enmity with God;" an enmity no less bitter in the nineteenth than in the first century. The walls of adamant which inclose the sinner's heart, can be demolished with no other enginery than was used in the days of the apostles, when they went everywhere, the Lord working with them. In the accomplishment of the great things we have seen the church has not been idle. She has not slept and awoke and seen the change. Sacrifices have been made, and labor performed proportionate to the results. Let us then unitedly labor, and guard against abusing the mercies of God.

10.—ATTAINMENT OF SPIRITUAL STRENGTH.

W. G. CROCKER.

How, in our large churches, where individuals seem to have so little to do, shall they grow in grace, and instead of being weak, puny infants, blown about by every wind of doctrine, become strong, healthy men, prepared to endure hardness as good soldiers of Jesus Christ? The answer is evident. They must engage with all their powers in the conversion of the world. There are exigencies which demand all the energies of the church, and God has given this spirit of activity to meet these exigencies. He has made accessible hundreds of millions of our fellow-creatures, who are now perishing for lack of vision, and he calls upon every individual member of the church, to put forth all his efforts to save them. Do any wish to grow in grace, let them engage in this work with all their might. It is not by running after every new preacher, and taking up with every novel sentiment, that they will attain the faith and hope of primitive Christians; but by imitating their zeal in seeking to save a perishing world. Spiritual food is not what they need; they are in fact fed to the full. What they need is exercise; and for want of this they are moral dyspeptics, capricious and depraved in their appetites. Let the farmer, the mechanic, the merchant, and the professional man, set before him the conversion of the world as the great object for which he should employ his hands and his head; and his secular employment, which now proves a snare to drag him down to earth, would all contribute to his advancement in holiness. Then, by the daily exercise of his Christian graces, the spiritual food, furnished him by the ordinary privileges of the sanctuary, would be well digested, and his soul be in health and prosperity. Never, till Christians take this view of their duty, and act accordingly, shall we see the church shining forth in the beauty of holiness.

11.—CAUSES OF DECLENSION IN THE CHURCHES.

T. HUME.

We propose to state some of the causes of a declension of spirituality in our churches. And we find that one of these is, the character of much of the preaching of the present day. It is scarcely necessary to say, that the preaching of the word has been appointed, not only as one of the great conservative agencies of the church, but as a chief source of her nourishment and her strength. If then there be defect in this, its results must be sadly injurious. And must we not mournfully confess that such, in some respects, is the case? Has not carnal-mindedness made large demands upon the pulpit, which have been too often met, greatly to the dishonor of God's truth? We must be allowed to say, that it has succeeded in very many instances, to form and direct our ministrations with reference to one great end—*to become popular ministers.* And can there be a prevailing impulse more injurious to the minister of Jesus Christ, or more fruitful in evils to the church than this? How must he become popular? Shall he open the fountains of eternal truth, the clear streams of which only reflect the full image and form of guilty and polluted man? Rather, must he not affect the eloquence of words, the gorgeous display of language, the polish of manner, the neatly turned period, the fine-spun sentimentalism, or the skilful play upon the passions? Truth in the simplicity of her garb, must not be set forth to commend herself to the heart and conscience, but must be decked with meretricious ornament—that she may charm by a vicious loveliness. O, how must the spirituality of our churches die under such pestilential influences!

But there are other kinds of preaching, the tendency of which is, injuriously to affect the spirituality of those under its influence. Especially do we refer to that which omits the frequent and clear enforcement of the distinguishing doctrines of the gospel. We need not *preach error*, in order to secure its presence among the people of our charge. Let us *omit to preach the whole truth*, and we shall find error flourishing as in a congenial soil, and under propitious influences. Such omission will, of itself, throw out of joint and proportion the form of the gospel; will be an evisceration which will leave a putrid carcass to spread disease and death. Where are the enforcements to practical piety, where are the real and overpowering persuasives to a holy life, if not in the doctrines of the gospel? Shut out these, and we close up the fountains of life, and of strength to the church. We are so "old-fashioned," as to desire that the time may speedily return, when the ministrations of the pulpit shall be seasoned with sound doctrine as in the days of Flavel, and Howe, and Owen, and Bates. Otherwise we must expect that our church-members will attain at best but a slender growth, and that feebleness will mark all their demonstrations.

Another cause of the declension of spirituality in our churches, is the passion for their mere numerical increase. This feeling has a growing tendency in the present day. It needs but little argument to show that it is fruitful in the production of the most radical errors, and the most corrupting practices. Let us instance one error that it cherishes—namely, that professedly unconverted persons should become members of the church. Where will the evil stop, which proceeds from this mistaken and mischievous sentiment? Through the influences of it, the ordinances of the gospel are perverted—baptism becomes regeneration; the Lord's Supper, the elements of which are affirmed to be the body and blood of the Lord Jesus, "is life-sustaining;" and the administrators of these are a peculiar race of beings, whose "succession" is a question of life to the human family. Thus, false and ruinous issues upon the subject of religion are made up, and their assumed verity takes the place of every other question. From these things you turn, with a disgust which is only checked by the pity you feel for those thus deluded, and assert that the teaching of the Bible is contrary to all this, and that the distinguishing views we hold as a denomination, are very much based upon the sentiment that a profession of faith is essential to participation in the ordinances and membership in the church. We rejoice that this ground is occupied by us, and we are jealous of every influence that may in the least degree tend to remove us from it. Yet may we not fear that we have, in some respects, practically affiliated with the errors in question? Have not the terms of admission been softened; have not equivocal evidences of conversion been too often received; and has there not been indiscretion countenanced in gathering individuals into the church? If these things are true, in the least degree, they are to be lamented. And if they have prevailed, we have just occasion for alarm. Let us be cautioned. Let us correct the mistaken feeling that a mere numerical increase of our churches is a supreme object, and a real occasion for unmingled rejoicing. What is the addition of numbers without piety? As the swelling of the body with diseased flesh produces suffering and death, so must we fear that a similar unwholesome influence exists in our churches, causing their present sad declension, and threatening other and aggravated evils.

The evils lamented by us may be justly attributed to some of the means used to promote the revivals of religion. These demand more of specification and careful analyzation than we can devote to them at present. We shall involve a good deal, however, when we say, that some new and eccentric modes of preaching, some novel and attractive measures, and some very startling results, constitute the popular idea of a revival. The accomplishment of good in the church, whenever spoken of, carries forward the minds of many to "a protracted meeting," when as an integral part of the same, there are to be present some strangers, or rather some *strange men.* Then, without reference to the preparation of the church, and with a kind of confidence which is presumption, the conversion of souls is looked for as a matter of course. As a sure consequence of these efforts, all other means are apt to be despised, and a vitiated appetite is formed, the certain precursor of leanness and feebleness, because it loathes the substantial food of the gospel. Pastoral ministrations are rather endured than esteemed, unless, indeed, this perverted taste is consulted, and topics of hortatory address, and means of moving the passions, are used to the exclusion of closely studied exhibitions of the doctrines of the gospel, and a plain yet faithful enforcement of "the truth as in Jesus." The great evil of all these peculiarities is, that they tend to exclude those forms of action and influence, which gradually bring up a church from weakness to broad and deep efficiency. A kind of hot-house system will be adopted, and plants of an unnatural growth will fill up our churches, which will wither away, and be soon succeeded by desolation. We might trace these influences, and contemplate them in other respects, so as affectingly to confirm us in the opinion that revivals, so called, are often brought about, and sustained, by a course of means calculated seriously to affect the spirituality and real prosperity of our churches.

The only additional cause we shall now mention of the declension of the spirituality of our churches is—an undue regard for, and reliance upon, mere accessaries, such as wealth, worldly influence, and others of a like character. We have no objection that these should occupy their proper places in the churches. Let them be subordinated to more essential influences, and sanctified to the advancement of the Divine glory, and then they will have their real importance. But if these are regarded as matters of supreme necessity to the advancement of the cause of truth, there will follow a train of influences, subversive of the true power and glory of the churches of the Lord Jesus. A system of expediency, and a religion of formality, would work out the ruin of the church sooner than any other given causes; and these will inevitably prevail where there is undue regard for the things of which we now speak.

And in the feeling which prompts to these mistaken reliances, there is a spirit manifested which is fatally sure to secure the destruction of our churches. Does it not entail upon it the curse of Almighty God? is it not a self-sufficiency which his word denounces, the folly and guilt of which his judgments will awfully confirm? O, let us be instructed by the sad results which have ensued to others, and whose history teaches us, that nothing can more effectually secure the downfall of a people than their undue dependence upon mere worldly agencies.

12.—GOVERNMENT OF THE CHURCH.

W. B. MAXSON.

We must take heed how we govern the church of God. Our Lord usually called the church "the kingdom of God," and "the kingdom of heaven;" and he has not been less careful in providing for its government, than for its enlargement. The church is not permitted to make rules by which its members shall be disciplined, any more than to invent doctrines and institute ordinances. The scriptures afford all necessary instruction on this subject. On this point a responsibility as weighty as eternity rests upon the church. Her official members are made stewards of their Master's house. To them has he committed his treasures, to them has he given a charge to feed, instruct, and correct his children, and he will not fail to avenge the wrongs practised upon them. If we say, Our Lord delayeth his coming, and shall begin to beat our fellow-servants, he will come at a time when we look not for him; and he has informed us that we may expect no mercy at his hand. We have, therefore, no less need of caution in this particular, than in those already noticed. It should be impressed upon the mind of every member of the church, whose duty it is to judge in the church, that he take heed *how* he acts in the discharge of this duty. On this subject our attention is called to a number of particulars.

1. We should be faithful in noticing what may be

considered small deviations from the Christian character. Custom may have removed the reproach from some sins, and they may be termed trifling offences; but custom can never sanctify sin, or make right that which is wrong; nor can a perseverance in what is wrong ever bring our Lord to consent to it. We are not willing to resign the small pecuniary claims we hold against those with whom we have dealings, nor allow our property to be purloined in small articles, or pass unnoticed small insults upon our persons, or slight aspersions upon our characters. Why, then, should we be less particular with the interest and honor of our Divine Master, when they are committed to our care? God has said, "Thou shalt in any wise rebuke thy neighbor, and not suffer sin upon him."—Lev. xix. 17. The scriptures are a sufficient standard by which we may determine what is proper to be allowed in the church. These little unnoticed *foxes* spoil the tender vines of the church. They characterize the worldling, and point out to the observation of all, the loose professor of Christianity. Our own faults may not be urged as a reason for indulging others in theirs. This would be a mutual encouragement to sin, and a kind of mutual insurance against its consequences. Mutual faithfulness will promote the general health and the increase of the church.

2. In the government of the church we must be prompt. Faults should be noticed as soon as they are known. They are not likely to correct themselves; but will increase in strength and number, by letting them pass unnoticed. Besides, this, the worldling and the delinquent will be led to the conclusion, that such errors are intentionally tolerated in the church. If a sin be considered trifling, and a solitary individual only be concerned in it, if connived at, it will probably become general, until, by its long continuance, and the numbers implicated, it becomes hopeless to attempt a correction. In this manner have all the

corruptions of Christianity obtained their standing in the church. And thus the honor of religion, and the reputation of the church, materially suffer, and perhaps the unfortunate member perishes. It is therefore needful that the remedy be applied as soon as the disease appears.

3. We should be impartial in the government of the church. No person should be privileged to do wrong. In this particular we are exceedingly liable to err. It is difficult to reprove the faults of those whose friendship is needful to us, or whose relatives are numerous and honorable, or whose age and former usefulness entitle them to our particular regard. We may fear that a faithful course, in such cases, will result in the withdrawal of pecuniary assistance, or in family disaffection. But whatever may be the consequence, we must not forget the admonition, to "know no man after the flesh." The members of the church have equal right to justice. Although this equal administration of discipline may sometimes be painful, the health and prosperity of the church require it. To permit a faulty member to live in such a manner as to impoverish his own soul, and bring it to ruin, is a wrong method of manifesting our kind feelings, either for him or his connections. It is well known that persons in such circumstances do not wish to be reproved; but our covenant engagements bind us to do it; and if we neglect it, we shall incur the displeasure of our Master. The faithfulness of the prophet Nathan with king David, 2 Sam. xii. 7—14; Micaiah with Ahab, 1 Kings xxii. 17—21; and John the Baptist with Herod, are noble examples of Christian duty. "Open rebuke is better than secret love." And,

4. We must be meek, spiritual, and scriptural in the discipline of the church. "Brethren, if a man be overtaken in a fault, ye which are spiritual restore "such an one in the spirit of meekness; considering thyself, lest thou also be tempted."—Gal. vi. 1. To

be unkind or overbearing in such cases, would be the direct way to harden and disaffect the unfortunate brother. The object to be had in view in all our labors of this kind, should be to "gain our brother." And we should be scriptural in what we do. There have been many discipline makers, and many rules have been made for *what offences*, and in *what manner*, we shall deal with our delinquent brethren. But not much credit is due to those who have affected to be wise above what is written. The rules the scriptures give will be found, in the end, to be the best calculated to effect the desired object. We assume an awful responsibility when we depart from them. There are but few, comparatively, who are invulnerable to acts of kindness and a tender Christian solicitude. We must also be unwearied in our efforts to reclaim a wandering brother—not less so, than when we attend on a brother who may be sinking under a literal sickness. In this case, if the first or second dose of medicine prescribed for him has not the desired effect, we do not abandon him, to fall a prey to his disease; but persevere in our efforts while life remains. And should we be less patient and persevering in saving a soul from hell, than we are in restoring a body to health? Certainly not. And "he that converteth a sinner from the error of his way shall save a soul from death, and shall hide a multitude of sins."—James v. 20.

13.—ADVANTAGES OF CHRISTIAN DISCIPLINE.

W. WALKER.

THE discipline of a church, if it be conducted according to the law of Christ, will be characterized by harmony, simplicity, and regularity. That law leaves nothing doubtful, in respect either to the mode of disciplinary action, or to the spirit in which it should be performed. It points out distinctly, and in its natural order, whatever is to be done, together with the most direct and easy method to do it. Nothing complex or confused is contained in it, or can result from it. While it is understood, and its authority acknowledged, no difficulty need be apprehended. There can be little occasion of disagreement among those who have only to obey; little room for disorder, where every movement is described by a fixed rule. But suppose that rule to be disregarded, and every thing to be left to discretion. The discretion of a church is the discretion of all its members. These will be likely to differ widely in their views of the expediency and propriety of any proposed measure. Some, perhaps, will give the preference to a method of preaching, which, in the apprehension of others, must lead to most disastrous consequences. Complicated and difficult questions may arise, and lead to unprofitable strifes. Thus divided in judgment, and contending for the mastery, there is reason to fear that the decisions of the body may be swayed by party zeal, rather than by a conscientious regard to truth and righteousness.

In proportion to the strictness with which the discipline of a church is conformed to the Christian law, will be its effectiveness. That law prescribes the method which our Lord himself has judged most happily adapted to accomplish the ends in view. Who, then, will presume to say that his judgment was erroneous, and that some other method will answer equally well? Those who adopt another method, practically say this. Those who neglect to observe the rule, are guilty of this presumption. But, aside from the adaptation of the measures enjoined by the law to effect the objects which it contemplates, the fact that the disciplinary acts of the church are performed in strict obedience to that law, will give a force to its admonitions, and a weight to its censures, which it can derive from no other source. The church will feel a confidence in so acting, which could not otherwise be felt. A consciousness that, in what they do, they are sustained by Divine authority, will relieve the disciples from that hesitancy and indecision, which they may well manifest in pursuing a different course from that indicated in the rule. At the same time, the offender cannot but regard what is done in strict accordance with Christ's instructions, as having received already the highest possible sanction; in fact, as being done, in some sense, by Christ himself.

Among the advantages resulting from a faithful observance of the Christian law of discipline, the happy reflex influence, exerted upon all who have occasion to bear an active part in such discipline, ought not to be overlooked. Though they may be justly grieved, perhaps deeply injured, they can scarcely entertain a feeling of resentment towards the offender, while engaged in earnest and repeated efforts to promote his highest good. A service so Godlike is utterly incompatible with the indulgence of malevolent passions. In the due performance of that service, these passions must be restrained and held in check; and he who is thus acquiring the power to rule his own spirit, is at the same time attaining to a higher measure of greatness than he who taketh a city.

In short, a band of Christian disciples, yielding a consistent and uniform obedience to the foregoing rules, exhibits the most attractive combination of moral strength and moral beauty that this world can afford. Such a church is like a well-trained and victorious army. Skilled in the use of the spiritual armor, and accustomed to act in concert, its members, at the bidding of the Captain of their salvation, move forward in one unbroken phalanx to the conflict with the powers of darkness. In the name of Jehovah they set up their banners, and the weapons of their warfare are mighty, through God, to the pulling down of strongholds. Negligence, on the other hand, of the salutary rules of discipline ordained by Christ for the observance of his people, must inevitably be productive of disastrous results. By introducing corruption, disorder, and dissension into the churches, it will mar their beauty, and sap their strength, until rendered incapable of united, vigorous, and well direction, they are prepared to fall an easy prey to their enemies.

14.—REMOVALS OF CHURCH MEMBERS.

THOMAS F. CALDICOT.

It is the duty of churches to teach that all things be done, and the duty of members to do all things, for the glory of God. It is the duty of churches to inculcate, and of members to resolve, that they will seek first the kingdom of God in the increase and prosperity of Zion. These are the conditions of their discipleship, the fruit of their union to Christ; the performance of penitential and baptismal vows; the reasonable service of creatures who are redeemed with a price, who are no longer their own, but are saved by a love that constrains them to live no longer to themselves, but unto Him who died for them.

Christianity is organized for the very purpose of its promotion and extension. Christians become a part of this organization—the church—for the express purpose of being used for its prosperity. They first give themselves to the Lord, and then to his people; thus they relinquish their individual selfish interests to the greater interests of the church of God. The church, through her ministers, should instruct them how to do this—and it is their duty to hear and obey such instruction. This is especially necessary in the removals of members from one place to another; such removals are very frequent, and they are frequently the cause of important effects, both to the churches and the individuals themselves—and not unfrequently do they produce *such* results.

Churches and members should also make themselves well acquainted with the influence of this wide-spread habit. It is frequently injurious to the churches which they leave. Many once flourishing churches—churches that were exerting a salutary and powerful influence around them, that were doing nobly for the cause of benevolence—have become feeble, inefficient, scarcely able to sustain the means of grace among themselves, much less to do any thing toward extending the Redeemer's kingdom abroad, and not from a lack of talent or faithfulness on the part of the minister, or devotion on the part of the church; but solely by the removal of members to places more congenial to their tastes, or that promised more effectually to promote their own pecuniary interests. The members that more generally remove from our cities and large towns, to find a pleasanter and cheaper abode in the country, are the men to whom the church looked for pecuniary support—on whom she depended in the conference room and the Sabbath school. But by their removal, she has been exceedingly reduced, weakened, and has become almost a blank. But where have these members gone? what are they now doing for the cause of God? If they have gone to churches and places, where they were more needed, well! If they are doing more now to promote the interests of Zion, well! If the cause of God is more widely extended, well! If they have increased their facilities for doing good, and are doing it more effectually than before their removal, it is well! But if it be otherwise, then is there something radically wrong in this practice; for it is wrong for the disciples of Christ to retard, to injure his cause.

It is frequently injurious to the member who removes. If he go where there is no church, unless it be for the express purpose of planting one, he must suffer from the want of that spiritual culture which nothing but the public and social means of grace can supply. If he go where there is a church, and do not unite with it, and become as active and be as benevolent as when in the one he left, then he must suffer loss from want of spiritual companionship, and the practice of those religious duties which are essential to the health and vigor of the soul. If he be less active he will have less strength; if he be less benevolent, then does he subtract from the amount of his usefulness. Many individuals have by removal sundered themselves from the church of Christ. In all our cities, persons may be found who have come from the country for the sake of gain, not for the cause of Christ—who keep themselves unknown to others as the disciples of Jesus, and who, being separated from their own church, are in their influence a dead loss, or a positive injury to the cause of God.

15.—IMPORTANCE OF CHRISTIAN UNION.

DANIEL SHARP.

"MIND the same things." Never forget that union is strength; and that division is weakness. In his ever memorable farewell address to his countrymen, Washington said; "United we stand; divided we fall." And a far greater than Washington had said, "A house divided against itself cannot stand." "If ye bite and devour one another," says the apostle Paul, "take heed that ye be not consumed one of another." Such has been the experience of churches in all ages. And yet, with all these warnings against disunion, and all these incentives to union, and with all your own good principles and purposes ; you, my brethren, are not free from danger. There is so much of personal importance, and self-seeking, and self-will, even among good men, that you will all need to be vigilant, lest, in sustaining good objects, you do not seek your own self-glorification.

Hence the injunctions ; "If it be possible, live peaceably with all men. Let the peace of God rule in your hearts, to which ye are called in one body." Whenever you are tempted to strife, think of what your Saviour has said : "Blessed are the peace-makers, for they shall be called the children of God." A modest estimate of your own judgment and position ; a considerate regard for the feelings of your brethren ; a conviction of the evils which follow personal bickerings and insinuations, and of the great benefits which flow from dwelling together in unity ; will be sufficient to keep the peace, if you all cherish these sentiments and feelings. One Diotrephes, however, may destroy the peace of the church. It is a melancholy fact, that some men must be first, or they will do nothing. They will rule or rage ; and the misfortune is, they rage if they rule. May God preserve you from such good men. May you live in peace, and the God of love and peace will be with you.

16.—CHRISTIAN ZEAL CHERISHED BY ETERNITY.

M. J. RHEES.

We expect greater things than other men in the eternal world. Without considering the solemn fact, that the hopes of the unbeliever and hypocrite will all perish ; what are those hopes, if they should be realized ? Annihilation, or an eternity of sensual enjoyments, is the height of their desires or expectations. There is no joy arising from the love of God, the presence of Christ, the society of the redeemed, the worship and the work of heaven. These are not "dreamed of in their philosophy." But the Christian, though he cannot fully understand what God has prepared for him, can, with the eye of faith, gaze into the future, and in the light of revelation see the glory of the New Jerusalem. He can listen to the music of that song, which he is even now learning, and which is sung in perfect harmony by the redeemed out of every nation, kindred, tongue, and people—"Salvation to our God, which sitteth upon the throne, and to the Lamb." He looks upon the mansion prepared for him in his Father's house by his Advocate and Redeemer, and expects it to be his everlasting dwelling place. He expects, for he has God's promise that it shall be so, to be like Christ, to be with Christ, to be engaged more perfectly in serving and honoring Christ. He expects to understand more fully those things which are now beyond his comprehension; to see more clearly those things which are dim to his present vision; and to do in perfect purity those things which are now so much mingled with sin. Nor does he expect to be stationary in his heavenly condition, but anticipates the expansion of all his powers of intellect and heart, and their being filled, when most expanded, with the knowledge and love of God his Saviour. And as he stands before the throne, and casts his crown at Jesus' feet, and looks upon the glory of the Eternal, he expects to be drawn upward, and for ever upward, by the attractions of that glory, becoming for ever more and more assimilated to Jehovah himself. All this, yea, more than tongue can express, or heart conceive, we expect, if we are Christians. Ought not these things, then, to impel us to do more than others? They have their portion here; let them be devoted to temporal interests and pursuits. Their inheritance is here; let them contend and fight, and oppress each other to attain that inheritance. We, as Christians, should pursue a more excellent way. We should live like Christ, live for eternity, and never be satisfied till we awake in Christ's likeness.

17.—FORMS OF CHRISTIAN BENEVOLENCE.

G. I. MILES.

As the field of Christian effort is the world, the forms of benevolence must be diversified, as the aspect of human want and wo is varied. Hence at home and abroad, though all form one grand whole for the exhibition and exercise of Christian feeling and action, it is right there should be various objects to elicit them, and various channels in which they may flow. They are as wheels within a wheel, not one of which can be deficient without affecting the action of the whole. The want of the seemingly unimportant cog may derange the whole operation, or a failure to supply the sufficient oil, retard the proper movement. And, we may ask, with which can we dispense? Let one say with this, and he will soon discover in the saddened countenance of a valued coadjutor, that it would be sundering a chord from his heart upon which the love of his Saviour vibrates with thrilling pleasure, and his most cherished hopes depend, and to which he therefore clings with exquisite emotions of pious tenacity.

No, brethren, the times are too hard in this guilty world, to dry up one channel through which pity and salvation may flow; too hard, to set aside one almoner of religious bounty; too gross the darkness, to extinguish one light; too heedless the passing throng, to summon one watchman from his post; and yet too inviting the field, to stay the hand of the sower or the reaper; too sweet and encouraging the promises, to hang one harp on the willow, or suffer any to sit by the river and weep; too fiercely also rages the battle, and too certain the conquest, to propose a truce, or call one warrior back, while we hear the great Captain say:—

"Fight on, my faithful band,
Nor fear the mortal blow;
Who first in such a warfare dies,
Shall speediest victory know."

18.—PRIMITIVE LOVE TO THE TRUTH.

HENRY DAVIS.

THE steadfastness and continuance of primitive Christians in the simple and unadulterated doctrine of the gospel, was a means of the rapid increase of Christ's kingdom. There is an energy in the doctrines of the gospel which is lost whenever any thing derived from other sources is mixed with it. It is the Gospel, as left by our Lord Jesus, unaided by any of the contrivances of men, which is to destroy all other systems of religion, and to fill the whole world. For this reason, God has most positively forbidden the intermixture of any human productions with its ordinances or with its doctrines. The system of religion published by Jesus Christ and his apostles, is perfect. Burden it with any additions, and its march is retarded. Take from it any of its simple rites, and its force is blunted. It is equally improper to strive to steady the ark of Christ, as it is to attempt to hurl it from its station.

The adherence of primitive Christians to the simple truths of Christianity, was a most powerful means of the rapid spread of the gospel. Doubtless, they were anxious that the kingdom of Christ should be extended, but this desire did not lead them to alter the gospel, that it might meet with a more ready reception. To render it more consonant with the feelings and superstitions of the Jews, they would not blend some of the ceremonies of the Mosaic law with its rites. They would not allow their Divine Master to be placed on a level with Moses and Elias. If Jews received Christ, they must renounce obedience to the ceremonies of Moses and the prophets, and must build the tabernacle of Jesus by itself. To render the gospel more agreeable to Pagans, primitive Christians did not mingle idolatrous customs with their religion. Pagan nations were commanded to turn from such vanities as their religion presented to the living God. They would not allow their Divine Master to be received at Rome, upon a level with the gods of the Pantheon. If Rome accepted Jesus, she must cast her "idols to the moles and to the bats," and must crown him "Lord of all."

The constant adherence of primitive believers to the doctrine of Christ, rendered them everywhere victorious. Rejecting all the armor furnished by the policy of this world, they took the weapons prepared and proved by the great Captain of salvation, and went forth to meet the enemies of the armies of Israel. Though the swords of the champions of idolatry had been glutted with the blood of philosophers and theorists, yet they could not reach the soldiers of the cross. Being guarded by the shield of faith, they quenched the fiery darts of the adversary. Wielding the sword of the Spirit, they conquered the enemies of Christ. This sword was not blunted by the sophistry of this world, but was quick and powerful, piercing even to the dividing asunder of soul and spirit, and to the joints and marrow, and was a discerner of the thoughts and intents of the heart.

The steadfastness of the primitive Christians in the plain doctrines of the gospel, could not be shaken by the most dreadful persecution. Every method which the malice of their enemies could devise, was tried to make them renounce their religion. "They had trials of cruel mockings and scourgings; yea, moreover, of bonds and imprisonment. They were stoned, they were sawn asunder, were tempted, were slain with the sword." In the midst of such direful persecutions, when agonizing in the flames or on the cross, life and its comforts were offered them if they would renounce the doctrines of Jesus. But on such terms they would not accept deliverance. Death, even in its most appalling forms, was preferred to a renunciation of that gospel, which to them had proved "the power of God unto salvation." Their enemies must have been astonished when they beheld their steadfastness, and frequently must have been convinced of the truth of that religion for which such sufferings were endured.

The opposition to the cause of Christ gained nothing by its greatness. Had primitive Christians been less steadfast in their attachment to the doctrine of the gospel, they would have been appalled at the number and hatred of their enemies. But being established in the faith, and preferring it to life itself, they were not afraid of them "that kill the body, and after that have no more that they can do." Had they been less established in the doctrine of Christ, they might have been induced to seek other means by which to appease their enemies. They might have had recourse to philosophy. Or, like Peter, when his Divine Master was attacked, they might have drawn the carnal sword against their enemies. Had they done thus, defeat would have been inevitable. It was not by false philosophy, or by the sword, that God had designed to spread the gospel. But while primitive Christians wrestled "against principalities, against powers, against the rulers of the darkness of this world, against spiritual wickedness in high places," "being rooted and grounded in the faith," taking to themselves the whole armor of God, and casting away all the weapons of this world, they stood invincible and victorious.

But the steadfastness of primitive Christians enabled them not only to suffer, but to *contend* "earnestly for the faith." Had they been less established in the gospel, never would they have ventured to declare it, in the face of such imminent danger. Had they possessed but a slight conviction of its truth, they would have sought to conceal their sentiments, or to exchange them for less dangerous ones. But, being steadfast in the faith, they ever "spake the word of God with boldness." It was this steadfastness that emboldened Peter and John to charge the Jews with having crucified the Lord Jesus. It enabled them to declare that Jesus was the only Saviour, and that "there is no other name under heaven, given among men, whereby we must be saved." The steadfastness of Paul led him to preach boldly at Damascus and at Jerusalem, in the name of Jesus. It caused him to stand with confidence before Felix, and to preach till the tyrant "trembled."

19.—DECLINE OF CHRISTIAN ZEAL.

HORACE FLETCHER.

How painful to look abroad over the church at the present day, and to perceive how few professing Christians, yielding to the entreaty of the apostle, have laid themselves upon the altar of God a living sacrifice! How faint and dim seems the impress of discipleship! How few seem to have any just conceptions of the extent of the obligations imposed by the name they bear! But it was not always thus. The time was when Christians acted under a full and lively consciousness of their responsibilities. You are all familiar with that stern fidelity of the early Christians, which, after lives of unwearied, unslumbering activity in the cause of Christ, fearlessly incurred the most revolting death. Such was the zeal and sacrificing spirit of Paul and his fellow-laborers, that they filled the world with the news of salvation through a crucified, but risen Saviour, in the brief period of their lives. It has been truly said that they "possessed the grand secret of giving up all for Christ, and yet accounting themselves rich." And is it from such Christians that we profess to have descended? Is it true that the cause for which they toiled and died has been committed to our custody? And who has exempted us from a life of equal devotedness? Where are our vouchers that we have the privilege of wasting life in idleness and inaction, or in the eager and exclusive pursuit of the world, while the early friends of the same precious cause toiled and died to spread its triumphs? Will any one say that we have less to do? When did this fallen world need more the salt of Christianity than at the present time? When before did it seem so much like one vast grave of piety? When before did sin and its concomitant woes so emphatically convert this world into a valley of tears? When before did the pestilential and poisonous malaria of sin so fearfully threaten the extinction of the last principle of piety, and the death of every plant of grace? Aside from the appalling condition of Christendom—enough truly to sicken the heart of devotion—think of the teeming millions who are perishing for "lack of vision;" upon whose ears has never fallen a single accent of mercy and salvation. There are doubtless more heathen now in the world than at any previous period. What a comment is this, my brethren, upon the zeal and activity of modern discipleship—of modern Christianity? If the spirit of primitive consecration had descended with the name which the disciples first took at Antioch, would eighteen centuries have gone by, and still three-fourths of the world be enveloped in pagan darkness, and its miserable population remain unblessed with the light and the hopes of the gospel? The zeal which once filled the world with the news of salvation, had it been perpetuated, would never have rested, until the banner of the cross had waved in triumph from "sea to sea, and from the river to the ends of the earth." With what feelings, brethren, do we who have done so little, anticipate a meeting with those faithful, ancient disciples of the same Lord and Master? If they are now permitted to look down upon the prevalence and ravages of sin in the lost world they once toiled to save, how little could they discover of that aggressive war upon the dominions of darkness, which they once prosecuted with such untiring and successful vigor! How many places would they discover, where they once planted the standard of the cross—where flourishing churches of primitive zeal and piety were established—that have been reconquered and made trophies to the prince of darkness! At Ephesus, where, in apostolic times, a Christian church sent forth its radiance, instead of the banner of the cross, may now be seen the turban of the Turk and the crescent of the false prophet. Look at Corinth, Colosse, Philippi, Galatia, Thessalonica and Laodicea, and you will perceive that not only has Time been busy with his corrosions and desolations, but the decline and extinction of Christianity will furnish abundant cause for weeping over the disappearance of that Christian zeal and heroism which early lifted high the banner of the cross, and there planted the lofty standard.

20.—WASHING THE FEET OF CHRISTIANS.

J. L. DAGG.

A PROOF that the washing of feet performed by our Saviour was a part and specimen of a whole class of duties, may also be derived from a passage, John xiii. 8—"Peter saith unto him, Thou shalt never wash my feet. Jesus answered him, If I wash thee not, thou hast no part with me." The true import of this passage seems to be—If I may not wash thy feet, (so the word here used implies,) I may not, on the same ground, render to thee any of the great benefits resulting from my humiliation, in which I came not to be ministered unto, but to minister, and to give my life a ransom for many. If I may not perform to thee acts of condescending kindness, thou hast no part with me. As, in this declaration, the washing of Peter's feet was made by the Saviour a specimen and representative of all his acts of condescending kindness; so the washing of feet, enjoined upon Peter and his fellow-apostles, was intended to include all the acts of condescending kindness which they could perform towards their brethren. "A new commandment I give unto you, that ye love one another; as I have loved you, that ye also love one another."

If, after a careful consideration of the subject, we have satisfactorily ascertained that our Saviour designed that his disciples should perform towards each other every needful act of condescending kindness, even the smallest and most servile, let us be ready with promptness and pleasure to fulfil his will. If we know these things, happy are we if we do them. If we have the spirit of Christ, we shall be ready, when need requires, to lay down our lives for our brethren, or give them a cup of cold water, or wash their feet, or render them any other comfort. In so far as by any of these means we seek to promote the happiness of a disciple of Christ, our good deeds will be remembered; and the great Judge in the last day, omitting all mention of our most labored religious ceremonies, will bring that act of kindness to mind, and will say, "Inasmuch as ye did it to one of the least of these, my brethren, ye did it unto me."

21.—CHARACTER OF THE BAPTISTS.

T. C. TEASDALE.

The Baptist denomination, to which we happily belong, my brethren, commends itself to the filial veneration and favorable acceptance of all, by many powerful arguments, and many affecting claims. What has been so confidently asserted of another church, may be said with much greater truthfulness of our own—"She is Apostolical in her ministry, pure in her doctrine, and beautiful in all her forms." She has always aimed to follow most scrupulously the divine model, even as Moses followed the pattern shown him in the mount. She has never been willing to bow down at the shrine of mere human authority in matters purely religious; nor to venerate the traditions of erring religionists, as though they were the commandments of God. Requiring a "thus saith the Lord" for all her practices, she has been happily exempt from the whims and fancies of fallible mortals, and her distinguishing performances have been as immutable and uniform as the essential principles from which they are derived. Herself entirely free from a spirit of persecution, she has been subjected to the most cruel sufferings which the ingenuity of men and devils could invent. More than any other people, the Baptists have experienced the truth of the Saviour's declaration—"If they have persecuted me, they will also persecute you." But notwithstanding they have been thus afflicted and abused, they have maintained a steadfast adherence to their distinguishing doctrines and practices, and have evinced a moderation and charity, which cannot fail to command the highest respect and veneration of every intelligent and unbiased mind. Well established in the truth and excellence of their principles, they commend them in kindness to all, but desire not to force them upon any. A fundamental principle in the constitution of the Baptist church is, that the Christian dispensation acknowledges no tie which can unite a human being to the visible kingdom of God on earth, except a voluntary profession of faith in Christ. This involves, as an essential part of true Christianity, the idea of religious liberty. No one can be *forced* to a voluntary profession, to a cheerful obedience. Hence results the sentiment, that the magistrate has no right to interfere in the affairs of conscience—hence the disconnection of the church and the state. This, too, of course, excludes infant baptism in the present dispensation, which is adapted only to intelligent, free, responsible beings."

22.—PECULIARITIES OF THE BAPTISTS.

SEWALL S. CUTTING.

WE claim that the position of Baptists is defined by a harmony with man's intellectual and moral constitution, and by a development of the idea of the Reformation. If others claim that we occupy this position in common with themselves, and inquire, where then are we peculiar? we reply, that our peculiarities consist in our adherence to this position *in those points where they abandon it.* We suffer no legal enactments to violate the freedom of individual choice; we deny that any man may rightfully create for his child a bond of union to the church of Christ, in which that child had no voluntary part, and for our culture and polity we rely upon the Bible alone, and upon the Bible interpreted independently of ecclesiastical authority. These are our peculiarities. By these we demand to be judged—and by these we stand or fall.

It has been said that we should find it difficult to impress upon the public mind, that Baptists are greatly peculiar in any thing except their demand for immersion, and restriction of communion at the Lord's supper to their own order. Charity will overlook the misconceptions of those who are ignorant of the facts of the case. But, for the candor of the man, who, claiming a sufficient measure of intelligence to comprehend principles, can affirm these to be our peculiarities, we entertain little respect. We hold that immersion is the baptism which was practised by our Lord and his apostles, and is taught in the word of God. But thus hold the Greek and Asiatic churches; thus have they ever held. Indeed, it is believed, that at this day *the majority of the Christian world practises immersion.* This is the baptism universally found, save in those regions which have been devastated by the superstitions of the Nicene period, and the subsequent tread of the giant foot of Romanism.

We believe that our principles belong to the truth as in Jesus, and we have faith in their prevalence. The elements of religious difference are resolving themselves into a very simple issue. On the one extreme stands the Roman Catholic, claiming that the church is a divine institution clothed with authoritative powers—on the other the Baptist, recognizing the Bible alone as supreme, and the individual conscience as its interpreter—the middle ground being occupied by those who approximate the one or the other. Every great collision of the religious world advances our views. We may retire from the strife, and as spectators of the battle scene, behold their triumph. Our principles will survive. These principles indicated their workings, while as yet the name we bear was not used to designate a sect, and these principles, we have not a doubt, will live, when all sects shall have become merged in the one Christian church—the church one in form as well as spirit—and humanity shall reach the high destiny to which the redemption in Christ Jesus so rapidly advances it.

23.—IMPORTANCE OF CHURCH DISCIPLINE.

A. W. CHAMBLISS.

THE discipline of the church in primitive times was exceedingly strict. In the estimation of the apostle, who was inspired to prescribe rules for the regulation of the house of God, it was a sufficient ground of excommunication, that a member was the cause of dissensions and factions in the church; or that his deportment was calculated to bring scandal and reproach upon the cause of the Redeemer. Nor could it have been otherwise with him, who charged it as a crime upon the Jews, that the name of God had been blasphemed through them. He who taught others, must needs teach himself. He who blamed the Jewish church for so acting as to bring dishonor upon the Divine glory, could not allow such conduct in Christian churches as would cause the name and the way of Christ to be evil spoken of.

In the Apocalyptic vision, the Spirit said to the Ephesian church, by way of commendation, "Thou canst not bear them which are evil."—Rev. ii. 2. This was honor enough for one church; and it formed a striking contrast to the rebuke which the same Spirit administered to the church at Pergamos—"I have a few things against thee, because thou hast there them which hold the doctrine of Balaam, who taught Balak to cast a stumbling-block before the children of Israel, and to eat things sacrificed unto idols, and to commit fornication. So hast thou also them that hold the doctrine of the Nicolaitanes, which thing I hate "—verses 14, 15. In this church were some base, mercenary souls—of a covetous, temporizing spirit, similar to ancient Balaam—who, for the sake of gain, did not scruple to sacrifice the best interests of the people of God. Also, were retained in the communion, some, who, under the notion of Christian liberty, did not hesitate to run into licentious indulgences—a set of Antinomians, who despised all rule and all authority—or, to use a modern phrase, who, "because they were free, claimed the privilege to do just as they pleased." The retention of such persons in the church, the Son of God said, "I hate." "Such serve not our Lord Jesus Christ." "Wherefore," said he, "repent," that is, reform, turn them out, "or else I will come unto thee quickly, and will fight against thee with the sword of my mouth."

It is a striking fact, which has doubtless occurred to every one familiar with ecclesiastical history, that the periods of the declension of pure and vital religion in the church, in all ages, and in all countries, have been characterized by a corresponding laxness in discipline; and that the revival of religion has been similarly characterized by a revival of the wholesome discipline which God has instituted for the government of his house. An example of this, worthy of attention, is recorded by Milner, the historian, in relation to the condition of the church in the third century. "It deserves to be remarked," says he, "that the first grand and general declension, after the primary effusion of the Divine Spirit, should be fixed about the middle of this century." The cause of this declension was the neglect of church discipline, as the Decian persecution was esteemed by Cyprian to be its chastisement. Cyprian was elected bishop in the year 248. He found the church, at that time, in a wretchedly lapsed and declining condition; and in a treatise concerning the lapse, he said: "If the cause of our miseries be investigated, the cure may be found. The Lord would have his family to be tried. And because long peace had corrupted the discipline divinely revealed to us, the heavenly chastisement hath raised up our faith, which had almost lain dormant: and when, by our sins, we had deserved to suffer still more, the merciful Lord hath so moderated all things, that the whole scene rather deserves the name of a trial, than a persecution." Here was the cause of the persecution; and here the consequence of inattention to the discipline of the church. Let it be neglected, and a blighting and a mildew will result, which will not fail, ere long, to induce the Divine judgment upon us.

If, therefore, the apostolic injunction—if the authority of the Son of God—if the testimony of ecclesiastical history—if all these together, have any weight—then, by them, "I beseech you, brethren, mark them which cause divisions and offences contrary to the doctrine which ye have learned, and avoid them; for they that are such serve not our Lord Jesus Christ."

24.—THE PURITAN FATHERS AND THE SANCTUARY.

N. N. WOOD.

OUR fathers, in coming to this land, were deeply impressed with the sentiment that the best possible security for their country, their hearths, and their homes, was the security which an enlightened sanctuary could give. Hence the wilderness soil was first warmed by their altar-fires. And as they went forth from the shores of the ocean to plant their homes, the sanctuary was the first beacon of settlement, and by its side was the school-house. The sanctuary was the radiant point around which they gathered their dwellings—it was the central bond of their feelings, and interests, and hopes. In the hour of danger and of dread, they gathered there for prayer. Was drought, or famine, or pestilence in the land, *there* from fervent lips went up the soul-sprung prayer. And when their sons and their strong men were upon the battle-field, the daughter and the matron and the aged sire were hastening to its sacred walls to lift up to a listening God their ardent prayer. And it was *there*, when the note of victory was heard, that the incense of a thousand grateful hearts ascended to "the Lord of Hosts," mingling with the solemn voice of prayer. A constant sense of the prime authority of God, and the proper dignity of man made them FREEMEN; and by this sense were they sustained in all their struggles for freedom. This sense was the latent inspiring principle which wrought out and diffused over our land all the distinguished blessings of a free people—and thus alone shall these blessings be perfected and perpetuated in all coming time.

But if a cloud ever do gather over our history—if God in his wrath shall ever will the subversion and ruin of this land, depend upon it, its first symptoms will be seen in a deserted and despised sanctuary, and a desecrated sabbath. And these, in turn, reacting upon their authors, will hasten and deepen the ruin—a ruin over which liberty and humanity would mourn—a ruin over which angels might weep.

Be careful, then, that the influence of the sanctuary go out and pervade our institutions, enter into the spirit of our laws, and sanctify the purposes of our people; and then we shall be bound together by a bond stronger and brighter than a chain of triple gold. We shall hedge around our land a tower of strength, surer and firmer than a fortress of adamant.

25.—THE HAPPY CHANGE.

J. S. BUZZELL.

I HAVE been standing on the walls of Zion watching for souls, and proclaiming this gospel, for five and forty years; and now, brethren, I know that I must soon come down—yes, my age assures me, being sixty-seven, I must soon come down, brethren; but not, I trust, I hope not, till I have seen Babylon, the mother of harlots, fall; not till I have stood long enough to preach a funeral sermon for Babylon, and pronounce it over her ruins. Oh! she must come down, and if I read prophecy aright, it must be very soon. Dear young brethren, pray for and aim at this great consummation. "As a young man marrieth a virgin, so have I married thee." Yes, the Lord Jesus married the church in these lands when she was a poor despised virgin; but see how beautiful she has grown now! I remember when all the people we could muster together amounted to only forty; now see what thousands assemble to worship and glorify their Lord! The watchmen are not to keep silence day or night. Not by *day;* I think this may refer to times of comparative prosperity; let us remember the church has had her dark times in this land. They were dark and difficult seasons when I traversed the woods forty years ago, with an eminent brother minister now in glory, and we threaded our way by the spotted trees through the forests, then uncut and uncleared, to search for persons to preach to, and places to preach in; when we used to lie down in the woods by night, in the blankets that covered our saddles for a bed, and the saddles themselves for a pillow. But, blessed be God, we kept not silence then—we kept not silence day or night; and I speak it for your encouragement, dear young brethren! it has often been found, and I have often felt it, that when ministers have their worst times in preaching, they have been really the most successful. I remember that on one occasion in particular, I was so shut up and so miserable in my own soul in preaching, that the words seemed as if they would not come forth—they were like icicles freezing in my mouth; but still I struggled on and on, and in the midst of my embarrassments, I secretly said to God, if he would but help me, and grant me but one, one soul for my hire, I would never be unbelieving again, as I had been when I begun; and lo! the result was fifty additions in a short time. Oh, keep not silence—go on, go on in your darkest times.

26.—IMPROVEMENT DERIVED FROM CHURCH HISTORY.

JOHN O. CHOULES.

How many of the good men who formerly composed this church, would be pained, if pain could enter heaven, to see those who bear their names and fill their places on earth, neglecting the great salvation, and even wanting the form of godliness! With some before me it is high time that they awake from their apathy on religious subjects, and become imitators of their worthy ancestors, who through faith and patience are now inheriting the promises.

I would ask the members of this church seriously to examine themselves, in order to ascertain if, under various administrations of the gospel of grace, they are really growing in grace and the knowledge of Jesus Christ. Has your faith been increased—your hope brightened—your love inflamed? Do you abound in good works? Are you found in the discharge of all the relative duties which devolve upon you in the closet, the family, the church, and the world?

The church of God in the present day has her station on commanding heights, and her prospects are more plain and glorious than in former ages. She is commanded to lift up her eyes, and behold the world white to the harvest; and, my beloved brethren, let us unite our energies with other churches in striving to propagate the gospel of Christ. In this sacred task, I pray you to remember that you are in holy fellowship; you become co-workers with the noble army of prophets, the goodly company of apostles—you unite in purpose with the glorious Redeemer, and you imitate the God of heaven himself.

If you feel thankful at the remembrance of God's goodness in raising up for you a succession of pastors and teachers, O show your gratitude by affording your prayers and support to the schools of the prophets. If vain complaints of the inutility of colleges and theological institutions were but superseded by fervent prayers that God would pour out his Spirit upon them, would it not be a blessed exchange? Let us pray and labor that in our denomination the ministry may be characterized by acknowledged piety and general information.

I cannot but congratulate you as a church and society, on the sweet peace which we are permitted to enjoy. Let our "camp" be marked by union, our "house" by brotherly love. Long may we be able to say with satisfaction to beholders, "Go round about Zion, tell the towers thereof, mark ye well her bulwarks, consider her palaces, that ye may tell it to the generation following!"

The aim of the gospel ministry is to "present every man perfect in Christ Jesus." I greatly fear that some of my dear hearers have never yet received the Saviour! The gospel has hitherto been to you only a savor of death unto death. You have had line upon line, precept upon precept, from one messenger after another; and the Master says, "What could I have done for you that I have not done?"

I feel much for your condition. You have heard much and thought but little of Jesus. I feel for you when I think of the march of death through this congregation. *There*, when I came, sat youth and health; and *there*, sat intelligence and virtue; and *there*, I saw the hope of heaven on the brow; and *there*, alas, but too much thoughtlessness of life's great end; and all, all have passed into the silence of the grave.

I see the king of terrors yet in our assembly; and I fear lest his sudden and sad summons should agonize your hearts before you have listened to my message. O, I "beseech you that you receive not the grace of God in vain."

27.—CLAIMS OF THE SABBATH SCHOOL.

W. C. CHILD.

If classes in the Sabbath School dwindle in number, and are irregular in attendance, the fault is not unfrequently in the teacher. It is generally found, that where the teacher is interested himself, his class will share in the same feeling, and if he succeed in interesting them, they will ordinarily be regular and constant in their places. It is not to be expected that scholars would attend the Sabbath school with pleasure and profit, if there was nothing in the spirit, or manner, or communications of the teacher, that would secure their attention, and elicit their love. On the contrary, it is not difficult to see how an attendance, in such circumstances, might be positively tedious to them, and how they might come to absent themselves altogether from the school.

But as a glowing piety, and a sense of the greatness of the object to be effected by the Sabbath school, will give ardor to the spirit in this work, it will generally be found to be the case that these characteristics will make successful teachers. In some cases, there may be, by nature, such disqualifications as nothing can remove, and in regard to them we must think that Providence decides what is duty; but these are the exceptions, and by no means the rule. Most Christians have the faculty of communicating such elementary truth as is taught to the young on the Sabbath; and unless they have lost simplicity of character in a wonderful degree, they will be able to interest them. But, as the faculty for giving instruction *can* be improved, and *is* improved, by exercise, even a want of the highest degree of success should not prove a source of discouragement to those who would engage in this enterprise.

Our churches must manifestly furnish teachers for our Sabbath schools. It were vain to expect the world to take the lead in this enterprise. This is the church's business. From her, as a centre, should go forth an illuminating and hallowing influence, which should operate upon all minds that come within her reach. If she is not to be depended upon entirely, in ordinary circumstances, we can have no encouragement to hope for the continuance of any scheme of usefulness.

If the church must supply teachers for the Sabbath school, in ordinary circumstances, and if devotion to God and a sense of the importance of the work must be the foundation of that interest which will secure and retain the services of teachers, we can see that our duty has reference to the church. If there be not sufficient devotion to God to induce our members to engage in this work, sad indeed is the state of things, and irremediable by any human power. But instrumentally, it is the duty of those who are interested in this work, together with the pastor, to present right views, touching this matter, and to render prominent the importance of this institution. Sermons should be preached with reference to it—Sabbath school concerts should be held, and other means employed, to create a correct sentiment in regard to this enterprise. In this manner, by familiarity with this department of Christian exertion, right views will come to prevail; and if they can be connected with a warm-hearted piety, we shall find no lack of teachers, if there are members enough in our churches.

Another thing it may be well to notice. The Sabbath school enterprise ordinarily seems to be given up to the younger part of the church. Now, is there any necessity for this? Is not the wisdom of experience and of age as important in this work as in any other? Is it not to be presumed that those who are parents themselves, if their circumstances will admit, will make as good, if not better teachers, than those who have had but comparatively little to do with training the minds of the young? It is well worthy of consideration, whether those who are in mature life should not be engaged in this cause. If they were, the force of their example, at least, would be afforded to secure and retain the co-operation of those who are younger.

Hence, the only way to secure and retain the services of teachers in our Sabbath schools, is, to excite a deeper interest in this institution throughout the church, and to enlist in the work of instruction all who are competent to teach. The first will be an *internal* stimulus, the stimulus of a glowing piety, enlightened by Divine truth; and the last will afford the powerful influence of example. In this way, the sentiment will come to be entertained, that the Sabbath school must be fostered and sustained by the *whole* church, and hence our members will come to feel that to engage in the work of instruction is an imperious duty, a duty required by the solemn vows which they have taken upon them to be God's.

JOSEPH BELCHER.

Edw[d] H. Fletcher, Publisher.

Lith of F. Michelin 180 Fulton St

28.—GOD THE AUTHOR OF PROSPERITY.

JOSEPH BELCHER.

It is scarcely possible, my brethren, to conceive of a scene more interesting than that of a great monarch, like the king of Israel, bowing, at the head of his people, before the throne of the Supreme Governor of the universe. Imagination here presents to our view the thousands of the descendants of Abraham, engaged in the public worship of Jehovah: some important event occupies their attention as a nation; they earnestly desire the prosperity of their country; and hence, their beloved sovereign, as the representative of the whole body, prays, "Save now, I beseech thee, O Lord: O Lord, I beseech thee, send now prosperity." It is ever important to remember that national prosperity is the gift of Heaven; and while statesmen devise means which appear adapted to promote extensive happiness, the Christian, who has been taught to feel a lively interest in the happiness of his fellow-men, and to desire the welfare of his native land, looks up to the Giver of all good for the blessing which alone can make the best selected means conducive to the desired end.

Nor is the prayer contained in our text exclusively appropriate to the Christian patriot. The principle on which the petition proceeds is applicable to us in our individual state, and to every connection we form in society. As He who possesses all good, is its sovereign and sole dispenser, we must ask it at his hands. In vain does man seek real happiness apart from God. Neither wealth, nor honor, nor pleasure, can contribute to our felicity without His blessing, who maketh rich, and addeth no sorrow. To Him, then, we entreat you to look for whatever may contribute to your personal enjoyment, or that of your families: God requires you to recognize him as the disposer of your affairs, and the author of your peace; if you fail in this duty, and are negligent in asking for his mercies, he frowns upon you—you are unhappy—and ultimately die, to endure his eternal wrath.

If the petition which forms our text be suitable for our adoption in reference to the enjoyments of individual and domestic life, it is not less appropriate for the use of good men in the expression of their best desires on behalf of the Christian church. Thus to describe our wishes for the happiness of Zion, is no abuse of the text; for it requires no ingenuity to prove that the inspired psalmist had his attention now directed to the period when Jehovah should bless the earth with the presence of his Son; who should establish a new kingdom, and favor the world with the knowledge and enjoyments which tend to convert its barren wastes into the garden of God.

And can any of you, my brethren, think of the advent of the Son of God—hear the interesting and sublime doctrines he published—see him offering himself as a sacrifice for sin—and rising from the dead to establish a spiritual and eternal kingdom, on the principles of the Divine glory, designed to illustrate the nature of his doctrine, and promote the best interests of the human race, without a most ardent prayer to Heaven, that this kingdom may flourish and extend itself, till every descendant of Adam be enrolled among its subjects, and share its blessings? From our hearts do we pity those unhappy men, who can contemplate the coming of Jesus into our world without shouting Hosanna to this son of David; or who can witness the commencement of his kingdom, without the most ardent desire that he may go on "conquering, and to conquer," till the whole earth become subject to his moral government.

While we pray for the peace of Jerusalem as a whole, we must have an especial regard to our own district of the city. As he is the best patriot, who diffuses happiness in his own immediate locality, so we regard that Christian as the most loyal subject of the King of Zion, who, while he entreats for the diffusion of the truth over the whole earth, especially seeks its interests within his own circle. When the wall of an ancient city was to be raised, every man built over against his own house.

29.—CHARACTER OF GENUINE REVIVALS.

A. BENNETT.

THE providence of God developed his purpose of mercy, and called forth human action. The agency of the church followed in the wake of Divine influence. In all these precious seasons of ingathering to the church of God, *He* led the way. He put his own sheep forth, but he went before them, and it was their joy and pleasure to follow him. The agency of the Holy Spirit was signally manifest in preparing the saints for their duty, and delightful labor in these revival seasons, and in reproving sinners for their unbelief, and in quickening and raising them up, prepared to sit together in heavenly places in Christ Jesus. The means employed were prayer, the ministration of the gospel, and ordinances of God's house, and exhortations, both from experienced Christians and young converts. All this was combined with united, extensive Christian effort, put forth in visiting from house to house, connected with personal appeals and fervent prayer, as far as practicable, in every family. The saints in addresses to the people, whether in the public exhibitions of the gospel, or in their social exhortations in the conference room, and family visits, did not approach them in a menacing tone, bearing down upon the impenitent, or backsliders, with a fault-finding, or even commanding style ; but with that penitent, subdued, affectionate, and expostulating manner, which reached the heart through the understanding. Or, if it did not reach the heart at once, it convinced the judgment, that the appeal was made by a friend, and from the best motives, while it was sustained by the most weighty reasons.

Instead of descending on the soul like an avalanche, carrying all before it with frowns and terrors, the address seemed to come *up* with the breathings of a heart stationed near the cross, or throne of God, with melting accents of kind entreaty, showing they were prompted by the Holy Spirit; so the proud sinner was reached, like Zaccheus in the tree, and called upon to *come down*, while the spirit and humble demeanor of the person who addressed him, presented a striking contrast to his own character, and seemed to challenge imitation.

By union of Christian effort, we do not mean any combination of influence by agreement, either among members of the same church, or of different churches, but a most hearty co-operation among the people of God, in the work, *as* the work of God, or as because it *was* the work of *God*. In neither of those great revivals mentioned in this discourse, it is not believed, the spirit or feeling to any great extent, prevailed, that it was a Baptist or Presbyterian revival, or that the revival was among any denomination as such, but among the citizens of Homer, *as sinners against God.*

The preaching in those revivals, was distinctly marked with that truth which vindicated God's government over his creatures, and charged the sinner with the guilt of violating his holy law. It was that kind of preaching which seemed more careful to please God, than to be approved of men; which showed the sinner that while his misery was the result of his own choice, his salvation and ultimate happiness depended entirely on God's choice. Of course it was his only hope and indispensable duty to repent and believe the gospel, and look to God through the atonement of Christ for pardon and justification as an act of his sovereign grace.

Convictions of sin were deep and pungent, both in saints and sinners, and at times it was hard to know in which they excelled, for backsliders returned in deed and in truth, and not in word only. The conviction of the sinner arose at first from a sight of his life; he had done wrong, and he feared justice, and awfully trembled in view of hell, but soon saw his heart was worse, much worse than his life had been, and was the seat of the difficulty, for it was enmity against God—that the imaginations of the thoughts of the heart were evil, and had been evil continually, and therefore there was no hope but in the *mercy* of God. Truth led them to discover, that nothing but the righteousness of Christ imputed to them, could give them such a character as they needed for acceptance with God, and even to enjoy pleasure themselves. The length of time conviction of sin continued, varied from one day to three weeks—generally from one to two weeks. It was not a common thing for a convicted sinner to find peace of mind in public meetings. Few, it is believed, dated their conversion in the conference room, or while others were praying with them. The greater number gained evidence of pardon from God, against whom they had sinned, while they were alone in humble prayer, reading the Bible, or in silent meditation.

The prevailing exercises of the converted were love, joy and peace. Love to God, as the Sovereign of the world; to Christ, as the Saviour of sinners; to the Bible, the people, and service of God. The holy law of God, which was their chief trouble before, now afforded exquisite delight. That very law which they found to be unto death, was now adopted as the rule of life, as the only rule by which they desired to walk; and its statutes became their song. They would often say, "O, how love I thy law, it is my meditation all the day." But Christ, the blessed Christ, was the theme on which all loved to dwell. Each seemed to vie with the other in adoring, extolling, honoring, loving, and praising Christ. He seemed to occupy most of the thoughts and affections, and out of the abundance of the heart the mouth spoke. Christ formed the ground of encouragement, and constituted the chief argument in prayer. Christ crucified occupied a large place in all the exhortations and addresses, in which the saints gave vent to their feelings in the public assembly, and by which they sought to win back their fellow-sinners from the paths of the destroyer.

30.—THE OBJECT OF THE CHRISTIAN MINISTRY.

R. E. PATTISON.

WHAT is the end of your mission? To the achievement of what object have you endured years of preparatory toil? To gain a name? You may gain one. But the most successful method will be to forget yourselves. Is it to cultivate in your church and congregation intelligence? or to promote general intelligence in the community? This would be a useful work, and the minister of the gospel can contribute much towards such a result. But this is not Christ's commission. It has not been on these subjects that your minds have been agitated with the question of duty. When, after much prayer, you came to the deliberate conclusion that Christ had a work for you to do in his church, and you, with much trembling, made a solemn covenant with him to do his will, was it that you should render a service of this kind? Was it not that you would do all in your power by preaching his gospel, to save men from sin and its serious consequences? I am confident that each heart responds to

.he latter. Do you inquire how this is to be done? On this subject a volume might be written? But there is one general principle, which, if rightly understood, and never lost sight of by you, will contribute much to your success.

If you would accomplish a good and great work, act on the principle that you are addressing the gospel to sinners who cannot be saved by mere moral corrections. Men are condemned sinners, and need pardon. They are the enemies of God by wicked works, and must be totally changed in their moral dispositions. They are not merely to be made better men, but they must become new men in Christ Jesus. The old doctrine, you must be born again, and except you be converted you cannot enter into the kingdom of heaven, should be your grand point. You must see every thing in this light and through this medium.

I would not be understood to intimate that the work of the minister terminates with the conversion of his hearers. This is a vicious doctrine, which, though avowed by none, is practically believed by too many, who act as if there was a strait gate, but no narrow way. My object is only to show, that however important it is to train the church in holy living, all efforts are vain if we start wrong. You cannot raise a church, or any portion of its members, from a sinful life, except as they have been converted by the Spirit of God. Do all that is in your power to educate them to a holy life, to invite them to imitate the Saviour; but rest your hope of success on the fact that they have been made alive in Christ.

You will not only find it necessary to have distinct views on this subject yourselves, and to keep them habitually before your own mind, but you will need to carefully enlighten the people on this point, and so to hold these doctrines before their minds, that they cannot lose sight of them. The greatest evil which has ever befallen Christianity has been the neglect of this doctrine. The line of demarkation between the converted and the unconverted has often been obliterated. Seriousness has been taken for piety; a profession, for faith in Christ; submission to the ordinances, a fulfilment of the conditions of salvation. In the administration of the ordinances, and in the reception of members to the church, while you should exercise the most tender Christian charity, you should also direct a *discerning* and searching eye to the religious affections, which are the fruits, and so the proofs, of the presence of the Spirit of God. Be not deceived; you cannot gather figs of thistles. You might as well attempt to educate a dead man, as to train an unconverted church to pious living.

These three points, therefore, I wish, brethren, to fix in your minds. It will require habitual progress in knowledge to sustain yourselves as preachers. Your studies, though not confined to theology proper, should have a concentrated bearing upon the duties of the ministry. And lastly, labor to secure the conversion of sinners to God, by faith in Christ, as the first step in religion, and as laying the only foundation for successfully training a church in practical piety. He who labors to make the people of his charge godly in life, before their hearts have been renewed by the grace of God, will do as little execution as he who explodes powder upon the surface of a rock. The heart must be penetrated by the Spirit and word of God.

31.—CLAIMS OF THE MINISTRY ON THE CHURCH.

J. J. FINCH.

THE duties of the ministry impose a corresponding duty on the church at large. When God commands the performance of any thing, the command embraces whatever is necessary to its accomplishment. He has commanded the preaching of the word—the preaching of the word to all men. But the word cannot be preached without preachers; how, then, are they to be obtained? God must provide them, is the answer, and this is true—but how does he provide them? Has Christian instrumentality nothing to do with it? God provides our daily bread, but has our activity nothing to do with its attainment? If we are instructed to pray for our daily bread, we are also instructed to pray the Lord of the harvest to send forth more laborers into the harvest.—Luke x. 2. But what a man prays for, he is bound to use proper means to secure; when a man prays for bread, he exerts himself to get it; and looks for an answer to his prayer, in the blessing of God *upon* his labors, which renders them successful. So when Christians ask the Lord to send forth ministers, if they would be consistent, they must seek them. Here is the point where Christians fail—they expect spiritual blessings in a manner totally different from that in which they get their temporal supplies. They offer a few cold prayers to God for ministers and grace, but do not labor for them; while they do not trust to such prayers, unaccompanied with exertion, for food and raiment. While, therefore, we rightly look to God to provide ministers, let us not overlook the means by which he operates in providing them. Christian labor and seminaries of learning, are among these means. God could as easily carry on his work without ministers, as he can provide ministers without Christian instrumentality. If as Christians, you say God has no need of your help, why may not ministers say the same? And if God converts sinners through the instrumentality of preachers, why may he not raise up preachers through the instrumentality of Christians? Christians, therefore, must admit *their* obligation in this matter, or say that the preaching of the gospel is not a *necessary* instrument in saving the souls of men; but as this would be a direct contradiction of the scriptures, no Christian can say it.

32.—DUTY OF THE CHURCH TO THE RISING MINISTRY.

R. RYLAND.

It is a principle established from time immemorial among our churches, that they have, in themselves, the privilege of investing with the sacred office any whom they may judge competent. This feature in our government, clearly recognized in the scriptures, and therefore dear to all our hearts, has still, in its operation, proved a source of perplexity. It has thrown on the churches a responsibility demanding greater wisdom and energy than many of them have exercised. It has been abused, by neglecting to encourage proper gifts, by sanctioning those that are unsuitable, and by not furnishing due facilities for the improvement of licentiates.

It is the duty of the churches to seek out and bring forward such young men as promise, by their piety and talents, to be useful in preaching the gospel. Shall I be told, that it is the exclusive province of "the Lord of the harvest," to send forth men to this work? This is not denied. But it is equally true, that the same Being convinces men of sin, subdues the pride of their hearts, and brings them into subjection to his Divine authority. Who believes, however, that this last doctrine supplants the necessity of pungent appeals to the consciences of men? It encourages and requires such appeals. He who feels the most dependence on the arm of the Almighty for success in his work, will always address the most urgent motives, the most pointed, affectionate, and powerful expostulations to the hearts of men. In like manner, we contend, that the Bible presents no view of a Divine call to the ministry, which renders it inconsistent, that suitable persons be urged to devote themselves to its labors. It may be assumed, as a religious axiom, that there is no duty which men ought to perform, that cannot be justly made the subject of exhortation. All the truths of the Bible belong to the church, and should be brought to bear on the minds of men, as incentives to action. Whatever it is right that a man should do, it is equally right that I should use suitable arguments to persuade him to do. Hence, when a church contains a member possessing useful talents, it is as much her duty to encourage him to exercise them, as it is to call on sinners to repent and believe the gospel. The whole arrangement of Divine grace is emphatically *a system of means.* Let our young men be taught the necessities of the world ; let them be enlisted in the Sabbath school enterprise ; let them be gathered into Bible classes ; let them be invited to speak in the social meeting. And should any of them exhibit signs of decided promise, let them be kindly cherished by the brethren. Instead of pursuing this course, we have too long acted on the presumption, that the duty of preaching the gospel is the only service to which man will yield himself unbidden. To all other sacrifices he must be allured by eloquent persuasion. But he must devote himself unaided to this delicate and responsible department of benevolence. What has been the consequence ? Men of fine sensibility and good talent often retire into the shade, and conceal themselves under the mantle of conscious unworthiness, while the presumptuous obtrude themselves into the awful work. Has not the cause of Christ lost many able defenders, and been annoyed by many feeble and arrogant upstarts, through this policy ? Human instrumentality is not inconsistent with Divine sovereignty in this matter. While, therefore, you pray for more laborers, remember, that prudent diligence must succeed prayer. That graceless men are, by corrupt establishments, introduced into the ministry merely as a means of livelihood, is not a good reason why we should fail to exhort holy men to come up to the help of the Lord.

33.—DUTIES OWING TO A PASTOR.

J. FLETCHER.

THE first duty of a church to its pastor is that of submission to his righteous and scriptural authority. That the exhortation addressed by Paul to the Hebrew believers, to obey them that had the rule over them was intended to refer to ministers, is evident from the fact that the word here expressive of authority corresponds with one of the titles applied to them—that of bishop or overseer; and that the churches are exhorted to remember them that had *spoken* to them the word of God, or, in other words, preached to them the gospel. Every one acknowledges a minister to be an officer, and a principal officer in the church; and an office without authority is a solecism. But the authority of a pastor is neither that of a lord, nor a lawgiver; but he is the organ of the Divine law, and possesses executive power. The rule, *then*, to which a church is required to yield obedience and subjection, is not the will of the *minister*, but the will of *Christ.* The minister goes forth as the ambassador of Christ, to enforce his laws, and preside over the interests of his militant kingdom. He is clothed with authority from the throne, and whosoever refuses to obey him, while he adheres to his written instructions, refuses to hear and obey Him that sent him.

It is the duty of the members of a church to attend regularly upon the ministrations of their pastor. The great object for which a church call and settle a pastor, is, that he may prepare for them from week to week a spiritual repast; and if he fails to do this, rather than treat his ministrations with contempt, and thus bring into disrepute the sacred office, let him be dismissed from his charge.

It is said by an eminent writer on etiquette, that "a dinner engagement should be regarded as particularly binding, and as imposing an obligation to be strictly punctual." But how many church members are there who, in such a case, would allow no ordinary incident to disappoint the expectations of a friend, and who, for no trifling reason, would violate the rules of etiquette; yet, for the slightest cause, do not hesitate to absent themselves from the spiritual repast prepared for them by their pastor, and thus treat him who has cherished the most anxious solicitude for their eternal welfare, and tasked his powers to the utmost for their good, as though he had no sensibility. Suppose a neighbor should express a wish to dine with you, and you had been at the trouble and expense of making suitable preparation, and fixing on a day named by himself—would it not wound your feelings were he subsequently to make another engagement for the same time, and comply therewith, to the neglect of the previous one? How, then, do you suppose the steward of the mysteries of God feels when you slight the entertainment which, by the direction of the Great Master of the feast, he has prepared, and in the preparation had special regard to your highest, your eternal interests?

It is not only the duty of church members to attend *upon* the ministrations of their pastor, but they should attend *to* them. Their decorous deportment and serious attention should evince an ardent desire to receive the truth in the love of it. No listlessness nor sleeping should be indulged during the solemnities of divine worship. A member of a church who sleeps under the dispensations of Divine truth, not only renders God a spiritless sacrifice, but offers a public insult to his pastor, and owes a public apology to the congregation.

3. Another duty of church members to this pastor is to remember him in their prayers. It indeed appears strange, that so plain a duty as this need be enjoined upon any church, or any Christian. We would naturally suppose if a professor of religion ever prayed *at all*, or for *any thing*, it would be for him from whom he expected spiritual instruction and Divine consolation. But alas! it is not so. How often do the members of our churches assemble together professedly for prayer, and offer their supplications before the throne, without *even remembering him* on whom rests the responsibility of feeding them with knowledge and understanding? Can such Christians feel their dependence upon Divine influences? Do they realize that, without Christ, their pastor can do nothing? The duty of a church to pray for their pastor is most forcibly enjoined by Divine authority. We hear an inspired apostle, with great importunity, saying, "I beseech you, brethren, for the Lord Jesus Christ's sake, and for the love of the Spirit, that ye strive together with me in your prayers to God for me!" As though the prayers of the church were of the greatest, yea, of the very last importance to the successful labors of a minister of the gospel, we hear even the chief of the apostles, with much entreaty, saying to the church at Thessalonica, "Finally, brethren, pray for us, that the word of the Lord may have free course and be glorified." Yea, these ancient preachers, though inspired, did not expect any *freedom* in their ministrations, without an interest in the prayers of the saints. Hence we hear them saying, "Pray for me, that *utterance* may be given to me, that I may open my mouth boldly to make known the mystery of the gospel." If, then, these inspired men

of God were so dependent on the Spirit's influences for success in preaching the gospel, and those influences were secured only in answer to the prayers of their brethren, how can the ministers of the present day even hope for a blessing to accompany their labors, unless the church help together by prayer to God for them? Oh then, my brethren, if you would have the labors of your pastor prove a blessing to you, and a blessing to the world, remember him in your prayers.

But remembering them who have the rule over you, who have spoken unto you the word of God, means something more than merely praying for them; or merely saying, "Be ye warmed, and be ye filled, while you give them not the things which are needful in this life." Hence we remark:—

4. That it is the duty of a church to give their minister a competent support. This is a duty founded upon the principles of common justice, and enforced by the express authority of the sacred scriptures. Hence the apostle reasons, "If we have sown unto you spiritual things, is it a great thing if we reap your carnal things?" If an individual should risk his life to save your child's, would it be too great a demand on your gratitude, for him to require of you the hospitalities of your house, or a suit of clothes even, if his necessities demanded? And shall the servant of God, who devotes all his energies to your spiritual benefit, and to the eternal salvation of your children, have less claim on your gratitude, than he who saved the life of your child? The duty of supporting a minister is enjoined upon the church, both under the old and the new dispensations.

34.—PASTORAL CLAIM TO SUPPORT.

W. WHITE.

It is your duty, individually, according to your several ability, to do what in you lies to make your pastor easy and comfortable, at least, in his circumstances; and where a church is wealthy, I do not see why a faithful and deserving minister should not be enabled to lay up something for his children. It ought to be remembered by a church, that such talent as is requisite to make an able minister, if given to business, would most likely secure an independence to the family of the person enjoying it; and can it be thought that a minister has not the same feelings for his children that you have, or that *his* children alone are doomed to be without partial aid? To withhold is unjust, for his time is as valuable as yours. If you will not labor one day without a compensation, is it reasonable or just, to expect your minister to give all his time and bodily strength to you without remuneration? Because it is his duty to preach, and he dare not disobey, are you at liberty to neglect him and leave him to starvation? Hard indeed would be the lot of the servants of God, if this was the order established by their great Master; hard indeed for the wife and babes of such a man; in that case, the popish doctrine of clerical celibacy ought to prevail, for marriage would prove a source of misery. It is to be feared that the pretended scruples of men to support the preachers of the gospel, originate more in avarice than in conscientiousness. This duty is enforced, Gal. vi. 6; 1 Cor. ix. 9, 11; Luke x. 7.

The passages relied on to prove they have no right to a support, have been wretchedly tortured; they are John x. 13, and Matt. x. 8. The first passage refers only to such as have no other motive for preaching, than "hire," or gain; and goes to show, not indeed that hire is unjust, but that a person actuated only by such motive will desert the gospel when it becomes his interest to do so. But will you compare such with one whose motive for preaching is love to souls, and draw an argument from it to his disadvantage? Strange reasoning this! The last passage has nothing to do with preaching without reward, but to the temper of mind which ought to actuate a man of God, and is designed to inculcate that he ought not to engage in the work with reluctance, but cheerfully and freely. But if ministers are bound freely to give, does this impair the obligation of Christians freely to impart to them all good things? Who would ever dream of inferring, if avarice were not concerned, that because one man is enjoined to be bountiful, this is exonerating all others from the duty?

It is your *interest* properly to sustain your pastor. In proportion as your minister has time to improve himself, he will improve his hearers; a judicious and well-informed ministry makes a well-informed people. An hour's conversation with the pastor of a church will show what sort of a people he presides over. It is your interest, because your means of support will be in the ratio of talent the preacher has. If the minister is instructive, his hearers will be numerous, and of course the burden of his support will be less felt. And this due support is your *honor*. No greater disgrace can be imagined than a church suffering their minister to want. How happy that servant of God who can, when interrogated, say, "I live among a liberal and affectionate people."

35.—THE SUPPORT OF THE MINISTRY.

J. F. HILLYER.

THE apostolic day is passed, the door of prophecy is closed, special miracles are at an end, the direct inspiration of the Holy Ghost is no longer to be looked for; and therefore, in all our church operations, God will use simple and ordinary means only. And apostolic usage establishes, that the church ought to support the ministry in whatever field they are called to labor. In the ninth chapter of the first epistle to the Corinthians, Paul claims this in language perfectly unequivocal. "For it is written in the law of Moses, thou shalt not muzzle the mouth of the ox that treadeth out the corn. If we have sown unto you spiritual things, is it a great thing if we shall reap your carnal things? Do ye not know that they which minister about holy things live of the things of the temple? and they which wait at the altar are partakers with the altar? Even so hath the Lord ordained that they which preach the gospel shall live of the gospel." It is true that he did not claim this from them, and that, upon the ground of expediency, he made the gospel without charge to them. But in his second epistle to these Corinthians, he says, "I robbed other churches, taking wages of them, to do you service. And when I was present with you, and wanted, I was chargeable to no man; for that which was lacking to me, the brethren which came from Macedonia supplied." This agrees with what he says to the Philippians: "Notwithstanding, ye have done well that ye did communicate with my afflictions. Now, ye Philippians, know also that in the beginning of the gospel, when I departed from Macedonia, no church communicated with me as concerning giving and receiving, but ye only. For even in Thessalonica ye sent once and again unto my necessities." These passages of scripture prove incontestably that it was the practice of this church to support Paul, wherever he went, while he preached the gospel to the heathen, in order that it might be without charge to them. The nature of things requires the establishment of this principle. We cannot expect the heathen to make the least contribution for an object of which they are totally ignorant, or to which they are, from force of education, violently opposed. Is it not, then, the duty of the churches to support those whom they send to preach the gospel in heathen lands? If God has ordained, "that they which preach the gospel, shall live of the gospel;" do we resist the decree of God when we send our contributions to our brethren in heathen countries? Paul calls it an odor of sweet smell, a sacrifice acceptable, well-pleasing to God. There are a few passages of scripture, very familiar indeed, but very forcible, in relation to the reward held in reservation for the cheerful giver. The subject of liberality is treated of at length in the eighth and ninth chapters of the second epistle to the Corinthians. Let them be carefully considered. "He which soweth sparingly shall reap also sparingly; and he which soweth bountifully, shall reap also bountifully." "God loveth a cheerful giver." "There is that scattereth, and yet increaseth; and there is that withholdeth more than is meet, but it tendeth to poverty." "The liberal soul shall be made fat, and he that watereth shall be watered also himself." "The liberal deviseth liberal things, and by liberal things shall he stand." "Will a man rob God? Yet ye have robbed me. But ye say, Wherein have we robbed thee? In tithes and offerings. Ye are cursed with a curse; for ye have robbed me, even this whole nation. Bring ye all the tithes into the store-house, that there may be meat in mine house, and prove me now herewith, saith the Lord of hosts, if I will not open the windows of heaven and pour you out a blessing, that there shall not be room enough to receive it."

As stewards of the manifold grace of God, we are required freely to minister the same to one another. Then, brethren, do not withhold your hands, do not restrain the generous emotion with which the theme may inspire your minds.

36.—CHRISTIANS CO-OPERATING WITH THEIR PASTORS.

S. P. HILL.

In order to render a pious and devoted minister's labors useful and efficient, there must be on the part of his people a spirit of sympathy, and of kind co-operation. He is but a man, a weak and imperfect man at best; a man of like passions with others. Take these things into consideration. Where you can, make allowance for him; put, if possible, the best construction upon his conduct; and try to uphold and guard his reputation. If this is taken away, the right arm of his influence is broken, the moral sinews of his strength are paralyzed. He must have a good report of them that are without, and his good name is infinitely more precious to him than the costliest ointment. Do not take it away from him. Do not watch for his halting. Do not wrest his words. Do not misrepresent his actions. Do not exaggerate his faults. Do not seek to pick flaws in his character. Do not make or listen to insinuations against his motives. Do not conspire against his peace. All this is unworthy of those who bear the Christian name, and directly contrary to the express commands of the word of God. Your minister, whoever he may be, is a man. Your kindness to him may make him a better and more useful man; but his faults, as I have somewhere lately seen it said, increase like snowballs, by being rolled about; and when you have once spoken against him, you feel compelled, right or wrong, to substantiate it. Try, therefore, to deal kindly and candidly with him. Encourage him. Come with your families, like Israel's tribes, to the house of God, and animate his heart, and your own, by the sublime spectacle of a thronged sanctuary. Go out and invite guests to come in, and throw open your doors with cordiality to the stranger. Fix the eye, and open the ear, enjoin silence, and, above all, seek for the preparation of the heart which is from the Lord, and your minister will be animated. But coldly enter, and carelessly sleep in the house of God, or lock up the heart in the gloomy and frozen cells of indifference and worldliness, and what zeal, though it be the zeal of a seraph, could survive in the midst of such discouragement? With an aching and broken heart, he would utter the mournful lamentation of the prophet: "I have labored in vain. I have spent my strength for nought." Unless a people sustain a minister by their sympathies, their prayers, their exertions, and their holy lives, his ministry will not be efficient, the church will not be in a prosperous condition. No preaching on earth could be rendered effectual under such circumstances. And though an angel from heaven should preach the gospel, which the imperfect man must now preach through much weakness of the flesh, still the effect would be the same. It is no difficult thing, and I fear no uncommon thing, for the members of a church to defeat entirely the great ends of the ministry in this way. The beloved John felt this, and therefore exhorted in his day: "Look to yourselves, that we lose not those things that we have wrought among you, but that we receive a full reward." The apostle felt this, and therefore cast himself on the prayers of the brethren, and besought the fellowship of their sympathy, so that the word of God might have free course, and run, and be glorified. The Lord Jesus himself refers to this, when he exhorts the church of Sardis to be watchful, and strengthen the things that remained, that were ready to die; for he had not found their works perfect before God.

37.—PRESENCE OF CHRIST WITH HIS MINISTERS.

S. F. SMITH.

To whom was the promise of our Saviour—"Lo, I am with you alway, even to the end of the world"—made? Who may expect to have Christ thus with them? We answer, beyond a doubt the eleven disciples, and others, if such there were, to whom the words were primarily addressed. If the five hundred brethren to whom Christ showed himself at once, before his ascension, were those who were assembled to witness his glorification, they might claim the promise till the last of them was dead. Years and years might pass away; the strange events of the Saviour's life and death might have vanished from the memory of man; the sacred feet which trod the steps of Jerusalem, and were pierced on Calvary, might have long forsaken their well-known paths; the polished Greek and the haughty Roman, the self-righteous Jew and the wise philosopher, might think, if they thought at all, of Jesus of Nazareth, as an impostor who once rose like a meteor on the world, and set again, and was now nearly forgotten; but as long as one of the disciples to whom the promise was made lingered on earth, fulfilling his part of the missionary covenant, so long the words of Christ were valid, "Lo, I am with you alway, even unto the end of the world." He is not a man that he should lie, nor the son of man that he should repent. Hath he said, and shall he not do it? Hath he spoken, and shall he not make it good? The Redeemer of men had said these words under the most solemn circumstances. He that cannot lie had left the words of this covenant, his last bequest to his friends and brethren, his apostles and followers. They understood them as containing the promise of his perpetual presence. They so acted on them, and they experienced the truth of what he had promised. On Mars Hill, in the dungeon of Philippi, in the castle of Damascus, in the court-prison at Rome, in perils oft, in hunger and thirst, in cold and nakedness, in perils by land and sea, in trials of cruel mockings and scourgings, the angel of his presence departed not from them. Under the solace of the Saviour's presence, they fought the good fight, they carried on a successful warfare, and are now enthroned, crowned, and glorified. "They rest from their labors, and their works do follow them."

But the covenant descends in its provisions to their heirs and successors. The first disciples could not finish the work. They who come after them, engaging in the work in the same spirit, and assenting to the conditions of the covenant, may expect the same succor. It is no more unlikely that Christ should extend his promise and fulfil it to a disciple, living five years after the apostles, entering into their work in their spirit, than that he should fulfil it to the apostles themselves. For it was one work, though extending through ages. Its nature is one. Its end is one. And if the promise was fulfilled to a disciple, an immediate successor of those who witnessed the ascension from Olivet, why should it not be to *his* successors also, down to the end of time? Jesus Christ having pledged his promise in the year 33, adheres to it to the end of the first century, and he will adhere to it till the end of the last. He who was with Paul, and Peter, and John, according to his promise, according to the terms of the same promise was with Swartz, and Brainerd, and Carey, and Boardman, and Martyn, and Gordon Hall; with the persecuted converts of Madagascar and of Burmah; and he will be with all their successors in the same enterprise and sufferings. Jesus Christ, the author of the promise, "Lo, I am with you alway," is "the same yesterday, to-day, and forever." When was the pledge annulled? When was the promise taken back? When, and under what circumstances, was it declared to the disciple that he must henceforth withdraw his confidence from his Master? Never—no, never. They, therefore, who take their lives in their hand and go to the heathen, may well depart in peace. We follow them with our benediction. It is all that we can do. We minister to their wants, at distant intervals sending them the pledges of our affection, and assuring them that they yet live in our hearts. But we cannot stand by, to bathe the fevered head, to cool the burning brow, to console the riven heart; we cannot weep with them precisely when they weep, or rejoice with them when they rejoice, or sympathize with them when they suffer. They may be consumed by the fires of persecution, subjected to indignities, torments, and death, and our hand is too weak to reach to their succor. They may be decaying in the grave, struck down by an early doom, long before we have ceased to pray for them. While we plead for them on earth, they may be rejoicing in heaven. But though they are removed from our sight, there is one from whose sight they are never removed. Our consolations may fail to reach them, but Jesus Christ, their Redeemer, their best friend, is with them always. In their trials, discouragements, privations, solitude, sickness, pain, persecution, sinking and dying—there he stands, with his gentle words, his benignant countenance, his affectionate interest in their welfare and their work, with his thoughts of love, with his sustaining strength, with his everlasting arm. And forever, amid the roarings of the tempest, or the tumult of victory and success, or amid the faintings of sinking nature, the music of his voice sounds like a melody from the skies, echoed and re-echoed without end—" Lo, I am with you alway."

38.—THE PRIMARY QUALIFICATION FOR THE MINISTRY.

W. HOOPER.

The Christian minister is supposed to have tasted the forgiving love of God, and in return to love God much because he has had much forgiven. Thus will he be constrained, by the strongest ties of gratitude to that Redeemer who saved him, and gave himself for him, and of love and pity to his fellow-sinners, to publish the proclamation of mercy, and as an ambassador for Christ, to make it the business of his life to beseech men to be reconciled to God. This love to Christ, begotten in the soul by his matchless love to us, constraining the soul to all acts of reciprocal love towards him and his cause, is the primary qualification of a Christian minister. When our Lord was just ready to ascend to heaven, and to delegate the care of his beloved flock to his apostles, that he might show them what he required as the most satisfactory evidence that they would be true to the sacred trust, he put to Peter that heart-moving interrogatory, " Simon, son of Jonas, lovest thou me?" Not satisfied with one assurance of his affection, he pursues Peter with the same searching inquiry, and extorts from him a second and a third solemn declaration of his devoted attachment. Then, at last, having taken a triple pledge of the apostle's love to himself, did he give over into his hands his blood-bought treasure. 'Here are the sheep for whom I laid down my life ; dear are they to me as the apple of mine eye ; to none but safe hands would I commit them ; take them, feed them ; guide them ; rule them with love ; protect them ; and finally present them all to me safe in heaven.' For the want of this love to Christ, no splendor of talents, no acquired learning, no eloquence, can compensate. Thus is a bishop to become "apt to teach," first by being himself taught from above the great doctrine of Christ crucified, and then, under the powerful constraint of pious duty to God, and of glowing charity to man, to teach to others what he has learned himself, under the tuition of the Holy Ghost. In other words, he must feel something of that holy necessity which impelled Peter to say to the Jewish rulers, in spite of their solemn prohibition, "We *cannot but speak* the things which we have seen and heard;" or which drew from Paul the emphatic declaration, "Necessity is laid upon me; yea, wo is me if I preach not the gospel;" and which made that apostle, while in the city of Ephesus, "cease not by the space of three years, to warn every one, night and day with tears."

39.—SELF-DENIAL OF THE CHRISTIAN MINISTER.

J. M. CARPENTER.

SELF-DENIAL is inseparable from, and indispensable to the Christian character. Between the men of this world and the disciples of Jesus, there must be drawn and maintained a distinct line of separation. The latter should be governed by different principles and maxims, cultivate different tastes and habits, and follow different pursuits. Even their secular calling should be prosecuted from different motives. In short, their whole lives should be such as to form a perfect contrast with the spirit of the world. Indeed, this principle should actuate them when opposed by their dearest earthly friends. Fathers and mothers, sisters and brothers, wives and children, are to be forsaken, when a compliance with their wishes will interfere with the claims and glory of Christ. In the observance of this duty, however, the private Christian is seldom under the necessity of sundering any tie which binds friend to friend. He can remain in the circle of his acquaintances and relatives, enjoy the society of affectionate parents and of others dear to his heart. He can continue in the church endeared to him as his spiritual birth-place, among the Christian brethren and fathers who sympathized with him when in deep distress for sin, and after he had experienced Divine forgiveness, and under the fostering care of the pastor, whose ministry was blessed to his conversion. Amidst all these he may live and labor, and acquire a comfortable subsistence, if not wealth; amidst these pass his seasons of joy and trial, die and be buried by those who care for him. It is not so with those called to minister in holy things. In addition to the self-denial incumbent on them, in common with their private brethren, they must sacrifice many of the endearments of life. Called of God, the conscientious minister feels that a wo is upon him, if he neglects or refuses to preach the gospel. He seeks direction from heaven. Divine Providence turns the attention of some church towards him. After much deliberation and prayer, he listens to their solicitation and becomes their pastor. Then comes the trying moment. All considerations which endear home to his heart, crowd into his mind. The thought of parting with affectionate friends and relatives, of leaving the church he first joined, and bidding farewell to his kind pastor, awaken in his bosom the most painful emotions. But the vows of God are upon him, and he must go, leaving all behind. He must go, perhaps across the ocean, to form new friendships among strangers. He must relinquish all lucrative pursuits, lest they so entangle him with the affairs of this life as to counteract his religious influence, and displease Him who hath called him to the ministry. His privations do not end here. That he may win souls to Christ, for Zion's sake he is destined to spend his days in adding sacrifice to sacrifice, from which other brethren are exempt. At last, probably, he must look back, on the verge of the grave, upon a fond and soon to be widowed companion, and fatherless children, unprovided with means of subsistence. And why are they to be left in such circumstances? Did not the husband and father possess advantages for gaining wealth? Had he not capacities for engaging in profitable business? Yes; but God, in his wise and holy arrangement, called him to employ those talents in watching for souls. Brethren, consider, we beseech you, the sacrifices incurred by your pastors for your sakes.

40.—THE MINISTER'S LOVE FOR SOULS.

W. F. BROADDUS.

If a preacher of the gospel would enjoy the approbation of his Lord in the great day, and have many souls given him as a reward for his toils in the vineyard, he must excel in love for souls. It is one of the strongest evidences of one's own gracious state, to love the souls of others, and earnestly to desire their salvation. Indeed, if we do not ardently desire the conversion and salvation of others, we may take it for granted, that we have erred in calling ourselves the friends of Christ; and on the other hand, if we sincerely desire the salvation of others, it may be to us consoling evidence that we ourselves have tasted the sweets of redeeming love; for why should we, out of good-will to others, be anxious that they should enjoy a blessing, which we do not ourselves enjoy? But the Christian minister has *peculiar* need of this ardent love for souls. Not unfrequently, he meets with discouragements which, in the absence of some powerful motive to counteract them, would lead him to abandon his arduous work; and then, unless his bosom burn with ardent love for the souls of men, he would retire with mortification from his office, and seek in some other way to glorify his Divine Master. Take, for example, the discouragement arising from the want of co-operation on the part of the church. Often, the minister has the mortification to see that the members of the church have become so filled with the world, as to manifest but little regard for the advancement of Christ's kingdom. The house of God is comparatively neglected, the prayer meeting deserted, the minister's salary diminished, or unpaid, and in short, every thing connected with the cause seems to be retrograding. In this state of affairs, how natural for the minister to reason thus:—"My brethren will not aid me in my labors to build up the kingdom; I can do nothing alone; my temporal interests, neglected by those who ought to provide for them, require all my attention; what, what shall I do?" It is then, that he needs some motive operating *immediately* upon his mind, to counteract those withering discouragements. The love of souls supplies such a motive. "I see," says the afflicted servant of the Lord, "my fellow-beings wandering in the paths of sin; I cannot bear to witness their ruin; cost what it may, I must pursue them, and warn them of the wrath that is gathering around them; and if others will not aid me, I must go out in the name of the Lord, and invite the perishing hundreds around me to shelter themselves in the provisions of God's grace. I will cast my wife and little ones on a faithful Providence, and with poverty staring me in the face, I will labor day and night to persuade men to forsake their sins, and accept the gospel salvation."

Very frequently, sinners, themselves, manifest a degree of indifference, and even repugnance, to the religion of Jesus, which may well be expected to discourage the man who lives and labors to bring them to Christ. In such a case, how natural for the minister to come to the conclusion, that those who thus lightly esteem his anxiety for them, will not be likely to heed any thing he can say; and how reasonable for him to determine that he will not waste his solicitudes or his labors upon those who do not appreciate them. Many, under such circumstances, would retire disheartened from the field, and seek, in some other way, to fill the measure of their obligations to their Divine Master. But ardent love for souls will rise even above these appalling discouragements, and inspired with the hope of being able to recover some one sinner from his moral degradation, and restore him to the favor of God, the faithful servant of Jesus Christ resolves, that the possibility of saving even one soul shall justify him in expending all his strength, and devoting his whole life to the work appointed him by his Divine Master.

Besides all this, the sovereign pleasure of God may, and no doubt, sometimes does, deny to his most zealous and faithful ministers such an amount of success in their labors, as their wishes and their hopes had contemplated. Without attempting to account for it, it may be safely affirmed, that God's sovereignty is engaged, both in giving and withholding those influences, without which no amount of talent, nor of labor, nor of self-consecration, will avail any thing in the great work to which the minister is called. It is not designed by this remark, to insinuate that God withholds or gives in mere sovereignty, and without adequate motive. On the contrary, it is certain that he gives or withholds because it is *right* that he should do it; and because evil would result from a contrary course on his part. But then, his reasons or motives often lie beyond the reach of mortal investigation; and he crosses the expectations of his people, in cases which, to them, are utterly unaccountable. This often comes to pass in the experience of ministers. For years they labor in the vineyard of the Lord, exerting all their strength, exhausting all their energies, and still, as if the hand of the Lord were turned against them, they are left to cry, "Who hath believed our report, and to whom is the arm of the Lord revealed?" Now under these discouragements, what but the love of souls could constrain a man to persevere? But he who is accustomed to estimate the soul's value in the light of Divine revelation, will find his anxiety to do them good increased rather than diminished, as the difficulties in the way of success are multiplied; and consequently his labor will abound, as the trembling apprehension increases upon him, that after all his labors *may* be in vain.

41.—PATIENCE IN THE MINISTRY.

J. WALKER.

To acquire knowledge on any subject is no easy task. Music, even with all its entrancing powers, when studied scientifically, demands intense application. There must be repeated trial, or there can be no proficiency; like the miner delving for the precious metals, the student must often strike into the same pit. Most minds, from indolence or a natural obstinacy, are wanting in docility. They must be kept to the subject under consideration with some severity, or there can be but little success. I have heard of some machinists, who were surrounded with models, had on hand always a number of machines partly completed, but could never make any one of them answer exactly the purpose for which it was designed. So in the studies of some preachers; almost every shelf and drawer contains the unfinished skeleton or manuscript of a sermon. Why are not these carefully reserved for future use? Why have we the head without the body? I am persuaded the reason is, not so much for want of genius or talent, but for lack of patience. This will appear evident, if we examine the manuscripts. Here, then, is the exordium. It conducts us with ease and dignity to the subject. The subject is just that which arises naturally out of the text. The argument, so far as it goes, is sound, The style is graceful, and the language chaste; and we are convinced from this specimen, that the man who proceeded thus far, *might* have gone much farther. But we are stopped in the dark! The train of thought, like the trail of a comet, is lost in the mist. We can trace it no longer.— Why this abrupt termination of so noble an enterprise? Ah! the mind became wearied. Truth could not be found without painful reflection. The mind begged a respite, and a respite was ingloriously granted; in other words, there was a lack of patience. Now, making due allowance for the difference of natural temper, I maintain that patience is to a great extent acquired. It becomes strengthened and confirmed by habitual perseverance. What can better settle this essential quality in the mind of a young minister, than the instruction of the college? In the college, study is made a business for a term of years. This lays a foundation for that patience which he will need all his life. At first, the mind, perplexed with the intricacy of language and science, may be fretful; but soon it is soothed and reconciled to the investigation of the most abstruse subjects. As the ox bends to the yoke, and toils steadily all the day, so the mind, accustomed to some exercise, will contemplate in the deepest abstraction, till truth is found, and the topic for discourse thoroughly understood. Robert Hall, it is said, possessed the power of abstracting his mind at pleasure in an eminent degree. Doubtless this became a habit, through constant discipline and a matured patience. A good workman can complete what he undertakes.

42.—IMPORTANCE OF A FULL EXHIBITION OF THE TRUTH.

C. EVANS.

NOTHING would tend more to predispose our hearers to receive the errors of the present day, than a defective, partial, one-side presentation of the truths of Divine Revelation. The facts, that these errors have been extensively embraced only in those sections of the professing Christian church, where we conceive that truth has been defectively exhibited, and that very few, from amongst ourselves, whose views of truth were clear and comprehensive, have been drawn aside by them, testify the great importance of fully declaring the whole counsel of God. Nor can I refrain from expressing my conviction, that if, in this respect, our preaching had universally resembled that of Flavel and Howe, of Edwards and Fuller, the peace of our Zion would have been less disturbed, and fewer defections would have occurred.

To a partial or imperfect exhibition of truth we have many temptations. The carnal heart rises in opposition to those doctrines of the gospel which have the most direct tendency to humble the sinner. To some of our hearers, perhaps the most influential, these doctrines may be very unpalatable. They may contrive to let us know this, and we may be tempted to keep them in the back-ground. The bias of our minds towards particular branches of theology, as favorite subjects of study, may also tempt us to give these subjects an undue prominency in our ministry. And we may likewise be tempted to dwell almost exclusively upon one class of truths, in hope of being thereby more useful. To this we are more liable from the circumstance that most of the recorded sermons of the apostles are of this description; and if we, like them, on the occasions of these recorded sermons, were preaching to sinners who had seldom or never heard the gospel—or if our congregations consisted, almost exclusively, of unconverted persons, we should do well to be constantly dwelling upon the first principles of the doctrine of Christ. But we should remember that we have also the epistles of the apostles, which were written to instruct the churches more fully in the truths of the gospels—to refute the errors propagated by false teachers, and guard the disciples of Christ against their pernicious influence; and as our assemblies comprise a large proportion of professed believers, it is surely incumbent on us to set before them all the truth that God has revealed, and defend it against the heresies which are coming in upon us like a flood. Our only hope of continued and increasing prosperity is a firm maintenance of the whole truth. Let us, therefore, always bear in mind the great importance of a full exhibition of Divine truth—of preaching to our hearers, both the sovereignty of God, and the responsibility of man; the election of grace, and the duty of the sinner to repent and believe the gospel; his depravity and guilt, and the fulness of salvation which the gospel reveals; his utter impotency, and the readiness of God to work in him both to will and to do; the necessity of holiness, and the entire absence of human merit; the certainty of a judgment to come, and the eternal duration of the punishment of the wicked, and the blessedness of the righteous. I scarcely need say that we should guard against placing any of these truths in such connection that one may neutralize the other. Nor will you understand me as intimating that all these topics should occur in every sermon. What I mean is, that the whole truth should come out fully in the course of our preaching, and in the relations and proportions in which we find it in the word of God.

43.—THE MINISTER'S EXAMPLE.

E. G. ROBINSON.

CHRIST should be taken as the minister's pattern, because he is the only perfect model; the only one who can always be imitated, and always with safety. Imitative as we all are by nature, and certain as it is, that we all, to some extent, are copyists of others, too much caution cannot be exercised in the selection of those by whose examples we may choose to be influenced. The nearer our models may come to perfection, the more closely and with the greater safety we may follow them. Jesus Christ alone, of all the dwellers on this earth, was perfect. Stretch your eye out as far as vision can extend over the sacred history of the redeemed who lived before the coming of Christ, culling the worthiest; survey the whole range of scripture characters from the patriarchs throughout the lengthened line of the prophets to John the Baptist, singling out the most perfect of their number, and place them each in comparison with Jesus of Nazareth. Patriarchs and prophets all stand out against the horizon of their day, in broad and beautiful lines of distinction from the mass, models of excellence in particular departments of morals, patterns of individual virtues, and objects of universal admiration and praise, like the higher points of distant mountains lifting against the sky in clear, distinct outlines, wrapped in their garments of snow, enchanting the eye with their sun-lit slopes and glittering summits, but revealing along up their sides many a dark line of shade, reminding us of the fearful chasms and deep ravines, where the sun's rays but seldom if ever penetrate, and where beasts of prey may lurk in concealment. If we scan the New Testament in search of an exemplar, we find a mild, a loving and confiding John; an eager, ardent, and impetuous Peter; a bold, unwearied, severely earnest, and deep-thinking Paul. But the more closely we study the example of either of these, the more plainly we discover the shades of their individual temperaments—their mental and their moral idiosyncrasies. The character of each has its elevations and depressions, its points of effulgence, and lines of shade. Not so is it with the character of Christ. In him every virtue is mature and proportional. Each trait harmonizes with all the others; the whole forming in combination a character of such exquisite symmetry and beauty as to constitute him "the brightness of the Father's glory, and the express image of his person." He stands out among all nations and through all time unequalled and matchless, comparable to no earthly object, but rising before us in such absolute perfection, in a manner so superior to all terrestrial imagery, or even human conception, that we can only adore and humbly aim to imitate him; and the closer the resemblance we attain, the more do we behold to fill us with wonder, and allure us on to attainments yet nobler. No one virtue in him peers above its fellows, engrossing the attention of his followers, and betraying them into forgetfulness of others of equal importance. In him we may find all the mildness and affection of John, all the energy and ardor of Peter, all the boldness and assiduity of Paul, without the imperfections of either. No little fault, made luminous by surrounding excellences, throws out its stolen lustre to catch the eye and cheat the heart of the follower. The dangerous propensity of our nature to copy the blemishes, rather than the beauties of another's character, finds nothing in him with which to be strengthened or excited. The pupils of Basil the Great, in profound admiration of their master, might imitate his tardy, drawling speech,

> —— "Those who could speak quick and rapidly,
> Turning their own perfection to abuse,
> To seem like him;"

but the disciples of Christ can find nothing in their teacher which they may not imitate to the fullest extent, and with perfect safety. If, as the ministers of Jesus, we stumble, we can find no corresponding misstep in the example of our Master with which to console ourselves. A patriarch or a prophet, a Moses, a David, or a Peter, might afford us comfort, and lessen our vigilance in future. A John or a Paul might lead us to cultivate some one virtue or more to the exclusion of others. But in Christ, our Saviour and example, we discover no defect, no excess, no misdeed, no parleying with temptation, never the minutest departure from perfect rectitude.

44.—THE MINISTER'S MESSAGE TO THE IMPENITENT.

W. LEFTWICH.

To the impenitent sinner our message is plain and pointed. "The wrath of God abideth on him." He stands condemned by the decision of the Judge of quick and dead, as a transgressor of his righteous law. The sword of justice is unsheathed, and even *now* while I speak, is it brandishing over his guilty, devoted head. But while vindictive justice lingers, mercy bends from the eternal throne, intercedes, entreats, weeps, and pleads, "Turn ye, turn ye from your evil ways, for why will ye die?" The preaching of necessity of "repentance towards God, and faith in the Lord Jesus Christ," is due to the impenitent, as a part of his portion, and also, that except he is born again he cannot see the kingdom of God. We see him sleeping on the verge of damnation, while fiery billows roll beneath his feet. He closes his eyes against the light of heaven, and stops his ears to the voice of mercy, the sweet, melting strains of Calvary, and the thundering denunciations of Omnipotence.

Will he plead his inability to obey the command of God, that "all men every where should repent?" This is to impeach the justice of his Creator, in his final overthrow. Let it be ours, ye heralds of salvation, to expose this false refuge, this stronghold of Satan, by unfolding to the sinner the documents of heaven, by which he shall be made to see and feel his responsibility; and that the circumstance of his being a sinner, is something more than a mere misfortune—that it is highly criminal, and that his impenitence is continually aggravating that criminality. Thus will he learn that his inability to repent and turn to God wholly consists in the aversion of a heart full of enmity against God, possessing no inclination or desire to obey his command.

Should he plead, that he derived his depraved nature and sinful propensity from our common father Adam, and forasmuch as he acted from an inherent principle, he ought not to be held responsible: this would be pleading just what every rogue would plead, who was so unfortunate as to be the son of a dishonest father. Such a plea would not only be unavailing, but an aggravation of guilt. The principle involved, is the only just ground of reward or punishment; *this* being the basis of all good laws divine or human.

Our business then, brethren, with impenitent sinners, is, if possible, to make them *see* their danger, to make them *feel* their responsibility; not to compromise, not to give place, "no, not for an hour;" but to warn, reprove, entreat, admonish, and command them by the authority of Heaven, to repent *now;* tomorrow may be too late, the die may be cast forever. My brethren, whatsoever our hands find to do, let us do it with all our might. Sinners are dying around us, and dropping lower than the grave. "The King's business requires haste." Here I might enlarge, and enlarge *much*, but must pass on to another part of the sinner's portion, which dying in his sins, he will most assuredly receive, for the veracity of God is pledged. He must receive his *final* portion in the lake that burns with fire and brimstone, and while eternity shall revolve its ceaseless cycles, it will still be his portion, the due reward of his own hands. It is his portion now to be warned of the awful fact. Oh! impenitent man, impenitent woman, let me say to you as in view of the judgment bar, "Choose you *this day* whom you will serve." If it should *now* be your happy lot, to determine heartily and honestly, on the side of God and truth, Christ and his salvation are yours, and yours forever. But alas, if you are so unwise, so lost to your best interests, as to put this subject far from you, and still resist the overtures of mercy, and reject an offered Saviour; O, then, prepare for the awful, heart-rending consequences! If heaven with all its ineffable glories, should be your deliberate choice, your choice you shall have; but if not, there is but one alternative, the lake—the *awful* lake, burning and still burning, kindled by the wrath of an angry, incensed God, is yours, and yours forever. There, in the society of wicked spirits and devils, to reek

"In flames that no abatement know,
Though briny tears forever flow."

And here, my dear brethren in the ministry, if after having endeavored, according to the instructions of our Divine Master, to give impenitent sinners *their* portion in due season, we feel acquitted from the charge of their blood being found on our skirts; and having followed them with the sound of redemption through a Saviour's blood, to the very confines of the grave, and seen, according to the testimony of Heaven, their final doom, what more can we do? "O, that my head were waters, and my eyes a fountain of tears!" then indeed I could weep day and night, for the awful desolations of a ruined world! Here, brethren, we must leave them, and turn away our eyes from beholding the agonies of black despair, and stop our ears at the shrieks and cries of horror, issuing from the awful pit, and mingling with the huge columns of smoke, from the torment of spirits abandoned of God, ascending up forever, and *forever!* O, my soul, be thou not gathered with the ungodly, when the great day of God's wrath shall come and shall burn as an oven; but be thou, in time and in eternity, a companion of those, however here despised, that fear God's holy name, and obey the voice of his servants; a companion of them that trust in the Lord forever, and stay themselves upon the mighty God of Israel. *Here,* brethren and friends, and here alone, is firm footing, a solid foundation, a rock on which to build higher than the stars, a kingdom that cannot be moved, an ark of perfect safety, a ship that rides out the storm, and goes safely into port, though it be amid conflicting elements, "the wreck of matter, and the crush of worlds."

45.—PUNGENT PREACHING.

S. B. SWAIM.

PUNGENCY is the power to pierce the mind. Preaching on the day of Pentecost, when three thousand were pricked to the heart, was an illustration of this kind of preaching. A pungent presentation of truth lies between the extremes of preaching mere morality and preaching none. Maintaining the five points in Calvinism, without *pointing* them at the conscience, is what an Antinomian would do. Our fathers, whose effective pulpits we occupy, into whose flourishing parishes some of us have entered, were not generally bookish men. But they preached Christ Jesus and him crucified, in a downright and unsophisticated manner. Their sepulchres are not only with us, but their example, their direction to prepare our sermons on our knees, before the mercy seat. Baxter was not alone in the experience that he communicated the distempers of his own soul to his flock. Are not some of the requisites to pungent preaching wanting in the ministrations of the few last years? It is not the character of the times only which has prevented the success of the ministry. We have not tasked ourselves in our general, so much as in our special preparations for the pulpit; nor have we shown the vigilance of a never-tiring endeavor.

The dependence of the Baptist ministry, and of the church, is on the power of the truth which they proclaim and adorn. We can safely fall back upon nothing else. We are a plain, unpretending, republican people, making no profession of authority over men's consciences. We, of all others, can never dispense with that preaching which reaches the heart, with the faithful dispensation of that word which is the fire and the hammer that break the flinty rock into pieces.

46.—POINTED PREACHING.

J. KNAPP.

Some years ago, there was a vessel stranded on the shores of Scotland, and as she was tossing and heaving in the howling tempest, and becoming a perfect wreck, hundreds of people collected on the beach, gazing upon the noble ship as she was heaved and tossed by the roaring billows: presently the poor sufferers on board saw to their amazement, that they were throwing bomb-shells at the ship, and they wondered they could be so inhuman as to undertake to kill them off with bomb-shells; but soon one reached the deck, and to their joy and surprise, they found a rope was attached to it, and one end made fast to a tree on the shore; and they made the other end fast to the top of the main-mast, and then making fast another rope to the deck, which was sent to them in the same way, they let down the life-boat, took hold of the rope, and in that way pulled themselves over the raging billows, till all were safely landed on shore. Now, why is it that sinners are so opposed to have truth presented in such a manner, as that they will feel its force, and yield themselves up to its convictions, though it be clothed in a manner not the most pleasing to the carnal heart. I have used that language in my discourses, and those figures, which I considered best adapted to carry the truth home to your consciences; and will you disregard the truths of the living God on account of the *shell* that contains them? The dreadful tempest is raging around you, and the ship, fitted up by the great Builder of the world, and designed to bear your immortal spirit into the harbor of eternal felicity, is liable every moment to be dashed on the dark mountains of death, and the cargo which cost the Captain of your salvation his life, is in danger of being swallowed up in the fiery billows that roll around you. And when I see my Master's vessel, with the priceless cargo on board, liable to be engulfed in the abyss of sin, I must obey my commission and cry out, "Ship ahoy! there are breakers ahead!" "Trim sail!" and "lay" for the star of Bethlehem; "reef the topsail" of vanity—"take in the mainsail" of sin, and lay "hard to" the promised land, or you will be dashed eternally on the rocks of Atheism and Infidelity. This, sinners, is what I am commissioned to do, and I am not at liberty to turn to the right hand or to the left, till I have by some means arrested your attention, and made you sensible of your imminent danger. I *must* do it, though for the time you may deride, and persecute, and laugh me to scorn. It is no worse treatment than my Master received, when on earth ; it is no worse than you treat him now, and "the servant is not greater than his Lord ; nor he that is sent greater than he that sent him."

47.—THE MINISTER'S FAREWELL.

LOTT CARY.

I AM about to leave you, and expect to see your faces no more. I long to preach to the poor Africans the way of life and salvation. I don't know what may befall me, whether I may find a grave in the ocean, or among the savage men, or more savage wild beasts on the coasts of Africa ; nor am I anxious what may become of me. I feel it to be my duty to go, and I very much fear, that many of those who preach the gospel in this country, will blush when the Saviour calls them to give an account of their labors in his cause, and tells them, "I commanded you to go into all the world and preach the gospel to every creature," and the Saviour may ask, "Where have you been? Where have *you* been? What have you been doing? Have you endeavored, to your utmost ability, to fulfil the commands I gave you? or have you sought your own gratification, and your own ease, regardless of my commands?"

48.—A RETIRING PASTOR'S COUNSEL.

LEONARD TRACY.

Receive, brethren, the word of exhortation, that when you shall have obtained a pastor, you help him. Let him not bear burdens alone. Stand by him. Co-operate with him. Encourage him. Meet promptly your obligations to him. Give him your kindest sympathies. At the point where he fails—and he will fail somewhere—there especially lend him your aid. If he fail to please you always in your personal notions, turn not from him. The question with him will be, as yours in respect to his work should be—*Is the Master pleased?* Think not, if he should happen to differ from you personally in his opinions and plans and mode of action, that therefore he must be unrighteously under the influence of some one whose opinions you disapprove. Remember that he may have the right of a question, and yet side neither with you nor your neighbors, who, on the point at issue, may be your antipodes. In no sense make a slave of your minister. Allow him to be independent.

If you would study the comfort of your pastor—and that of his wife, if he have one—say as little in their presence as possible, either of a favorable or unfavorable character respecting their predecessors. Too frequent praises will be regarded as implied invidious comparisons, made to the detriment of the new comers. Implied censures will be regarded as indicating a captious spirit, and will unavoidably give rise to the thought—"Well, our turn will come." No wise man feels himself safe in the society either of fulsome flatterers, or constant censurers of their fellow-men.

When another pastor is given you, you will not forget that, as God has established human identity, there will be many things in respect to which you cannot have change and novelty from week to week. The same physical form, same voice, similar gesticulation and style, you will expect in the same man. Those who regard what is *new* in respect to these things more than they do *thought* in a sermon, will soon look on the pulpit performances of a pastor as stale and uninteresting. In order to be edified, the hearer must love thought, and accustom himself to reflect, must pray, feel the force of truth, and have the spirit of the gospel, as well as the preacher. May you in this manner hear the gospel, and be blessed.

49.—MINISTERIAL FELLOWSHIP.

J. W. OLMSTEAD.

FELLOWSHIP imports affinity, not an affinity grounded on a simple belief of conversion to God, or of devotion to his cause. The thousands of other denominations than our own, we believe to be included in this condition—ministers and private members—and for them we truly, as born of the same Spirit, do cherish fellowship. It is, however, in strictness of meaning rather a Christian than a church fellowship. Ministers inducted into the sacred office in Baptist churches, I suppose to hold the same great truths as well relating to the order of Christ's house as to doctrine in general, held by their brethren; the same precious, blood-bought, immortal principles. Were we in doubt here, the present would be a sad occasion. I shall, then, regard fellowship as implying between brethren a truthful affinity. More than this even. As two cannot walk together except they be agreed, certainly in all great essentials, I ought to be warranted in supposing that this fellowship will involve concert and harmony, or that we shall strive with a good conscience to promote these in all the relations which our action will have on our brethren around us. It is obvious enough, that while we hold, or profess to hold the same fundamental doctrines, we may yet pursue a course—alas! too often pursued—most detrimental to the common unity, which is "as the dew of Hermon." Should we go forward, especially where churches are contiguous, in a reckless carrying out of certain measures, to which, in great conscientiousness it may be, we might become committed, avoiding fraternal consultation with our brethren, refusing to defer to our seniors in years and experience, intent on our own will, overlooking other and general interests; should we do this, one consequence must follow—the spirit of an active and uniting fellowship will be lost. Let me not be misunderstood in this, as uttering aught against a position of proper mental and moral independence. Enlightened Christian brethren are always prepared to award much, all indeed that is consistent, or that should be demanded. What I desire to make plain is, that the rupturing of affinity will often follow as truly from the general measures and policy which we adopt—our practical theories of operating, as they affect all around us—as from the principles of belief which we incorporate into our doctrinal system. Something, surely, ought to be meant in giving the hand of fellowship. It ought to imply that there will be the *cherishing* of fellowship as an object in the relations of ministers, especially of pre-eminent value, and as, hence, an object which it should be ever our sedulous aim to guard as the very heart, the very life-centre of our holy religion. How much have the beauty, the glory, and the overcoming power of this religion been marred and diminished, by the absence of a true Christian and fraternal fellowship! And who can doubt that a spirit ensuring this has been, among all classes of Christians, and especially among ministers, too little cultivated?

The value of a strong tie of ministerial fellowship,

we shall be prepared to appreciate. Amid buffetings from without, fears and failings from within—under a burden of care and responsibility—amid, it may be, desertions in the faithful performance of duty, the consciousness into which we may retire of endeared and confiding union with our brethren in the Lord, whose bosoms we may make sharers of our misgivings and sorrows, will be sweet to the soul. God has provided it as a sheltering refuge for us. I am glad to believe that we shall fully prize it, and aim ever to render ourselves worthy of it. We will throw its strong arms about each other, and our prayer to God shall ever be, that each may be upheld and shielded, sustained by kindred sympathies, but above all "by the power of His might."

Around the throne of light on high, dwell the myriad companies whose intercourse, animated by one prevailing inspiration of holiness, one beating heart for God's glory, no discordancy of thought or of feeling ever mars. One pure, golden chain binds them all to the Father and to the Lamb slain. To that beatified company, thus "knit together" by one sympathy, we hope as Christians and as ministers soon to be joined. The spirit, then, by which we are now united, should be a satisfying earnest of the ultimate and forever unbroken union that awaits the redeemed. As the clouds of angels and of saints, the prophetic, the ministering, and martyred dead, are now "perfectly joined together in the same mind," be it ours ever to invoke upon us from them, as they are ever our surrounding beholders, their approving view. So with them, our fellowship will be with the Father, with his Son Jesus Christ, and one with another. So will

> "Our fellowship of kindred minds
> Be like to that above."

50.—THE AMERICAN BAPTIST MINISTRY A CENTURY AGO.

A. G. PALMER.

THE ministry of this period seem to have been endued with a remarkable degree of wisdom, prudence, and piety. They were men, evidently, whom God had selected and fitted for the weighty responsibilities and arduous work to which they were called; men who were able and willing to take the oversight of the church of God; to guide her amid the perils through which she was passing; to lead her up from the darkness in which she had long been wandering, into the full light and liberty of the gospel. Theirs was the responsible work of combining elements; of separating the precious from the vile; of discriminating between the true and the false, both in doctrine and practice; of collecting, arranging, fitting, and harmonizing, materials for the establishment of the church of God, as the pillar and ground of the truth, upon the foundation of apostles and prophets, Jesus Christ himself being the chief corner stone.

They were called upon, not only to preserve the ordinance of baptism which they had received in special trust, in its primitive relation to the church, but also to cast a mass of mind, just emerging from the darkness of a false theology, into the peculiar mould of gospel truth, into the form of sound evangelical sentiment, and of equally sound evangelical practice; and of the manner in which, under God, they met this responsibility; of the consummate wisdom, prudence, and fidelity, with which they discharged their high and sacred duties; of the correctness of their decisions in most matters of faith, practice, and discipline; the present condition of the denomination, is, perhaps, the best criterion; for it has advanced to its present state, guided and guarded by those simple principles of ecclesiastical economy, in which they so faithfully instructed the churches committed to their charge. And in no way, perhaps, has the wisdom of their successors in the ministry been more happily exhibited, than in attempting no innovations concerning these important points of order in the church. Wherever an improvement has been attempted, it has most signally failed; both individuals and churches have found themselves constrained to return, and retire within the prescribed limits of an ecclesiastical fellowship, based upon the truth as it is in Jesus. The reason of this is obvious. The light which guided our early ministry in the formation and discipline of the church, was the New Testament. This was their law, their canon, their rule of faith and action. They did not study the fathers, or the decrees of councils, or the decisions of synods, but the teaching of Jesus Christ, and the acts of the apostles. Here they found the grand model of the Christian church, or rather the Christian church itself, as constituted and regulated under the immediate teachings of the Holy Ghost; and to this they strove in all things to conform the spiritual temple which they were called to rear. Hence, under their hand, the building rose with something of the simplicity and beauty of the apostolic church. It stood out before the world, reflecting, in all its prominent features of doctrines, ordinances, and discipline, the light of a pure, primitive Christianity. Let it not be supposed, that our veneration for our fathers in the ministry is excessive; we venerate them because they venerated the New Testament; we follow them because they followed Christ. We speak of their religious principles, because they were drawn fresh from the fountain of truth, the living oracles of God; we speak of their acts, because they were conformable to the precepts of the gospel, and as such are worthy of our perpetual imitation. We admire their spirit, the elevated tone of their piety, their unwavering fidelity to truth, their strict and undeviating conscientiousness, their patient endurance of suffering, and their manly resistance of religious despotism. They were indeed extraordinary men, but were made so by the grace of God; by the peculiar circumstances into the midst of which they were thrown; and above all, by the sufferings, privations, and persecutions which they were called to endure. That they were great men we do not claim, at least in the ordinary acceptation of this phrase; and yet, if purity of mind and character, deep and ardent piety, strong attachment to truth, correct and comprehensive views of the gospel, a thorough acquaintance with the word of God; together with an ability in illustrating and applying the same, in an extraordinary degree successful in winning souls to Christ, as well as in edifying the church of God; if these qualifications in any degree constitute true goodness, and true greatness, then were *they* truly good and great men. They were men of a plain, common education, yet of strong, vigorous intellects, of sound practical sense; and thence brought to the study of the scriptures that peculiar artlessness and simplicity of mind so essential to a right understanding of the word of God. Books they had none. The Bible alone was the man of their counsel, their great and almost exclusive study; and hence they became "mighty in the scriptures," thorough and correct expounders of the doctrines and precepts of the gospel. They were unlearned in many of the modern modes of interpretation, untaught in many of the nice distinctions of a speculative theology; but were not, therefore, we imagine, the less evangelical in their sentiments, the less successful in their ministrations.

They seem to have received the scriptures in their most plain and obvious meaning, without seeking to conform them to their prejudices, or to bend them to the support of a denominational creed. Indeed they had no such creed; and if prejudice at any time they had, it was a prejudice consequent to, and dependent upon a diligent and prayerful study of the Bible, and might, therefore, be supposed to be in harmony with truth. Doubtless, like all other good men in similar circumstances, they were not aware of the greatness of the work they were performing, of the far-reaching influence of the principles which they had embraced, and were laboriously inculcating. Hence the absence of all policy in their proceedings touching the future. They left truth where the apostles left it, not to be transmitted by means of creeds and heartless subscriptions, but to be handed down from generation to generation in the experience of those who should embrace it, trusting in God that the line of the true spiritual priesthood would continue unbroken, and the church thus be perpetuated to the end of time.

We are disposed, however, to trace all this to the superintending providence of God, to the guardian influence of the Holy Spirit. To us it seems evident that God, through the agency of these men, was preparing to give the world a practical illustration of that great truth, which the church has ever been so slow to learn, namely, that the Bible understood, the Bible believed, the Bible loved, the Bible practised, is the best, the only safeguard to ecclesiastical purity.

51.—RULE OF CHRISTIAN AGENCY.

J. A. MC KEAN.

In the commission, we have the extent to which we are to go, "*into all the world*"—those to whom we are to proclaim the good news, "*every creature*" —and in the words accompanying the commission, the plan to be pursued, "BEGINNING AT JERUSALEM." What, then, is the principle that is to govern our plan of operations?

Is it not plain that the principle developed in this last command is, that the *force* and *course* of Christianity is to be *centrifugal?*—that the word of the Lord was to sound *out from* Jerusalem? Do not the parables of the grain of mustard seed and the leaven in the measures of meal, spoken with reference to the same subject, convey the same idea? This, then, is the DIVINE PLAN, and we have only to apply this principle to the subject, and the answer to the question, What is duty? is obvious.

But this principle must be regarded, not merely as it applies to missions. It governs the whole subject, and it is at this point that many of us fail. I would speak with deference, my dear brethren, but I submit it to you. How many of us, in obedience to the spirit of this command, "*begin at Jerusalem?*"

If the view here presented be correct, this principle points out the course to be pursued with regard to all that is entrusted to us—our property, our time, our influence, health, abilities—all! all held for God! and held for Him, in view of the evangelization of the world—"*beginning at Jerusalem.*"

This presents to us a chain of influences extending from each Christian's heart to the limits of the whole earth. It passes from his own heart first, through the particular church of which he is a member, thence through the state society or association, thence through the General Home Mission Society, and thence through the Societies for Foreign Missions, passing out and reaching even to the utmost bounds of the earth. Hence, we see that the Christian who neglects, or in any wise impairs *his own personal piety* (this being the fountain from which, under God, these influences flow), in just so much wrongs the church of which he is a member, and the association of which it forms a constituent part, and the general interests of missions; in fact, every *personal dereliction*, whether it concerns his spiritual or his temporal affairs, is felt throughout the whole chain. Every failure to begin at Jerusalem, cuts off the supply of influences *at its source*, and must therefore be ruinous in its effects.

52.—THE MODERN MISSIONARY.

B. M. HILL.

REGARD the modern missionary of the cross, as he labors in his work of weighty responsibility. The house of his birth, the fireside of his parent, the society of his youth, the local beauties which delighted the ripening energies of his mind, and implanted in his heart the sweet sensations peculiar to a native home, have all lost their powerful attractions in his eyes. His Divine Master has said to him, "follow me;" and, deeply imbued with the spirit of his Master, remembering that he is, while here, but a pilgrim and a stranger, behold! he leaves all, and follows him. He looks around upon the desolations of Zion; he sees the heritage of the Lord scattered upon the mountains; he beholds the unrelenting enemy exerting his destructive power over the souls of men; he gazes with astonishment and grief upon the wide extended progress of sin and vice; and with a heart wrung with anguish known only to such as himself, he bids farewell to worldly ease and honors, that he may subserve the cause of Christ, and rescue ruined man from wo; "choosing rather to suffer affliction with the people of God, than to enjoy the pleasures of sin for a season." And now follow the indefatigable man as he prosecutes the objects of his mission. See him climb the bleak and rugged mountain, or tread the lonely glen. Accompany him, when the wintry tempest howls around him, or the midsummer heat oppresses him. Visit with him the obscure and decaying cottage of the poor and needy; partake of the lonely repast, and lodge upon the uneasy pallet, which are sometimes the only thank-offering to be found in these habitations of sorrow and affliction. If you have the courage, penetrate with him the haunts of dissipation and vice, and the abodes of wretchedness, where disease and filth pour forth their pestilential vapors. If his expanded soul bid him extend his toils, encounter with him the perils of the ocean, the rudeness and caprice of heathen; the unbelief and opposition of idolaters; the danger of unhealthy climates; and the social, intellectual, and spiritual sacrifices incident to such a situation; and then determine what, besides love to God, love to the church, and love to the souls of men, could induce this man thus to labor and to spend his strength.

Is it for ease and comfort? He expects and finds none, but such as strengthen and support his heart, and allow his soul a free taste of that bliss, which will be his portion when he has ceased from his labors, and his works do follow him.

Is it for wealth? Ah! let his humble equipage, his scanty wardrobe, his simple fare, and his numerous wants, tell the story of his earthly possessions.

Is it for honor? Indeed, if being despised and considered weak; if being reviled, persecuted, and defamed; if being made as the filth of the world, and the offscouring of all things are honors, then do honors thickly blush upon him. No, my brethren, these are not the motives or objects of the evangelical missionary. He aims at cultivating the wastes of Zion, and winning souls to Christ. His labor is to correct the vices, and to enlighten the darkness of the world; and though he endure the "heat and burden of the day," he feels encouraged to prolong his toils, if, when looking over his field of labor, he can discover here and there a plant, cultivated by his hand, whose fresh and fruitful boughs assure him that he has not labored in vain, nor spent his strength for nought.

And this is the spirit, and these are the objects of every evangelical missionary operation. The men who aid this cause are men of kindred spirits; they drink from the same spiritual fountain; they breathe the same divine atmosphere; and the congenial feelings of their souls mingle in the same moral element. It is the fountain from which the apostles drank—Christ and his cross; it is the atmosphere of the Bible; it is the element of truth. This strong resemblance, which modern missionary labors bear to those of primitive times, is proof of their evangelical nature.

53.—CHRISTIAN TRIUMPH IN THE SUCCESS OF THE GOSPEL.

J. O. TURPIN.

LET us remark now on the result, the *triumph* of believers; not a mere conquest, but a *triumph;* not a heartless, but a *grateful* triumph. This triumph is not effected by human agency—"*God* causeth us to triumph." It is not temporary—"God *always* causeth us to triumph." It rests upon no mutable basis—"He always causeth us to triumph *in Christ.*"

Believers are recognized in the text, as the instruments of diffusing the savor of divine knowledge. God is represented as the agent, and Christ as the medium of their triumph. As believers can do all things through Christ who strengtheneth them, so in their success and triumph they recognize him. No joy can equal that of bringing souls to Christ; making them "meet to be partakers of the inheritance of the saints in light." What reward can be richer than this—"They that be wise shall shine as the brightness of the firmament; and they that turn many to righteousness, as the stars forever?" Well may we be willing to go "forth weeping, bearing precious seed," if we can return again, bringing our sheaves with us. There is supposed to be an allusion, in the text, to the triumphal processions among the Romans. According to Macknight, the apostle represents Christ as a victorious general, riding in a triumphal procession through the world, attended by his apostles, prophets, evangelists, and other ministers of the gospel, and followed by all the idolatrous nations as his captives. Among these the preachers of the gospel diffused the savor of the knowledge of Christ, as fragrant flowers and perfumes were liberally scattered in a Roman triumph. The conqueror's joy sinks infinitely below that of the soldier of the cross, who has gathered around him trophies of grace as seals of his ministry. The apostle refers, with heavenly satisfaction, to this source of *his* joy. "For what," asks he," is our hope, or joy, or crown of rejoicing? are not even ye in Christ Jesus? For ye are our glory and joy."

The apostles frequently referred to the results of their labors as the fruitful source of their bliss. John says, "I have no greater joy than that my children walk in the truth." Paul says, "Ye are our epistles known and read of all men." To the Colossians he says, "For though I be absent in the flesh, yet am I with you in the spirit, joying and beholding your order, and the steadfastness of your faith in Christ." These grateful joys are realized by the believer in the present state, but their richest fruition is reserved for the kingdom of glory. It is impossible in the present state, for a Christian to know the full results of his labors and influence. Doubtless, very erroneous calculations are made upon this subject. It remains for eternity to disclose these results. The solemn councils of the last day will enable us to form a correct judgment, and to understand and appreciate the richness of that benediction—"They that be wise shall shine as the brightness of the firmament; and they that turn many to righteousness, as the stars forever and ever." Then, while the consistent and laborious Christian contemplates the various and happy results of his labors, with a spirit overwhelmed with rapturous astonishment, he will inquire, "Can all these be the children which the Lord has given me?" "Now I see," he says, "obscure as I was in yonder world, humble as was the sphere in which I moved, the Lord's eye was upon me, marking my course, and his hand blessing my labors." He will then see, that those exhortations and warnings, made not only in the great congregations, but under the roof of the humble poor, and in the ears of the stranger upon the highway, the Divine Spirit rendered effectual.

While the ransomed spirit contemplates the glorious bearing of all his self-denials, works of faith, and labors of love, and as he hears that these are acknowledged as rendered to the person of Christ; with a feeling approaching incredulity, he will inquire, "When saw we thee a hungered, and fed thee? or thirsty, and gave thee drink? when saw we thee a stranger, and took thee in? or naked, and clothed thee? or when saw we thee sick or in prison, and came unto thee?" Prophets and patriarchs will there see the fruit of their toils. In the morning they sowed their seed, and in the evening they withheld not their hand. They knew not which should prosper, whether this or that, or whether both should be alike good. All shall be made plain in eternity. Peter will see the seals of his ministry, from among the Parthians, and Medes, and Elamites, and the dwellers in Mesopotamia, and in Judea, and Cappadocia, in Pontus, and Asia, Phrygia, and Pamphylia, in Egypt, and in parts of Libya, about Cyrene, and strangers of Rome, Jews and proselytes, Cretes and Arabians. And if we take into the account the savor which these people shed upon their respective countries on their return, how vast the "works following" up this apostle to the throne of God! Paul will see and know his converts from Rome and Philippi, from Corinth and Antioch; and who can describe his joy as he cries, exultingly, but gratefully—"Thanks be unto God, who always causeth us to triumph in Christ, and maketh manifest the savor of his knowledge by us in every place." Coming down to the present generation, how widely is this savor extending itself! Carey, and Boardman, and Judson, and Mason, and a host of others—among them many devoted females—having gone forth toiling and weeping, bearing precious seed, shall doubtless return again with rejoicing, bringing their sheaves with them.

54.—MINISTERS AT THE JUDGMENT DAY.

N. KENDRICK.

EVERY individual who has taken part in the ministry will have a prominent place assigned him, in the arrangement for the judgment day. He will be examined in the presence of those who have been the subjects of his ministry, and his work will be tried by fire. The motives which induced him to undertake the work, the amount he has accomplished, and the manner in which it was done, will then be made known. All the feelings of his heart will be laid open, which he has ever had towards saints and sinners, and his secret sins will be set in the light of God's countenance. The authority and worth of the word, and the use he has made of it—the eternal interests of souls, and the sense in which he has regarded them—and the plenitude of Divine glory, and the reference he had to it in fulfilling his ministry, will all be brought before him, and placed in the light of eternity. We know not how many will then appear who have never submitted themselves to the righteousness of God, but from mercenary motives, have entered the ministry not sparing the flock; counting gain to be godliness, and making shipwreck of the faith, teaching for doctrine the commandments of men. Their superior advantages in the ministerial office will give a stronger character to their crimes, and sink them deeper in darkness, where "they shall be punished with everlasting destruction from the presence of the Lord, and from the glory of his power." With them will be contrasted the "good stewards of the manifold grace of God." "In all things approving themselves as the ministers of God, in much patience, in afflictions, in necessities, in distresses—by pureness, by knowledge, by long-suffering, by kindness, by the Holy Ghost, by love unfeigned, by the word of truth, by the power of God, by the armor of righteousness, on the right hand and on the left, by honor and dishonor, by evil report and good report, as deceivers and yet true, as poor yet making many rich, as having nothing yet possessing all things." In the judgment day, the testimony of both saints and sinners to the faithful discharge of their work, the witness of the Holy Spirit, the approbation of the Father, and the plaudit of the Lord, will unitedly appear in their favor. Having been faithful unto death, and finished their course with joy, they will receive a crown of life; and through the exceeding riches of his grace, enter mansions of glory prepared by the Saviour.

THE BAPTIST PULPIT.

VI.

THE DUTIES, DANGERS, AND PROSPECTS OF SOCIETY.

1.—POLITICAL INSTRUCTIONS OF CHRISTIANITY.

WILLIAM HAGUE.

CHRISTIANITY holds to Politics the relation of a divinely commissioned prophet and teacher. She declares the principles on which the destinies of nations turn. She utters them without fear or favor. She is constantly expounding the principles of rectitude, truth, and justice; announcing the consequences of obedience and disobedience, asserting the free agency and accountability of all, at the same time exclaiming to every nation and community, "Behold I set before you the blessing and the curse, life and death, therefore choose life, that you may live." Appearing in the world without a sword or sceptre, she holds, nevertheless, a commission like that of the prophet Jeremiah, to announce to all people their duty, their reward, or their doom; and in this majestic character she is "set over the nations to root out and pull down, to destroy and to throw down, to build and to plant." Rejoicing in the welfare of all, she yet stands, like Daniel in the court of Babylon, serene amidst the wreck of empire. She makes her abode with the humble, and fosters pious hope in the heart of the peasant or the slave; but with a voice like the voice of many waters, and the voice of mighty thunderings, she declares to the principalities and powers of earth, "The nation that will not serve the Lord shall perish." She has beheld the fall of states, kingdoms and commonwealths, but her eye beams keen with hope as she glances towards the future, in full expectation that the Most High "will turn and overturn, till he shall reign whose right it is." She sees that He who, while in bonds at Pilate's bar, said, "I am king," is now enthroned in heaven, and knows that he will subdue his enemies by a moral sway, and behold a world in prostrate adoration at his feet.

And what, practically considered, is the amount of all her teachings to us as a people? It is that we bow beneath her sceptre; that it be our supreme care to mould the laws and doings of our government into conformity with the eternal principles of the kingdom of Messiah; lest, if it jar against their harmony, we be at first broken, at last ruined. While she declares the Messiah to be the Prince of peace, and that the consummation of his reign shall be a state in which men shall learn war no more, and in which the lion and the lamb shall lie down together, she yet points to the oracle of prophecy which said that nations should unite in the resolve, "let us break his bands asunder, and cast away his cords from us," and that all such he would rule with a rod of iron, and dash them in pieces like a potter's vessel, and scatter the fragments like the chaff of the summer's threshing-floor. Therefore she puts forth the voice of warning—"Be wise, ye kings; be instructed, ye judges of the earth! Serve the Lord with fear, and rejoice with trembling! Submit to the Son, lest he be angry, and ye perish from the way when his wrath is kindled but a little.

2.—OUR DUTY TO OUR COUNTRY.

B. BRIERLY.

The relation we sustain to our country, imposes upon us peculiar obligations to labor for its welfare. There was a period when this statement would have been universally received as a truism, but we have fallen upon other times. In our days, men have arisen who, claiming to be citizens of the world, have cut themselves loose from the ties of country, and by pen and speech have branded patriotism as a crime, and love of one's native land as a base-born passion. Regarding, upon this subject, neither the teachings nor the example of Christ or his apostles, they recognize no special obligations to the country in the midst of whose institutions they live, and by whose government they are protected. We admit, as freely as these men, the existence of a common relationship which binds us to our race, and imposes upon us obligations to do good unto all men. We would burn the brand of infamy as deep as they upon the worse than heathenish sentiment, "Our country, right or wrong." But while we hold common ground with them here, we cannot burn out the impression which our hearts have long since received, that He who instituted families, also instituted nations, and that the love of the latter may be a virtue and a duty, as well as the love of the former. Both have propriety, utility, and we believe divine authority, to commend them to our regard. As the parent owes duty to his children, which he does not owe to others; as the child owes affection and service to its parents, which it does not owe, to the same extent, to others—so, on the same principle, the citizen owes service and love to his country which he does not owe, in the same degree, to other countries; and for him to withhold these seems well nigh as unnatural as if the child should break away from parental restraint and filial obligations, and give to the mother who bore it, and the father who provided for it, no service, love, or respect, except such as it lavished with equal profusion upon all men.

The error and absurdity of the views to which we now object, become evident the moment they are tried by the following principles, which are prominently developed in the moral government of God; *First*—The measure of our ability and opportunity, is invariably the measure of our obligation. Now, as God has committed the interests and destinies of our nation into our hands as he has not committed them into the hands of any other nation, we owe to it duties which no other people can owe it; and as its destinies are entrusted to us, as those of other nations are not, we owe to it duties which we do not owe elsewhere, to the same extent. We can all of us remember some sheet of water, by which we played in childhood, whose smooth surface was ruffled by the falling pebble, which in childhood's glee we cast upon it. We gazed with eager interest upon the increasing and widening circular waves, and noticed how each receding circle became more faint than its predecessor, till the tracery became so indistinct that we could no longer detect it. Some of us, too, can recollect how we were startled by the announcement of what was given as a philosophical fact, that not a particle of air could be set in motion without agitating the whole atmospheric mass—so that the swearer's oath, the infant's merry laugh, and the wood-bird's song, each had power to move the whole mass of atmosphere that surrounds our globe. But if we admitted the statement to be accordant with sound philosophy, we saw at once that the agitation would diminish as the particles increased their distance from the point where the impetus was given. Here we have illustrations of human influence. Other things being equal, it acts with greater distinctness and power upon those near to us, than upon those more remote. Because of this, in part, we owe special service to our families, our kindred, our neighborhood, and our nation. So that while our benevolence, like the atmosphere, should encircle the globe, yet, as our influence cannot act with equal power in all places, and upon all nations, we are under greater obligations to some than we are to others. The *second* principle is this :—While our obligation is proportioned to our ability and opportunity, our accountability is proportioned to our obligation. Now on the principle stated above, as well as from other considerations, it is evident that the civil and religious interests of our country are entrusted to us, as they are not entrusted to the citizens of Europe, Asia, or Africa; and that, consequently, God holds us responsible here as he does not hold them. Neither argument nor illustration can be needed to explain or enforce this.

3.—INFLUENCE OF RELIGION ON SOCIETY.

N. W. WILLIAMS.

LET no one think that a thorough reformation from sin can be produced merely by human agency, nor that even an extensive change of public sentiment in favor of pure morals can be effected without the concurrent influence of religion. The depravity of the human mind is too deep to be eradicated by any power that cannot reach the heart. If, then, you would see vice eradicated, and virtue take root throughout the land; if you would see the prevalence of an efficient morality throughout the mass of society, *pray —ardently, constantly pray*, and employ every appointed means, that revivals of religion may be multiplied, that the regenerating power of the Holy Spirit may give effect to the word of God, and conversions be daily multiplied—and by the influence of religion in the community, that stern integrity, chastity, and fidelity to the Divine law, may distinguish our citizens; and by the same influence, intemperance, that moral plague of the land, profane cursing and swearing, gambling, and sabbath-breaking, may cease from among us.

4.—THE SOCIAL UNION OF ALL MANKIND WITH ONE BIBLE.

ORRIN B. JUDD.

THAT all nations of men, dwelling upon the face of the whole earth, are destined to be united in one society by the religion of the Bible, is evident from the catholicism, the exclusiveness, and the assimilative power of the Divine word.

1. The catholicism of the Bible appears from the universality of its address, its adaptation, and its design.

The Bible is adressed to all men. It speaks to man as the creature of God; and this itself involves the idea of a revelation that is universal, the knowledge of which is as important to one as it is to another, to all as it is to any. That God should reveal himself to me as *my* Maker, in order to give me a knowledge of my relation to him as his creature, naturally and necessarily induces the belief, that he will reveal himself in like manner to all, and that the Book which contains that revelation was addressed to all. It speaks to man as a sinner in the sight of God; and this involves the conception of a character which belongs to the whole race of Adam, the knowledge of which is equally important to all. It speaks to man as salvable, and proffers a ray of hope to relieve the darkness of despair. Who that considers the darkness which, without the Bible, would shroud the world, can avoid the conviction, that this guiding star was fixed in the firmament of the church to fling its light over all the earth, and to conduct the wandering pilgrim of every age and nation, of every class and condition, not to the babe of Bethlehem, in the land of Judea, but to the cross of Christ, the hope and the home of the world? It speaks to man with invitations of universal application. "Come unto me all ye that labor and are heavy laden, and I will give you rest." "Look unto me and be ye saved, all the ends of the earth; for I am God, and there is none else." To what man, or nation of men, can such invitations be confined? It speaks to man with commands of universal obligation. "The times of this ignorance God winked at, but now commandeth all men everywhere to repent." If God commandeth all men everywhere to repent, and the Bible alone contains that command, it is clear as the sunbeam that the Bible is the voice of God to universal man.

2. The assimilative power of the Bible arises from the revelation of one God, one Mediator, one worship, and one communion.

The Bible reveals *one God*. The world has been for ages distracted by the conflicting claims of polytheism. From the earliest estrangement of man from his Maker, objects of religious worship have been multiplied as were the dialects of Babel. But the Bible, universal in the province of its power, and unique in the supremacy of its authority, proclaims to all nations that Jehovah is God alone. Let this book be given to the world, and the most formidable institution of idolatry, will fall before the Bible as did the Dagon of the Philistines before the ark of Israel's God; the Mussulman shall no longer revere the name of Mahomet, the Brahm of the Hindoo shall be execrated, and the Boodhist shall despise the memory of Gaudama. Jehovah shall be God alone. In every language His name shall be the symbol of all that is supreme, the designation of all that is divine.

3. This union is beautifully drawn in the delineations of the Divine Word. It is proclaimed by the prophet, when he declares that "the mountain of the Lord's house shall be established upon the top of the mountains, and shall be exalted above the hills, and all nations shall flow unto it." It is set forth by the Saviour in the beautiful figure of the Shepherd and his flock, in which he also designates the Bible as one of the leading instrumentalities by which that union is effected; "They shall hear *my voice*, and there shall be one fold and one shepherd." It was breathed in a sublimer strain by the Redeemer, as he was about to enter the garden: "Holy Father, keep through thine own name those whom thou hast given me, that they may be one as we are." * * * "The glory which thou gavest me, I have given them, that they may be one, even as we are one; I in them, and thou in me, that they may be made perfect in one."

O! how transcendently sublime and glorious the union, when the vast population of our own continent, with the millions of Europe, and Asia, and Africa, and the islands of the sea, are all united by the Bible in one God, one Mediator, and one worship; and when, with the daily circle of the sun, the voice of prayer and praise shall encompass the earth, and, with a golden chain from the sweetest music of the soul, bind all nations into one.

Who that knows the blessedness of union; who that loves the harmony and happiness of his race, will not give his heart and hand to the devotions and duties of the religion of the Bible?

Its work is the noblest work of man. Its reward is treasured among the jewels of the Lord of hosts, which will ere long adorn the diadem of the world's Redeemer.

5.—INFLUENCE OF CHRISTIANITY ON FREEDOM.

J. N. GRANGER.

WHEN we look at those countries where Christianity has existed in its purity, and where the church has faithfully labored at its great work—the work of personal religious improvement—we find that Christianity has been favorable to the peaceful prosecution, by the State, of all the lawful ends of national existence. It has unfolded that Divine government which is the model of a free human government. It has constantly familiarized the minds of the people with those elemental ideas of rule, obedience, and equal rights under authority, upon which all governments must be established, which are intended for the preservation of civil liberty.

There are other considerations which might be urged to show how, in other ways, religion befriends liberty. It does so by keeping alive the idea of God, and thus restraining the turbulence of passion; by directing towards him the supreme homage, which, under a despotic rule, is always given to princes; by promoting a generous spirit of philanthropy, which makes us as jealous of others' rights as we are careful of our own; by diminishing the necessity for public restraints, and for the use of force in the administration of justice. This it does just to the extent that it perfects private character, and governs the soul by the fear and love of God.

I have not detained you with these remarks, for the purpose of reaching a worn out eulogy upon the free institutions of our beloved country. I can, however, safely say, that for whatever advantages we possess over other nations, we are indebted, not to our higher social civilization, or our developed native talent, not to our learning or our wealth, but to our religion—the religion of our Lord Jesus Christ, widely embraced and freely professed among the people. And I may also say, that if we would perpetuate these advantages for our children's benefit, we should educate them as Christians; we should teach them to become free in Jesus Christ, by loving him, professing openly his religion, and doing what they can to convey its blessings to others.

6.—THE POWER OF PRINCIPLES.

E. L. MAGOON.

By high self-culture we reach the spirit of our age and move it by the power of principles. He who deeply *feels* the riddle of the world is in a good way to unravel it. One spark may kindle a conflagration which shall destroy the temples of liberty and justice. Such is the fanatic who hurls his torch on high and vaunts himself a philosopher, when he is only a madman. One spark of hallowed fire may set rubbish in a blaze, from whose flashy and blasting heat rich products may flow, as Corinthian brass was first formed amid the cinders of a voluptuous city. One little word embodying a nation's spirit—one speech glowing with the inspiration of the age—may fall on combustibles which oceans cannot quench. Old John Adams, when a college student, chanced to be in Boston, and heard a patriotic speech, one of the first sparks struck by the genius of American Liberty from his Majesty's oppressive throne. That seed of fire was not lost. It fell in the already glowing heart of him whom a great rival frankly termed "our Colossus in congressional debate." What the worth and power of the principles then broached were, is indicated by Mr. Adams' declaration—"I say in the most solemn manner, that Mr. Otis' Oration against Writs of Assistance breathed into this nation the breath of life."

Martin Luther found a bible unencumbered by traditions, and read it in secret, panting after truth until the bright vision burst upon his enraptured heart. In the light of a new and nobler principle than was possessed by his cotemporaries, his cell became more glorious than grandeur's most magnificent saloon, and he deeply felt that no man should hide what God designed all men to know. Inspired by holy truth, he could but inspire, and those reachings of his soul went forth conquering and to conquer, until he had kindled the surrounding atmosphere into a canopy of magnificence, inspired contiguous minds with his own ardor, and left the world all blazing from his torch, to assume hereafter a crown compared with which the laurels of selfish heroes are but weeds.

And yet the reformation was not complete. Latimer and Ridley struck for a still nearer approach to undoubted right. For their fidelity they must share in the peril and glory of all great advancements. "Fear not, Master Ridley," said the heroical Latimer, as both in chains were going to the stakes," for by the blessing of God we will this day kindle such a flame as shall never go out!" No! it shall not go out. Each new principle discovered and proclaimed, is a new and imperishable luminary added to the moral heavens.

To support an unjust war, Charles I. of England taxed his subjects illegally and without just cause. Hampden resisted the trifling assessment of twenty shillings on his vast landed property, and stood up the mightiest among the mighty to defend a down-trodden principle of justice, and ceased not until he had brought from the dust the cry of liberty, and rendered *ship-money* in all men's ears a hated word.

There is another and still more striking illustration of the service rendered to one's age, and to all ages, by the discovery and defence of profound and original principles. Sir Edward Coke, the distinguished lawyer—for it was fashionable for lawyers to go to church in those days—one day discovered a lad taking notes during divine service. Being pleased with the modest worth of the lad, he asked his parents to permit him to educate their emulative son. It is said that Coke sent him to Oxford. He drank from the fountains of knowledge, and in those draughts he found

> "The sober certainty of waking bliss."

As the hart panteth after the water brooks, he longed for the wisdom that rouses the might which so often and so long slumbers in a peasant's arm. He communed with the past, and with his own startling thoughts. He summoned around him the venerable sages of antiquity, and in their presence made a feast of fat things—

> "A perpetual feast of nectared sweets,
> Where no crude surfeit reigns."

At the fount of holiest instruction he cleared his vision, and from the mount of contemplation breathed in worlds to which the heaven of heavens is but a veil. But his soul was too free for the peace of his sycophantic associates; his principles were too philanthropic for the selfishness of his age; the doctrines which he scorned to disavow were too noble for old England; and he sought an asylum among the icy rocks of this wilderness world. He came

> "To plant the tree of life,
> To plant fair Freedom's tree;"

and was driven from the society of white men through wintry storms, and savages more lenient than interested factions, to plant the first free colony in America. That boy was the founder of Rhode Island; that man was the patriot who stooped his anointed head as low as death for universal rights, and ever

> "Fought to protect, and conquered but to bless."

That Christian was Roger Williams, the first who pleaded for liberty of conscience in this country, and who became the pioneer of religious liberty for the world. Such lovers of truth and justice are the pillars of society and the benefactors of their age. They expel popular fears, steady popular fickleness, expand narrow prejudice, and sink factious tempers in their enlarged wisdom and public spirit. Such service is neither transient nor spasmodic. Thoughts born in solitude and agony most frequently convulse or console the world. In the lightning-gleam of intellect, which in the murky gloom of his indigence and neglect created in the mind of Columbus the conclusion that the earth is spherical, and that the Indies might be reached by sailing due west, America, with all her vast domain, inhabitants, and history, was discovered!

But we have had moral explorers who, striking out a new and successful voyage, have returned with "rich argosies" of inestimable wealth. Fifty years ago, [1792,] a few Baptist preachers assembled in a small parlor in the retired town of Kettering, England. After spending a season in prayer for Divine direction, they resolved to form an association for diffusing religious knowledge in the heathen world, and from their scanty means they contributed thirteen pounds sterling as alms to accompany their devotion. This was the beginning of the great work of modern missions. The germ has grown to a mighty tree overspreading the earth. There are now [1842] fifteen hundred missionaries in the field, aided by five thousand native teachers. These are laboring around twelve hundred central stations and fifty printing establishments. One hundred and eighty thousand have already professed conversion to the Christian faith, and two hundred thousand more are daily taught wisdom, human and divine, in the missionary schools. William Carey struck the first blow at home, and kindled the first beacon light on the shores of the kingdom of darkness abroad. He rose to be the first scholar and foremost philanthropist in India. He emulated every excellence, and became the purest among the great, the greatest among the pure. The government, which first opposed him, came at length to acknowledge their obligations to true religion, and on the 10th of August, 1842, a great concourse of British statesmen and native patriots in Calcutta resolved to signify their gratitude and veneration for great services and exalted worth, by ordering the form of Dr. Carey cut in marble. But neither they nor the angels above can fully estimate how wisely and how well he served his generation.

Robert Raikes, the industrious and benevolent printer of Gloucester, having acquired a fortune, set about subordinating it to the benefit of his age. Happily he struck upon a new principle, by gathering the vicious and ignorant into a Sabbath school. A great light has sprung up and spread from that heavenly spark, and millions are now blessed in that institution, of which, since God himself is the President, every matured Christian should be a teacher, and the whole world of youth the alumni.

Clarkson out of Parliament, and Wilberforce in it, with their tongue and pen, like Howard with his heart and hand, served their generation in the advocacy of justice and mercy, and won fame and glory which shall be luminous and immortal when the names of their calumniators shall rot in the caves of eternal infamy and oblivion.

Another illustration, the strongest and most striking of all, will stand prominent in the history of this eventful age. It is that those six inebriates in Baltimore, when drunk, should have staggered upon the only true principle of sobriety—a principle which, had it been acted upon, would have prevented previous dissoluteness, and which is hereafter destined to rescue the abandoned drunkard from his hell, and elevate the moderate drinker into the condition of a temperate and virtuous man.

The influence of true service to one's age goes on multiplying. Washington and his compatriots went to "war against a preamble;" behind a small but unjust requisition they detected the presence of tyranny, and dragging up from the deep well of truth an old but undiscovered antagonist principle, they first felt its worth, authenticated its justness, and then went to the struggle of death in its defence. What are the results? The principle has survived its first patrons, and is now circling the globe. From us to the south pole, from sea to sea, almost every foot of soil is disenthralled from European rule, the peasants of the vales and hardy mountaineers of the old world snuff the air of liberty from our shores, and pant for the blessings we enjoy.

What has done this? Opinion—mind aroused, and stimulated into action. It is a fearful power to unloose, but it is more fearful when arbitrarily confined. When ardent truth has once fallen where it kindles, and latent thought has been drawn from the quickened mind, it thenceforth becomes a sword of lightning which no material scabbard can sheathe.

7.—SYSTEM IN BENEVOLENT EFFORT.

HENRY C. FISH.

System is a characteristic requisite in successful benevolent effort. Without this no good and great enterprise can be successfully prosecuted. Its importance is felt and acknowledged in all the concerns of this life. It is universally conceded as a self-evident truth, that in the professional, commercial, mechanical, or agricultural pursuits, method or system as to the time and the manner of disposing of all matters of moment are essentially necessary.

The order and efficiency of our military and marine forces, and for which a well-disciplined ship's crew are proverbial, afford but imperfect illustrations of the immense advantages growing out of a regard for method, and a rigid adherence to a minutely defined system. Yet, notwithstanding its acknowledged importance, how many of our churches seem to have lost sight of it in their works of faith and labors of love! Most of them are accustomed, besides their monthly or annual collections from the promiscuous assembly, some time in the year, to make a personal application to some of the members, to contribute something for the various objects of benevolence deemed worthy of their patronage. But with very many here it ends.

Now it is certain, that each church must decide for itself, what the particular features of a plan, by them to be adopted, shall be. But some system, every church would do well to adopt. Moreover, it should be such a system as will reach the entire membership. Let the name of *every individual* be obtained as a contributor, and when additions are made to the church, let those added be at once solicited to enroll themselves as contributors to swell the amount of its benefaction. The youngest, and the poorest of the flock, should not be neglected. Their "mite" will be acceptable to God, and in feeding others, they likewise will be fed. And let all be called upon to *specify* what they will do, even though it be but the merest trifle. Again—let it be a plan by which the amount they subscribe shall be called for at *stated intervals*. Let it be also at *short intervals*. This is of the *highest importance*, and here is a very common and serious fault. Annual or semi-annual contributions may not be abandoned, but it is worthy of remark, that the Divine method of charitable contributions was that they should be made *weekly*. "*Upon the first day of the week* let every one of you lay by him in store as God hath prospered him." There is wisdom in this arrangement, as might be anticipated, since it emanated from such a source.

In doing this, the Christian is frequently reminded of his obligations to Christ and his fellow-men; it keeps his heart warm, and creates and fosters the habit of giving. Besides, more can be realized and with greater facility by this, than by any other process. Given at short intervals, and consequently in small amounts, it is not felt by the donor as when paid in the aggregate. With the majority of individuals it is much less difficult to contribute a few cents each week, than several dollars at one time. If those who labor to advance Christ's religion, have lost sight of this fact, there is no lack of proof that the men of the world, especially in our day, have not. Neither has the gospel's great opponent. Rome very well knows that in no way could she gather such almost incredible sums of money for the propagation of her faith, and mostly from those who are absolutely poor, than by demanding it at short intervals and in small amounts. To careful observers of her policy and plan of operation, it is not surprising that Catholics never lack for funds. The mother of abominations has appropriated to herself the plan dictated by Divine wisdom for the people of the living God. *This* is the secret of her success.

It is not for want of ability in the church that the whole earth is not filled with the knowledge of the glory of God. The truth is, the Christian world does not realize the extent of its resources, and is not conscious of the prodigious influence believers in Christ are capable of wielding, by means of their possessions. Wealth is not wanting, neither is willingness to give wanting, to the extent that many imagine. But to reach that wealth and make it available, and to cultivate and incite to a proper expression that willingness to give; *this* is the labor, *this* the work required. And this object shall have been attained when *every member* of the *family* of Christ contributes *something*, and each in *proportion to his ability ;* when he does it from *Christian principle*, and does it *systematically.*

8.—THE AGE OF CONFLICT.

T. G. KEEN.

THE present age, my brethren, exhibits strong and striking indications of its close proximity to that era, in which will be the last conflict of great principles—in which the Christian religion shall stand triumphantly vindicated from the base scurrility and invective abuse, which have been so profusely heaped upon it. The clouds of persecution and of popular indignation have enveloped the church in obscurity for many centuries ; but the Sun of righteousness is rapidly dispersing them, and she promises soon to stand forth in her original grandeur and in her pristine beauty. The day of letters has dawned upon her, and the light of sanctified intellect is fast illuminating her doctrines.

We live, my brethren, under a government and at a time, peculiarly favorable to free inquiry and independent action. Here is no national priesthood, no spiritual hierarchy to rule over or bias the minds of men ; but all the liberty of conscience which the gospel vouchsafes, is guarantied to us by our national constitution. Here is no partition wall reared by hereditary rights and exclusive privileges—here is nothing to prevent the intercommunication of thought, and reciprocal moral action. Any individual, however obscure his origin, however humble his attainments, who wishes to bring a moral influence to bear upon society, has the entire nation before him. If he possesses intellectual and moral worth, and has any thing to say, and can communicate it intelligently, he will meet with attentive ears, let him go where he will.

If he cannot traverse the entire country and address himself to communities in person, the press, so powerful and diffusive in its energy, comes in to his aid, and gives him free access to the homes and firesides of the millions scattered over the length and breadth of the Union. Here, then, are peculiar facilities for the propagation of opinion, and the free use of our mental and moral powers. Every barrier, civil and religious, is taken out of the way, and a bright prospect is open before us: a whole nation of intelligent minds, susceptible of the finest moral culture, and fit for the reception of religious truth. This, therefore, is an age, which not only demands vigorous action, but presents inducements for the development of all the faculties of the mind. Shall we embrace these advantages? Shall we avail ourselves of surrounding circumstances, and thus the sooner show to an incredulous world, that Christianity is indeed of Divine origin, and must stand acknowledged, when infidelity and all the doctrines of Antichrist shall be overthrown, and obliterated from the memory of man? Or shall we sleep on, till the enemy has fully invaded our ranks, gathered her spoil, and tauntingly called upon us to show our faith? We cannot, we dare not disregard the calls of God, retire in ease and mental indolence, when the foe is all around us. Never, since the establishment of the church in America, has she been watched with such attentive anxiety as at the present day. She now stands upon the vantage ground; but let her step from her eminence and place of protection, her faith is obscured and her strength impaired.

When looking over our country we see no conflicting elements which threaten a storm of desolation and death. The clangor of the trumpet has been hushed, the glittering sword has been replaced in her sheath, and the banner of peace waves happily and triumphantly over our land. No excuse remains for us; we are bound by the sacred obligations of the gospel,

WILLIAM W. EVERTS.

Pastor of the Laight St. Baptist Church, New-York.

Edwd. H. Fletcher, Publisher.

F. Michelin, Lith.

and by the circumstances of the age, to rush forward until the victory is won.

There is not only a common struggle for the general and fundamental doctrines of Christianity, but there is also a contest for Denominational distinction. All appeal to the standard of truth for the proper adjustment of ecclesiastical differences; while some, mingling too much the philosophy of the world with the elevating principles of the Bible, retire from the field unsatisfied and unenlightened. They are unwilling to receive the truth, unless it harmonizes with some peculiar principle of interpretation, or some cherished sentiment of philosophy. We should be able and ready to meet them on their own ground, show the fallacies of their argument, the unreasonableness of their deductions, and with a masterly hand, compel them, by the pungency of truth, to admit the falsity of their hypothesis and the unsoundness of their demonstrations.

We, as a denomination, occupy high ground; but it is the place our Master has assigned us. Many, presuming we have unwarrantably assumed this position, have set themselves in array against us. They have made the attack upon us, while attempting to show to the world that they are acting on the defensive—that their defeat may not appear so glaring, or that their victory, if gained, might appear the more signal. Every advantage which sophistry and false inductions could give, has been seized with the greatest avidity. This, my brethren, is not a false representation—it is truth, as fairly witnessed and recorded in the history of our Denomination.

We are in the world strangers—unprotected by any power, save the strength of Almighty God. We cannot expect the esteem of the world; for she has long since declared war against Christianity, and against every thing that is part and parcel of it. We cannot look for the sympathy of those who oppose the progress of our body; for long since have we received nothing but cold reproof, unkind and unfeeling epithets. We have then, brethren, no friend but God. We enter the field single-handed, to contend for the faith, and, under the guidance of our Leader, we expect—and reasonably, too—the triumph of our principles.

9.—RESPONSIBILITIES OF THE AGE.

J. B. TAYLOR.

WHAT are the most effectual means of supplying the necessities of the age? In deciding this question, we are irresistibly led to the conviction, that they consist mainly in the mental and moral training of the rising generation. This is the great desideratum. We will not disparage other means. While those whom God has counted worthy, by putting them into the ministry, are to prosecute the work of feeding the flock of Christ, and preaching his gospel to all ages and conditions of men, and while we should be unwilling to derogate from the paramount importance of this office, we are convinced of the truth of the assertion just made. Light must be poured upon the mind of the rising age. The biography of thousands of the most estimable of human kind attests, under the blessing of God, the power of an early moral training. To the nursery are to be traced many of the best impressions of which the heart is susceptible. The reverse of this is also true. The ungovernable passions and unholy habits which distinguish a large portion of men, have their origin in a defective education, as well as a depraved nature. And it is a notorious fact, that even when the grace of God triumphs over the depravity of the heart, and a profession of religion is made, a marked deficiency of Christian character is often to be ascribed to inveterate habits formed in the beginning of life.

If, then, we would exercise a general and salutary influence on our dark earth, we are invited to diffuse widely and rapidly the light of science and gospel truth. Thus shall we find a remedy for the evils to which allusion has been made. Enlighten the public mind, and give the ethics of the Bible the prominence they deserve in the formation of public sentiment and manners, and you give the best guarantee that our political rights and religious privileges shall be handed down unimpaired to other generations. You will anticipate and neutralize the influence of Romanism and infidelity of every shape. The morals of our country would be purified, while to the most distant nations of the earth we might expect the tidings of salvation to be sent. What we have thus said is in perfect accordance with the doctrine of the entire alienation of the carnal mind from God, and of supernatural agency in the conversion of the soul. None more than ourselves are ready to plead for the necessity of Divine influence in this great work, or to urge continual prayer for success in every effort to lead the young to God.

10.—DUTIES OF AMERICAN CITIZENS.

W. W. EVERTS.

The cause of the race in future ages, and in all lands, is narrowed down in its problems to the compass of a single city. Our hope for the better does not preclude fear, or the necessity of vigilance, precaution, and effort. If the present experiment of American society prove more auspicious than those of the old world, it must be by some wiser regulation or amelioration of the condition of large communities. The decay and ruin which have come successively upon ancient cities, must be traced, in an eminent degree, to the insufficiency of any false religion, and to the insufficiency of the true even, when grossly perverted, as a means of sustaining a high tone of social morality, along with an advanced state of civilization. Our hope, then, as exposed to all the dangers which have proved so fatal through the past, must have respect to our better faith, its superior wisdom, and more earnest philanthropy, as the momentous element, which alone can operate as a preserving leaven through the great substance of universal society. This leaven of energetic, conservative Christian influence, must be deposited in the heart of great communities; or in them will accumulate and concentrate a combination of destructive elements that will explode and scatter in fragments the consolidated structure of universal society. If their intelligence, subordination to law, and general morality, keep pace with extending population, luxuries of wealth, and refinements of arts, the star of empire will rise, and from its zenith continue to shine upon the new world with benignant promise. If lawlessness and demoralization prevail in them, it will suffer disastrous eclipse, and at length sink in darkness and blood.

In wise recognition of the concentration of wickedness in large cities, Judaism concentrated its moral forces in the temple, ministry, worship. and festivals of the empire city, to confront and repress demoralization in its most formidable manifestations at its source. In approbation of that policy, the Messiah directed his attention chiefly to the larger communities of Judea; and the first preachers under his instructions went first to the cities of Palestine, Asia Minor, Greece, and Rome.

It is important to remember, some at least of the evils of the old world may be obviated or mitigated in the new, by the combined vigilance of medical, legal, and moral police over these rising communities. We would fasten here and there a buoy, and rear here and there a lighthouse, along these dangerous roads and stormy capes of the sea, where so many tempests sweep; so many furtive currents set in towards the gulf stream; so many sunken reefs lie; so many wrecks of vessels of state hang upon the sounding rocks. We would point those who desire to co-operate in the stupendous work of reforming and saving the world, to the importance of concentrating the highest moral agencies to repress depravity and vice where their outbreaks are most to be apprehended, and most disastrous; of raising barriers and dikes against iniquity and demoralization, where they come in like a wild, desolating flood.

Numerous association is not necessarily an evil; and is made such only by the ascendance of depravity, and its enlarged facilities of temptation. Diversified and indefinitely extended association, regulated by temperance, justice, benevolence and piety, might proportionably augment the happiness of social beings.

Such association is a feature of the heavenly world, prefigured by a golden city with streets and gates of pearl. Its worship is the *united* homage of an innumerable company of angels and the redeemed, and the blended sounds of its choral praise, are as the noise of many waters.

When benevolence, instead of selfishness, becomes the law of human association, a city will be the glory of the earth as well as a type of heaven. It will be the place of many offerings of beneficence to man and of worship to God. Instead of the voice of obscenity and blasphemy swelling on the gale of night, the incense of gratitude will perpetually rise from the metropolis, as the incense of a nation's worship from the ancient temple.

While anticipating such amelioration of the condition of cities, we already trace its great preparation, in the exalted type of piety and the enlarged plans of benevolence developed in them. From them will rise an exceeding great number, who have kept themselves unspotted from the world, and washed their robes and made them white in the blood of the Lamb, to receive the brightest crowns reserved in heaven for the faithful. There the amplest opportunities of usefulness may be found, and the most exalted communion with God enjoyed.

11.—PATRIOTISM PROMOTING TEMPERANCE.

E. W. FREEMAN.

PATRIOTISM prompts us to enlist heartily and practically in the cause of temperance. A love of country we all profess, and I trust we all feel the fire of patriotism kindling in our bosoms. There let it be cherished—let it burn deep and last long. Let the day never come when the hallowed flame shall be extinguished! But who proves himself to be in sincerity a patriot? Who gives undoubted testimony that he is a lover of his country? He who professes merely? He who is noisy in his pretensions? He who grows clamorous over his cups about patriotism, and about public men and public measures? He who is most eloquent at the retailer's shop, or at the bar-room? O no! The spirit of patriotism and the spirit of the bottle are opposites. They are at war with each other. Let, then, the spirit of patriotism carry on the war against the fiery spirit! Let this be a war of *extermination!* Let the enemy have no quarters! Let all that is patriotic in us be roused up, and enlisted in this glorious conflict, until the deadliest foe of our land shall be completely conquered! If the characters I have just mentioned are not patriots, if they prove the truth of the maxim that "profession is not principle," shall we exhibit the spirit of patriotism if we sit calmly and behold this dark and wasting desolation in all our land, while we move not to arrest it? But in what, you ask, does the mighty conflict consist? Shall we take the field with powder and balls? Must there be the alarm of war and garments soiled in blood? Or must there be any thing of coercion? None of this. All we are to do is to abstain. All that is necessary to efface the broad and glaring blot from our national character; to roll away the burning tide of misery and death from our beloved country; to silence the wailings and to hush the sorrows which are now in the land; to render permanent and healthy all our civil and literary and moral institutions; to send abroad, as far as the boundaries of our national compact, a salutary and cheering influence; to lay a foundation for our future glory, which nothing can shake; to present our country, our whole country, to the world as the happiest and the loveliest land on which the sun shines; we have only to "touch not, taste not, handle not."

12.—CONNECTION BETWEEN MEANS AND THE END.

A. SHERWOOD.

God has inseparably connected means with human salvation. The gospel must be preached in order that sinners may hear; for "how shall they *hear* without a preacher?" We have no reason to expect God will work miracles, or rain down bibles to instruct and convert men—they will be instructed in the ordinary way by those who have been "begotten through the gospel." There is no ground to hope that God will respect his covenant, and rescue from the miseries of heathenism, without the active exertions of his people; as the *end*, salvation is ordained—so also the *means;* but the end cannot be attained without the means. When God ordains an *end*, he looks to the instrumentality which is to accomplish it. True in temporal—true also in spiritual things. He has ordained that there shall be "seed-time and harvest:" but take away the human instrumentality which should sow and reap—set men down contented in their houses waiting for a miracle to gather in their grain—and you destroy the doctrine that a crop is ordained: so in spiritual things.

This connection God has controlled in every age of the world to gather in his chosen people. He designed to save sinners in Pisidia, and commissioned Paul and Barnabas to accomplish the object. We cannot perceive how "as many as were ordained unto eternal life," in that region, could have been constrained to believe, had not the gospel been preached to them—had not the means been put in operation. "How shall they believe in him of whom they have not heard, and how shall they hear without a preacher?" Paul seemed to discover no other than the ordinary way to save men; that is, through preaching and believing. He had not pried into the secret plan of producing effects without adequate causes, which distinguishes some ministers of the present age—a glorious plan indeed, which keeps men *idle* lest they should be *proud*, and rob God of the glory of converting sinners.

God designed blessings for our rising nation; so he influenced our pilgrim fathers to bring with them the Bible to instruct and sanctify. Knowing the influence which truth would exert on many minds, and the capabilities of such for self-government, the Lord infuses into the pioneer settlers courage to contend successfully with tyranny, and patience to endure all the trials and sufferings incident to the desperate struggle they were making for freedom. But was it ever ascertained that a nation of ignorant, idle cowards were ever predestined to be a free and happy people? No—their character must be changed before they could achieve their independence, or maintain it after the bloody work of revolution had been accomplished.

What would restrain from fatal insurrections twelve millions of people [1835] in a mild government like ours, were it not for the light which the Bible sheds upon all, and the wisdom exhibited by many who fear and serve God? All these ends were descried by the All-seeing eye, and means put in operation to accomplish them. May we never, by our ignorance and vices, spoil the fair fabric, which has sprung up so far the admiration and wonder of the world. But unless we continue to increase in virtue and knowledge, in a ratio with our rapid increase of population, our civil and religious liberties will not survive the present century. It is possible the wave of Papal influence will be permitted to sweep over the land, to convince us of our ingratitude—to show us how easy it is for God to take away privileges, which we have undervalued, and which we dreamed would be perpetual without means.

Of what avail would have been the Declaration of Independence, if our fathers had not gone on to *achieve* it? It required something more than predetermination to shake off the galling yoke—it required *action*, bold and bloody, and courage too, which defied death in its most dreadful forms. In the use of the weapons of war, we became free and independent.

God did rain down manna for the Israelites in the wilderness; but this fact in their history, did not induce that highly favored people to infer that always after they were to be fed without industry. No, when they entered Canaan, the land was divided out by lot, on which each, except the priests, was to earn his bread by the sweat of his brow. Much as their faith may have been strengthened by the special interposition of God's power in their behalf, it did not sink into stoic fatalism when the day of miracles had passed away. And now, since the miracles which were requisite to establish the Christian religion in its infancy, are no longer necessary, the work of converting sinners must go on in the ordinary way which the Saviour has ordained—namely, the preaching of the gospel. While we proceed in this way, we may expect the promised influence of the Spirit to subdue and sanctify the heart. In this way God will control the connection of means and ends to save lost men.

13.—PATRIOTISM AND INFLUENCE.

JOHN M. PECK.

A PATRIOT is one who is actuated by the love of his country, and who will sacrifice his own interests rather than the interests of the people. Private interests are merged in public good. True patriotism does not annul or counteract the duty of universal benevolence; for it does not call us to regard our country's interest exclusively, at the expense of the general happiness of mankind. It does not abrogate the Divine injunction to love all mankind—to love our enemies. The laws of universal justice and equity require no one to promote the interests of the country, state, town, or neighborhood, where he resides, at the expense of justice, humanity, and the happiness of mankind. A nation is exalted only by righteousness, and not by rapine, injustice, and artifice. "Equal justice to all," has been recognized as the sentiment of this nation.

True patriotism, in a citizen, displays itself in zealously supporting the honor, interests, and prosperity of our country, and government, on principles of equal justice. It never engages in plots and conspiracies to overturn or pervert constitutional principles, though individuals, equally patriotic, may honestly differ in opinion about the extent and application of those principles. It never seeks to bring the government, or its constituted authorities, into contempt; and though it may approve of one set of measures, and disapprove of another—it may seek to elevate this man, as more fitted to rule than that—yet it never takes pleasure in exposing the errors of rulers, or in defaming their characters. A dutiful son may see faults in his father, and affectionately remonstrate; but until all affection is extinguished, and self-respect is lost, he will not take pleasure in exposing him. So with the real patriot; he delights not in exposing his country's faults.

But the man in office, above all others, is expected to be a true patriot. He must exhibit that unquenchable love of country which will prompt him to a cheerful sacrifice of his own interest, when placed in competition with the public good. This will appear the more necessary, when it is noticed that men of wealth, as well as of influence, are frequently selected for the higher and more important offices. If such persons are not influenced by the spirit of the real patriot, the temptation to sacrifice the people's interest to their own will too easily prevail.

It is unnecessary here to particularize instances where the most elevated patriotism existed. Their names are found scattered over the records of antiquity. One of the most brilliant examples is that of Moses; for in renouncing the pleasures and riches of Egypt, and his title, as the adopted son of Pharaoh's daughter, to the throne, and in preferring the interests of the Hebrew nation in their vassalage, his patriotism was not less conspicuous than his piety was elevated. The page of our revolutionary history furnishes evidence of entire devotion to the welfare of the nation. He, then, only deserves the name of a patriot, who enters into public office with the fixed principle of promoting the good of his country, and his fellow-men—and who continues to be governed by that principle. And however important are natural talents, a well-cultivated mind, self-control, mngnanimity and high-souled feelings, and decision of character—if patriotism is wanting, he may be a *great man*, but we dare not pronounce him a *great statesman*.

"None of us liveth to himself," is the declaration of an inspired apostle. We are not insulated beings. Our example, influence, wealth, talents, and prayers are all to be employed for useful purposes, and should be directed in the way that will lessen the most misery, and promote the most happiness in the world. Whatever be our rank, whether as legislators, jurists, magistrates, ministers of the gospel, or private citizens, we are capable of doing immense harm, or immense good, and the influence of this good or evil is not expended upon the present generation merely. Ages to come will feel the effects. It will follow in the continuous line of succeeding generations, and future millions will arise to call us blessed, or invoke anathemas on our memories. The laws that are now framed—the moral influence exerted—the national or state improvements attempted—the schools established—the churches gathered—the preachers ordained—the appointments to office—the public and private example of all—the humblest walk of the humblest citizen of the state, will prove the means of happiness or misery to the individuals and the community, for years to come. Filled and overwhelmed with a sense of this weighty responsibility, let each one act well his part in life, that blessings may water his memory when his ashes have commingled with their kindred dust.

14.—PROPRIETY OF NATIONAL THANKSGIVING.

J. MIDDLETON.

The duty of assembling annually in the temples of Jehovah, to render him an expression of public gratitude, arises not only from the recommendation of executive wisdom, but is in strict harmony with the finer feelings of the patriot and the Christian; inasmuch as it furnishes to the world and to our Creator a national acknowledgment of the mandates of revelation, or an abiding consciousness of an over-ruling providence, from whence flow unnumbered mercies. It well becomes us in a special manner to offer thanksgiving unto God, for with what nation has he so kindly dealt as with us? That beautiful composition, the hundred and sixteenth psalm, is generally acknowledged to be the production of the sweet singer of Israel, and sung by the assembled congregation on days of thanksgiving. The sentiment it breathes must commend itself to the heart and conscience of the most hardened. The spirit of gratitude is becoming all created intelligences, especially those who have forfeited the Divine favor. Its distinctive traits I conceive to be—a sense of the blessing received—a feeling of reverence and affection for the benefactor—and a desire to render unto him some acceptable offering for the benefits conferred.

15.—DEMORALIZING TENDENCY OE UNIVERSALISM.

A. PERKINS.

A RELIGION destitute of Christian piety, cannot be expected to promote healthful morals; and who ever heard of a pious Universalism? The promotion and success of Christian morals has ever depended chiefly on the renewing and sanctifying influence of the Holy Spirit; but where, and when, was a community, adhering to Universalism, known to be blest with an outpouring of the Holy Spirit, a revival of religion, and the conversion of sinners? Have not the pious everywhere, and the friends in general of good order and correct deportment, dreaded the entering in of Universalism, as a signal for raising the flood-gates of iniquity, and corrupting the public morals?

The statement here made, that Universalism encourages in sin, may seem unkind and severe; but it is by no means so intended; we regard it as a *fact* of very alarming import, that such is its natural tendency; and it would be recreant, and uuworthy, should we on this topic hold our peace. But very probably the statement may also be objected to as unfounded and untrue; be this as it may, we appeal to the common sense of the community, whether any position can be more self-evident than the following—"If it be said, and published from the pulpit, that the Scriptures teach that all men shall be finally saved, every sinner, whatever be his vicious courses, is encouraged to expect eternal life; and though he should persist in sin till death, is warranted to hope and rejoice in the prospect of all being well with him at last. For any man to deny this position, is to deny what is self-evident, and there can be no further reasoning with him."

The doctrine of Universalism is dangerous. Did it only peril the present life, and eventually kill the body, the danger and the death would be comparatively nothing: but souls are deceived, and by it being induced to observe lying vanities, they forsake their own mercies. Its advocates cry "peace, peace," when God has said, "there is no peace to the wicked." The sinner is taught to believe there is no danger—nothing to fear; but the word of truth assures him, "it is a fearful thing to fall into the hands of the living God." The impenitent, as such, are by it encouraged to hope for heaven and happiness, though they should die impenitent and unpardoned; when the eternal God has said, the very "expectation of the wicked shall perish, and his hope shall be as the giving up of the ghost." Thus deceiving and leading its votaries blindly onward, the advocates of this doctrine "weave the winding sheet of souls, and lay them in the urn of everlasting death." Again we warn the sinner of the impending danger. Thy feet, being on slippery places, must shortly slide, and hell from beneath shall be moved for thee, to meet thee at thy coming. Thy covenant with death shall be disannulled, and thy agreement with hell shall not stand; and, continuing in thy sinful course, "This," saith Jehovah, "shalt thou have at my hand; thou shalt lie down in sorrow."

16.—IMMORALITY OF MODERN LITERATURE.

A. S. PATTON.

IMMORALITY is an alarming tendency of our modern literature.

To deaden and destroy any of the kind or tender feelings of the soul, can be no light offence against a pure and holy God. Nor can he be a friend to his race, who, under the potent dominion of selfishness, would scatter the withering blight of impurity over the virtuous principles and moral sentiments of our nature. Yet there are those who, coveting reputation rather than truth, and fearless of Heaven's threatened wo, "call evil good, and good evil; that put darkness for light, and light for darkness; that put bitter for sweet and sweet for bitter!" and then enjoy, with a high, though malicious relish, the alarm excited by their gross and wicked perversions.

This open hostility, however, is confined to the few, who have resigned themselves to the wasting desolation which has passed over all their nobler principles and affections; while other authors, by their efforts to enlist our sympathies in behalf of depraved and vicious characters, exhibit a more secret, but not less inveterate, hatred for some of the settled principles of morality. In this connection, we might allude to the works of Lord Byron, whose vulgar Don Juan has, perhaps, done more to corrupt the mind, and weaken the restraints of virtue than any other book of the past century; and whose Childe Harold, by its cheerless, but sublime misanthropy, has contributed to the most serious social ruptures, and taught thousands to regard every exhibition of generosity and friendship as heartless hypocrisy.

But if from our standard literature, we turn to the floating and fictitious effusions of less noted authors, we shall discover in them the same alarming tendency. Their prominent characters are invested with peculiar interest, and lauded, though identified with the most base designs. We read of the contrivance of some clever sharper to elude justice; some intriguing politician to accomplish his purpose; some needy impostor to succeed in passing as an honest man; or of an accomplished villain, whose life and talents are devoted to the subversion of female virtue; and while we openly detest their wickedness, we fear their detection or applaud their success. Now, when it is considered how often our worldly interests place us in circumstances in which the desire of the natural heart is to secure a present pleasure, it cannot be made a question, but that our weak principles are in imminent peril from the polluting recollection of instances in which truth and virtue have been violated, without exposure, or visible retribution.

Or, to view the subject in another light, if it be dangerous to associate with low characters in real life, can it be safe to hold converse with them in the secret "chambers of imagery?" If the perfect portraiture be admired, how can the original be despised? If "evil communications corrupt good manners," what reason have we to anticipate a different result, when wicked sentiments are thrown before us in a more tangible and permanent form?

17.—PLANS OF SATAN.

W. PARKINSON.

It appears, that in order to produce a general belief among the Thessalonian Christians that the day of Christ's second coming was at hand, Satan worked in three different ways. First, "*by spirit;*" that is, by counterfeiting the Spirit of God, in making communications, either in dreams or by suggestions, that the coming of Christ was drawing nigh. These dreams or suggestions he might communicate to some who were gracious persons, that they might thereby be shaken in mind and troubled; though it is more probable that he communicated them to such men and women, whether in the fellowship of the church or not, as pretended to be prophets and prophetesses, and who, being deceived themselves, supposed they had them by Divine revelation; and, as such, delivered them to the church and the world. Thus Satan, by Divine sufferance, acted as a lying spirit in the prophets of Ahab.—1 Kings xxii. 22, 23. Second, "*by word;*" either some word or saying, falsely reported to have been uttered by one or more of the apostles, intimating that the day of Christ was at hand ; and which, coming to the ears of the saints, might stagger and trouble them ; or rather, some word or sentence in relation to the coming of Christ, which Satan either took from scripture, or invented to answer his purpose, and directly or indirectly communicated to credulous persons in the church, who might think they had it from the Lord, and speak of it accordingly. So this adversary of truth and righteousness imposed on the man of God who went out of Judah to Bethel, and probably upon the old prophet himself, who was the instrument of this imposition.—1 Kings xiii. 18. And Third, "*by letter ;*" that is, by prompting some evil-minded person or persons, to forge a letter or letters in the name of Paul, or some one or more of the other apostles, announcing that the day of Christ was at hand ; the pretended originals of which they might send to the church, and copies of which they might circulate more generally.

18.—DUTY OF CHRISTIANS TO THE WORLD.

RUFUS BABCOCK.

As Christians would I address you, and by all that is sacred in those not unwelcome ties that bind you to consecrate your all to Him who freely gave his life for you, I would plead the claims of his great commission, "*Go, preach the gospel to every creature.*" All that is binding in this authority, all that is precious and salutary in this gospel, and all the infinite worth of the immortal souls to whom you may cause it to be made known, should impel you not to disregard these claims.

Look around you on a guilty world now perishing in unbelief, who can never hear the gospel without preachers, and to whom none have yet been sent, or are now prepared to go. Take into view, also, the many desolations of Zion at our own doors, the destitute churches and waste places, where so many of the lambs of Christ are scattered abroad, having no skilful and faithful shepherd. And then let the kind and holy sympathy you feel for all their wants and woes, lead you to pray with more intense earnestness for an increase of laborers, and to act in accordance with your prayers. Never can you so well study your Maker's will, or promote your own spiritual interests, as when you inquire the path of duty, with a crucified Redeemer in your eye, the groans of a dying world for whom his blood was spilt, vibrating on your ear, and your lips repeating his mandate, "What thy hand findeth to do, do it with thy might."

Yes, my brethren, do it with your *might*. If ye are strong and the word of God abideth in you, put forth that strength in his service. Content not yourselves with offering a meagre and stinted pittance, for which your better feelings shame you, and on which Heaven must frown. Show, also, the fruitfulness of that abiding word. It was planted in you to yield a large emolument of praise and glory to its Author—and of blessings to the world. Let it not be barren, lest in righteous indignation he say, "Why cumbereth it the ground?"—But I will not thus weary you with persuasives to the performance of duty. You know the object, and to you with cheerful confidence do I commit it. You will act worthy of it, and of yourselves; and God, even our own God, will bless you.

19.—PROSPECTS OF THE WORLD.

I. T. HINTON.

Glorious prospect! The earth redeemed from the grasp of its tyrants, shall soon be regenerated by the truth and power of God! The angelic song, Peace on earth and good will among men, shall then be verified; and when thus the oft-repeated prayer, "thy kingdom come," has been fully answered, the will of God will be "done on earth, as it is in heaven." Nations shall be born in a day, and millions on millions of human beings, happy in the love, and under the rule of their Saviour, shall occupy the earth; civilization, virtue, and religion, being universal, the number of earth's inhabitants shall be greatly enlarged; but on the altar of every heart shall burn the incense of thanksgiving, and upon earth's wide domain, arise one universal symphony of praise.

Onward, then, with the work of mercy! loud proclaim the glad tidings! The earth's jubilee is at hand! Let the light shine amid the darkness of the nations; let the sound of Jesus' name resound amid the rocks and vales of every clime; in every spot accessible to the soldier of the cross, let the banner of redeeming love be planted. Let the pure and unadulterated word of God be given to all the human race. Be not discouraged, ye who are gone forth to prepare the way of the Lord, by the massive bulwarks of Satan's power which darkly frown upon your efforts—their strength is gone; nor startle at the renewed activity of the legions of the enemy. It is true they did "make war with the saints, and overcame them;" but rather than they should again triumph—rather than the results of your devoted labors shall be crushed, even for a season, the Lord himself shall appear, and show that the year of his redeemed, the time of their final triumph is come.

Let all who love their Saviour and their fellow-men, consecrate all their energies to this great work of communicating to a lost world the knowledge of the only Saviour. "Blessed is that servant whom his Lord shall find so doing."

20.—IMPORTANCE OF HISTORY.

J. TEASDALE.

We live in an ever-changing world. Kingdoms and nations spring up, flourish, and pass away in rapid succession. Individuals, distinguished by intellectual vigor, by great valor and glorious achievements in the battle field, or by eminent piety and usefulness in the world, appear upon the stage of action, and anon they are gone. And but for the pen of the faithful historian, we should have known nothing of them—nothing, on the one hand, of what is censurable and to be avoided—on the other, of what is praiseworthy and to be imitated.

Infinitely above all other historical records is that of the Bible. In all human productions, there are imperfections and defects, and in too many instances gross misrepresentations. But the Bible is a record of facts recorded under the immediate direction and control of the unerring Spirit of God; for "Holy men of God spake as they were moved by the Holy Ghost."

The communications of truth made to the prophets and apostles, were not more important to them, and the people of their day, than to all succeeding generations. Hence their transmission to us. The language of the apostle John is, "that which we have seen and heard, declare we unto you." They would snatch from forgetfulness the most thrilling incidents connected with the kingdom of the Redeemer in their day. Had the same spirit continued from that time to the present, what a vacuum in the history of the church would have been supplied! But churches, associations, and other religious bodies, of our own denomination, have been remiss in the duty of transmitting to posterity an account of their doings in the cause of benevolence and truth.

21.—GOD, THE UPHOLDER OF NATIONS.

J. N. MURDOCK.

We are impressively reminded on this occasion that our *only sure dependence as a people is in the favor and protection of the Almighty.*

The fate of nations is in his hand. He sets up and casts down empires. He "bringeth princes to nothing; he maketh the judges of the earth as vanity." "He shall blow upon them, and they shall wither, and the whirlwind shall take them away as stubble." "He breaks the bow of the strong, and confounds the wisdom of the wise." These are truths which should be deeply impressed on all our hearts. As a Christian people, we should feel that GOD is supreme. If we have wise and great statesmen, let us be thankful and rejoice. They are the gift of God to the nation. They are sent to execute his counsels. They stand, in a manner, in his stead, and are his agents. How seldom do we realize—how rarely do we pause to think, who has given us this glorious land, and reared, and cemented, and guarded the mighty structure of our federated empire. We scarcely ever look beyond the prowess of our warriors, and the policy of our statesmen. We forget that God drove out our enemies before us, and directed the movements of our fathers—that he nerved the arm of the soldier in battle, and sustained the confidence of the sage in council. He raised up the men, and inspired them with wisdom and strength for the work of rearing our great confederacy. Our fathers were constrained to acknowledge, in the language of the monarch of Israel—"Both riches and honor come of thee, and thou reignest over all ; and in thy hand is power and might ; and in thy hand it is to make great, and to give strength unto all."

God presides over the destinies of our country still. 'Tis only by his favor that we are preserved. Trust in the wisdom of the legislator and the might of the warrior, as we will, it is still God who upholds us, and makes us great. He can take these vain dependences from us by a stroke as sudden and unexpected as the one which has removed him whose death we deplore. Their breath is in their nostrils. While he smiles, they live: when he withdraws his countenance, they die. How solemnly does this mournful event admonish us to trust in God rather than in man. Man is weak, but he is mighty: man vanisheth like the vapor, but he endureth forever. The people who make God their trust will never endure the reproach of a vain confidence. Based on "the Rock of Israel," their superstructure shall survive the fury of the tempest, and the shock of the earthquake. "Happy is the people that is in such a case ; yea, happy is the people whose God is the Lord." By this mysterious providence, as well as by his word, God now says to this great nation—"It is better to trust in the Lord than to put confidence in princes." Great Ruler of the nations ! "keep this forever in the imagination of the thoughts of thy people, and prepare their heart unto thee."

C. W. HODGES.

www.ingramcontent.com/pod-product-compliance
Lightning Source LLC
LaVergne TN
LVHW020918110826
845150LV00004B/711

* 9 7 8 1 4 2 5 5 5 5 2 6 9 *